CONTENTS

~~~~~~

Further praise for
Louis Armstrong's New Orleans

"A thoughtful and enjoyable study of an artist as well as the disparate and fascinating setting that nurtured him."
—Yoshi Kato, *Downbeat*

"Brothers unpicks brilliantly the hierarchies of class and colour that Armstrong had to negotiate to succeed as a musician."
—Mike Hobart, *Financial Times Magazine*

"This is a book of tremendous significance. Brothers manages to bring together the most recent scholarship on both New Orleans the city and Armstrong the man in a way that brings both vividly to life. It seems that they remained—make that remain—inseparable. It's a timely reminder of how indebted our national identity is to them both." —Loren Schoenberg, executive director, The Jazz Museum in Harlem

"Brothers does a beautiful job of exploring the musical world that Armstrong inhabited before he ever learned to play an instrument."
—Dennis McNally, *News and Observer*

"Five stars. . . . If anyone needs further proof of just how much was lost, first to Hurricane Katrina and then to the tidal wave of incompetence and indifference that has all but drowned New Orleans, it's all here in this wonderful book." —Merrell Noden, *MOJO*

"One of the best primers on jazz you'll ever read." —*Time Out*

"Brothers paints a word picture of New Orleans during Armstrong's youth, making this book a good read not just for jazz fans, but for anyone interested in the history of New Orleans."
—Cliff Bellamy, *Sunday Herald-Sun* (Durham, NC)

"The word 'entertaining' doesn't usually show up in reviews of deeply researched works, but [*Louis Armstrong's New Orleans*] is an exception." —Charles Suhor, *Jazz Notes*

"A thought-provoking and ground-breaking study of musicians' lives 100 years ago."　　　　—Brian Priestley, *Jazzwise Magazine*

"Brothers has attempted to do for New Orleans what James Joyce did for Dublin in *Ulysses*: make it live in every detail for those who never saw it. Given that Louis Armstrong is at the center of this work, and that most of the neighborhoods in which he moved have now been destroyed, this important book is all the more essential."
　　　　—John Szwed, author of *Blues for New Orleans: Mardi Gras and America's Creole Soul* and *So What: The Life of Miles Davis*

"This is an astonishingly smart book, one that scholars of jazz and historians of New Orleans can't afford to overlook."
　　　　—Lawrence N. Powell, *Duke Magazine*

"*Louis Armstrong's New Orleans* is a detailed and insightful look at the formative years of the most influential figure in American music. Thomas Brothers seems to have absorbed everything written on the subject, and is especially good at illuminating influences of the church and parade rituals. You may not agree with all his interpretations, but you would be hard-pressed to ignore the array of facts and the rich tapestry he makes of them."
　　　　—Gary Giddins, author of *Natural Selection* and *Weather Bird*

"Four stars. . . . This is . . . a gripping account."
　　　　—Siobhan Murphy, *Metro*

"[Brothers's] methodical analysis—which is nevertheless hugely enjoyable to read—cuts through the fuzz and gives us the best glimpse so far of how this amazing art form emerged as well as its undisputed first great virtuoso . . . a sparkling and compelling account of one of the most important epochs in the history of music told through the perspective of its most dazzling star."
　　　　—Damian Rafferty, *Fly*

Louis Armstrong's New Orleans

THOMAS BROTHERS

W. W. NORTON & COMPANY

New York · London

For information about permission to reproduce selections from this book,
write to Permissions, W. W. Norton & Company, Inc.,
500 Fifth Avenue, New York, NY 10110

Manufacturing by RR Donnelley, Bloomsburg
Book design by Charlotte Staub
Production manager: Amanda Morrison

Library of Congress Cataloging-in-Publication Data

Brothers, Thomas David.
Louis Armstrong's New Orleans / Thomas Brothers.— 1st ed.
p. cm.
Includes bibliographical references (p.   ) and index.
ISBN 0-393-06109-4 (hardcover)
1. Armstrong, Louis, 1901–1971 2. Jazz musicians—United
States—Biography. 3. Jazz—Louisiana—New Orleans—History and
criticism. I. Title.
ML419.A75B78 2006
781.65092—dc22

2005030672

ISBN 978-0-393-33001-4 pbk.

W. W. Norton & Company, Inc.
500 Fifth Avenue, New York, N.Y. 10110
www.wwnorton.com

W. W. Norton & Company Ltd.
Castle House, 75/76 Wells Street, London W1T 3QT

1 2 3 4 5 6 7 8 9 0

For Leo & Roger

PREFACE

~~~~~~

In the early 1990s I had the good fortune to begin work on an edition of
Louis Armstrong's unpublished writings, eventually published as
Louis Armstrong, In His Own Words. As I tried to contextualize what
Armstrong was saying, I realized how much American musicology
has neglected the early period of jazz in New Orleans. Some excellent work has been done, but by a very small number of people. I
traveled to New Orleans, visited the archives, and got a sense of the
possibilities. Now that I have finished the present book, the range of
possibility seems even greater than it did when I started.

Armstrong produced dozens of accounts of his early life, in interviews and written memoirs. To these we may add autobiographies
written by a few of his contemporaries, plus hundreds of extended
interviews with many more of them. The result is an extremely rich
body of first-person accounts. This diverse collection of memories
gives us a chance to view the emerging world of jazz from the inside.

The body of first-person accounts for early jazz in New Orleans
is exceptional, yet this information is hardly without problems.
Most of the accounts were generated decades after the events that
concern us. Memory can fade and it can be substantially restruc-
tured. In the end, however, using oral histories is no different from
using any other primary source in the sense that the historian must
assess the information, weighing it against all other sources and try-

ix

ing to understand how it was shaped and what interpretation it will most responsibly serve.

I have tried to provide a substantial set of references to the oral histories I have used, with the goal of assisting scholars. It would be wrong to regard the references cited here as "proof" of any assertion in my text. This book is not the place to explain every decision regarding the validity of the evidence, but the reader should realize that such decisions were constantly made. It would please me immensely if the references provided here assist future investigation.

Bibliographic citations are of two kinds, "general" sources (mostly published works, with the exception of a few dissertations and unpublished research papers) and unpublished sources held in archives; the latter are distinguished by an abbreviation referencing the place where the document is held, inserted after the author and before the date (e.g., Keppard HJA 1957). References in the endnotes are keyed to the main body of the book through a system of page numbers and key phrases.

Acknowledgments

Olly Wilson's views on jazz as part of African-American history have shaped my thinking ever since my first semester in graduate school. That same semester I also met Scott DeVeaux, who, over the years, has taught me more about jazz than anyone. Rich Crawford first suggested that I visit the Hogan Jazz Archive, and I am grateful for all of his generous support. Charley Kinzer has shared his deep knowledge of New Orleans, jazz, and Louisiana with me; he was kind enough to read a draft of the present book, improving it immensely. Jim Manheim, who has, for a long time, shared with me his insights into American culture, did the same. At Norton, I am deeply indebted to Maribeth Anderson Payne, whose loyalty and commitment to this book have been sources of inspiration, and to Mary Babcock, whose meticulous copyediting has been a marvel to behold.

Early presentations of parts of this book were read at McGill University (my thanks to Julie Cumming), the University of North Carolina at Chapel Hill (thanks to Jim Ketch), and a conference on Louis Armstrong in Milan (thanks to Stefano Zenni and all the participants). Lawrence Gushee, whose work on New Orleans continues to set musicological standards, gave helpful advice at several turns. Jeff Taylor, Brian Harker, Eric Simpson, Jairo Moreno, Anthony Kelly, T. J. Anderson, and Paul Berliner all helped me by either providing materials or talking through parts of this book with me. I am also indebted to Michael Cogswell of the Louis Armstrong House and Archive, Dan Morgenstern of the Institute of Jazz Studies, Nathan Salsburg of the Alan Lomax Archive, Wayne Everard at the New Orleans Public Library, John Magill at the Williams Research Center, and John Druesedow of the Music Library at Duke University. My research trips to New Orleans and New York were generously supported by grants from the Arts and Sciences Council for Faculty Research at Duke University.

Work on this book benefited immensely from a fellowship at Duke University's John Hope Franklin Institute, supported by a grant from the Mellon Foundation called "Making the Humanities Central." Fellows Rick Powell, Lee Baker, and Maurice Wallace were especially generous with their knowledge. A Duke Endowment fellowship allowed me to further my inquiry through a fellowship at the National Humanities Center, where a wonderful group of scholars read and commented on parts of this book; I wish to thank Jim Peacock, Brad Weiss, Elizabeth Kennedy, Lew Erenberg, Jordanna Bailkin, Carol Summers, Lee Baker, Jeffrey Kerr-Ritchie, Brian Kelley, and Gabrielle Foreman. At the NHC I also benefited from a musicology reading group with Wendy Allanbrook, Susan Youens, and Larry Zbikowski. I am grateful to Sam Floyd not only for his scholarship and his personal support but also for a year of stimulating lunchtime conversations at the NHC during our time there together.

I know what it means to miss New Orleans, since I've spent a good bit of time there researching the material for this book. Connie Atkinson, Tony Cummings, John Joyce, Jack Stewart, and Tad Jones were all gracious with their hospitality and generous with their knowledge. So were the staffs of the two main archives I worked at, the Williams Research Center and, especially, the Hogan Jazz Archive, where Charles Chamberlain, Lynn Abbott, and Alma Freeman were of tremendous help. Richard and Debbie Snyder and Giuseppe Gerbino helped me in many ways during my visits to New York City.

Charles Chamberlain, formerly on the staff at the Hogan Jazz Archive and now at the Louisiana State Museum, has been a steady source of local and global knowledge. He read this manuscript and offered numerous suggestions. And finally, it is a pleasure to acknowledge the greatest scholarly debt I incurred while writing this book, which is to Bruce Boyd Raeburn, curator of the Hogan Jazz Archive, who gave me something of a personal tutorial in the intricacies of his archive and early jazz. Without Bruce's deep knowledge and generous spirit, this book simply would not have been possible.

My greatest personal debt is to my family, to Tekla, as always, and to Leo and Roger in this case, especially.

INTRODUCTION

~~~~~~~~~~

In the early twentieth century, New Orleans was a place of colliding identities and histories, and Louis Armstrong was a gifted young man of psychological nimbleness. The city and the musician were both extraordinary, their relationship unique, their impact on American culture incalculable.

He loved to reminisce about New Orleans. He believed that he was born on July 4, 1900, though we now know that his birth took place a year later, on August 4, 1901. His young parents, unwed and barely acquainted, left him in the care of his paternal grandmother, Josephine. His mother, May Ann (short for Mary Ann), fifteen years old at the time of his birth, moved to a different part of town; Louis did not see much of her or his father, Willie, for the first five years of his life. Josephine took the responsibility for raising him, and he had strong, positive memories of her. He was sorry to leave her when it came time to join his mother and his little sister, Beatrice, also known as "Mama Lucy."

For the next six years, the three of them lived in a two-room house in the area around Liberty and Perdido streets, a neighborhood Armstrong described as the "cheap Storyville"—that is, a downscale prostitution district. It was also alive with African-American music. During the day, parades circulated through or near the area, and so did advertising wagons, each with a little band. At night, music poured out of dance halls and honky tonks, little places for gambling that often had a musician or a small band.

Armstrong grew up poor, but he had easy, constant access to all of this music and more. He learned the names of musicians and noticed the growing reputation of cornetist Joe Oliver. His own music making started in a Sanctified church, with his mother, where he learned to sing while the congregants applauded his efforts. He hung out with a "rags-bottles-and-bones" man named Larenzo who held him "spellbound" with talk about music. In the evenings he peeked through cracks in the walls of Funky Butt Hall to watch the dancers and get familiar with the cornet styles, and he sometimes snuck into honky tonks at night to listen to blues. By age ten or so he had formed a little vocal quartet with some friends. The people in his community loved to make music, and they typically did so without much training or equipment—just a lot of heart and willingness, Armstrong would later say.

He was not closely supervised at home, and though he did have memories of school, he probably did not attend very often. He spent a lot of time on the streets with his buddies, following parades and hunting up mischief. It all caught up with him on New Year's Eve in 1912. While he and the quartet were out on one of the biggest nights of the year, hustling tips in the real Storyville, he was arrested for firing a gun and sentenced, on January 1, 1913, to the Colored Waif's Home for Boys. He spent about eighteen months there and emerged with a cornet and enough technique to impress not only his friends and neighbors but also a local honky tonk owner, who hired him, at the tender age of fourteen, to play blues late into the night.

For the next few years he held various jobs—collecting rags, delivering coal, delivering milk, washing dishes, loading boats on the docks—while trying to advance his cornet playing. He continued to live with his mother and sister and various "stepfathers" (as he playfully referred to May Ann's boyfriends) and was proud to bring home his first small earnings through music. As a substitute in bands he took the odd musical job here and there trying to find his place in the huge network of ear-playing musicians who likewise held common labor jobs and played music on the side. Around age fifteen he gained a clear advantage over most of them: Joe Oliver decided to take him under his wing. Oliver gave him lessons in his home and stopped by places where he was playing. He made it clear that Louis was welcome to hang around his band, both on parades and in dance halls, and he gave him a cornet. According to Oliver's widow, Stella, Louis was the only "scholar" Oliver ever took on. Oliver must have seen a bit of himself in the dark-skinned, impoverished child who had minimal training but a good ear that was now in evidence.

In 1918, at age seventeen, Louis married Daisy Parker, whom he met on a job where she was working as a prostitute. During the same year, a huge break for him came when Oliver decided to leave New Orleans for Chicago. Since Armstrong knew all of Oliver's solos and had been hanging around the band, Kid Ory, the band leader, yielded to the opinion of the other band members and, against his initial inclination, decided to give the spot to Louis. The job with Ory gave him broader exposure, and he came to the attention of Fate Marable, who was organizing a band to play on riverboat excursions that departed from the Canal Street dock in the evenings. When, in the spring of 1919, Marable invited Armstrong to move northward with the boat band, which was based in St. Louis for the summer, Armstrong accepted. Life with Daisy was difficult, and he sensed that the boat job would broaden his musical skills.

Over the next few years, he worked on the boats during the long summer season, then picked up gigs in New Orleans during the winters. He thrived in both settings, which demanded very different kinds of music. By the time he left the city for Chicago in 1922, he had achieved a local reputation. His fame was probably not equal to that reached by Oliver before he left in 1918, and it may not have even been at the level of Freddie Keppard or Sidney Bechet, but he was rapidly reaching maturity. In Chicago and New York City during the next few years, his musical gifts would blossom in ways that were instantly recognizable as belonging to New Orleans, even while they moved musical style forward into new territories for jazz solo playing.

✧ Armstrong grew up in an environment of low expectations, as controlled by the growing reach of Jim Crow legislation and vigilante terrorism. The famous Supreme Court case *Plessy vs. Ferguson* of

1896 was based on an incident that happened in New Orleans. In spite of its easygoing reputation, the city was not immune to the violent side of white attempts to maintain the myth of racial supremacy. This was the downside of the social situation in which many descendants of slaves found themselves in 1901, the year of his birth.

His mother was one of some forty thousand immigrants who left hundreds of plantations in Louisiana and Mississippi and headed for New Orleans during the last decades of the nineteenth century. They brought with them a culture that had been strongly shaped by legacies from various parts of Africa. In the city, they settled alongside African Americans who had been living there for some time, and they all discovered what they had in common. Something similar had happened in New Orleans during the early decades of the nineteenth century at the famous Place Congo, where as many as six hundred slaves clustered together by tribes, the Minahs, Congos, Mandingos, and Gangas staying apart from one another around the fringe of the performing circle and gradually, over the years, forging a shared African-American culture. By the 1840s the African dances of the old days were gone; they had yielded to African-American hybrids. On slave plantations the same process played out in rituals like the ring shout, where a synthesized African-American religious culture was formed out of disparate African and American traditions.

In New Orleans around 1900, the freedmen and their descendants were discovering common ground at Funky Butt Hall, in storefront churches and in street parades and funerals. These were Armstrong's early training grounds, places where the musical culture that had been formed during slavery, the African-American musical vernacular, was preserved. The word "vernacular" (from the Latin *verna*, meaning "slave") carries associations of class; it is everyday music made and appreciated by lower-class people—indeed, enslaved people. And it is mainly music made with no recourse to notation, existing purely in an oral (or aural) tradition. Armstrong lived a childhood of poverty, on the margins of society, and this position put him right in the middle of the vernacular traditions that were fueling the new music of which he would eventually become one of the world's greatest masters.

What was Armstrong's relationship to this culture? To how much of it did he remain loyal and how much did he modify as he developed into a professional dance-band musician? Further, and more provocatively, how was his music shaped by the complex social forces surrounding him, the forces of Jim Crow oppression, most obviously, but also of Creole separatism, of a passionate interest in the masculine articulation of dignity, and of the determination of the freedmen to symbolically assert cultural autonomy? These questions guide the present inquiry.

My main thesis is that Armstrong was immersed in the vernacular music that surrounded him much more thoroughly and extensively than biographers have acknowledged. This has remained obscure for several reasons. We are dealing with prehistory in the sense that early jazz made by African Americans from New Orleans was not documented on sound recordings until 1921, a year before Armstrong left the city. The history of any vernacular music is difficult to work with, since the music belongs to an oral tradition and since it is made by people whose lives tend not to be well documented. Armstrong's image has often been tied up with stereotypes of noble-savage primitivism and God-given talent that is born and not made, but it is more interesting to discover how he was shaped by the musical and social complexities of New Orleans. Many of the people who nurtured him—the "ratty" people, as one Creole of color referred to them—were impoverished, illiterate, and from broken homes. Not only were they confined to the back of the trolley car, like all other African Americans, but also many of them suffered from additional prejudices against people with relatively dark skin, which signified both a history of severe suffering under past structures of white supremacy and the near impossibility of escape from the position of subordination those structures were designed to ensure.

The story of how, out of this milieu, one of the greatest musicians of the twentieth century emerged is uniquely African American and therefore uniquely American. To understand jazz as American in this way is to work with a social conception of the music that is quite different from the familiar story of jazz as an American musical gumbo, a melting pot of many different ethnicities.

This book is not exactly a biography; it is, rather, about one musician's experience of a complex city. To the extent that it is a biography, it is a highly decentered one. The details of Armstrong's experience open up topics relevant not only to his musical development but also to the history of jazz. Thus, the book is organized around the flow of his life, but the discussion often moves laterally, into the larger context.

Armstrong was shaped by total immersion in the central traditions of African-American vernacular music. Furthermore, in New Orleans, and indeed throughout his life, he showed no interest at all in assimilating to white culture. He understood the advantages of seeing the best in people, but he despised those who "put on airs." His sharpest criticisms were directed at Negroes who were "dicty"— African-American slang for someone who pretentiously imitates

Music float, Mardi Gras, 1901 (New Orleans Public Library,
photo by Cornelius Durkee)

Street scene in New Orleans, ca. 1910
(Courtesy of the Hogan Jazz Archive, Tulane University)

whites. Eventually he learned how to play many different kinds of music, including music socially marked as white. But it is important to understand his reasons. His interest was partly professional: the more versatility a musician had, the better his options for employment. And it was partly a matter of creative curiosity about materials of sound to which he was exposed. He got from white music what he wanted, what he needed for success and what his sonic curiosity drew him to.

The point is crucial for understanding his musical accomplishment. Like virtually all African-American musicians of his generation and generations long before and long after, he was fully prepared to provide any kind of music a paying audience called for. His goal was not to *be* like white people; the goal was to *get paid by* white people. But that was a long-term project. His strength, for a long time into his maturity, was playing to black audiences, and when he did that he foregrounded a distinctively African-American set of stylistic features and values. Had it been otherwise, he would have turned out to be a very different musician.

That he was not interested in cultural assimilation is an indication of psychological security and confidence. It may also be taken as a

political stance. To insist on the value of vernacular culture and to
reject assimilation of white culture was not an idle position to take.
There were considerable ideological pressures working in the other
direction. The *Times-Picayune* of New Orleans published an arrogant
little bit of social-cultural Darwinism in a 1918 article about what it
called the "mansion of the muses." Melody is said to occupy the great
assembly hall; harmony, the sacred inner court; and rhythm, the
basement, the servant's hall, where one hears the "Negro banjo, ragtime and jazz"—"It's musical value is nil, and its possibilities of harm
are great." Some dicty Negroes undoubtedly agreed. By promoting
vernacular practices, Armstrong and people like him asserted a different political position.

Because he was committed to vernacular practices, and for other
reasons too, the story of Armstrong's musical development is shot
through with the impact of social experience. And vice versa: music
was used to cast and recast social outlook. Music was hardly neutral
in a social-political sense; it was not something to be admired in isolation in a concert hall or through a CD player. Armstrong learned
music according to various musical-social configurations ranging
from the communal nurturing of church members in a Sanctified
church to in-your-face dancing in the streets. During the early years
of Jim Crow, when vigilante terrorism rose to historically high levels,
there were plenty of opportunities for this social-musical dynamic to
be inflected in various directions.

🎵 Social tension was not the kind of thing that Armstrong and his
colleagues spoke about freely, so these conditions must be teased out
from their accounts. That the matter is obscure does not diminish its
importance. To the contrary, the social uses of music were particularly
important in the environment Armstrong grew up in. Some of this
richness is revealed by putting under a microscope a biographical
moment from 1921, near the end of Armstrong's time in the city. It is a
moment Armstrong, looking back decades later, regarded as a shining
triumph. A single parade with the Tuxedo Brass Band gave him the
feeling that he had finally arrived at the top in the city of his youth.

CHAPTER ONE

Tuxedo Brass Band, 1921

When I played with the Tuxedo Brass Band I
felt just as proud as though I had been hired by
John Philip Sousa or Arthur Pryor.
                                    —Louis Armstrong

Isidore Barbarin had a reputation as a dependable marcher, and for a man
who spent most of his working hours plastering walls, that was perhaps honor enough to live for. His love for brass bands drove him to
find a way, when called upon, to take time off from work and show
up promptly, music under control and uniform looking nice. Still, at
age forty-nine, even he must have favored certain seasons over others. In autumn—Armstrong tells us only that it was "toward the end
of 1921"—the weather in New Orleans can be uncomfortably hot
and very wet. The city's dirt streets were routinely transformed by
heavy rains into slogging paths of putrid, sewage-ridden mud. Many
musicians hated marching no matter what the weather. Emile
Barnes refused to parade unless he owed somebody a personal favor.
Hypolite Charles thought that marching had removed a few years
from his life. Aaron Clark was convinced that he had contracted
what would be his final illness from marching; his dying request was
that his son never become a musician. Walter Blue Robertson actually did die in a parade, as did a few other musicians whose identities have faded into the mist. Piled on to fears of parade-induced
illness was the objection that parades were plagued by violence from
onlookers.

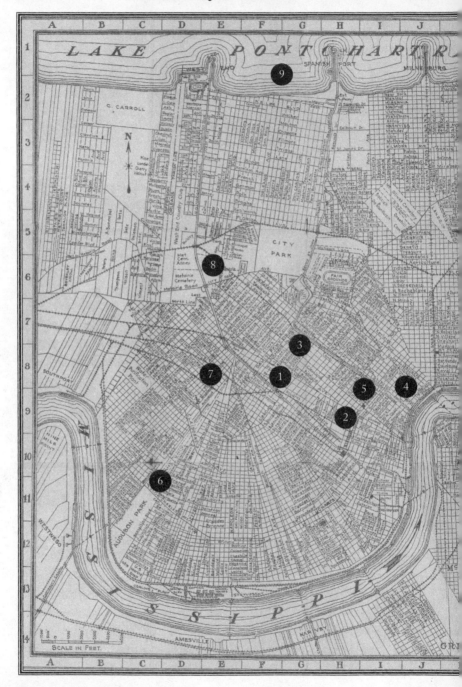

New Orleans, 1924 (New Orleans
Public Library)

1. Jane Alley, Armstrong's
   birthplace
2. Liberty and Perdido streets,
   where Armstrong grew up
3. Canal Street
4. The French Quarter
5. Storyville
6. Tulane University
7. Lincoln and Johnson Parks
8. Colored Waif's Home for
   Boys
9. Lake resorts

Isidore Barbarin (Courtesy of the Hogan Jazz Archive,
Tulane University, photo by Ralston Crawford)

If any of this concerned Barbarin, there is no evidence that it detracted from his pleasure in performing brass-band music. He usually played with the best. He learned his instrument from Charles Scior, bassoonist at the French Opera House, and by the early 1890s he was playing with the distinguished Onward Brass Band. By the late 1910s he had joined the Tuxedo Brass Band. His instrument was the "peck horn." Officially known as alto horn, the nickname came from the monotonous rhythmic punctuations on offbeats the player was required to produce—along the lines of oompah repetitions, with "peck" replacing "pah." Peck, peck, peck, tune after tune, block after block, year after year. Glory went to the cornet, duty to the peck horn. You could not have a first-class marching band without a solid peck horn, and players were not easy to find. Barbarin's dedication made him a valuable man.

Barbarin had probably heard about the substitute cornetist who would be joining the Tuxedos that autumn day in 1921. Most musicians knew about him by now. And though the idea of dutifully pecking behind the flashy playing of a twenty-year-old uptown

dark-skin may have caused Isidore a moment of hesitation, he probably recognized and appreciated a mutual enthusiasm for marching.
By this time, Armstrong had played in some fancy places—at the
New Orleans Country Club and most recently at Tom Anderson's,
where the money was very good indeed. Nevertheless, he shared this
pleasure with Isidore Barbarin, with whom he did not share very
much else. For him, there was no greater happiness than marching
in a parade. "I really felt that I was somebody," Armstrong wrote
thirty-two years later. "When I played with the Tuxedo Brass Band
I felt just as proud as though I had been hired by John Philip Sousa
or Arthur Pryor."

Perhaps you marched in a parade band when you were young.
Probably you enjoyed it, but it is unlikely that you remember the
event as one of the musical highlights of your life. When Armstrong
reflected back on this moment, he was fifty-two years old and sitting on top of the most successful career jazz had ever known. So it
is something to think about, this parade and why it meant so much
to him.

Free to Move

A parade is, by definition, a performance that moves through a
public space. For Armstrong and his community, such an event carried special significance. With his 1921 success with the Tuxedo
Brass Band, Armstrong believed that he had solved, through his
growing musical ability, the problem of trouble-free movement
through a dangerous city.

It was not uncommon during these times for people with dark
skin to be harassed when they walked through unfamiliar parts of
virtually any town in the United States. But wasn't New Orleans
different? From the start there was greater tolerance, more integration, and less restriction than perhaps anywhere else in the South.
New Orleans had slavery and all the brutality that went with it, but
in its early years the city gained a reputation for relatively relaxed
racial relations. That changed when Americans started to arrive in
large numbers after the purchase of the Louisiana Territory in 1803,
bringing with them a more vehement attitude of rigid exclusion.

The Civil War intensified the threat. In 1865 a defeated Confederate soldier returning to New Orleans described his vengeful mood: "I hope the day will come when we will have the upper hand of those black scoundrels and we will have no mercy for them we will kill them like dogs. I was never down on a nigger as I am now." New Orleanians today will tell you that there has always been tolerance, and maybe that has been true in a quirky, individual way. But it has not been true uniformly, and for someone like Armstrong part of life's challenge was learning how to deal with the problems that came from being dark-skinned, poor, and disfranchised.

In 1921, the most notorious incident in anyone's memory was the July 1900 shootout and riot involving Robert Charles. Charles was an admirer of Bishop Henry Turner's back-to-Africa movement, and he had learned during his youth in Mississippi the utility of a gun in the face of lawless, racially charged violence. The catastrophe in New Orleans started when Charles was visiting someone in an unfamiliar part of town. Questioned why he was there by an intimidating policeman, Charles drew his revolver and fired.

Fleeing to a second-floor apartment barely ten blocks from the neighborhood where Armstrong grew up, Charles relied on a Winchester rifle and a stockpile of bullets, homemade with his portable furnace, to fend off a huge mob of white citizens. Before they killed him, he shot twenty-seven people. In response to his one-man insurrection, three thousand whites produced twelve hours of indiscriminate rioting, burning, beatings, and killing throughout African-American neighborhoods. All of this happened barely a year before Armstrong was born. A commemorative song circulated, but, as Jelly Roll Morton pointed out, it was wise to forget the song "in order to get along with the world on the peaceful side." It did not take citywide rioting to make African Americans aware of the unwritten laws governing their movement, but the event certainly stood as an enduring emblem of what those laws were all about.

Another terrorizing occasion was the defeat of the boxer Jim Jeffries—known as the "Great White Hope"—by the Negro Jack Johnson on July 4, 1910. Johnson's victory caused white rioting throughout the country, and New Orleans was no exception. Armstrong remembered hiding in his house while gangs wandered

New Orleans Item, *August 2, 1900, satirizing the heroism of Corporal Trenchard in the face of Robert Charles*

through the neighborhood in search of random targets on whom to release their rage. Such was the New Orleans into which Louis Armstrong was born.

These events did not trouble lighter-skinned Creoles in the same way. Guitarist Louis Keppard was asked in the 1950s if his father had been threatened during the Robert Charles riots. He answered no, that his father "could pass around the streets," that he wouldn't be bothered because he was Creole and "kind of bright" ("bright" meaning light-skinned). For a Creole like Isidore Barbarin (b. 1872), the threat of racial violence was apparently remote. Asked to reminisce about his childhood, Barbarin recalled, "I didn't know I was colored until, I mean, well later years—I didn't know I was colored." That statement speaks volumes about the different experiences of Creoles and Negroes like Armstrong. For there was never a time when Armstrong or any member of his family did not know that he or she was colored.

His first experience of what it meant to be colored was sharply etched in his memory. It came with his first ride in a trolley car, in 1906 at age five. Accompanied by an adult friend of the family, the five-year-old boarded the trolley and decided to play a game. Instead of sitting with his guardian, he moved to the opposite end of the car, straight past the sign—which he could not read, of course—that marked the boundary of racial seating. He never forgot his guardian's panic as she seized him and dragged him back. She was so frightened, he remembered, that she "turned colors" (pun intended), and cursed him, "SIT DOWN DAMMIT." Here was the child's first taste of the institutional guarantee of disadvantage that he would live with, in one form or another, for the rest of his life. In his guardian's panic he got a glimpse of how terror reinforced the legal side of Jim Crow.

He wrote about several incidents that occurred during his teenage years, when walking through unfamiliar sections of the city was tinged with danger. At age seventeen he took a job across the river in Gretna that required him to return home very late. The scene made him apprehensive: "Just a few drunks, white and colored . . . Lots of times, the both races, looked like they were going to get into a scrap, over just nothing much . . . And down there, with something like that happening, with just a few 'Spades' (colored folks) around, it wasn't so good . . . Even if the colored are in the right—when the cops arrive, they'll whip your head, and then, ask questions." Two years later his wife Daisy took a job with a white family who provided the couple with a small apartment behind the main house. The first night that he returned home late after a gig, Louis was terrified he would not be able to explain his presence to the "watchman." Daisy gave notice the next morning and the couple promptly moved.

Armstrong was not given to dwelling on social problems, and he rarely mentioned them in public. But near the end of his life he wrote the bluntest possible account of racial relations in New Orleans, confirming that the intense hatred held by the returning Confederate veteran remained an active force:

At *ten* years old I could see—the Bluffings that those Old *Fat Belly Stinking* very *Smelly Dirty* White Folks were *putting Down*. It seemed as though the only thing they *cared* about was their Shot Guns or those Old time *Shot* Guns which they had strapped around them. So they get full of their *Mint Julep* or that *bad* whisky, the poor white Trash were Guzzling down, like water, then when they get so *Damn* Drunk until they'd go out of their minds—then it's Nigger Hunting time. *Any* Nigger. They wouldn't give up until they would find one. From then on, Lord have mercy on the poor *Darkie*. Then they would Torture the poor Darkie, as innocent as he may be. They would get their usual Ignorant *Chess Cat* laughs before they would shoot him down—like a Dog. *My my my, those* were the days.

One of his youthful passions was second lining, the practice of following a parade as it made its route through the city. Second-line gangs carried homemade weapons—"drum sticks, baseball bats, and all forms of ammunition we'd call it to combat some of the foe when they come to the dividing line," according to Jelly Roll Morton. It was while second lining that Armstrong learned all about foes and dividing lines. The Irish Channel, uptown and near the river, was notoriously hostile to Negroes who did not live there; "if you followed a parade out there you might come home with your head in your hand," he wrote. Creole neighborhoods also marked their boundaries efficiently. Many Creoles were forbidden to second line due to the violence regularly associated with it. Benny Williams, a parade drummer universally known as "Black Benny," was sought after not only for his musical skill but also for his ability to match blow for blow with a heavy blackjack that he pulled out when necessary. "Nobody would do us nothing," said bass player Ed Garland. "He used to take care of us." Armstrong figured out a less dangerous way of dealing with the problem. If he could gain the privilege of carrying the horn of Willie "Bunk" Johnson, Joe Oliver, or some other cornetist, neither the police nor neighborhood toughs would bother him. By performing this little service, the unsupervised child could stay with the band on its entire route. Later, in his mid-teens as a hired cornetist, he was known to break away from his parade steps in order to chase down and flail hecklers.

Freedom of movement was a rare privilege that antebellum slaves had cherished highly. Beyond a small handful of yearly holidays, a slave could visit a neighboring plantation only when his master allowed; more daringly, he could break the law and make a visit without permission. After Reconstruction, whites adapted earlier techniques for repressing movement. Similarly, so did the freedmen and their descendants bring to New Orleans a sense of pleasure in being able to move freely from one place to another. With his 1921 march with the Tuxedo Brass Band, Armstrong felt that his musical ability had granted him a passport for safe passage throughout the city.

Within his community, that was a notable triumph. Black Benny was "the only man, musician or not, who dared to go anywhere, whether it was the Irish Channel, Back O' Town, the Creole section in the Seventh Ward or any other tough place," he wrote. "He was not afraid of a living soul." Guitarist Danny Barker described Black Benny as "six foot six inches, 200 pounds of primitive African prime manhood" (a description that says as much about Barker, a Creole, as it says about Williams). What made movement difficult for Williams and Armstrong was the dark complexion of their skin. Joe Oliver, Armstrong's mentor, experienced the same problem. Jelly Roll Morton's taunting nickname for Oliver was "Blondie." But in Armstrong's mind the 1921 parade had solved the problem for him. "I too could go into any part of New Orleans without being bothered," he wrote. "Everybody loved me and just wanted to hear me blow, even the tough characters were no exception. The tougher they were the more they would fall in love with my horn." First, the child gained mobility through the protection of adult musicians, by carrying their horns; later, he learned how to fight and rely on strong allies; finally, he earned the reward of unmolested passage thanks to his musical skill. As jazz fanned out across the country, more than a few musicians were drawn to the profession because it brought them that same opportunity. When Armstrong left New Orleans in 1922, he started traveling on a grand scale, and in a sense he never stopped until his very last years in Queens, New York.

On one level, a parade through unfamiliar territory stands as a symbolic victory: it accomplishes the goal of unrestricted motion while preserving the "real" status quo, the otherwise rigidly enforced restrictions. But the parade is more than symbolic because it moves through the actual battlegrounds of class conflict. And it is also structured as a moment for asserting cultural autonomy, to literally broadcast vernacular culture over the entire city, through the hostile Irish Channel and the Creole Seventh Ward, through the blood-stained streets of the Robert Charles riots, the very streets where fat-bellied, stinking white folks hunted down targets of revenge after Jim Johnson's victory and where Jim Crow laws scripted the performance of a social structure of subservience and exploitation by requiring rear seating in trolleys.

Late in his life Armstrong grew fond of the idea that his music was capable of dissolving racially charged violence. He remembered a 1948 performance for an integrated audience in Miami: "I walked on stage and there I saw something I thought I'd never see. I saw thousands of people, colored and white on the main floor. Not seg-regated in one row of whites and another row of Negroes . . . These same society people may go around the corner and lynch a Negro. But while they're listening to our music, they don't think about trouble. What's more they're watching Negro and white musicians play side by side. And we bring contentment and pleasure. I always say, 'Look at the nice taste we leave. It's bound to mean something. That's what music is for.'" His feeling that music issues an antidote to violence appears to have had its origins in New Orleans.

Yet that was largely a conceit, a comforting homily to be called on when needed. More salient were the many incidents when the threat of racist violence intruded on his music, literally surrounding it and shaping many career decisions. Though it pleased him to look out from a stage and see smiling white folks, he may never have completely left behind his internalized fear of white violence. What sociologist John Dollard wrote in the 1930s certainly held for Armstrong: "Every Negro in the South knows that he is under a kind of sentence of death; he does not know when his turn will come, it may never come, but it may also be any time." After he moved in 1922 to Chicago, where there was a degree of racial mix-ing and also an increasingly assertive self-image among African Americans, he remained shy and deferential. White musicians idolized him. They gathered around the bandstand to admire his brilliantly spun licks, and they gradually got to know him. Eventually they invited him to a party. He accepted the invitation; nevertheless, when he arrived he could not be persuaded to leave the kitchen.

Music in the Open Air

The value Armstrong placed on unrestricted movement is linked to another reason why he remembered this 1921 parade with the Tuxedo Brass Band so fondly: the most important venues for music, for him and the people he grew up with, were located outdoors rather than indoors. Today we appreciate his musical legacy in our homes, on the CD player, or perhaps on television. The tradition of jazz that flowed out of New Orleans came to be performed in venues that imitate, to one degree or another, the European model of classical music in the concert hall, which in turn imitates the contemplative atmosphere of church worship in the West. Indoor music stands at the top of our pyramid of values, street music on the bottom. In the New Orleans of Armstrong's youth this relationship was turned on its head.

A cabaret has walls that limit the size of the audience, which must pay to listen; the audience for street music is unlimited and the music is free. To a child growing up in poverty this made all the difference. With the exception of church, most of Armstrong's early musical influences were absorbed outdoors, on the streets every day. Men collecting junk for recycling played blues on tinhorns, and bands played on advertising wagons and in parades. As he wandered around town, he could even listen to music from dance halls and honky tonks as it freely flowed through open windows and cracks in the walls. If violence provided the brutal push, the barrier to free movement, then music provided the seductive pull. Violence and music were thus paired as opposing forces of repulsion and attraction ripping through the vertical organization of society.

Music outdoors was always interactive. Parades are the famous example. Louis rarely saw his father when he was growing up, but he sometimes watched him perform as the grand marshal in parades. "All the chicks would swoon when he'd pass by with his high hat, tails, and a long beautiful, streamer hanging down by his side," he wrote. "It would just send me to watch my dad, sort of, put his hand towards the middle of those streamers, and casually hold it (a little) as he would strut like a Peacock." Marchers in the second line interacted with the grand marshal, with the music of the band, and with each other. In the famous New Orleanian "funeral with music" the band played hymns, slowly with grief on the way to the cemetery while the community of mourners sang along. On the celebratory return, they played up-tempo ragtime, spiking the crowds in number and excitement.

Jessie Charles, a Methodist unsympathetic to extroverted styles of worship, described the scene: "Second line—that's the life of the parade and a funeral . . . Dancing in Sanctified Churches is like the second line. The Baptists do a shout." The ring shout was the most important religious-musical ritual during the period of slavery, and Charles is recognizing its lingering importance in New Orleans. A slow, shuffling circle dance, with clapping and singing in call and response between soloists and the group, the ring shout may well have been the central arena where slave culture was born as a synthesis of disparate African and American traditions. It was based on the many circle-dance traditions of West Africa and performed with an intense focus on musical-kinetic interaction. The practice was designed to bring out emotions in ecstatic, communal display. It promoted a style of spiritual engagement that continued to mark religious practice among Baptists and the newly found Sanctified sects. In New Orleans, second lining brought the ecstatic behavior of the ring shout into the streets. One New Orleanian musician put a nice finish on this church analogy when he said how important it is to look nice in a parade because "you gonna have a congregation of people lookin' at you."

Parades thus offered disfranchised Negroes a chance to assertively move their culture through the city's public spaces, the very spaces where African Americans were expected to confirm social inferiority by sitting in the rear of trolley cars and by stepping aside on sidewalks to allow whites to pass. In many parts of the South after the Civil War, African Americans had chosen to demonstrate subversive rudeness instead—brushing shoulders on the sidewalk, for example, or

Alfred T. Bricher, "Religious Dancing of Blacks, Termed Shouting,"
engraving from The Black Man of the South and the Rebels
by Charles Stearns, 1892

failing to yield altogether. In the early years of the twentieth century, shoulder bumping was largely a thing of the past. ("Good darkies" move into the gutter when a white person approaches, a smug South Carolinian was pleased to report in 1905.) It was much safer to assert dignity symbolically. The city of Place Congo, where slaves had gathered in the hundreds to perform African dances accompanied by African music played on African instruments, now accommodated the equally public display of African-American vernacular culture on parade, which often included a flashy set of pseudomilitary gestures borrowed from the French—uniforms for the marching club members, plumed hats for the grand marshal, the muffled snare imitating a military kettledrum, even sabers. It would not have taken much to regard the whole thing as a symbolic act of resistance to Jim Crow hegemony, which may partly explain why second lining was so consistently associated with violence.

The people Armstrong grew up with understood music as a medium of social interaction, and since they performed outdoors so often, the range of that social interaction easily opened up to the intense political oppression that stifled their daily existence. The context is therefore fundamentally different from that of European art music, in which "art" is conceived in isolation, by the cloistered composer, for the equally isolated, imaginative interpretation of every member of the art-hall audience. That model makes no sense in Louis Armstrong's New Orleans, where the "artist" is a public performer who thrives on direct visual and aural interaction. These dimensions of cultural practice did not survive the Great Migration of jazz out of New Orleans to points north, east, and west. Or at least they did not survive in precisely the same form. Armstrong, as much as anyone, would be responsible for changing the music and the terms of its reception. But before he left New Orleans he received his greatest recognition in the open-air space of immediate and public interaction.

It was not just whites who were targeted in public displays of symbolic resistance. Manuel Perez, an old-line Creole, was disgusted by the intensity of the second line: "Lots of people dancing, misbehaving, it drove him out of music," said Hypolite Charles. Danny Barker told a similar story about Chris Kelly, a cornetist born on the Magnolia Plantation downriver, who "played for those blues, cotton-picking Negroes, what they called in the old days 'yard and field Negroes' who worked in the fields, worked hard. When he would play a street parade, mostly advertising, all the kitchen mechanics would come out on the corner, shaking. The Creoles would hate to see that." Armstrong wrote about a parade from around 1918 when he, Kid Ory, and a few other improvising musicians were hired to supplement a band of Creoles led by John Robichaux. Subtly but surely, the Creoles made known their sense of superiority, causing Armstrong to turn to Ory and wonder, "You dig what I'm digging?"

According to Armstrong's memory, the Creole arrogance dissolved when he and Ory swung the band so beautifully on the uptempo return from burial that the second line demanded an encore. He viewed that moment as a social and musical victory: "We proved to them that any learned musician can read music, but they all can't swing . . . Nice lesson for them." This publicly issued lesson brings us to what was probably a third reason for Armstrong's treasured memory from 1921: in that parade he achieved friendship and respect from the old-school Creoles, perhaps for the first time.

Color and the Creoles

The earliest surviving document written by Armstrong is a letter he wrote from Chicago dated September 1, 1922. He had just arrived from New Orleans in August, and he was already busy writing to his friends back home. This letter is addressed to "Mr. Barbarin, Dear Friend"—that is, Isidore Barbarin, the peck-horn player in the Tuxedo Brass Band. Armstrong reaffirms their mutual fondness for marching: "The boys [in Chicago] give me H . . . all the Time because [I'm] forever talking about the Brass Band . . . They say I don't see how a man can be crazy about those hard parades." It is clear that the two had established a friendship. Given Barbarin's social and musical biases and Armstrong's background, this is noteworthy, for Barbarin was a downtown Creole, Armstrong an uptown Negro. In musical circles of the time those labels of social distinction carried tremendous weight.

Like most cities in the United States, different sections of New Orleans have been historically associated with different ethnic groups. Since 1836, when the city was partitioned into three municipalities, Canal Street has provided the central boundary of this kind. The original French settlers located their village—the area now known as the French Quarter—on a sharp bend in the Mississippi River that gave them a good view of trouble approaching from either direction. Because of this and other riverbends, the city cannot be negotiated with a compass; the streets spin out in directions that are rarely north, south, east, or west. Canal Street became the main point of orientation. Still today, residents speak of the downriver side of Canal Street, beginning with the French Quarter, as "downtown," and the upriver side as "uptown." But the boundary of Canal Street was much more than a point of orientation. Beginning with the 1836 partitions, the uptown side was also called the "American section," and downtown the "French section." These terms were used by musicians from our period, and these basic geographic-demographic facts of the city were part of the social texture that played such a huge role in the history of early jazz.

The downtown population that concerns us—because it is the population that concerned Armstrong—is the group of people who had mixed ancestry, French and African. Armstrong knew them simply as "Creoles"; at times they have also been called "Creoles of color." Creoles were French-speaking Catholics. They controlled superb traditions of musical pedagogy, deriving from the French Opera House and ultimately from the Paris Conservatoire, at a level that is very hard to find in the United States today. They also embraced the American fondness for brass bands. Out of their numbers came a few musicians who gained national attention, including Arnold Metoyer, with whom Armstrong played during his last few years in New Orleans.

On the other side of Canal Street, the uptown "American" side, the last decades of the nineteenth century brought continual social flux. Yankee immigrants had been arriving in huge numbers since the Louisiana Purchase of 1803 and they continued to come; so did the Germans and the Irish. As the turn of the century approached, these groups were joined by alarming numbers of Italians and Jews. Even more alarming was the massive influx of freedmen and their descendants arriving from the rural plantations of Louisiana and Mississippi. This was Armstrong's group. Creoles were wary of these plantation immigrants. As they watched them arrive in imposing numbers, the Creoles asserted a multidimensional sense of cultural difference. They produced a package of social barriers that Armstrong was forced to deal with if he wanted to advance musically.

As Danny Barker's description of Black Benny Williams—"six foot six inches, 200 pounds of primitive African prime manhood"— indicates, the Creole sense of difference included appearance. Barker belonged to a younger generation, and he does not usually reveal the Creole snobbishness that typically marks the generation of his grandfather, Isidore Barbarin. The fact is that people on both sides of Canal Street routinely thought about people in terms of relative lightness and darkness of skin color. Perhaps you did not think that the infinitely varied shadings of skin color mattered so much *within* the African-American population, with everyone thrown into the same miserable boat named Jim Crow—especially within the African-American population of New Orleans, with its legendary tolerance and social relaxation. Unfortunately, it did matter. In New Orleans, perhaps even more than most places in the United States, differences in skin color were constantly noticed and regarded as primary markers of social difference.

The following sampling of descriptions of some of Armstrong's contemporaries, most of them from Armstrong himself (others are so identified), highlights the period's sense of shaded distinctions:

BLACK BENNY WILLIAMS: "a very much good looking, real smooth black, young man"

JOE OLIVER: "There are three kinds of blacks: A *black,* a *lamb* black, and a *damn* black. I'm black and I only seen two other damn people in the world blacker'n me" (Oliver describing himself)

CAPTAIN "SORE" DICK (policeman): "short, not too stout jet black guy, built like a brick house"

ISAIAH HUBBARD: "a real black man, with thick mustache, carried a pistol"

HENRY ZENO (drummer): "a little short, dark, sharp cat"

"SNOW" (criminal in Armstrong's neighborhood): "a real dark character"

NICODEEMUS (a "character who had me spellbound through my years in the third ward"): "jet black"

TONY JACKSON: "real dark and not a bit good looking" (Jelly Roll Morton)

CLERK WADE ("sharpest Pimp that New Orleans ever had"): "goodlooking, tall dark and handsome guy . . . He had a very nice smile . . . He was a real dark brown skin young man—who kept his hair cut real close (Konk wasn't known in those days). Clerk wore the very best of clothes and he also had diamonds in his garters for his socks"

LEONTINE RICHARDSON (daughter of Armstrong's cousin): "a nice looking brown skin gal . . . a little on the short side"

BUDDY BOLDEN: "brown, not dark" (Kid Ory)

ARTHUR BROWN (neighborhood boy dead at age fifteen): "a very much, good looking boy, with the prettiest brown skin (light brown)"

NELLY WILLIAMS (Black Benny's wife): "a real short, good looking, light skinned colored gal"

LORENZO TIO: "straight black hair and a copper-colored complexion" (Barney Bigard)

MORRIS MOORE: "A tall, real light skin'd-fellow, very much good-looking"

ISAAC SMOOTH: "Goodlooking light skinned boy"

MRS. MARTIN (caretaker of the neighborhood school) and her "three beautiful daughters, Orleania, Alice, and Wilhelmenia": "all were real light skinned . . . On the same order of the Creole type."

JOHN COOTAY (husband of Alice Martin): "He could easily pass for a white boy . . . But he couldn't be bothered"

DAVE PERKINS (musician and possible teacher of Joe Oliver): "very light, like a white fellow" (Warren "Baby" Dodds)

JOHN ROBICHAUX: "could easily have 'passed' for Caucasian" (Edmond Souchon)

Armstrong's description of his fourth and last wife, Lucille, helps to round out his reading of the color chart: "When I first saw her the glow of her deep-brown skin got me deep down. When we first met, she was dancing in the line at the old Cotton Club and was the darkest girl in the line . . . I suppose I'm partial to brown and dark-skinned women, anyhow. None of my four wives was a light-colored woman."

The event of the dark-skinned Armstrong playing along-side light-skinned Creoles like Barbarin in the Tuxedo Brass Band must be understood in a context where racial appearance and cultural practice were not necessarily separated in people's minds. Musicians in New Orleans, like most Americans of the time, conflated the two unless they had a good reason to think otherwise. When Creole musicians looked at Armstrong, they saw racial markers and thought about a whole set of cultural differences. We know a little bit about Barbarin's own biases from his grandson Danny Barker, and they are not surprising, given what we know about other Creoles of Barbarin's generation. "Isidore referred to musicians who played jazz music in the many six-piece jazz bands about the city as 'routine' musicians," wrote Barker. "It was a slur. To him, 'routine' meant playing by ear, with no music, in the now 'classic' jazz pattern: melody, then variations on a theme . . . I heard Isidore once say of [Buddy] Bolden, 'Sure, I heard him. I knew him. He was famous with the ratty people.' I soon learned what ratty people, ratty joints and dives meant: it meant good-time people, earthy people, who frequent anywhere there's a good time . . . So, ratty music is bluesy, folksy music that moves you and exhilarates you, makes you dance."

So another good reason for Armstrong's strong feelings about his 1921 appearance with the Tuxedo Brass Band would be his successful integration with downtown Creoles. Not just any Creoles, but the older generation like Barbarin, who embraced Eurocentric musical standards and scorned everything else. One does not have to read too deeply between the lines to understand who the ratty people were: they were poor and uneducated, direct descendants from slaves, recent arrivals from the rural plantations, often with dark skin and holding cultural values that were distinctly not Eurocentric. Armstrong was very much a product of the culture Barbarin disdained. "Bluesy, folksy music that moves you and exhilarates you, makes you dance"—that was the kind of music he grew up with, day in and day out.

Before 1921, Armstrong's contact with Creoles seems to have been slight, though he did have some professional acquaintances and even some friendships. But now he found himself alongside established figures in the downtown tradition. William "Bebé" Ridgley and Oscar "Papa" Celestin were not at all Creoles but immigrants from the plantations to uptown New Orleans ("We were both country boys," Ridgley said). In 1917 they formed the Tuxedo Brass Band and the Tuxedo Dance Band with the aim of competing for the very best jobs. Celestin joined several fraternal clubs with an eye toward using his contacts to land jobs, and Ridgley opened up a line of work by befriending a "white gentleman named Sim Black who was Scoutmaster for Boy Scout Troop 13." Together they booked their bands "almost everywhere in the city of New Orleans and the state of Louisiana that a colored band could go," said Ridgley. Their success allowed them to hire some of the old-school Creoles like Barbarin and Alphonse Picou, thus producing an "integrated band," with members from both sides of Canal Street.

❧ On the day of his remembered march, Armstrong was greeted by Papa Celestin's warm welcome and also a bit of caution. This was the first time he had ever seen a lyre for holding notated music, and Celestin worried about his ability to read the music. Armstrong took this in the best way: "That was a good deal of encouragement for a young fellow without too much brass band experience." His first fully professional position, a couple of years earlier, was with Kid Ory's nonreading band, surely an exemplar of Barbarin's idea of ratty and routine. Drummer Warren "Baby" Dodds said that "the [uptown and downtown] musicians mixed only if you were good enough." Armstrong had become good enough by 1921.

What makes the history of early jazz so rich is the need to parse "good" according to two different standards of valuation—one for downtown Creoles, the other for uptown Negroes. Downtown, "good" meant precise intonation, a round and full timbre, and the ability to read music fluently. Just a couple of years earlier, Armstrong had been so intimidated by the idea of playing with a good reading band that he drank himself sick with cheap wine. But his note-reading skills, as well as other dimensions of his cornet technique, had advanced considerably during the intervening years, thanks mainly to his jobs on the riverboats beginning in 1918 and running intermittently for the rest of his time in the city.

The standard of "good enough" cultivated in Armstrong's uptown circles constitutes one of the main topics of this book. Canal Street is very wide, and the cultural gap it represented was wider still. It must have been clear to Barbarin and everyone else how far Armstrong had come by the autumn of 1921. What he brought to the Tuxedo Brass Band and eventually to the world was the product of years of tutoring in a musical culture that has not been well understood. It was a culture based on blues, on communal singing in church, and on the string-band tradition of ragging tunes. It held a special place for improvisation. Its skills emerged from a set of values and practices quite different from those fostered by Eurocentric practices. It was a culture that consciously extended practices formed during slavery, in secret in the woods or in public for the benefit of the planters. A culture that, in sum, carried a strong African legacy.

The social dimensions of Armstrong's experience were both restrictive and liberating, as they always are for artists, but with a special twist for a dark-skinned child living in poverty during one of the most violently oppressive periods in the nation's history. There were comforts in life, music being the strongest of them all. Armstrong had the good fortune to grow up among people who granted music a prominent place, music of any kind, but especially music that had some direct social purpose and especially music that had soul.

CHAPTER TWO

The Saints

It all came from the Old Sanctified Churches.
—Louis Armstrong

Everybody in there sang and they clapped and
stomped their feet and sang with their whole
bodies. They had beat, a powerful beat, a
rhythm we held on to from slavery days, and
their music was so strong and expressive it
used to bring tears to my eyes.
—Mahalia Jackson on the Sanctified Church

When Armstrong was asked late in life about his religious beliefs, he responded, "I'm a Baptist and a good friend of the Pope's and I always wear a Jewish star a friend gave me for luck." This clever answer communicates on several levels. Behind it lies the fact that Armstrong was exposed to all three religions—Baptist, Catholic, and Judaism—during his childhood. Only his experience with Baptists—along with the collection of sects that will be referred to here as "Sanctified" and whose members are known as "Saints"— had a fundamental and lasting impact, however.

Catholicism came first. Sponsored by his paternal great-grandmother, Catherine Walker, Louis was baptized at the Sacred Heart of Jesus Church on August 25, 1901, three weeks after his birth. It would be a mistake to place much emphasis on these Catholic connections. In New Orleans during his youth, Armstrong's name was pronounced "Lewis" rather than "Louie," contrary to his national reputation; as his widow Lucille wryly observed, "He wasn't French," and we have already glimpsed the implications of that distinction. In spite of Walker's commitment to Catholicism, her daughter Josephine does not appear to have continued the faith. The boy lived with Josephine for the first five years of his life, and she made sure that he got to church and Sunday school. "That's where I acquired my singing tactics," he wrote. "I did a whole lot of singing in church . . . my heart went into every hymn I sang." The reference to hymns and to active congregational singing implies Baptist rather than Catholic services. It is likely that after his baptism he did not enter a Catholic church again until long after he left New Orleans in 1922.

His early experience of Judaism and Jewish culture is more unusual and harder to assess. In an impassioned memoir written just before he died, he claimed Jewish singing as one of his youthful inspirations. A family named Karnofsky provided his main and perhaps only Jewish connection in New Orleans. He worked for them as a teenager, picking rags and hauling coal. They may have even been the only "white" family he knew very well. They fed him in their home and tried to improve his pronunciation of standard English, encouraging him to say "this" and "that" instead of "dis" and "dat." His later career brought him into contact with many Jews in the music business, and he grew close to some of them, especially his manager Joe Glaser.

In any event, the impact of Judaism and Catholicism on Armstrong was slight compared to that of the Baptist and Sanctified churches he attended as a child. The Baptist Church and its newly found offshoots provided many African Americans in the Deep South with their main social networks, and they were also places of intense personal fulfillment. Young Louis was no exception.

From Baptist to Sanctified

While Josephine was raising Louis, decisions about his upbringing must have been her responsibility alone. Armstrong always referred to his mother as "May Ann," which probably indicates the early maternal bond with his grandmother; African-American children raised by a grandmother often call her "mother" and the biological mother by her given name. It is not unusual in nonindustrial societies for grandmothers to rear young children while parents and older children work. The arrangement is practical and serves cultural stability; it creates a situation in which the inflexible minds of the elderly impart values and traditions to the youngest and most malleable minds. Since Louis's mother was fifteen years old when he was born, and his father never took much interest in him, it must have seemed to Josephine like a decree of destiny that the early childrearing should fall to her.

With a bit of inference it is easy to imagine the surrounding details. When Louis does eventually move in with his mother, she is living not in the peripheral, "Back of Town" district where his grandmother lived, but in the heart of the colored prostitution district, near the corner of Liberty and Perdido streets. Life was an adventure since he and his sister never knew when May Ann might disappear for several days, in which case the children depended on neighbors and their Uncle Ike, May Ann's brother. A succession of "stepfathers," as Armstrong jokingly referred to May Ann's boyfriends,

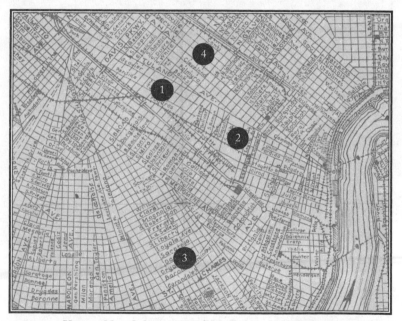

Uptown New Orleans, 1924 (New Orleans Public Library)
1. Jane Alley   2. Liberty and Perdido streets
3. Site of the Robert Charles shootout   4. Canal Street

came and went. "If my mother was Hustling, I could not say," he wrote, which seems to be a way of saying that she did indeed work as a prostitute.

Mahalia Jackson, the great gospel singer and Armstrong's near contemporary, spent her childhood in New Orleans, just a few miles upriver from where Armstrong lived. She once explained that if a young girl was going through a time of temptation, the family looked to their preacher for help. The preacher would visit the girl and "try to keep her out of the bad houses—bring her back." Perhaps Uncle Ike sought this kind of help for May Ann, for we find her "getting religion" sometime around 1910. Louis witnessed

River baptism, 1940s (Historic New Orleans Collection, Acc. No. 1976.139.26)

the conversion. The preacher, Elder Cozy, "had the whole church just rocking . . . May Ann started to shouting, knocked me off the bench, and as stout as she was, she shouted so much until it took six of the strongest brothers to grab hold of her and pacify her." The conversion was followed by baptism in the Mississippi River. The intensity of the ritual overwhelmed the child: "the preachers had to duck May Ann under that water so much and so fast, until I had to turn my head." The conversion must signal May Ann's abandonment, at least for a time, of prostitution. Income would now come through domestic work for white people, the most common occupation by far for female members of Sanctified sects during this period. "All of you wash-ladies understand the necessary need of every garment being perfectly clean," preached Rev. J. F. Forest of Atlanta. "And *you* is a garment for God."

Church could not have been entirely new to her. May Ann was probably raised Baptist like the majority of her neighbors who had moved to New Orleans from the plantations. She grew up near Boutte, about fifty miles west of the city. Her parents had been slaves and were "all but slaves," as Armstrong phrased it, at the time she was born. We might look again to Mahalia Jackson for a family history that moved in parallel to Armstrong's. After emancipation Jackson's maternal ancestors remained on a cotton plantation about a hundred miles northwest of New Orleans where they had been enslaved. They left for New Orleans in the last decade of the nineteenth century. Uncle Porter was the first to go; he left in disgust after a request for shoes to keep his feet warm in winter was refused. He found work in New Orleans as a crewman on a steamboat, then as a cook, and then as a waiter. His success inspired the rest of the family to follow. They had been Baptists on the plantation, baptizing new members in the Atchafalaya River, and they continued their Baptist faith in New Orleans, where Mahalia grew up attending the Mount Moriah Baptist Church.

Emancipation promised the freedmen of the South many things, but it took decades and even lifetimes for most of those promises to be fulfilled. There were the promises of literacy, of land, of voting rights, and of political power, just to name a few. The swirling, tumultuous forces of southern hostility, northern corruption, and, above all, American willingness to sacrifice the welfare of the freed-men to accommodate southern demands tragically caused the collapse of Reconstruction. But of all the promises implied by emancipation, one was kept and exploited fully. That was the opportunity to establish independent churches. To be free of white religion, while taking from it whatever fit, whatever was useful and adaptable—that was the great, uncompromised blessing of the troubled last decades of the nineteenth century. No more of the "cold and proper" religion of the white folks, taken in from a remote church balcony. No more need to meet secretly in the damp and chilly woods. During these post-Reconstruction decades, spiritual energy was bursting out in all directions, articulated through some of the most potent forms of expressive culture ever created.

The Baptists succeeded beyond all other denominations in their missionary efforts among the freedmen. They offered the experience of conversion, with ecstatic displays of spiritual communion and the symbolic use of water, each matching up with African rituals that had been important in slave religion. They offered a preaching style designed to engage the worshipper emotionally. Baptists had no interest in centralized, denominational control, which made it easy for Negro lay preachers with little or no formal training to form their own congregations. It is estimated that 62 percent of all African-American churchgoers in Louisiana were Baptists in 1890. Here was a welcoming space for African-derived traditions of worship.

Charles "Sunny" Henry (b. 1885) grew up on the Magnolia Plantation downriver from New Orleans, where his Baptist congregation clapped hands and danced vigorously enough to make "jubilee time," as Henry described it. Sometimes a brass band performed right inside the church to augment the congregational singing. Harrison Barnes came from the same plantation, and he described how the congregation sang: "They'd word it out, then they'd sing that strain. Then they'd word it out again and sing some more, you know? I don't know how to call that . . . Sometimes they would start to clapping their hands on the jubilee. Sometimes the sisters would shout, you know, just like a person would dance there . . . it wasn't dancing, it was so near dancing I don't know what it is." Barnes is talking here about the two main religious-musical practices that emerged from slavery: first, solo lining out of the hymn followed by a slow, heterophonic rendition by the congregation; second, the ring shout. New Orleans had its own traditions of ecstatic worship, and the plantation immigration was strengthening them. The city directory listed twenty Baptist churches in 1885 and nearly fifty by 1900.

During those same decades, however, Baptist houses of worship were feeling the winds of change. Northern missionaries' new goals for the freedmen went beyond conversion and salvation to include assimilation and social uplift. The missionaries worked this agenda through the new Negro colleges and secondary schools dotted throughout the South. Zealous graduates fanned out to promote Victorian values, their collective vision reaffirmed annually at the National Baptist Conventions. The missionaries targeted the morals and habits of the masses in tracts with titles like *Take a Bath First*, *How to Dress*, *Ten Things the Negro Needs*, and—one that must have caused more than a few laughs in New Orleans—*Anti-Hanging Out Committee*. The Shiloh Baptist Church in Washington, D.C., demanded in 1914 that any member caught dancing or drinking stand before the church and be censured. But the missionaries inevitably found services inside of the church building much easier to control than the day-to-day personal habits of their members. They discouraged the kind of ecstatic music and dancing that Henry and Barnes grew up with on the Magnolia Plantation. At the First Baptist Church on St. Simon's Island, Georgia, "noisy" worshippers were asked to leave the building. By the time Mahalia began attending Mount Moriah Baptist Church in the 1910s, congregational singing had been cut back in favor of anthems sung by the choir and by soloists. While the choir sang, the seated congregation clapped their hands and tapped their feet. Mahalia described the singing as "sweet."

It is interesting to speculate about what May Ann's reaction might have been to these Baptist changes. We know that she brought Louis to both Baptist and Sanctified churches. Armstrong recalled the communal scene in his Sanctified church, with the pastor leading off hymns: "Before you realized it—the whole Congregation would be *Wailing*—Singing like mad and sound *so* beautiful. I being a little boy that would 'Dig' Everything and every-body, I'd have myself a Ball in Church, *especially* when those Sisters would get so carried away while Rev (the preacher) would be right in the middle of his sermon." We are not told when and why May Ann changed between Baptist and Sanctified, but the trends that mark this period suggest an explanation. She may have initially joined the Baptists, the church she knew from her youth in Boutte. Perhaps she then turned in dissatisfaction to one of the newly found Sanctified congregations, for turn in dissatisfaction is what many lower-class Negroes indeed did. The Baptists aimed to uplift the "crude and undeveloped" emotionalism and superstitions of the poor, and if one did not accept this, there was little to do but leave. Lay preachers were now being replaced by trained preachers, so their new opportunity was to form Sanctified congregations that they could lead free of missionary intervention.

This splintering from Baptist to Sanctified took on firm associa-tions with social class. John Birks "Dizzy" Gillespie ranked the churches in his hometown of Cheraw, South Carolina, and his analysis would fit many towns in the South. Presbyterians occupied the top rung on the social ladder. In descending order from there came Methodists (the denomination Gillespie grew up in), Baptists, A.M.E. Zion, and finally, at the uncontested bottom, Sanctified. So one way to read Armstrong's childhood situation is that May Ann made a choice about where she belonged. She brought her son into the emotional-communal world of *her* tradition, not the assimilative tradition of the new Baptists and definitely not the French tradition of the Catholic Creoles, but the one that was closest to the ring shouts of slavery, the one that featured communal focus on a direct experience of the Holy Spirit, the one that cultivated vigorous rhythms that made your body move and deeply felt melody that made your heart pour out—the tradition that in many ways trans-mitted the core values of vernacular African-American culture in the South.

Gillespie took in Sanctified music by peeping through the win-dow of the little building used by the Saints on the corner, down the block from his house. He was captivated by the percussion section, formed by the preacher's four sons who played bass drum, snare

"I first learned the meaning of rhythm there" (Courtesy of the
Hogan Jazz Archive, Tulane University, photo by Ralston Crawford)

drum, cymbal, and triangle. Out of this ensemble flowed an invigor-
ating web of four different rhythmic patterns, to which the congregation added singing, clapping, and foot stomping, the latter
boosted by resonance from the loose floorboards. "I first learned the
meaning of rhythm there," Gillespie remembered.

In New Orleans, the differences between assimilative Baptist
and uninhibited Sanctified were also important to Mahalia
Jackson. She too took lessons from the Saints by standing outside
the building and watching through a window. "Those people had
no choir and no organ. They used the drum, the cymbal, the tambourine, and the steel triangle," Jackson said. The Saints used their
bodies in a way that contrasted dramatically with the discreet foot
tapping of the Mount Moriah Baptists. "Everybody in there sang
and they clapped and stomped their feet and sang with their whole
bodies," said Jackson. "They had a beat, a powerful beat, a rhythm

we held on to from slavery days, and their music was so strong and expressive it used to bring tears to my eyes." Jackson summed up her musical debt to the Sanctified Church in this way: "First you've got to get the rhythm until, through the music, you have the freedom to interpret it."

Louis Armstrong, unlike Dizzy Gillespie and Mahalia Jackson, did not need to peep through a window to gain access to Sanctified musicality. He lived at the bottom of the social ladder, and this put him at the center of the ecstatic traditions of worship that had been worked out during slavery. In church he learned how music was a means for shedding all emotional inhibitions. Rhythmic intensity played a big role. Jackson's premise—"First you've got to get the rhythm until, through the music, you have the freedom to interpret it"—would seem to lie equally as a foundation of both jazz and gospel. "Louis was very strong in rhythm," clarinetist Joe Muranyi once understatedly observed. Armstrong probably learned how to use rhythm early in life, and his Sundays in church surely helped bring him along, if, in fact, they did not provide the formative tutorials.

Sanctified churches are famous not only for rhythm and movement but also for communal participation. The doors of the building are open to anyone, regardless of status or appearance. Everyone— every child, novice, and tone-deaf adult—is encouraged to sing, move, clap, shout, and testify. Armstrong said he learned to sing in a Sanctified church, and that the congregants applauded his efforts. Throughout the African diaspora, music has been conceived as being tied to bodily motion. There are several purposes, beyond the sheer pleasure it brings, to this synchronization of sound with moving bodies. For one, it makes unity visible. The physical, tangible realm of the body is united with the nonmaterial realm of music and spirit. The body moves as the first step that carries the worshipper along the path toward spiritual engagement. And there is unity on the communal level as well; each moving person is visibly united with every other moving person. Synchronized movement acknowledges mutual obligation, a nonverbal confirmation that "I'm with you." Kid Ory told a story about a Sanctified congregation in New Orleans that jumped up and down so hard that they knocked the church building off of its foundation. Exaggerated or not, the story surely communicates the intensity of group momentum, the collective synergy that feeds on spontaneous yet organized interaction.

Novelist and literary scholar Melvin Dixon has a nice way of recognizing how important the group was for slaves during the early stages of African-American Christianity, when people from different regions of Africa worked to find common ground: "the slaves were not converting themselves to God, but *were converting themselves to each other.*" Music was the keystone that held the group together. For the Ewe people of West Africa, musical performance is saturated with values of proper social behavior and ethics. Though many metaphysical details of African religion were lost in the United States, the deep vein of musical-social-spiritual synthesis not only survived but flourished. A favored technique for bringing individuals together was heterophony, meaning the practice of simultaneously singing multiple versions of a single melody. Heterophony allows room for each worshipper to inject his or her own version of the spiritual or hymn. The result is a collective rendition of the tune that is both spontaneous and socially organized, coherent yet richly diverse.

"I always did love the way the congregation sang the song—it had a different tone quality than the way the choir sang," remembered Mahalia. Zora Neale Hurston added a technical observation in her study of the early Sanctified Church: "The jagged harmony is what makes it . . . The harmony of the true spiritual is not regular. The dissonances are important and not to be ironed out by the trained musician. The various parts break in at any old time . . . *Negro songs to be heard truly must be sung by a group, and a group bent on expression of feelings and not on sound effects.*" Various parts breaking in at any time, with emotionally charged dissonance and jagged harmony—that is a good description of African-American congregational heterophony, the history of which is poorly documented in sound recordings. "When I sang in church, my heart went into every hymn I sang," Armstrong wrote. At its most thrilling, heterophony produces a great mass of sound, with individual voices emerging out of the group as spontaneous articulations of the communal emotion. Never is there a pause in the musical flow. Individuals fill in around the breaks in phrasing of the main statement of the tune, which serves as the organizing principle for the entire performance.

An observer in 1863 may not have been entirely sympathetic with these goals but his description of slave singing frames the practice well: "The congregation joined in, not reading the music exactly as good old Tansure composed it, for there were crooks, turns, slurs, and appoggiaturas, not to be found in any printed copy. It was sung harshly, nasally, and dragged out in long, slow notes." Good old Tansure's melody was not the congregants' priority. His melody was little more than a contour of pitches that served to hold them all together. With reference to this shared contour, each individual poured out the vernacular practices that mattered most, the crooks, turns, slurs, appoggiaturas, and dragging that created a sonic world broader and deeper than any single person could imagine or achieve.

From Church to Dance Hall

"It all came from the Old Sanctified Churches," Armstrong once wrote in a letter, with "all" referencing jazz and more. It seems like dozens of musicians have said something similar, and when they make this assertion they are not simply thinking of rhythm. The historical connection—and the extent of it—may not be immediately obvious from this distance.

How did church music find its way into the entertainment world of sin-loving New Orleans? The infusion must have happened bit by bit, here and there, with some experiments taking off while others went nowhere. Brock Mumford took a small step around 1900 when he shouted, in the middle of his band's performance of a dance tune, "Oh Lord have mercy!" That interjection was taken straight from the storefront churches, and the women in the dance hall loved it. The musical detail is lost to us, but the band must have been playing in a way that reminded everyone of church. Around the same time, Buddy Bolden took a bigger step and included the actual repertory of church in his dance-hall routine, tunes such as *When the Saints Come Marching In*. It is easy to imagine why Mumford and Bolden found these church references so useful. A city culture was being born, and the time-honored, communally based practices of the plantations were the best foundation on which to build it.

Bolden also played slow blues, according to drummer Bill Matthews, with "a moan in his cornet that went all through you, just like you were in church or something . . . make a spiritual feeling go through you. He had a cup, a specially made cup, that made that cornet moan like a Baptist preacher." Mahalia used these very terms to describe preaching: "The preacher would have a singing tone in his voice. It was sad. It is the basic way I sing today, from hearing the way a preacher would preach, in a cry in a moan. It would have a penetrating quality." These references allude to a common stock of musical gestures that instantly communicate, on the basis of generations of practice, deep emotional intensity. Fifty years later, when Ray Charles experimented with a similar mix on a national stage, the results still proved popular, even though they also generated controversy within the African-American community. That the same mix was not only tolerated but embraced around 1900 in New Orleans indicates a great deal of social-religious change through the intervening decades.

One rhythmic detail that may have come to jazz from church is the "four-beat style" or "flat 4/4"—a steady background pulse of four undifferentiated beats per measure. This rhythmic foundation was first used by dance bands in New Orleans; it then wound its way in and out of jazz through the 1920s, eventually knocking out the two-beat style for good in the early 1930s, just in time to launch the swing era. The flat 4/4 was crucial for Armstrong's conception of rhythm (Chapter 12). Guitarist Bud Scott said that it came from church music, where the congregation kept "perfect rhythm" by clapping hands. Buddy Bolden used it when he played blues. Joe Oliver was associated with it in different kinds of dance music during the mid-1910s. All three musicians—Bolden, Oliver, and Armstrong—were raised with this rhythmic foundation in Baptist and Sanctified churches.

Cornetist Hypolite Charles remembered another technique that Oliver developed and in doing so caused Charles some grief. Seemingly oblivious to the varied accompaniment of the band playing behind him, Oliver liked to riff on a high note in a slightly syn-copated pattern. Charles demonstrated by scatting what Oliver played: "baah bap . . . baah bap . . . baah bap . . . baah bap . . . baah bap . . . baah bap." One note, the same syncopated rhythm, a few too many times—that was precisely the point. Hired to replace Oliver for a dance in the neighborhood known as the Irish Channel, Charles could not bring himself to imitate this or much else of Oliver's style, to the disappointment of the dancing patrons. "That's all he'd do—I couldn't see it," said Charles, meaning that he could not understand the appeal of the repeated riff clashing against the accompaniment, could not bring himself to play it, could not, per-haps, even accept it as *music*. Perhaps Oliver borrowed the idea from church. You can still hear it used there today. When a gospel soloist riffs like this, the congregation usually responds with shouts of encouragement. There is something about the stubborn repeti-tion that instantly indicates spiritual engagement. The repeated pitch ignores the harmonic accompaniment as if to also ignore Eurocentric culture and, at the same time, all the earthly compro-mises of quotidian existence. Jazz soloists today sometimes run the same technique, reproducing in a kind of vast temporal synchronic-ity the connection between dance music and church music that Oliver made around 1915. In my experience, African Americans in the audience typically applaud and smile in knowing recognition when a jazz soloist does this.

Amateur brass bands uptown provided one way for church prac-tices to enter jazz. Faced with the challenge of working up arrange-ments of parade tunes, amateur and nonliterate (in the musical sense) musicians could easily turn to the heterophony they had grown up with in church. That is one way to imagine the details of their ratty playing, which was, by many accounts, full of loud, rough dissonance and assertive, percussive attack, thus generating the kind of emotional intensity that Hurston admired in church singing and that downtown Creole musicians simply could not stand: a group bent on expression of feelings and not on sound effects. Bass player Louis James felt that musicians who played only by ear could "get more out of a piece by playing it 'wrong,' " thus giving them an advantage over those who read music. By playing hymns heterophonically in funeral processions, bands were essentially extending an invitation to mourners to sing along. Some of the musicians who brought church music into the streets also played for dances, thus connecting the links in this chain of venues. By the time Armstrong's mother began taking him to church, these links were firmly established.

Congregational heterophony is organized around the tune itself—old Tansure's melody—and the same is true for New Orleanian jazz. "The secret of good jazz music has always been to carry the melody at all times," wrote Baby Dodds. "The melody is supposed to be heard distinctly from some instrument—the trumpet, trombone, clarinet or violin. At all times." Everything that is added to the tune, the crooks, turns, slurs, appoggiaturas, slow dragging, and so on, is essential for a good performance yet ancillary in perceptual terms. In the classic format for "collective improvisation," the texture that as much as anything else distinguishes early New Orleanian jazz, the clarinet, second cornet, violin, and trombone fill these ancillary roles while the first cornet usually plays the lead melody. The clarinet, especially, often seems like a one-man effort to reproduce the heterophonic richness of a congregation, even though it also foregrounds instrumental virtuosity so fiercely that the resemblance to vocal practice gets covered up. Collective improvisation may thus be read as a stylized, instrumentalized, and professionalized transformation of church heterophony.

Jazz musicians also found in the Sanctified Church an example of how to think about music not in autonomous terms, as a thing in itself, but as sonic dialogue. The fate of old Tansure's melody was a common one: the emphasis was not on the faithful performance of a unique *piece* of music, but on using so-called pieces to organize the activity of performance. The conception is far from European art music and close to traditional African practice, and it has conditioned music making throughout the African diaspora. The piece— the spiritual, hymn, march, popular song—takes on a fluidity its creator did not imagine. Anyone who walks into the church or steps on the bandstand is invited to add something to it. Hurston said that an African-American sermon is not something "set"; rather, it is something "loose and formless and is in reality merely a framework upon which to hang more songs." The same analysis applies to the songs themselves, which become frameworks on which to hang the favored vernacular practices of the community.

The techniques of church and jazz alike are designed to promote musical-kinetic-social interaction. "The more enthusiastic his audience is, why the more spirit the working man's got to play," said Johnny St. Cyr, a New Orleanian guitarist. St. Cyr believed that interaction stimulates musical creativity: "And with your natural feelings that way, you never make the same thing twice." Those "natural feelings" on the bandstand must have been similar to those of the inventive congregational singers witnessed by Hurston. The approach was part of an African legacy that is a central concern of the Ewe people and others from sub-Saharan Africa: "To maintain their poise in their social encounters, Africans bring the same flexibility which characterizes their participation in musical contexts: they expect dialogue, they anticipate movement, and most significantly, they stay very much open to influence," writes ethnomusicologist John Chernoff. Valuation finds its focus not in the authentic rendition of a received text but in the qualities of performance expected from the interacting group.

Accommodation and Resistance

Most denominations pay lip service to the inclusive, universal goals of religion, but the Sanctified Saints are known to take that idea to heart. They bring to life a forgiving, optimistic, and embracing way of interacting with others. That is the context in which to understand a story about values that Armstrong told on several occasions:

Yea—I am just like the *Sister* in our Church in N.O., my home town. One Sunday our pastor whom we all loved happened to take a Sunday off and sent in another preacher who wasn't near as good. The whole congregation "frowned on him"—except one Sister. She seemed to enjoy the other pastor the same as she did *our* pastor. This aroused the Congregation's curiosity *so much*—until when Church service was over they all rushed over to this *one Sister* and asked her *why* did she enjoy the substitute preacher the *same* as our regular one? She said, "Well, when *our pastor preach*, I can look right through him and see *Jesus*. And when I hear a preacher who's *not* as good as ours—I just look *over* his *shoulder* and *see Jesus just the same.*" That applies to me all through my life in music ever since I left New Orleans. I've been just like that Sister in our Church. I have played with quite a few musicians who weren't so good. But as long as they could hold their instruments *correct*, and display their *willingness* to play as *best* they could, I would look over their shoulders and see *Joe Oliver* and several other great masters from my home town.

The shocking analogy—Joe Oliver as Jesus—shows how unreligious Armstrong turned out to be. It was not an analogy that would have occurred to every musician who worked with Oliver (especially those to whom he owed money), and it reveals the sense of indebtedness to his teacher that swelled within Armstrong during the last two decades of his life. Yet his point comes through. There is something immensely accommodating about the New Orleanian style. This sense of relaxed accommodation makes spontaneity possible, very much like the atmosphere in church, where there is more than enough room for every personal interjection. Cornetist Herb Morand

The Saints, 1950s (Courtesy of the Hogan Jazz Archive, Tulane University, photo by Ralston Crawford)

articulated this principle nicely: "I always stuck to good old New Orleans jazz, cause when you playing New Orleans jazz you don't have to be worried about anything, just whatever come in your head, you can make." To be sure, the situation on a bandstand is not exactly like church, since an expectation of professional accomplishment is built into any commercial setting. But anyone familiar with New Orleans jazz will understand what Morand is saying. To grow familiar with the style is to adjust aural expectations; one learns to listen differently. It is possible to listen as Armstrong listened, to grant conviction and passion a place in the first line of valuation, with technical sophistication pushed slightly to the rear. One can value *willingness* and learn to hear it, even to think about it as carrying a glimpse of spiritual or artistic purity—at a certain point it does not seem to matter how this is phrased.

And if there is something immensely accommodating about the New Orleanian style, that was also true of Louis Armstrong himself. His success was due in part to his ability to convey in performance something of his own warm and inclusive spirit. He could be as competitive and egotistic as any performer who craves the spotlight of center stage, but there are many accounts of his generosity and willingness to accommodate virtually anyone. When we are drawn to him, we may sense the nurturing of a young child in the loving warmth and encouragement of the Saints. He was once asked in an interview about how he was able to appeal to people all over the world, people who are so different. He answered, "They're not different as far as we're concerned." The interviewer came around again to the question, with a different tack: "Louis, you've been described as a musician, sometimes as a singer, an entertainer, even a comedian. You've always had a wonderful relationship with an audience. How would you describe yourself?" He answered unhesitatingly, "As one of them. I'm just the same as one of those people out there in the audience."

Where do politics fit into this universal vision of human harmony? The idea that Sanctified practices are built on a social conception of music is very specific: we are talking about music and its effects on the people *inside* the building. This says nothing about society at large, about the crushing forces of subordination that pervaded African-

American life in the Deep South of 1910. W. E. B. Du Bois understood how religion was mixed with politics in the minds of the freedmen, who were prepared to recognize divine intervention of the most dramatic kind. Many believed that God had caused emancipation, and who are we to say that they were wrong? In their worship one notes a potent conflation of energies: the energy of the immediate community, of God, of political assertion, and of musical-kinetic dynamism, all inseparable from one another in an experiential sense, all held together by their cherished practices.

It may be difficult in bourgeois, twenty-first-century America to identify with this conflation, and one might even argue that it would have been more productive to address political problems by isolating them as such. It is important for us to understand the Sanctified point of view of a century ago, to realize how thoroughly music was conditioned by this synthetic conception. Music fortifies the individual because it is capable of bringing forth the Holy Spirit, capable of emotionally bonding the community of worshippers, one to the other, and, by extension to that, capable of destroying the demonic injustice of slavery. The strength of music cannot be sliced into different parts, and it is all the more powerful because of that. It is no wonder that so many have cited the church as the central generating force for the vast, expansive momentum of African-American music, as it flowed out of the rural South, into the cities and far beyond.

At the same time that one can trace an attitude of universal accommodation through the Sanctified Church and into New Orleanian jazz, there emerges a stubborn sense of independence, a firm claim on cultural self-determination that has long been a source of strength for African Americans. I doubt that Louis Armstrong ever had an assimilative impulse of any significance. During his years with May Ann, no one was telling him to straighten his hair or bleach his skin, no one was interested in claiming *any* identifiable marker of white culture as a way to accrue cultural capital (the use of cultural practice for social or political advantage). His memory of the Karnofskys teaching him to say "this" and "that" instead of "dis" and "dat" indicates how exceptional this kind of advice was. His nonassimilative approach to life later caused tension with two of his four wives, Lil and Lucille. He was irritated by Lil's insistence on table manners—"a certain Spoon for this and a certain fork for that," he complained—and how she fussed when he sat on the made-up bed. Lucille could also impose social pretensions from above; he responded with the occasional outburst and with more than a few retaliatory affairs. All his life he carried his mother's disdain of pretension: "she [Lucille] still has a sense of airs that I've never particularly cared for—being raised around people who were just plain human beings, and love and at least respect for each other." He lived uptown Negro values with no trace of self-consciousness whatsoever. This complete lack of interest in cultural assimilation was part of the Sanctified vision.

Hurston takes that idea a step further and views the Sanctified renewal of ecstatic religion as a "protest against the high-brow tendency in Negro Protestant congregations." In a Marxist view, cultural practices either legitimize power or resist such legitimization, depending on one's class position. The Saints turned away from the new assimilative agenda of the Baptists, and Hurston reads that as an act of protest. Were the Saints also trying to undermine the vicious structure of domination to which they were relentlessly subjected through the cumulative burdens of Jim Crow legislation and vigilante terrorism? If May Ann chose Sanctified worship as an act of rejecting Baptist assimilation, then there may have been an ideological dimension of resistance to her decision.

Resistance may be read on another level as well. Art historian Robert Farris Thompson identifies "resistance to the closures of the Western technocratic way" in the asymmetric textiles made in Haiti, in the Deep South, and other parts of the African diaspora. He traces this textile tradition back to the Mande people of West Africa. Among the freedmen of Louisiana and Mississippi, the musical-social practices of slave religion were more ubiquitous, more central, and, perhaps, more powerful than the patterning of textiles. But Thompson has the advantage of being able to read visual designs in light of African religion and philosophy. "Why one red sock and one white sock worn deliberately mismatched?" an elderly woman in Ohio is asked. "To keep spirits away," is her answer. "Evil travels in straight lines" is how Senegambians understand the

problem, and their solution is the design principle of strikingly stag-
gered patterning and coloring, a visual syncopation between adjacent strips of cloth. A man in Haiti hires an expert to make him a
shirt in strips of red, white, and blue; his goal is to disrupt the evil
eye. Bob Wilber, who took clarinet lessons with Sidney Bechet, may
have been alluding to the same sensibility when he described
Bechet's style of dress in the 1940s: "It was something I noticed
other New Orleans musicians did. They would, almost perversely,
wear one item of clothing that didn't jell with the rest."

This form of resistance could be extended to music. It has been
argued that capitalism causes fragmentation and reification—the
effect of splintering culture and indeed all existence into isolated
parts and then creating the illusion that these splintered parts are
autonomous entities. The freedmen of the Deep South had lived
through a long history of exploitation, truly one of the most devious
economic programs ever conceived. They were besieged by the
dehumanizing effects of plantation capitalism—"capitalism with its
clothes off," as the saying goes—and music turned out to be one of
their most potent defensive weapons. Music for them was not
something autonomous, a thing in itself. On the contrary, it fostered
wholeness by bringing spirituality, communality, and politics into
the same performing circle. Their musical-social-spiritual practice
was a technique for resisting pressures to fragment and reify experience, just as it had been for their ancestors in slavery and in Africa.

If the ring shout was the place where the slave community was
born, synthesis was achieved, and experience became deepened
rather than fragmented, then the storefront Sanctified church was
the place for these activities in the New Orleans of 1910. Here was
where the twin evils of fragmentation and isolation were warded off.
Here was where Armstrong received one of the main lessons of survival passed on from slavery, and it was also where he learned how to
think about music. Some of this value system informed early jazz—
it is impossible to say how much. Sometimes the most important
things are left unsaid. But it would be a mistake to miss these
dimensions, which find resonance in other practices and situations
too and which we shall come across as we tour through the music
and places of Armstrong's youth.

I have argued that Armstrong's early musical experiences in church were formative. Yet his previous biographers have underemphasized the church, and there may be two reasons for that. First, very little information specific to Armstrong's experience of church survives; he did not talk about it extensively, and the present discussion has depended on reports of what was happening elsewhere. Second, as an adult, he was simply not very religious, as his ecumenical quip about Baptists, Catholics, and Jews would suggest.

In fact, his religious participation in New Orleans rose and fell in line with a fundamental shift in social orientation. When he was released from the Colored Waif's Home for Boys at age thirteen, he was placed in the custody of his father. He did not stay with his father long, but from then on the teenager spent more and more of his time with male colleagues and mentors. A fraternal network of musicians added layers of musical tutoring and life lessons to the loving warmth and encouragement he had received, primarily from women, before his placement in the Waif's Home. Sanctified churches were predominantly female, and Armstrong was raised by women for the first eleven years of his life, not just by his grandmother and May Ann but also by women in the neighborhood. "Old Lady" Magg, Mrs. Laura, and Mrs. Martin each disciplined him occasionally and reported back to May Ann. These "old sisters" stood in tears at the train station to see him off when he departed for Chicago in 1922.

The male network of professional and semiprofessional musicians that he would join during his teens was a thoroughly secular one. The saying "blues on Saturday night, church on Sunday morning" was not invented with this group in mind. It is true that some venues served as both dance hall and church. This could mean continuous use, from the beginning of the Saturday dance to its ending at dawn on Sunday, as worshippers arrived to set up the room for their services. Ed Garland said there was only twenty minutes between the end of the dance and the beginning of church at Funky Butt Hall. This makes the hall seem like an architectural symbol for the symbiotic importance of blues and church, but the turnover in the room must have been exactly 100 percent; the symbolism turns out to be nothing more than a need to take full advantage of scarce resources. Easter represented another kind of transition between secular and sacred. It was an important day for professional musicians, but not for the Christian reason. Ash Wednesday and Lent prepared Catholics for Easter, but professional musicians reversed the terms of the relationship: for them, Easter was important because it was the last day of Lent, which meant a return to dancing and regular employment.

The pattern one gleans from the oral histories is that musicians went to church only after they quit playing music professionally. I'm sure there were exceptions, but this must have been the overwhelmingly consistent trend. The inverted lifestyle of all-night work was enough to preclude church attendance. But in fact, the secular orientation of musicians was part of a broader pattern in which membership in fraternal clubs replaced church membership. Armstrong's lack of interest in religion as an adult and the shift of his attention toward fraternal clubs as a teenager were fully typical.

Yet the uptown community that nurtured Louis was saturated with the musical-social vision of the Sanctified Saints and traditional Baptists. Armstrong could not escape it even if he had wanted to. The historical reach of that vision is astonishing. Mahalia's Mount Moriah Baptist Church still stands today. The social position of assimilative Baptists that led to a preference for sedate singing and discreet foot tapping also manifested in a fondness for bricks and mortar. On the other hand, the nearby Sanctified church Mahalia listened in on probably disappeared long ago. Yet, even though their low-rent buildings are gone, the *musical* legacy of the Saints still holds a powerful presence. The long historical reach of this music flows from a central fact of slavery: by necessity, the slaves made a culture that did not depend on materiality. The experiential depth of their religion, the kind of social interaction it emphasized, and the musical style that energized it—these values could thrive even in complete impoverishment, in a brush arbor in the woods or in a low-rent storefront. The potent legacy of the ring shout extended in directions both sacred and secular far beyond the African-American community to touch virtually the entire world through jazz, gospel, and their various offshoots.

If the idea of jazz as classical music is remote from Louis

Armstrong's New Orleans, it is easy to see where it comes from. Jazz eventually took a position where it could make such a claim in settings that mimic the concert hall, which in turn mimics European styles of worship—contemplative, discreet, and largely private. So it is not without irony that jazz is usually enjoyed today by people who tap their toes, sway ever so slightly from side to side, and perhaps snap their fingers. They could just as easily be sitting in the Mount Moriah Baptist Church in 1910. My guess is that worshippers in that church abandoned such restraint long ago, following the lead of Mahalia herself, who, along with many others, helped bring Baptists in Chicago and other parts of the country back to their demonstrative roots. To this circle of irony may be added another loop: what Louis Armstrong accomplished as a solo improviser in Chicago, just around the time Mahalia moved there in the mid-1920s, eventually helped turn jazz in the other direction, away from its communal, participative origins and toward the concert hall. Such are the varied dimensions of the cultural legacy of New Orleans.

✣ May Ann must have had some trouble corralling her active child into church every Sunday, for he seems to have been happiest when he was free to roam the neighborhood. It was on the streets where he would find, from a surprising source, early tutorials in another vernacular tradition. It is there where he received his first lessons in the blues.

CHAPTER THREE

~~~~~~

Larenzo's Soul

Blues is what cause the fellows to start jazzing.
—Big Eye Louis Nelson

In an obscure passage from one of his many autobiographical writings, Armstrong remembered hanging out as a child with three different street musicians, known to him as Larenzo, Santiago, and the "Waffle Man." Larenzo collected old clothing, rags, bones, and bottles for resale. Louis admired how he drew people to him with music. He played "an old, tin, long horn, which he used to blow without the mouthpiece and he would actually play a tune on the darn thing," Armstrong wrote. "That knocked me out to hear him do that. He had a soul, too." Larenzo took an interest in the child and spent time talking with him—"the things he said, pertaining to music, had me spellbound." Santiago sold pies and publicized his wares with a real bugle. He too made an impression, for it was from Santiago that Louis "adapted the rhythm to blow the bugle out at the Orphanage." For Armstrong these were formative years, probably around age ten, and his account suggests that the two men provided important musical models. Indeed, who could have been more important than a musician who had soul and held Armstrong spellbound with his discussions of music? Or another from whom he learned rhythm? It was here on the streets, apparently, where the future virtuoso took his first lessons in playing a solo instrument.

This is all the information we have about these lessons, but it is important to realize how precious it is to have even this. For several reasons, these details have been ignored in previous accounts of Armstrong's life. Most writers have been more interested in lineages of great masters passing on genius, one to the other, than in the entanglement of jazz with everyday life. There is little room in such an idealized progression for a toothless old man puffing on a party horn. There is also a problem of access to the evidence, for when the typescript just quoted was edited to produce Armstrong's autobiography *Satchmo: My Life in New Orleans*, the references to Larenzo's soul and the adaptation of Santiago's rhythm were eliminated. The published account of these street musicians was reduced by almost half, giving the topic much less weight. We are indeed lucky that a copy of Armstrong's typescript survives.

His editors undoubtedly had their reasons for trimming the passage, but for anyone whose aim it is to imagine the musical and social conditions that shaped Louis Armstrong, nothing could be more important. It is possible to think about these street lessons as analogous to the rudimentary lessons in counterpoint and harmony young Mozart took at a similar age with his father. Knowing about them helps explain the direction his talent would take, and it eliminates the need to talk about unexplainable genius. Counterpoint lessons get written on paper, and sometimes that paper survives. Fleeting conversations between a street musician and a street child leave few traces. Yet these parallel moments of early tutoring may have been equally significant; certainly what we are told ties in well with other known details of Louis's childhood and his eventual rise through the world of professional musicians.

Though it may seem futile, one is bound to ask, What did Armstrong learn? Other reports of the same kind of street music will help us to imagine an answer to that question.

Work Songs and Blues

Kid Ory claimed that the legendary cornetist Buddy Bolden, whose popularity peaked just a few years before Louis began to hang out with Larenzo, "stole" musical ideas from a "rag man, used to blow a tin horn." "Some of the notes weren't true notes," Ory said about the ragman's playing. Jelly Roll Morton remembered how "rags-bottles-and-bones men" played "more lowdown, dirty blues on those Kress horns than the rest of the country ever thought of." Morton heard their music when he was visiting relatives uptown. The Kress horn got its name from the department store that sold it, and it was probably similar if not identical to the tin party horns used by Larenzo and the ragman who influenced Bolden.

Johnny Wiggs (b. John Wigginton Hyman, 1899), white and living uptown near Tulane University, remembered many details about these bottlemen-musicians who brought blues to his neighborhood on a regular basis. Their distinctive musical routines beckoned from a distance like the jingle of an ice-cream truck—except that the ragman had a small, rickety wagon pulled by an emaciated mule—and children came running with bottles, discarded clothes, and tin foil stripped from cigarette butts that they rolled up in little balls. All of this could be traded with the ragman for a piece of candy or a tiny toy. The long tinhorns cost ten cents each and were used by other people for celebrating Christmas, New Year's Eve, and Mardi Gras. They were about three feet long, with a soldered reed and a wooden mouthpiece on top of that. The bottlemen liked to remove the wooden mouthpiece so that they could manipulate the reed directly and produce the inflections of the blues, the "untrue" pitches, in Ory's description. Wiggs found them to be "the most gifted people in the world for blues . . . I guess only the most talented blues players went into the business, because the only ones I can remember played the most beautiful blues you could possibly imagine. It wasn't only one—they were all over town. And that sound later on I heard in Negro trumpet players. The same sound. The bending of notes which they are supreme on. No singing with the bottlemen. All of his talking was through his horn." Wiggs also heard African-American women singing to advertise the wild berries they had picked in the woods. He was moved by the way these women sang, but for this future trumpeter the horn-playing bottlemen were the best.

From this collection of memories emerges a general point already made with respect to church music: the vitality of the uptown bands

The flag covers the merchandise.

*Trading toys for bottles (Historic New Orleans Collection,
Acc. No. 1951. 78xi, drawing by Leon Fremaux)*

flowed through a connection with daily music making by ordinary people. Armstrong was thinking along the same lines when he said, in a separate discussion, that jazz "isn't anything new. At one time they was calling it levee camp music." Since Armstrong was exposed to these vernacular traditions at an early age—not only exposed but also tutored through Larenzo's spellbinding talk—he was in an excellent position to draw on their vitality when he became a professional cornet player. Through the complicated vicissitudes of his musical career he never lost this connection to the everyday music of African Americans, which accounts in part for his wide appeal among this social group for a good part of his career. The connection was strong until the very end, even after his African-American audience had largely abandoned him and even when he was making a living singing songs like *Chimchimery* and *Zippity-do-dah*.

Larenzo the ragman's music may be conceived as a subgenre of the *work song*. Musicologist Ernest Borneman believed that of all the different kinds of African-American music in the United States, work songs preserved the strongest link to Africa. Music in traditional African cultures has a functional orientation, and it is not surprising to discover how, in the slave society of the United States, this was preserved in work songs. Frederick Douglass described how planters encouraged slaves to sing while they worked. "This may account for the almost constant singing heard in the southern states," he wrote. Work songs can be performed in groups, as documented in the chilling recordings of chain gangs Alan Lomax made in the 1940s and 1950s, or by a soloist working in isolation. George "Pops" Foster remembered jail mates in New Orleans singing blues when they swept the floors and using the swish of their brooms as a rhythmic foundation.

Work songs have been classified into such subgenres as the street cry and field holler. *Street Cries of an Old Southern City*, compiled by Harriette Kershaw Leiding in 1910, includes drawings of singers in Charleston and an attempt to notate their cries, shouts, and chants. There is even a boy selling coal, the occupation Armstrong would take up just a few years later in New Orleans, and notation of his call. The author notes the "queer minor catch" that characterizes these melodies, and she did her best to document the subtle inflections of pitch; today it is easy to see the affinity with blues. Performed with a bit of flair, these songs could easily have resembled the lowdown, dirty blues that Morton heard from ragmen in New Orleans. They condense the distinguishing gestures of the blues, gestures that are also commonly referenced as "soul."

In the western "delta" of Mississippi, the region where guitar-based blues were beginning to flourish around just this time, the connection between work songs and blues was obvious to everyone. Musicians Lightnin' Hopkins, Son House, Sonny Terry, and Sunnyland Slim all noted it. "Blues come out of the fields, baby," said Hopkins. A specialist in field hollers named Henry Sloan shaped the emerging blues tradition directly when he tutored a young Charley Patton around 1903 at Dockery's Plantation. Patton combined the singing with his guitar and thereby influenced a whole generation of bluesmen. It may not be

"Blues come out of the fields, baby" (New Orleans Public Library, photo by George François Mugnier)

too fanciful to think of this mentoring relationship as analogous to that between Larenzo and Armstrong in New Orleans.

In the 1930s, composer and conductor John Work saw the connection between field hollers and blues in this way: "In these 'hollers' the idiomatic material found in the blues is readily seen; the excessive portament, the slow time, the preference for the flatted third, the melancholy type of tune, the characteristic cadence. As a matter of fact, with a little more formal arrangement many of these 'hollers' could serve as lines of blues." The Mississippi River was a gathering place for this kind of music, as workers from the plantations clustered there to build levees and move cargo, two occupations famous for work songs and early blues.

A New Orleans Specialty

To imagine Armstrong being tutored around age ten in bluesy work songs explains a lot about the musician he would soon become. By age fourteen or so he was gaining notice in a neighborhood honky tonk as a good little blues player. In fact, he couldn't play anything else, and when older musicians used him as a substitute in their bands, they had to work around his limited repertory. He was physically small and the prostitutes had fun with him. They were delighted, no doubt, by the amusement of seeing a young boy play such seductive music so well. They sat him in their laps, partly as a tease and partly in the same spirit of encouragement that he had received from the Saints in church just a few years earlier. How was it possible for a young teenager to impress prostitutes with his renditions of blues? It was possible, first of all, because blues performance was practiced and encouraged over a broad continuum, from amateur to professional. Anyone could do it—that was the key to the universality of the idiom. Only a few rose to the skill and fame of a Buddy Bolden or Joe Oliver, but even their virtuoso accomplishments were heard and interpreted within the broader context of ordinary amateur participation.

It is important to qualify that point according to the historical moment that concerns us. The genre of blues is sometimes thought of as a central, binding force that organizes virtually all of African-American culture. Our challenge is to sift through the details of a historical moment when that generalization makes no sense. It is a moment when W. C. Handy, for example, could grow up in Florence, Alabama, with little exposure to the blues. In 1903, at age thirty, Handy heard a singer-guitarist at a train stop in Tutwiler, Mississippi, and he found his slide guitar blues to be the "weirdest" music he had ever heard—this did not stop him from promoting himself as "father of the blues" a few years later, however. Singer Gertrude "Ma" Rainey, Handy's pseudogenerative counterpart who promoted herself as "mother of the blues," never heard them either when she was growing up in Columbus, Georgia. Her first encounter was in 1902 on tour in Missouri. Blues sounded strange but compelling, and she quickly figured out how to incorporate the sound into her act. Both of these important musicians grew up in the Deep South in environments where there was no blues. In Armstrong's neighborhood the scene was rather different, and the historical significance of Armstrong learning this melodic idiom on the streets around age ten cannot be overestimated.

In New Orleans around 1910, blues provided improvising musicians with a musical form—a pattern of phrases and a set of chords, both repeated in the background, over and over—that is still commonly used in jazz. This form is not what Larenzo was teaching Armstrong, however. For the tinhorn men, "blues" meant not a form but a set of gestures and a feeling for how to place them. Armstrong was learning the rudiments of a melodic idiom. Ethnomusicologist Gerhard Kubik traces the history of this idiom back through slavery to the savannas that run from Senegal and Gambia across northern Ghana and into Nigeria. There one finds subtle manipulations of pitch and time, a technique of merging together, in delightful ambiguity, the accents of speech with the accents of music, heterophony, and slight use of polyrhythms—slight, that is, compared to the polyrhythmic complexity well known from drum ensembles that predominate around the Gulf of Guinea. Timbre, a focus of expression, is manipulated, distorted, invented, instrumentalized, and vocalized. Work songs are especially important. Even the swinging triplet feeling so characteristic of blues and New Orleans jazz has been located here. Inflections of pitch are of great importance. Blues and gospel musicians refer to "bending" or "worrying" pitch, a technique so central to the idiom that it has given rise to the term "blue notes." The importance of blue notes was carried into early jazz: "The blue notes are the strongest notes you can play," according to bass player Pops Foster.

Music like this is best learned early, as part of daily life, through the inflections of speech that one soaks up in childhood. Shades of phrasing, precise effects of timing, meticulous bending of pitch at the right moment in the right way, judicious distribution of growls and distortions of timbre, all of it wrapped into linguistic dialect and pronunciation—these are the markers of skillful blues. Muddy Waters believed that these vocal nuances were the part of blues that white musicians could not duplicate. One observer said something similar about New Orleans during the early years of the twentieth century. Whites were interested in blues as a novelty, she remembered, but "they couldn't catch it."

Blues were played slowly in New Orleans around 1910, probably in deliberate imitation of the singing style the immigrants had brought from the plantations. A slow tempo puts emphasis on isolated gestures, which carry the expressive weight identified by Foster. All of us have been taught how to respond to music emotionally, and part of what Armstrong learned as a child was to understand the difference between church and blues, where similar gestures belonged to very different emotional configurations. The style of emotional engagement laid out for him by the Saints in church was deep and ecstatic—deep in the sense of being nonfrivolous and unordinary, a kind of experience that is not suited to everyday life, and ecstatic in the sense of an overt outpouring, a heightened emotional state of the kind Armstrong witnessed when his mother converted. We must imagine the musical codes of congregational heterophony—the scoops and slides, textural richness, rhythmic tension, and so forth—being *felt* in this way.

A very different emotional articulation was at work in blues performed in New Orleans. Blues have often been described with incorrect one-dimensionality as music designed to extinguish suffering. In New Orleans the idiom was much more firmly articulated as a music of seduction. Bolden's blues, for example, made "the women jump out the window," according to Bill Matthews (Chapter 2). Bolden is firmly associated with the tradition of playing slow blues after midnight, as a stimulant that brought the dance known as the "slow drag" to high erotic intensity. Armstrong recognized the idiom's seductive power early on. Shy with women as a teenager, blues were his aphrodisiac: women had "an admiration for the Blues that I played, [more] than anything else." In other settings blues were played with less eroticism but still as a way to magnetically draw one person to another. Bolden famously blasted his cornet for miles, calling audiences out to Johnson Park (Chapter 7), and in the same way, but on a smaller scale, Larenzo's tinhorn blues brought the children running with their recyclable scraps.

Blues on wind instruments became the African-American New Orleanian specialty. This was partly a matter of "taking advantage of the disadvantages"; novice musicians discovered how they could compensate for poorly functioning instruments, as well as weak control of scales and intonation, by bending pitch a lot. It would have been clear to everyone in New Orleans around 1910 that bluesy playing was bound up with bluesy singing, which was in turn bound up with a way of speaking. This continuum made it hard to say what, precisely, the difference was between speechlike blues and musically inspired talk. The talk was infused with rhythms, inflections of pitch, and shadings of loud and soft. Bass player Wallace Collins described the singing of an unnamed "junk man," and in the difficulty he had finding the right words, we may detect the sought-after ambiguity between speaking and singing I am alluding to: "He'd go around singing—he wasn't singing, he was talking but he was really singing." This blur between speech and music is characteristic of sub-Saharan, West African cultures, where tonal

Harper's Weekly, *1886*

languages—"tonal" meaning that a change of pitch reframes the definition of a word—mark the speaking end of the verbal-musical continuum.

What is being described here is a way of communicating that cannot be learned through writing, a process sometimes discussed through the term "orality," by analogy with literacy. If one is focused on learning music through notation, that focus will get in the way of mastering the techniques of orality, which can only be learned by direct imitation. White observers who tried to notate slave music found it impossible to document the strange nuances of pitch and rhythm and were left to simply remark on how ubiquitous they were. Blues scholar Robert Palmer has provocatively suggested that the kind of blues that foregrounds these nuances so prominently—*deep* blues, in Muddy Waters's phrase—is a practice in which only people who are verbally illiterate can excel: "Literacy, which trains one to focus on the linear continuity of words and phrases rather than on their intonational subtleties, tends to obliterate such minutely detailed and essentially nonlinear modes of expression," he writes. That is a difficult idea to work with, partly because most people do not feel comfortable with the idea that there is a positive side to illiteracy. Yet if one assumes that in expressive culture there is always a loss for every gain, then there may be something to attend to in Palmer's hypothesis.

For our investigation of New Orleans the important points are first, that blues thrived in a nonliterate environment where musically inflected speech was practiced, and second, that Armstrong learned the idiom early on, probably before he learned to read. Certainly he became a good blues player before he learned to read musical notation, which was not secure until his extended stay on the riverboats, late in his teenage years and long after he had absorbed the vernacular idioms that were stimulating the new dance music in New Orleans. His initial immersion in orally based idioms made his early training fundamentally different from that of most Creole musicians downtown, who typically began with intensive instruction in musical notation.

There has always been controversy about where jazz came from, but no one has ever doubted the social origins of the blues. Isidore

Barbarin would have said that the idiom came from the ratty people. A prostitute named Carrie, who worked in Armstrong's neighborhood during the years he was growing up, was passionate about the blues, and she had a good perspective on musical markers of social identity in the playing of pianists Tony Jackson and Buddy Carter ("hincty" in the following quotation means the same thing as "dicty"—socially pretentious, imitating whites): "I used to stay around by the Frenchman's when I wasn't in the crib. Mostly like three, four o'clock in the morning. Shit! I use to *drink* some of that Raleigh Rye! Listen to them dicty niggers playing and singing and carrying on. Bud Carter, that was my man! For playing *you* know. He played them blues *all* the time, nothing but them blues. *Low* blues, I mean, from *way* back-of-town! He *played* some blues! He wasn't hincty . . . All them dicty people used to hang by the Frenchman's like to hear that fruit Tony Jackson best of anybody . . . He play pretty, I give them that—but my man was Bud Carter."

Various lower-class references got attached to blues from early on: the music was performed in "dives"; the style was termed "gutbucket," after the chittlins bucket of animal intestines that poor people relied on for nourishment; it was also labeled "ratty music" or "dirt music." Upwardly mobile African Americans usually disdained the blues, partly because of its sinful texts and venues but mainly because of the genre's associations with illiteracy, sharecropping, and ultimately slavery. Blues probably had its widest impact through the ways that it shaped early jazz. "Blues is what cause the fellows to start jazzing," is how "Big Eye" Louis Nelson provocatively understood the history of this music, from his perspective looking across Canal Street at Bolden and the earliest uptown wind players of blues.

Blues and Jazz

Armstrong's early mastery of the blues signals his position in New Orleans society, his position in jazz history, and, indeed, his position in the history of African-American music. Blues separated uptown Negroes from downtown Creoles, just as heterophonic singing in church did. While Armstrong was hanging out with rags-bottles-and-bones men, soaking up their spellbinding talk and listening to them play more lowdown, dirty blues than the rest of the country ever thought of, Creole boys of the same age were being introduced to a pedagogical system of sight-singing, musical notation, and instrumental technique that had come to New Orleans directly from France, via the French Opera House downtown. Creole pedagogy typically started with singing solfège, the use of the syllables "do," "re," "mi," "fa," "sol," "la," and "ti" (which brings us back to "do") to mark out steps along the Eurocentric scale. The student trained in solfège for up to a year or more before he was allowed to touch an instrument. This training cultivates tremendous precision in hearing and negotiating intervals. And it does more than that: it fits the student's hearing into the melodic-harmonic system of Eurocentric theory, with its elaborate keys and chords. There are no blue notes, no bending or worrying of pitch, just an increasing ability to hear and perform with intonational precision and systematic rigor.

W. C. Handy was tutored in the same Eurocentric way in an Alabamian public school, by a recent graduate of Fisk University; he got so good at solfège that, as a student, he was able to sing through operas by Wagner and Verdi. It is hardly surprising that when Handy eventually heard blues, the idiom sounded truly weird. The two approaches easily seem mutually incompatible. Blues finds expressive depth through subtle shading and dramatic bending of pitch, while solfège is designed with just the opposite goal in mind—to internalize the distance between pitches with such precision that there is absolutely no deviation from the measured scale. The French pedagogical system produced "many a fine musicianer" in the Creole wards downtown, as Sidney Bechet put it. Bechet also acknowledged that Creoles were inferior to uptown musicians in their ability to play the blues. He himself came to blues as a young teenage rebel who bucked the Creole system and began hanging out with uptown musicians.

Tension between musicians who were educated in blues and those who weren't became part of the dynamics of jazz history. The pattern continued all the way through the swing era and into bebop, dieing out gradually, in the 1960s and 1970s, as blues began to recede in importance within the black community. African-American musicians from the Deep South who moved around the United States during the Great Migration discovered that blues gave them a marketing advantage, while musicians raised in the North struggled to catch on. In the 1920s, according to musician Garvin Bushell, "there wasn't an eastern performer who could really play the blues . . . We didn't put that quarter-tone pitch in the music the way the southerners did. Up north we leaned toward ragtime conception—a lot of notes." He could have extended the comparison to rhythmic practices, especially the technique of dragging slightly behind the beat to create a rich feeling of detachment from the underlying pulse. This is described well by Baby Dodds: "The trumpet or clarinet will sometimes delay and fall what we would call 'a step behind.' Although they are 'with it,' they are just a little behind, say 1/8th of a beat . . . The drummer has to keep right on the beat."

These South-North distinctions can be heard in recordings of the Duke Ellington band from the late 1920s. Bushell remembered how he and trumpeter Bubber Miley learned from one of the greatest blues players to come out of New Orleans: "Bubber and I sat there [watching Joe Oliver] with our mouths open." Miley advanced well enough to become Ellington's featured soloist. On Ellington's famous 1927 recording of *East St. Louis Toodle-oo*, his solos stand in sharp contrast to the ragtime melodies composed by Ellington. Ellington plays "a lot of notes," just as Bushell said the easterners tended to do, and they are rather stiff notes at that. Miley, on the other hand, is free and fluid in his quarter-tone inflections, vocalized timbres, speech-like rhythms, and staying "a step behind." Just a few years earlier, Sidney Bechet had been the first to bring New Orleanian blues to Ellington's ear. "I shall never forget the first time I heard him play, at the Howard Theatre in Washington around 1921," Ellington wrote. "I had never heard anything like it. It was a completely new sound and conception to me."

During the 1930s the same kind of contrast separates the great tenor saxophonists Lester Young and Coleman Hawkins. Young (b. 1909) grew up through age ten in Algiers, across the river from New Orleans, where, like Armstrong, he enjoyed constant exposure to outdoor music. The blues vernacular he internalized in New

Orleans developed further during his early professional years in the Southwest and Midwest. Young stubbornly resisted musical notation and cultivated a casual approach to the harmonic foundation, a technique designed to enhance the sense of bluesy detachment in his improvisations. Hawkins's (b. 1904) childhood in Missouri included classical training on piano and cello, which put him in a good position to later take harmonic complexity in fresh improvisational directions. He was anything but casual about harmony, though he lacked the kind of melodic ease that comes through in virtually everything Young ever played.

In the 1940s, the same distinction divides the central pair of bebop, Charlie "Yardbird" Parker and Dizzy Gillespie. Gillespie himself addressed the matter, and he used the adjective "deep," recalling Muddy Waters: "I'm not what you call a 'blues' player . . . I mean in the authentic sense of the blues . . . My music is not that deep—not as deep as Hot Lips Page or Charlie Parker, because Yard knew the blues." Gillespie, like Ellington and Hawkins, was a harmonic innovator. Ultimately, one must soften this binary approach to style analysis, since the musicians were constantly learning from each other. Yet it exposes fundamental issues that may be factored into a range of interpretations. Today the creative tension between players who grew up with blues and those who did not has disappeared, for the simple reason that blues no longer has the presence it once had in the African-American community. No one playing jazz today came up in the way Armstrong did, with impressive mastery of blues by age fourteen and layers of additional learning to follow, as a *supplement* to the blues foundation. No one playing today came up in a way even remotely close to this.

There are advantages to thinking about blues and jazz in the way alluded to by Bushell, Ellington, and Gillespie. Blues may be conceived not as the universal unifier of African-American vernacular culture but as one prominent tradition that influenced jazz at various times and places and to different degrees. The tradition of blues-oriented jazz had a beginning, it has had great innovators, and it has had secondary practitioners and imitators. An early training in blues taught the expressive gestures of bending pitch and dragging behind the beat, and it also provided an opportunity to focus on

melody, with few harmonic distractions. In its basic form blues are
built on three chords, which are used as signposts for the regular
flow of four-bar phrases. The main chord of the three is built on the
pitch that serves as a center of gravity for the soloist's melody; the
two secondary chords alternate with it, but only briefly. Thus, blues
harmony is much simpler than the harmony typically used in most
popular songs.

It has long been a mark of competence in jazz to be able to
improvise precisely against the background chords of whatever tune
is called, but in early blues the relationship between solo melody and
chords was, most likely, much more flexible than that. A strong tradition of blues practice allows the soloist to literally ignore the secondary chords and simply build an entire improvised melody around
the main pitch. This melodic independence can be heard throughout blues history, especially in guitar-based, "country" blues, but also
in jazz. In the blues Armstrong played around age fourteen with his
little band of cornet, piano, and drums, the three chords just
described were probably used over and over again, but he undoubtedly enjoyed the freedom to disregard the secondary chords. More
important than harmony was the ability to work the gestures of
blues into a coherent stream of melody. This lack of harmonic con-
straint made blues the perfect training ground for melodic improvisation. This training must have been a strong factor in Armstrong's
eventual emergence as a great melodist.

As Armstrong roamed around town listening to cornetists, he
discovered a variety of stylistic models. Bunk Johnson and Joe
Oliver, especially, showed him how to bring the blues sensitivity of
the ragman's tinhorn to a cornet, just as Bolden had done fifteen
years earlier. Lillian Hardin Armstrong said that Louis told her
about learning blues phrasing from Johnson, specifically the technique of getting behind and catching up, "a way of hesitating." He
certainly heard this in Oliver's playing too. Bolden may have been
the first cornet player to do this, sometime around 1900; certainly
the legends surrounding him imply that he was the first *great* cornet
player to do it. By 1915 the connection between street blues and
professional cornet blues was nothing new, and Armstrong was fol-

lowing the established uptown pattern of bringing everyday blues into a professional setting.

We are not told what Larenzo said in his spellbinding talk, but it is important to try and imagine the musical sensibility he transmitted to the child, in words and by demonstration. Training that is exclusively oral depends on apprenticeship and direct imitation, with little need for theoretical language or abstract constructions. The lack of surviving detail may give the impression of no tutoring at all, leading to the conclusion that Armstrong was the product of a primitive mentality that yields some mysterious advantage over cultivated minds. The most significant things in music are not always talked about, making it harder to identify them and all the more crucial to try.

Armstrong wrote that he admired Larenzo's soul, and that is surely a word to focus on. Besides indexing religious music, the direct reference for the word in the 1950s (when Armstrong was writing), "soul" signals emotional depth, expressed musically through nuance and gesture. In this depth merges a paradoxical combination of emotional sincerity and liberating detachment. It is as if the linear *progress* of the musical surface is inconsequential; what is important is the persuasive use of gestures that provide access to a vast, hidden interior. Easier to hear than to describe, the gestures are played evasively, indirectly, understatedly, as if to pull the emotion out. Cornetist Don Albert defined blues as a "soulful song," a matter of making each note count, of not playing too many notes and putting each one in the right place. The gestures must be made to seem to float. This is accomplished through phrasing and through nearly constant shadings of loud and soft. The analogy of depth created in painting through *chiaroscuro*— shadings of light and dark—may be helpful.

Following Robert Palmer, one may think about music performed in this way as nonlinear. Deep blues are more about the expressive markers than about moving toward linear goals. Once internalized, this sensitivity can be brought to the performance of any kind of music, no matter how goal-directed it may be in other aspects of its design. Armstrong and Parker—the two most influential soloists in jazz history—were committed to the bluesy approach as much as anyone was. "Louis will take a popular piece and if there's any chance of playing some blues in there, that will come out of his horn," said Johnny Wiggs. Soloists like Hawkins and Gillespie invented other means of achieving expressive depth. Their harmonically oriented techniques might be associated with blues at some point of reception, but they definitely did not belong to the deep blues tradition of the Deep South.

Blues started to be played on wind instruments in New Orleans around the same time that the distinctive dance music that would later be called jazz came into focus. When Big Eye Louis Nelson said that "blues is what cause the fellows to start jazzing," he asserted a historical analysis that is difficult to track in detail. Perhaps he meant to recognize the importance of blues as an improvisational genre (Chapter 9). Or he may have meant to emphasize how common it was for early jazz musicians to bring the expressive markers of blues to other repertories—hymns, marches, dance tunes—and how truly distinctive that was. There were blues singers in New Orleans, but they were not terribly important in the sprawling professional world to which Armstrong aspired. Cornetist Ernest "Punch" Miller sang blues to himself while he was plowing fields and making sugarcane in the countryside before he moved to New Orleans. "In the city they didn't do much singing—just played. They didn't sing the blues much," he said. Bass player Eddie Dawson (b. 1884) said that Bolden's band was the first he ever heard play blues, which must have been around 1900. This was probably a huge part of Bolden's success—the novelty of blues being played by wind instruments, and the possibilities that new idea opened up. Ragmen on the streets provided the daily, amateur-level counterpart to this New Orleanian orientation toward winds.

In rural Mississippi too, the genre of blues was beginning to take shape during these same decades, but mainly on string instruments and especially guitars purchased from the Sears and Roebuck catalogue. Piano blues flourished up and down the lower regions of the Mississippi River, from St. Louis to New Orleans, where the piano had a strong presence in uptown honky tonks and in the brothels of Storyville. But the dancing venues that provided most of the employment for uptown musicians did not usually have pianos, so ensemble music evolved without them. Instead, it developed through connections to various outdoor venues for music, the parades and picnics and parks, where wind instruments found their natural place. The piano is limited in its ability to render vocal nuances, which may also account for the New Orleanian preference for blues on winds. And in Armstrong's uptown neighborhood, the cornet ranked first among wind instruments.

❧ In his many reminiscences of his years in New Orleans, Armstrong told a few different stories about how he received his first cornet. In one version he picked up the horn, tinkered with it, and "realized that I could play *Home Sweet Home*—then *here* come the *Blues.*" Even if that was not exactly how it happened, we can easily accept that these were the strong childhood associations he brought to the instrument. By the time he got a cornet, he was already familiar with American popular songs, of which *Home Sweet Home* was perhaps the most popular of all. But a stronger association he brought to the instrument would have been the blues played by Larenzo on a long tinhorn. Once again we find the child hanging around the economic margins of society, and once again this also placed him at the center of African-American vernacular culture. Just as he was born into Sanctified musicality, so was he born into the nuances of the blues. It is hard to imagine that anyone thought in this way in 1910, but we can now see that by hanging out on the streets with Larenzo and Santiago, little Louis was in the right place at the right time.

CHAPTER FOUR

~~~~~~~

Street Hustler

Lots more music back then than today, more livelier—funerals, parades, saloons, every little advertisement, things, grand openings of a place.   —*Manuel Manetta*

All day Sunday the streets would be jammed with people. Wasn't nothing but fun.
          —*Punch Miller*

Growing up between ages five and twelve with his mother, in the heart of the colored prostitution district around Liberty and Perdido streets, gave Armstrong constant exposure to different sides of vernacular culture. At the same time, he enjoyed a little too much freedom to run around and get in trouble. In his memoirs he says very little about school, but a great deal about the outside world. His attendance at the neighborhood Fisk School was probably intermittent. "When I was coming up around Liberty and Perdido, Franklin and Perdido, I observed everything and everybody," he wrote. By modern-day American standards of childhood, the situation was imbalanced and out of control. But if we think about the successful adult that he would become, then we must assume that he experienced a fruitful combination of nurturing and stimulation, even if there were some rough moments along the way.

He often wrote about his mother and the life-lessons she imparted. On the day he arrived to live with her, at age five, she immediately had him take a "physic." The idea that a daily laxative protects against disease was common during these times. Armstrong remained faithful to the regimen for the rest of his life. Near the end, after a severe illness, he wrote a funny story about trying to

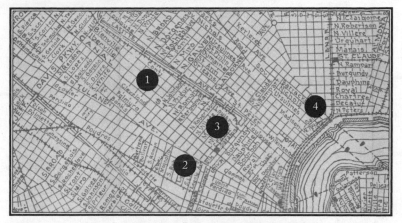

New Orleans, 1924 (New Orleans Public Library)
1. Canal Street   2. Liberty and Perdido streets
3. Storyville   4. Gallatin Street

convert the nurses in the intensive care ward to the laxative Swiss Kriss. May Ann had no money for store-bought laxatives, so she gathered pepper grasses around the railroad tracks, ground them to a powder, and served Louis a teaspoon followed by a glass of water, according to a tradition of herbal medicine that was widely practiced by slaves and certainly had some connections to Africa. Another all-purpose purge was Sweet Spirits of Nitre, which, when smeared on his lips, caused enough pain to make him "grab four bedposts." He believed that these treatments protected him from tuberculosis and other deadly diseases. For a sore throat his mother boiled cockroaches, strained the broth, and fed him a teaspoon. To ward off lockjaw it was again the pepper grasses, boiled down to a paste and rubbed directly into a wound. When he developed a daily marijuana habit as an adult, he thought of the drug as similarly herbal and purgative, a mental cleanser analogous to the physical cleansing of laxatives.

Red beans and rice, catfish heads, biscuits and molasses were the daily food staples. He and his sister gathered spoiled produce for their mother to salvage. Two loaves of stale bread from the baker could be purchased for a nickel. Boyfriend Tom worked at a local hotel and brought home scraps of beef or lamb. They all lived in one room, the children sleeping on a pallet on the floor, next to the bed for May Ann and her series of boyfriends (he remembered "at least six"). "Sex time" originally confused the child, who mistook passion for violence. He occasionally tried to intervene in fights between his mother and a boyfriend, throwing bricks once and pulling her out of a canal another time. Other than these few emergency interventions, he learned to "stay in his place" and not sass his elders.

This was poverty, but he did not feel deprived. May Ann taught the children to "never worry about what the *other* feller has *got. Try* and *get something your self*," he wrote. He remembered his childhood as a happy time. In the worldview he was acquiring, poverty could even be good for you. In Chicago he got to know one Andrew Hilaire, a Creole drummer of whom he had only been dimly aware in New Orleans. Hilaire grew up comfortably, not wealthy but "nigger rich," as Armstrong put it. But when Hilaire died young from tuberculosis, it appeared from Armstrong's perspective that this had something to do with his comfort and lack of struggle as a child. Impoverished children who had the "chance to rough it out" grew stronger than those with advantages. Clarinetist Barney Bigard put a musical spin on the same idea: "If you're poor you can realize more of something than if you are rich . . . So many of the guys that suffered because of the racial situation and the economic situation in New Orleans, for instance, they can't even read music, but they play with that feeling."

Beyond his family, Armstrong seems to have been well connected within the immediate community. To a degree, his upbringing was communal. Everything was out in the open, visible and public. In the backyard there were two common outhouses, one for men and one for women, and there were also rocking chairs where elderly neighbors sat and talked. He liked to tell the story of a neighbor calling into the backyard to retrieve her daughter: "Marandy, you'd better come into this house—you laying out there with nothing on top of you but that Thin Nigger." He got to know the local pimps and prostitutes, and a few years later, when he marched through the neighborhood with the Colored Waif's Home band, they showered the band with donations. His sense of family was less stable and more extended than is typical today. It was hardly a "wretched" childhood, as one recent biographer would have it. To think in that way is to impose the materialistic values of middle-class America onto a situation that was perhaps richer socially and artistically. (The comment also reveals the trappings of "black pathology" thinking.) His childhood was hardly free of suffering, but when he looked back on it fondly, he was not simply creating a fantasy.

Parades, circa 1910

The thrill that loomed largest in Louis's childhood was, unquestionably, a parade. A parade offered the unmatchable combination of hanging out with friends, wandering through dangerous parts of town, getting close to famous musicians, and, of course, grooving with the music. Parades first formed Armstrong's sense of what it meant to be a professional musician. They were the continuous presence brightening his childhood and packing it with lessons of styles of expressive culture as well as social structure. Enough descriptions from Armstrong and from his contemporaries survive to allow us to imagine in considerable detail how he experienced a parade.

Parades happen every Sunday and often on other days. Dr. Edmond Souchon, who would later become an important patron of jazz, remembered how notice of a parade made its way through the grapevine to his nanny, who took him by the hand to watch at First Street and Dryades, near Terrell's Grocery. For Armstrong, it was easy enough to pick up the music in the air and track it down. On big festival days like the 10th of May, St. Joseph's Day, or Labor Day, the parade begins as early as eight in the morning. It is led by the grand marshal, dressed in full splendor with the longest sash of any marcher, which reaches down to his shoe and blazes with gold bangles; shining emblems grace his shoulders. He walks in a fashion that also distinguishes him. In fact, he has gained the honor of this position through his ability to strut and prance. He is expected to strut creatively, to stimulate the crowd with his fancy, rhythmic steps, some familiar and some surprising. When his father is grand marshal for the Odd Fellows, Louis watches from a distance. He rarely sees him otherwise—there are no weekend visits, no child-support payments, no birthday greetings—so the moment is loaded with significance. He sees how Willie's strutting pleases the women, and he notices his passion for this public moment: "He was a *Freak* for being the *Grand Marshall*," Armstrong wrote.

Right behind the marshal march the aides to the club, also in full uniform, with silk ribbons falling from their shoulders. Sometimes they ride decorated horses. Behind them is the hired band, placed between the aides and the rest of the club members as if to shore up

George Palmer Holmes, Grand Marshal, 1892
(Historic New Orleans Collection, Acc. No. 1974.25.11.148)

the identification of the club with the musical display it is paying for. First among the members are the standard bearers, who carry the club banner and the American flag. Every member wears a button showing the name of the club and the club color. One club has uniforms that are entirely white, with white felt hats, silk shirts, and mohair pants. Of course, the band is also well dressed. Manuel Perez's Onward Brass Band, one of Armstrong's favorites, has tailored blue serge coats, white pants, and white hats. Joe Oliver, featured cornetist for the Onward, is visually distinguished by cream rather than white pants, and he positions under his hat a handkerchief that is pulled back to cover his neck to keep the sun off.

As Sidney Bechet said, "You want to *see* [a parade] as well as hear it." Nevertheless, if a band cannot afford fancy clothes, a strong musical performance will compensate. Professor James Humphrey made his living by teaching various band instruments to boys and young men in small towns. He called his ragtag band into the city on big holidays, when the demand for bands exceeded the supply. The country boys lacked uniforms and they felt self-conscious, but with youthful vigor and amateur passion they outlasted the better-dressed and more-established bands, coming on strong especially late in the afternoon to please the crowd. As many as fifteen bands graced the big parade days of the year.

In typical band formation the two trombones are in front, side by side. They are followed by baritone horn on the right and tuba on the left, and then clarinet on the right and alto horn on the left. Then come the two cornets, with drums bringing up the rear, snare on the right and bass with attached cymbal on the left. Everyone steps in time with the steady beat of the bass drum. Since the streets are full of holes, an established musician like Joe Oliver takes the liberty of moving over to the sidewalk during "take down," a break from playing. This is when Armstrong can wedge his way in and ask to carry Oliver's horn. The parade route is designed to wind through the neighborhood where the club members live. Sandwiches and whiskey are served at a designated stop, and Louis can snatch a sandwich if he has made a place for himself as horn carrier.

He runs the second line with his buddies—Black Benny, Nicodemus, Rainhead, Black Sol, Black Lute, Hobo Crookit, Big

Walter Bell, Cocaine Buddy, Ikey Smooth, Jakey Brown, Lips the
Camel, Big Sore Dick, Foots Ariel, and Nasty Slim. Like Louis,
most of them lack parental supervision; several will become well-
known toughs. Black Benny is particularly aggressive about claiming a place for himself as "grand marshal" for the second line. The
police sometimes disperse the crowd. But if Louis is able to carry an
instrument during take down, he can stick with the band and march
all day, which is what he likes to do. (The grown-up, dance-hall version of this service was for women to carry the instruments out of
the hall, after a dance. "That meant lay off, she was the [musician's]
main girl," said drummer Zutty Singleton.) He and his friends
notice how the Onward Brass Band, with Oliver and Perez, pleases
the crowd enough to earn a distinguished position in larger parades.
On Labor Day, for example, ten or twelve bands line up on Rampart
Street, described by one writer of the time as "the Broadway of New
Orleans negroes." Oliver dispenses bits of advice to children who
approach him; he is the only musician who does this, according to
Armstrong. The Onward Brass Band is awarded the rear position,
which means that at parade end the foregoing bands split apart their
two files, thus opening up the middle for the Onward to march
through playing *Maryland, My Maryland*.

There are many, many parades, but Mardi Gras is the most spectacular of all. Mardi Gras gives Armstrong a chance to see white
bands that play for the Rex procession up Canal Street. The people
in his Third Ward neighborhood have Mardi Gras traditions of
their own. Prostitutes buy expensive dresses and fancy stockings
that they stuff with dollar bills. They wear masks—it is legal on
Mardi Gras to wear a mask until six o'clock in the evening—and
they use the anonymity to randomly whip people with switches.
Some men from Armstrong's neighborhood wear Indian outfits,
drink "fire water," and meet at designated locations to violently settle old rivalries. His mother wears a costume that includes silk
stockings and a mask. His father wears a "big white monkey suit"
with a long tail. Louis puts together a children's costume of blackface makeup and old rags.

The main Mardi Gras attraction for him is the Zulu ensemble, first
launched in 1909 by working-class men in his neighborhood—"coal

cart drivers, bar tenders, waiters, hustlers, etc.," he wrote—who belong to the Zulu Aid and Pleasure Club. The first King Zulu wore a lard-can crown, blackface makeup, ragged trousers, and carried a banana-stalk scepter. "Zulu" was a common racial slur, used right alongside "nigger," "darky," "coon," and "monkey." From the start the Zulu ritual was loaded with double-edged symbolism, as signaled by the blackface makeup of minstrelsy, complete with white paint around the lips and eyes. King Zulu is not an African but rather a minstrel parody of an African. His true object of satire is Rex, the white Mardi Gras king. He does everything that Rex does, only upside down. Rex arrives by yacht—"get off of his big, fine boat looking like a million, which most of them have," wrote Armstrong—so Zulu arrives by a rowboat named the "royal barge." Rex is protected by the city police, King Zulu by his comical Zulu police. It is a classic example of carnivalesque release of class tensions with the special twist of African-American signifying. "Each member has a burlesque of some character they have in mind," Armstrong remembered, and in 1918, one of the Zulus parodied, to the delight of the crowd, a white policeman who had imprisoned Armstrong unjustly. In 1919, one of Armstrong's "stepfathers" was crowned king of the Zulus.

Rex toasting, Mardi Gras, 1901 (New Orleans Public Library,
photo by Cornelius Durkee)

King of the Zulus (New Orleans Public Library)

In 1932, as he was about to perform *I'll Be Glad When You're Dead You Rascal You* for the king of England, Armstrong jovially shouted from the stage, "This one's for you, Rex!" Everyone smiled at Satchmo's good-natured informality without realizing what it meant for an uptown New Orleanian to call the king of England "Rex." A year earlier, Armstrong had dedicated the same song to the city police of Memphis, Tennessee, who had just released him and his band from an overnight stay in prison. (Their crime was traveling on a bus with a white woman, their manager's wife.) Preston Jackson, the trombonist, remembered how terrified he was by Armstrong's rather exposed bit of signifying, and he had good reason: most of the police department carried membership in the Ku Klux Klan. But in Memphis too, Armstrong's jovial stage manner carried it off. After the performance several policemen told him, as Jackson remembered it, "You know, Mr. Armstrong, we have had a number of important jazz orchestras come through Memphis, people like Paul Whiteman and Jean Goldkette, but none of them ever thought enough of the Police Department to dedicate a song to us! We appreciate it, and we want you to know that at your next show we will be reserving the first several rows for ourselves and our wives."

The seed of royal aspiration planted in Armstrong's youth finally blossomed in 1949, when the crown of King Zulu infamously fell on him. Again, outsiders were unable to understand what was going on, though in this case they were plenty astonished as photographs circulated nationally of the famous trumpet player dressed in black-face makeup with broad white lipstick, a crown with red feathers, a red velvet tunic with gold sequins, black tights, gold shoes, and a yellow cellophane grass skirt. He and his drunken entourage collectively threw twenty thousand coconuts. Armstrong's image as a regressive, plantation-style minstrel—an image that, from the start in New Orleans, had been used for spirit-lifting subversion—was now firmly imprinted on the national consciousness. It would haunt him for the rest of his career.

How far does this kind of two-sided signifying, so perfectly captured in the Zulu ritual and in Armstrong's performance of *I'll Be Glad When You're Dead* for the king of England, extend through the music of early jazz? There are some attractions to thinking about jazz as carrying an ironic edge, especially during the period of early Jim Crow, when things were as bad as they could get and when other means of performing symbolic resistance were in play. The problem is a universal one for music: whenever instrumental music is played with no reference to words, irony is very difficult to analyze. Theoretically, even purely instrumental music offers the opportunity to create ironic distance between performer and material being performed. After all, weren't the uptown immigrants from the plantations riffing on white tunes—hymns, marches, dirges, waltzes, quadrilles, and so on—when they developed jazz? Might they not have been doing that in the same way that King Zulu was riffing on Rex?

My sense is that they were not doing this at all. I see no evidence that uptown musicians were interested in creating a sense of ironic distance between themselves and their musical material. Armstrong *could* be about that, on occasion. But he is more consistently about absorbing and transforming his musical material so that it becomes his. To riff on a waltz is to riff on the white power structure—it is a little too easy to think that way, being so far from the tensions and pleasures of the moment. Too easy and also too difficult to support in the absence of any hints from the participants themselves.

"Funeral with music"

Back to 1910. The spectrum of the parade ritual is filled out by the New Orleanian "funeral with music." All club members find a way to take the afternoon off from work to honor their deceased brother; they are fined by the club if they don't. Men join as many clubs as popularity and income allow, thus assuring a grand spectacle of marchers at death. Five or six clubs, each with a hired band, might accompany the funeral of a popular man. In a "perfect death" (Jelly Roll Morton's phrase) the funeral procession, led by a band, gathers at the club hall or meeting place. At first the band walks slowly while playing *Sing On, Just a Closer Walk with Thee, Just a Little While to Stay Here*, or perhaps *The Saints Go Marching In*—"a very slow 4/4 tempo," said Pops Foster, "it was gorgeous." An experienced band plays quietly during this initial stage. Behind the band come the surviving club members in parade formation. The colorful buttons they wear for festive parades are now reversed, to show black. The second line starts to gather. As it nears the church or house where the wake has been held, the band stops playing. Armstrong remembered the charged atmosphere of a wake: "While we were sitting around the corpse in the middle of the floor, the chaste sisters would come by. You get the spirit like everyone else."

The band waits outside while the club members pay respect. If there is a church service, the band disperses to nearby saloons; a child is sent to get them when the service is over. As the body is carried out and placed in a horse-drawn hearse covered in black shrouds, the band plays the hymn *Flee as a Bird*. "Bass drum, snare drum goes 'rum tum tum' and the procession begins," Armstrong remembered. "Someone is always singing." The grand marshal whistles to start the procession to the cemetery; the hymn of choice for this moment is *Nearer My God to Thee*. The procession moves forward, and when the band rests, the snare drummer rolls a stark, isolated cadence, the drum head muffled by a handkerchief underneath in order to mimic the sound of a kettle drum, a reference to high military style. The march tempo picks up a little during these kettledrum interludes, but otherwise the walking is very slow. People stand in reverent silence along the sidewalk as the hearse passes by.

At the cemetery the band slows the pace even more and begins to play a dirge, usually the hymn *What a Friend We Have in Jesus* at an extremely slow tempo. Here Louis is exposed to an emotional register that is not available to him in any other musical situation. The band members move slowly forward at the same time that they sway gently from side to side. The two files split to allow the hearse to pass between them, all to the accompaniment of the dirge. The cornet is now playing the lead melody straight, with almost no embellishment, while the clarinet adds obbligato counterpoint in a higher range. Clarinetist George Baquet, playing with Perez's Onward Brass Band, is famous for the emotional intensity he brings to dirges: "It would go so sweet and high," said Zutty Singleton, "really make you cry." And Perez himself is known for his powerful renditions of the lead melody in a dirge. In selecting this band as his favorite, young Louis follows popular opinion.

Funeral with music, 1950s (Courtesy of the Hogan Jazz Archive, Tulane University, photo by Ralston Crawford)

The body is carried to the grave while the drummer rolls on his muffled snare. As the body is entombed, the band plays another hymn, with mourners singing along. Three successive markers signal the end of the service: the preacher prays, "Ashes to ashes and dust to dust," the mourners moan and cry, and dirt is thrown on the coffin, the final gesture that "turns the body loose."

After a respectful pause, the grand marshal flips his sash over, from its black side to its colored side, and the club members do the same with their buttons. The snare drummer now removes his muffling handkerchief and he rolls the drum loudly, calling the rest of the band back into position. *Oh Didn't He Ramble* typically launches the famous New Orleanian rejoicing after death. In a recording from the 1950s Armstrong and his band reenacted a graveside scene—the preaching, the mourning, turning the body loose, and the rejoicing with *Oh Didn't He Ramble*. Though done with humor, the recording carries a degree of historical accuracy, including heterophonic rendition of the hymns. In a more reflective moment it seemed to Armstrong that jazz was born in this up-tempo rejoicing. "Yeah, Pops—jazz actually rose from the dead . . . the real music came from the grave. That was how jazz began. That's why it brings people to life." One Alex Christensen claimed in 1914 that "ragtime will always be popular—anywhere, everywhere—except, perhaps, at a funeral." Obviously, he had never visited uptown New Orleans.

Mourners, hearse, and preacher linger at the grave as the band turns around and marches back to the home of the deceased. Umbrellas come out, and the sounds of up-tempo ragtime cause the second line to expand dramatically. In the late 1950s, Roland Wingfield observed specific African retentions in a second-line dance: "The dancers moved with pelvis thrown forward, the upper body slightly tilted back, loose and responding freely to the rhythm, legs slightly apart and propelling a shuffling step with a subtle bounce—a step characteristic of Africa and found often in Brazil and the West Indies." Armstrong and his friends mimic the footwork of their favorite band, and they watch for the fancy steps that are reserved for turning corners. The grand marshal teases the second line and waits until the last second to indicate which direction

The grand marshal turns a corner while the second line stays in step, 1946 (Historic New Orleans Collection, Acc. No. 92–48–L MSS 520 f.298, photo by William Russell)

the procession will turn. The second line must then hurry, but they don't run; they *skip in tempo* as they try to catch up.

When more than one band is hired for a funeral (and also in parades), the second line is sometimes handed a special treat. The first band splits its two files, making room for the second band to march through the middle; both continue playing their different tunes in full Charles Ivesian anarchic splendor. The second band then splits and the process continues. "Forty instruments all bucking at one another," remembered Sidney Bechet. "Then came the beauty of it . . . the part that really took something right out of you. You'd hear mostly one band, so clear, so good, making you happier, sadder, whatever way it wanted you to feel. It would come out of the bucking and it would still be playing all together. None of the musicians would be confused, none of them would have mixed up the music, they would all be in time." One point of this demonstration is to see who is solid enough to hold the ensemble together through the cacophonous challenge. Musical winners are judged by applause. The victors march back to the house of the deceased, play at the front door for fifteen minutes, and then finish the afternoon inside with gumbo, ham salad, burgundy, and sangaree. The entire event, from initial procession until the last glass of wine, lasts about two hours.

Aside from the danger of it, second lining does not seem like such a bad passion for an eleven-year-old to have. When he followed parades and funerals, Armstrong was being brought into a collection of rituals that defined a set of meanings and emotions for music. Here too is the ultimate spectacle of social status into which the child is drawn, with his father marching as a flamboyant grand marshal and famous musicians allowing him to carry their horns. Here is a masculine identity for a boy to admire and grow into.

Hustling in the Neighborhood

During the evenings Armstrong could listen to music from his house if he wanted to. Actually, it would have been hard to avoid. It is clear from many accounts that music traveled great distances in New Orleans, aided by the low altitude, the humid air, the lack of tall buildings, and the absence of ambient noise from automobiles. Paul Barbarin (Isidore's son) said that bands could be heard from a distance of a mile and a half; others claimed three miles and more.

Near his mother's home around Liberty and Perdido there were clusters of honky tonks, each with a little band or piano pounding through the night. But Armstrong did not always stay home at night. There were curfews for children, and other musicians talk about having to race home to "beat the bell" that firehouses rang at nine o'clock, but Louis and his friends did not pay attention to the bell. Instead they went looking for gambling, fighting, and bits of mischief. "Mama didn't make us go to bed. We were afraid we might miss something," he chuckled to an interviewer. Bunk Johnson remembered Armstrong sleeping behind the piano of a honky tonk on the corner of Perdido and Franklin, waiting for Johnson to show up at four in the morning. On Saturday nights especially, his mother had a hard time finding him. His evening rounds brought him first and foremost to Funky Butt Hall, right down the block on Perdido Street, where the walls had cracks big enough for the children to gawk at the sexy dancing.

Through those cracks the child discovered more about a part of vernacular culture that he had already been introduced to in church—the firm association of musical gesture with moving bodies. But unlike church, the musical codes that Funky Butt Hall was known for—the codes of ragtime, rough counterpoint bordering on anarchy, passionate, vocalized timbre, and the sensuous gestures of the blues—were saturated with eroticism. Armstrong never forgot what he saw there as a child: "To a tune like *The Bucket's Got a Hole in It*, some of them chicks would get way down, shake everything, slapping themselves on the cheek of their behind. Yeah!" he wrote. What is not said may be taken for granted: the slap was rhythmically synchronized with the music. The conflation of musical and bodily gestures was part of the African cultural legacy that Armstrong was internalizing, both indoors and outdoors, at home and in church, in the streets and through the cracks of dance-hall walls.

This association comes through often in descriptions of slave dancing. From Louisiana in 1833 there is a report on "Congo" dancers "striking their thighs and their hands in time." A description from Jamaica in 1774 attends to female hips: "the execution of this wriggle, keeping exact time with the music, is esteemed among them a particular excellence; and on this account they begin to practice it so early in life, that few are without it in their ordinary walking." Here is another continuum between the mundane habits of everyday life and the formalized practices of expressive culture. The same continuum that links the inflections of everyday speech to the stylized utterances of blues also links ordinary walking with virtuoso dancing. Zora Neale Hurston discusses the everyday side of kinetic practice:

> Everything is acted out. Unconsciously for the most part of course. There is an impromptu ceremony always ready for every hour of life. No little moment passes unadorned . . . A Negro girl strolls past the corner lounger. Her whole body panging and posing. A slight shoulder movement that calls attention to her bust, that is all of a dare. A hippy undulation below the waist that is a sheaf of promises tied with conscious power. She is acting out "I'm a darned sweet woman and you know it."

It is sexual: she slaps her ass, wriggles her hips, calls attention to her bust. But she is *acting* all of that in stylized, culturally determined ways. The dance hall that Armstrong began to study as a child was the place for bringing increased form and virtuosity to these stylized movements of daily life.

Some slave observers noted how children were brought into these dancing traditions, even the lascivious ones, and this follows the traditional African inclination to initiate children into music and dance of all kinds. Thirty minutes in advance of advertised events in Funky Butt Hall, bands were required to play on the *banquette* (New Orleanian for "sidewalk") as a promotion. This gave children a chance to imitate the dancing they would watch later in the evening. Armstrong remembered hearing Buddy Bolden in this way, which would have been at age five or six. Bolden blew so hard that the child ached in sympathy with the tension in his face.

Armstrong took the dance steps he had been practicing in front of Funky Butt Hall and tried to make some money with them on the streets, as teenage boys still do in New Orleans. By 1910 he was also selling newspapers as a helper to a white boy named Charles, who had realized that he could make more money by farming out delivery to younger children. Armstrong picked up copies of the *New Orleans Item* at the corner of Canal Street and St. Charles Avenue and peddled them from streetcars. But newspaper boys were supposed to be white, according to Jim Crow, so the arrangement got him in trouble with the law, perhaps for the first time but not for the last. Running with older boys, he learned how to multiply his earnings through gambling, shooting dice, coon can, black jack, and African dominos. Gambling gave him change enough for a new pair of short pants.

There were other hustles. He cleaned graves on Decoration Day out at Girod Street Cemetery. He scraped brick dust and sold it to the prostitutes for fifty cents a bucket; they mixed it with their urine and scrubbed their steps as a way to bring good luck and ward off evil spirits. He passed out handbills for dances. A notice for Bunk Johnson's Eagle Band, which had just brought in fourteen-year-old Sidney Bechet, read:

> The Eagle Boys fly high
> And never lose a feather
> If you miss this dance
> You'll have the blues forever

Roaming through town in the evenings, Armstrong probably heard serenade bands hired to make surprise appearances outside of someone's window, in celebration of a birthday or other event. And almost every day he heard the ubiquitous advertising bands circulating on horse-drawn wagons, with the small group of musicians sitting on chairs. The advertising wagons always stopped at the buzzing intersection of Liberty and Perdido to promote a furniture sale, dance, boxing match, or anything else. "People ran out of their houses like it was on fire," was how Manuel Manetta described the scene. Best of all was when two wagons met by chance, sparking a little competition.

But the most important of Armstrong's childhood hustles was the vocal quartet he formed with his buddies. Children commonly put together bands in imitation of adults. Paul Barbarin had one; he used chair rungs for drumsticks while his friends whistled and played wax paper on a comb. They played on street corners until the police chased them away. Kid Ory led several childhood bands in LaPlace, Louisiana, on the sugar plantation where he grew up. Before they figured out how to patch together homemade instruments, Ory and his friends vocalized; Ory called it a "humming band." Armstrong and his friends used adult terminology to designate their respective vocal ranges: Louis sang tenor, Little Mack took the lead, Big Nose Sidney sang bass, and James "Red Happy" Bolton found his place on baritone. The quartet sang for tips—their "hustle," as Armstrong phrased it—in direct competition with street musicians playing guitar or mandolin. Their favorite song was *My Brazilian Beauty*.

The quartet worked on Rampart Street between Perdido and Gravier, but whenever possible they liked to wander into Storyville, not the cheap Storyville but the real one, just a couple of blocks away, where the best tips were thrown. They had a walking order, just like a brass band, with lead and tenor side by side in front, baritone and bass behind. Storyville was definitely off limits to African-American children, so they had to alertly stay one step ahead of the police, who had a heavy presence. "Policemen catch you down there, short pants, oh-oh, he should throw that club at you, run you into it and get your legs crossed on the club, and throw you down," remembered Montudie Garland. Armstrong and his friends tried to disguise themselves with long pants. Armstrong's performance pose was to cup his hand behind his ear while he sang and to move his mouth from side to side. It would be interesting to know whom he was imitating when he did this, for ear cupping is a technique found in Mississippi and also the west central Sudanic belt in Africa.

Though it may seem hard to believe, since it is so completely foreign to American life in the twenty-first century, it was not unusual for men sitting in barrooms to sing extemporaneously in quartet style. Armstrong heard "some of the finest singing in the world, listening to guys who hung around the saloons, with a cold can of beer in their hands, singing as they drank." When he became old enough, around age sixteen, to join the men, he took the lead with his tenor voice. He won their approval and they called him a good "ragtime singer." He was finding his way into an important tradition of vernacular song. Extemporized part-singing ran very wide throughout the South among African-American men. Historian Lynn Abbott has made the case that barbershop quartet singing originated with African-American men in Jacksonville, Florida, spreading out from there via minstrelsy and vaudeville. In New Orleans around 1910, Laddie Melton remembered, "It was typical, almost, for any three of four Negroes to get together and, they say, 'Let's crack up a chord! Let's hit a note!'" Dewberry's Shaving Parlor and Social Club, on Franklin Street not far from Armstrong's home, was a popular hangout for singers. In Kansas City during the late 1880s comedian Billy McClain recalled that "about every four dark faces you met was a quartet." In 1912, Irving Berlin published a song about the African-American phenomenon that included these lines: "When you find you can't afford / To be paying for your board / You can find a meal in ev'ry chord."

Armstrong's friend Black Benny Williams, described by Louis as a "jack of all trades," excelled not only at drumming, pimping, and fighting but also at singing tenor parts. His specialty was *Sweet Adeline*. Benny also sang *Mr. Jefferson Lord—Play That Barbershop Chord*, which was composed by William Tracey and Lewis Muir in 1910:

'Twas in a great big rathskeller
Where a swell colored fellow
By the name of Bill Jefferson Lord
Played the piano while he sang a song,
He just played and sang the whole night long,
'Til a kinky-haired lady
They called Chocolate Sadie
Heard him playing that barbershop chord,
She heaved a sigh
Every time she could catch his eye.

She cried, "Mister Jefferson Lord,
Oh, play that barbershop chord,
It's got that soothing harmony,
It makes an awful, awful, awful hit with me!
Play that strain
Aw, please play it again,
'Cause Mister, when you start
The minor part,
I feel your fingers tripping and a-slipping 'round my heart.
Oh, Mister Lord,
Oh, that's it!
That's the barbershop chord!"

Armstrong and his childhood friends were searching for those same beautiful chords, the ones they heard from the older men. Kid Ory said that his humming group in LaPlace sang in four-part harmony as much as they could, "like a barbershop quartet." That Armstrong and his friends designated themselves tenor, lead, baritone, and bass suggests that they had a basic understanding of the format. The ensemble technique was similar to that of church and early jazz: a standard melody was learned and parts were invented to go with it. The focus of quartet singing, however, was on harmonic experiments. "I have witnessed some of these explorations in the field of harmony and the scenes of hilarity and backslapping when a new and rich chord was discovered," wrote songwriter and novelist James Weldon Johnson about quartets he knew from Jacksonville.

It is this focus on harmony that makes the vocal quartet so important for Louis's musical development. Male quartets were much more adventuresome with chords than church singers could be. It is easy to miss this distinction, since in more recent times African-American male quartets are familiar mainly through gospel, which was how the tradition continued, in groups like the Dixie Hummingbirds; secular spin-offs like the Ink Spots and Temptations followed from that. Armstrong and his friends did not need to stay within the bounds of conventional harmony—just the opposite, the expectation was for unconventionality. Jelly Roll Morton remembered the "crazy ideas of harmony" in the vocal quartet he sang with in New Orleans, and in Nashville, Tennessee, Roland Hayes, later to become a great concert-hall singer, strolled every evening in a quartet with his teenage friends, making "personal discoveries" in harmony that were "good practice for the ear." This is precisely the training that I imagine Louis getting in his vocal quartet.

Louis's first opportunity to develop a feeling for vertical combinations of sound came in Baptist and Sanctified churches. The vocal quartet gave him an opportunity to move forward. He acknowledged how the ear training he gained there served him well when he began playing alto horn at the Waif's Home a year or so later. In quartets, the format of only one singer on a part encouraged harmonic precision. In a couple of years, the Karnofsky family would compliment him on singing with good intonation, the ability to control sound at a refined level so that pitch is tuned up precisely. Good intonation can be learned, though most great musicians are simply born with it. In the quartet, Louis's innate ability was challenged and cultivated by the unusual chords, which expose one's intonational ability (or lack of it). Precise tuning is appreciated even by untutored listeners who have no name for the phenomenon but can immediately hear the difference between good and bad.

The quartet also gave Louis a chance to practice a vocal technique that he would later develop brilliantly into a tradition of great importance. Here is where we first hear about him singing scat. The early history of scat is obscure and little studied. Much has been made of his 1925 recording of *Heebie Jeebies* with the Hot Fives. Jelly Roll Morton objected to the popular opinion that Armstrong invented scat in this recording. Morton claimed that he, Tony

Jackson, and a few others brought the technique to New Orleans after they learned it from a comedian named Joe Sims, who hailed from Vicksburg, Mississippi. Armstrong responded that he never claimed to have invented scat, and he agreed about the precedent of old comedians. It is interesting to think of scat originating as an extension of minstrel malapropism. As his vocal quartet walked down the street in formation, they experimented with the syllables "scat-do-beep-dedo, etc." Just a few years later, Red Happy Bolton made a name for himself by scatting in dance halls as a comic interlude to give the older musicians a break.

Armstrong and his quartet gained a small reputation, and musicians started referring to him as "Little Louis." They competed in an amateur show under a large tent. Bunk Johnson heard them somewhere, and he claimed later to have directed his young protégé Sidney Bechet to seek them out. Bechet would have been about fifteen years old, four years older than Armstrong. Bechet remembered how much the quartet impressed him, and he also remembered meeting Louis on the street one day and being so taken by the eleven-year-old's musicality that he invited him to come over to his house for dinner. Bechet was not one to have any qualms about the free invention of historical facts, and the scenario he creates here is bizarre: Two street boys who would each become globally renowned as the leading soloists to emerge from New Orleans, influencing virtually everyone who heard them during the 1920s and beyond, meet through the introduction of a common mentor. Bechet, the rebel from downtown, is living on the streets while working on both his musical career and his emergent alcoholism. Armstrong, from uptown, is a few years younger but largely unsupervised and occasionally in trouble with the law. The fifteen-year-old Bechet extends to the younger prodigy a genteel invitation to dinner.

But Bechet gave his story an unpleasant ending: rudely, Louis didn't bother to show up! More than forty years later, Bechet could not forgive the eleven-year-old: "It's a little thing, but there's big things around it." One of those big things was the fierce competitive temperament that drove the two into a long rivalry. This did not have much of a chance to develop in New Orleans, since Bechet left early, but it did surface during recording sessions from the 1920s, with Bechet sometimes landing musical victory. During the 1930s Armstrong's popularity soared while Bechet, like almost every other New Orleanian of his generation, failed to find a niche for himself in the swing era. Although Bechet eventually did well in France, he never got over that injustice. Perhaps his unforgiving story of the dinner invitation had its cause in the bitter taste of drifting out of fashion while Little Louis acquired stardom of global dimensions. It is also possible that the story indicates something about Armstrong that we know from other sources too: as a child and well into his teens, Armstrong would have been unlikely to cross Canal Street and befriend a Creole.

🞂🞇 Life was good for roaming Little Louis until New Year's Eve of 1912. The quartet set out to harvest pennies, nickels, and dimes on what could be their biggest night of the year. Louis brought along a gun. His story of being arrested for firing it is probably the most often-told tale of his New Orleanian youth. His recollection of the event always included elements of celebration and innocence, though occasionally he let slip a telling detail, for example, that this was not the first time he had found the gun, which his mother kept trying to hide from him. Why would an eleven-year-old be carrying a gun? In Armstrong's version of the event, he was using it as an upgraded firecracker, his personal contribution to the festive holiday atmosphere. More likely would be the scenario of a juvenile delinquent who was hustling money late at night in a dangerous neighborhood and doing what he thought necessary to protect himself and his cash. Many people carried guns in Storyville, and crime was common. Like inner-city youths today, Armstrong and his friends had learned the importance of self-protection. Early death from criminal violence was not unusual, and in fact Armstrong helped bury two of his friends during his middle teenage years.

A newspaper reported the arrest, labeling him an "old offender." Perhaps he had been caught selling papers on the Canal Street trolley. Or perhaps he had gotten into too many fights; certainly he was not reluctant to fight, and lower-class children in his neighborhood had no choice but to protect themselves, since threats were many and external protection nonexistent. He was locked up overnight, and the next day a judge from juvenile court sentenced him to live for an indefinite term at the Colored Waif's Home for Boys, several miles from his Third Ward home, out in the country toward Lake Pontchartrain. Landing in the Waif's Home—a kind of "jail," Armstrong called it—caused several big changes in his life. Gone was the unsupervised roaming, the thrill of public music mixed with danger. In place was military-like discipline and schooling in various subjects, including music. The transition caused his musical activity to turn abruptly away from singing and toward the shiny instruments of the brass band.

CHAPTER FIVE

Jail

The article reporting Armstrong's arrest is the first appearance of his name in a New Orleans newspaper; it would be a long time before he showed up in one again. He was sentenced to live in the Colored Waif's Home for Boys. It is not known how his father, Willie, felt about the matter. Since Louis rarely saw him, his father may not have even heard about this placement for a while. Neither do we know how his mother felt. It has been suggested that this was a difficult period for her, and that the judge sent him to the Home because parental supervision was lacking. Even if that is true, she must have been distraught, for it is clear from everything Armstrong wrote about her that the two were very close and that she nurtured him in many ways.

It *is* known, however, how Louis felt about being placed in the Colored Waif's Home for Boys: he was absolutely terrified. In the beginning he refused to talk much or even eat. The caretakers, especially Peter Davis, who taught music, were automatically suspicious of any boy from the Third Ward. They probably did not know about the first five years of his life in the "Back of Town" section of the Third Ward, known also as the "Battlefield." The nickname, Armstrong explained, came from the fact that "those bad characters would shoot and fight so much." Eddie Dawson said that the police were reluctant to go there because it was too dangerous. The Battlefield was also known as a place where Mardi Gras "Indian" processions came to an end for the purpose of taking gang rivalries to the level of violent confrontation. The area was torn down decades ago and football is played there now, inside the Superdome.

But Peter Davis wasn't thinking of the Battlefield when he judged Armstrong from a rough neighborhood. He was thinking of the colored prostitution district around Liberty and Perdido streets. Davis may have read about the cheap Storyville in newspapers, which sensationally condemned the "gambling hells of Franklin Street," where "male and female, black and yellow, and even white, meet on terms of equality and abandon themselves to the extreme limit of obscenity and lasciviousness." He probably already had experience with children from this neighborhood, for, as Armstrong admitted, "nothing but the toughest of kids came from Liberty and Perdido Streets." And as the newspaper report on his arrest implies, Armstrong had a reputation that Davis was surely briefed on. During his "breaking in" period, Davis gave him hand lashings for no good reason other than to instill a fear of authority. Armstrong felt like he had been sent to jail.

From Tambourine to Cornet

But eventually Louis would come to like the Home, and his departure left him full of regret. He came to like the pastoral set-ting ("contented cows . . . Yea," he wrote), his friends, the regular meals, Davis, and especially the brass band. He remembered the smell of honeysuckle blossoms drifting in through the window of his dormitory, mixing synesthetically with the sounds of Freddie Keppard's orchestra from downtown Storyville. The blended image of perfume and music, both carried seductively through the air, gives one a sense of what it means to miss New Orleans. The music called him back to Liberty and Perdido, to a place where he had followed brass bands and roamed with his vocal quartet, but the scent of the flowers enticed him to remain where he was. For the Home also offered the sensual pleasure of music, in the form of the brass band that would make his stay there an important moment of transition in his life. The Colored Waif's Home for Boys became a famous part of Armstrong's biography, and with good reason. Without it, Armstrong would not have found himself positioned to take a place in the uptown musical world after his release in the summer of 1914.

One thing that made the transition to the Home difficult was the drastic contrast between his lifestyle there and what he had grown accustomed to. The Home separated him not only from the people he was close to but also from his cherished freedom of movement. Only occasionally were the boys allowed to go out on an errand or an outing. Those who tried to run away met severe punishment on their inevitable return. One runaway was stripped naked and held down by four other boys while everyone else watched the director deliver 105 searing lashes. The cries in horror and pity from the onlooking children only inspired the director to make the beating more severe. The point of this and all other forms of punishment was to inspire acceptance of the new style of life; however brutal, the formula seems to have worked for Little Louis. When he recalled the Home in writings and interviews, he often moved through mixed emotions, at one point describing it as a jail, at another "more like a kind of health center or a boarding school than a boys' jail."

Forced to stay put, the boys learned how to read and write. It is certainly possible that Armstrong would not have become fluently literate without this schooling. (His contemporary Sidney Bechet, for example, apparently never learned to read.) He probably did not return to school after he was released from the Home, at age thirteen. That would not have been an unusual educational trajectory for the time. Johnny St. Cyr, who played guitar with Armstrong on the Hot Five recordings during the 1920s, said that he himself "played school" in New Orleans until he was ten years old; after that he actually went to a school and stayed until age fourteen, having passed through grade 5. Armstrong wrote that he too completed grade 5, and this seems to have been a common ending point for African Americans uptown. "I went to High School at the orphanage," he told an interviewer. His education at the Home also included singing.

Like most institutions of reform, the Home patterned its routine on military practice. The boys stood at attention near their beds for inspection, performed their daily jobs in a prescribed amount of time, and followed the array of bugle calls that summoned them to dinner, chores, and bed. Superintendent Joseph Jones was fresh from duty in the tenth cavalry; he drilled the boys every morning with wooden guns. Armstrong eventually gained the privilege of blowing *Reveille*, *Taps*, and *Mess* on the bugle. And with this military orientation came—inevitably for New Orleans in 1913, but also common to similar institutions in other parts of the country—a brass band for the boys, which carried the name Maple Leaf Band. The band played "a little of every kind of music," Armstrong wrote.

Before this, Armstrong's experience with instruments was very limited. Henry "Kid" Rena, who sometimes sang in the vocal quartet with Louis and also endured a stay in the Waif's Home, said that Louis only played one instrument before he went to the Home—Rena called it a "gitbox" made from a cigar box with four copper wires attached. Armstrong once said that before he went into the Home he wanted to be a drummer, certainly a common goal for little boys. Perhaps he played around with the ragman's tinhorn. Other than that, he sang and he whistled.

Davis brought him into the Maple Leaf Band gradually. First, he gave him a tambourine and then a snare drum. Louis's rhythmic skill impressed Davis, who pointed to him for a solo break during the band's rendition of *At the Animal's Ball*. Percussion instruments were basic both in a pedagogical sense, being the first instruments for many children, and in a practical sense, providing the rhythmic base for the ensemble. Elsewhere in New Orleans, Professor James Humphrey taught his brass bands for children by first rehearsing what he called the "battery," the bass, trombone, and drums, the foundation of the band in Humphrey's opinion. Once this group was playing the way Humphrey wanted it to, he added cornets to the rehearsal followed by the rest of the band.

From snare drum Louis moved to alto horn. He remembered that quartet singing had given him a sense of how the alto horn might participate in the brass band, which must have been taught without musical notation. "My better judgment told me that an alto is an instrument that sings a duet in a brass band the same as the baritone or the tenor would do in a quartet. So I played the alto very well indeed." Next, Davis gave him a bugle, and after that there was only one place to go—to the lead brass-band instrument, the cornet. Davis showed him how to play *Home Sweet Home*. Soon he was playing lead melody for *When the Saints Go Marching In*, which the band performed every Sunday morning to accompany the delinquent boys in their procession to church (let it never be said that the Colored Waif's Home for Boys lacked a sense of humor). Louis practiced hard on his cornet, and Davis rewarded him with regular lessons. His ascent up the Home's musical ladder eventually earned him the honor of bandleader. Thus, Davis successfully applied the simple formula of bringing the child gradually through various instruments and levels of status, as a spur to motivation. His system got Louis to settle down and acquire a set of musical skills that he probably could not have learned anywhere else.

Armstrong's time in the Waif's Home brought about two fundamental changes for him; together, they are what make his stay there such a central moment during his years in New Orleans. His stay occurred roughly midway through these twenty-one years: he entered the Home at age eleven and a half and left it at age thirteen. One change had to do with his musical orientation. Before the

*Armstrong's bugle and cornet from the Colored Waif's Home for Boys
(Historic New Orleans Collection, Acc. No. 92-48-L MSS 520 f.149,
photo by Charles Edward Smith)*

Waif's Home, during the years of his early childhood, his musical education was firmly located within the vernacular African-American traditions that surrounded him. The Home exposed him, for the first time, to Eurocentric musical pedagogy. The rudimentary training he received on the cornet opened up professional possibilities he would explore for the rest of his life.

The brass band became his overarching passion; it was his way of coping with an alien environment and it was also a vehicle toward greater self-esteem. His interest had already been activated, of course, through constant exposure to parades, where he was driven to find a way to carry the musicians' horns. Now he was in a band himself, and within the Waif's Home the status of the band was high since it was regularly used for fund-raising, with the director hiring it out to private parties, parades, and picnics on Lake Pontchartrain.

White patronage of amateur black bands during this period was commonplace. The practice was an extension of traditional southern paternalism designed to keep Negroes in their subservient place, the soft complement to Jim Crow laws and threat of vigilante violence. Bebé Ridgley, cofounder of the Tuxedo Brass Band, got his start in music through a band sponsored by white owners of the grocery store where he worked as a teenager in Jefferson Parish. Downriver from New Orleans on the Magnolia Plantation, Governor Henry Clay Warmoth sponsored a band that he hoped would lift the spirits of his exploited sharecroppers. In Waggaman, Louisiana, one Senator Brady hired Professor Humphrey to teach a brass band for which he had purchased instruments; among the terms of Brady's patronage was the expectation that the band perform for him and his friends every Saturday night. Policemen in uptown New Orleans sometimes donated their old uniforms to neighborhood bands. The Waif's Home band was part of this charitable trend. The institution offered the band as proof of how well it could train delinquent Negro children. The children proudly marched through town in their uniforms. The ultimate display of the Home's success would come a couple of decades later when Louis Armstrong's name started to appear in marquee lights and the hero himself made a triumphant return.

The crucial ingredient for Armstrong's musical development was

The Colored Waif's Home band; the arrow points to Armstrong (Courtesy of the
Louis Armstrong House and Archives at Queens College/CUNY)

instruction on the cornet with Peter Davis. This would have included basic instruction on how to finger, how to adjust tension in his lips and cheeks, and how to breathe. I doubt that he saw any notated music. He learned the fundamentals of sound production on the instrument, and the most distinguishing lesson he learned was tone— that is, how to make a beautiful sound on the instrument.

Armstrong had already, before coming to the Home, become sensitive to differences in tone between professional cornetists. Bolden's sound was too rough for him; Bunk Johnson's was sweet; Oliver could not match Johnson in tone, though he bettered him in everything else. So when Davis gave him a cornet, he already understood how important it was to pay attention to tone. The "first thing Peter Davis taught me [was] tone . . . He said 'a musician with a tone can play any kind of music, whether it's classic or ragtime' (that was the name of good hot music in those days)." It may seem like a simple thing, to blow into a piece of brass and flutter your lips to set vibrations through the air. Anyone who has ever tried knows that it is not that simple. Oliver once said that it took him ten years to develop a good tone. Armstrong was taught properly—"properly," that is, in accordance with European technique—and from this he eventually learned how to produce a sound that would be the envy of trumpet players around the globe. Preston Jackson, who also spent time in the Waif's Home, remembered that Armstrong's "ability was evident even though he wasn't but twelve years old then."

His shining moment was a parade made by the Maple Leaf Band through the old Third Ward neighborhood. The "whores, pimps, gamblers, thieves, beggars, in fact everybody who was anybody" came out; "they'd never visualize me with a cornet in my hand," he remembered. Someone ran to wake up his mother. His band hat was triumphantly passed around, and it filled up with donations so quickly that several other boys had to pass their hats too; they raised enough money for new uniforms and instruments. One observer remembered Armstrong improvising little runs in breaks (brief pauses for solos), thus showing off his good ear at this early age. But for Armstrong to stand out musically in this setting, the main distinguishing feature must have been tone, the beginnings of a firm, confident sound.

Technique and Male Identity

Peter Davis's emphasis was not on finding your own way or playing funky but on matching an external standard that was demonstrably white. Davis wanted Louis to be able to play any kind of music, not just uptown "ragtime"—which, as Armstrong and others tell us, was the closest his social group came to naming the music that would later be named "jazz" (Chapter 7). The experience of African Americans in the United States has been frequently touched by forces, some blatant and some covert, some repressive and some seductive, promoting the assimilation of white culture. Slavery was marked by repression of drum ensembles at the same time that musically gifted slaves were given European instruments and rewards for performing in a way that pleased white audiences. Edmond Souchon, the wealthy white patron of jazz and an early admirer of Joe Oliver, remembered his father's stories about the family slave they called

"Snowball" (ridiculing his dark skin). Even though he was a slave, Snowball was paid in cash to accompany the family's schottisches and mazurkas, which he turned out with magnificent "ten-fingered piano." This typical feature of the slave plantation continued into the sharecropping period, through the patronage of people like Senator Brady. Assimilative pressure was packaged subtly or less so, depending on the circumstances. It could depend on white businessmen who purchased instruments and lessons or, more simply, on the lure of a brass cornet glowing brightly in the harsh and restrictive setting of the Colored Waif's Home for Boys.

It is possible to play a brass instrument without any instruction at all, to simply pick it up and find your way around. The self-taught approach may even carry advantages if the goal is to work outside of traditional practice. In fact, this was a common preference in uptown New Orleans, where there was a strong tradition of creatively distorting timbre. Originating in Africa, this approach surfaced throughout the Deep South. In New Orleans the practice stood very much alongside the cultivation of a more traditionally "legitimate" and European sound. To be a full professional meant mastering both, and in this sense what was in part a matter of assimilation was more substantially a matter of professional advancement. Davis understood this, and he communicated the lesson to Armstrong: to learn a European instrument meant acquiring the potential to enter the white market, where there was an expectation of proper Euro-centric technique.

The European ideal of sound production was almost constantly audible in New Orleans, most prominently as demonstrated by the Creoles. The Creole musicians of the old school did many things well, but they were particularly admired for tone. Creole cornetist Don Albert described a light tone as a "peashooter sound." And he paid Armstrong the highest compliment when he described his tone as "big around as a bowl." The Creoles put their standards of tone production within audible range of uptown Negroes, but they did not necessarily grant them access to learning how it was done. Lessons of this kind—as opposed to lessons in the Sanctified Church from the Saints, or lessons on a tin party horn on the streets from Larenzo—were not easy for someone in Armstrong's position

to come by. Joe Oliver, who grew up in a different uptown neighborhood, was lucky enough to find a teacher who not only gave him
lessons but also put together a brass band for boys that Oliver
marched with around age fifteen. The lessons and the band opened
up the profession for Oliver. The same opportunities did not exist
for Armstrong at home with May Ann.

One intervention caused by his placement in the Home, then,
was the introduction of Eurocentric technique to his musical
upbringing, which had, until now, been firmly centered within
African-American vernacular traditions. The other involved musically articulated relations with women and men. This change,
alluded to in Chapter 2, was as profound as any musical redirection.
When he was brought to the Home, the child was removed from his
mother's custody, but when he left it he was released in the custody
of his father. Even though he stayed with his father for only a short

*Willie Armstrong (Courtesy of the Louis Armstrong House and
Archives at Queens College/CUNY)*

time, this shift is significant, for while Armstrong was nurtured primarily by his grandmother, his mother, the sisters in church, and the other women in the neighborhood during the first eleven years of his life, he was supervised mainly by men, especially Peter Davis, at the Home. It is not that he didn't know any men during his early childhood—there had been Uncle Ike, his mother's boyfriends, and even people like Larenzo before this. At the Home, however, male role models became much more dominant. Soon after he left the Home and the custody of his father, it did not take Louis long to find his most important musical mentor, Joseph Oliver, who turned out to be just the connection he needed to enter the fraternal world of professional musicians. The social transition represented by the Home is thus one of moving from a predominantly matriarchal world into a patriarchal and fraternal one.

Certainly the institution was designed with this kind of transition in mind. It was conceived as a place to give young adolescent boys fatherly attention that many of them lacked, thereby helping them grow into men. Some mothers who felt a boy slipping out of their control were known to ask for placement in this kind of setting. Armstrong's success was tied to his relationship with Peter Davis, who, he said, taught not only music but also "life in general." Eventually he was treated to personal visits at Davis's house, where he became "chummy" with Davis's daughter, Ida. The two went to shows together in town. He played cornet in the Davis family parlor, with Ida accompanying him on piano (anticipating by ten years his important relationship with Lil Hardin in Chicago). Davis gave him extra lessons during these visits, and Armstrong even slept at the Davis home at times, the two returning to the institution together the following morning.

When Louis heard that his father had arranged through his white boss to have him released, his first thought was to refuse the offer and stay where he was. So it is clear how important Davis was to him, and how wrapped up in music was this male identity that he was internalizing. This pattern would continue and grow stronger. After the Home, there would be no more church, no more rocking and shouting with the Saints, though the formative experiences that these women had given him were so strong that they continued to shape his sense of music and life. Now a masculine model of music making began to take over, in different settings and laced with different values. It had started earlier in the vocal quartet, but now his cornet helped him find a place inside a much larger network of mentoring and fraternal support.

He left the Home in June 1914 a fledgling cornetist, and though he continued to sing with his quartet, the professional world of music to which he aspired did not have a large place for singing. In his immediate professional future, singing would be bracketed as an eccentric novelty on stage, not only for the rest of his time in New Orleans but also in Chicago and New York during the 1920s. For his remaining years in New Orleans, his attention was directed toward the cornet, and with persistence and a touch of luck he found just the right mentor to follow Peter Davis. "When I got out, I went right into Joe Oliver," he said. For many reasons, Oliver was the perfect person to both bring along the teenager's developing chops and lead him through the psychological intricacies of the fraternal world of New Orleans musicians.

CHAPTER SIX

~~~

Lessons with Oliver

Everything I did, I tried to do it like Oliver.
—Louis Armstrong

Louis's father had a good reason to get his son out of the Waif's Home and into his custody: he had a new woman and a young family, and at age thirteen Louis could be counted on to bring in more than it cost to keep him. For whatever reason, the arrangement didn't work. Louis was soon back with his mother and his sister, back at the center of things, at Liberty and Perdido. It is possible that he attended school in the fall of 1914, but just as likely that he did not. (The chronology of events for his teenage years could easily be shifted a year or so later; often the evidence is vaguely located.) Around this time his "stepfather" Gabe got him a job delivering coal for the CA Andrews coal yard. He and his old friends restarted their vocal quartet. And, most excitingly, he was now able to expand his hustling possibilities by using the basic cornet skills he had acquired at the Waif's Home. Peter Davis had given him a horn, and he had been practicing.

His friend "Cocaine Buddy" Martin alerted him to a possibility at Henry Ponce's honky tonk, a couple of blocks from his house. A little older than Louis, Cocaine Buddy had begun to wear long pants and was now running errands for Joe Segretta's honky tonk, across the street from Ponce's. "What is the name of that thing you blow?"

Cocaine Buddy asked, and he told Louis about the job. Armstrong remembered how Cocaine Buddy framed the matter:

> "Henry Ponce is one of the biggest pimps in the red light district. Got a lot of whores working for him. And he ain't scared of nobody either. He wants a good cornet player . . . If you want me to, I will speak a good word for you, and maybe you can get the job. All you have to do is put on long pants at night, play the blues for the whores that hustle all night until 'fo' day' in the morning. They come in with a big stack of money in their stockings for their pimps. And when you play the blues for them, they will call you sweet names and buy you drinks, and give you tips."

It couldn't have been a difficult decision. He stepped into a little band of piano, drums, and cornet; Pops Foster called it a "kid band."

New Orleans, ca. 1900 (New Orleans Public Library,
photo by George François Mugnier)

Ponce agreed to find a better cornet for him in a pawnshop, the first of many such arrangements between Armstrong and an employer.

The job selling (illegally) newspapers on Canal Street may also have continued, but now his musical hustles were in the ascent. Armstrong's first recognition as a performer had come with the vocal quartet, his second with the brass band from the Waif's Home. He now felt ready to step out as a soloist. Thirteen may seem like a young age to be playing late into the night in rough places, but it was not unusual. Cornetist Don Albert started to play for money at age fourteen, though he had to be home by nine o'clock every night. For an employer the obvious advantage of hiring a child was that he worked cheaply or even for nothing. It was common for adult bands to use boys who had no experience at all when a contract specified a certain number of musicians. There are stories about fitting a boy with a uniform and giving him a baritone horn and a potato, which was placed in the bell of the horn to stop the flow of air; the instructions were to only pretend to play the horn, thus filling the position jokingly known as "potato horn." Boys hired as real substitutes tended to be reliable and enthusiastic. This was exploitation but it was also part of an informal system of apprenticeship, a way of providing a place for teenagers in entry-level positions. Armstrong remembered playing until daybreak, at which point he would have a beer.

Honky tonks—or "tonks" as the musicians usually say—were simple places that thrived on illegal gambling. Most tonks had a pool table with blocked pockets so that the surface could be used for shooting craps. When the police made their rounds, the table was instantly converted back to shooting pool. In addition to gambling, a tonk usually had some combination of prostitution, alcohol, food, and at least one musician, often an ear-playing pianist. Many, many ear pianists drifted in and out of the tonks, playing nothing but blues. Their names likewise float in and out of the oral histories—Jasper, Black Pete, Birmingham, Game Kid, Stack O Lee, Leon Alexis, Tink Baptiste, and so on. Cornets were not typical, though around Liberty and Perdido the tonks were a little more elaborate and sometimes brought in small bands. Armstrong remembered one gambler calling his cornet a "quail"—"Listen to that cat blowing that quail."

The corner of Liberty and Perdido streets, 1949 (Historic New Orleans Collection, Acc. No. 92–48–L MSS 520 f. 600, photo by William Russell)

Blues were so consistently associated with these venues that the idiom was known as "honky tonk music." This made the neighborhood tonk ideal for young Louis. Here he could play blues for hours and hours, essentially practicing his cornet in front of an audience. It was the perfect place to apply the gestures he had learned from Larenzo on the streets. In a way Armstrong was now acquiring a bit of musical range. Singing in church had taught him heterophony, singing in the quartet brought along his sense of chords, and the Waif's Home band grounded him in cornet technique. Now, in the tonk, he could work on the melodic idiom of blues.

He must have done well, for he came to the attention of older musicians. Foster remembered how his own band was looking for a substitute cornet player to help with the required advertising before the dance at night; Foster thought of hiring Little Louis. Armstrong eagerly rode along on the advertising wagon, which stopped every few blocks or so to play. But the band faced a dilemma, Foster said: "The only thing Louis could play then was blues, so we played them all day long. Louis played them good too." He played well enough that the band brought him along to the evening gig, even though that meant filling a night of dance music with little more than blues. They could get away with this because blues had become so extremely popular among uptown African Americans. According to Foster, "In

New Orleans if you didn't play any blues you didn't get any colored jobs . . . [whites] didn't care what you played."

Armstrong borrowed long pants and made a place for himself in the tonk. On the first night he proudly brought fifteen cents home to May Ann, only to have his little sister ridicule the small sum. He probably worked there for close to a year. As Cocaine Buddy had predicted, Ponce's prostitutes—"real beautiful women of all colors," Armstrong remembered—enjoyed hearing him. In an account that probably refers to a job a year or two later than this, he described prostitutes teasing him and urging him on while he played the blues. They called him over as soon as he put down his horn: "'Come here, you cute little son of a bitch, and sit on my knee' . . . They would almost fight as to whose lap that I was to sit in." That kind of attention goes a long way with a teenage boy.

Meanwhile, he continued to follow the professional musicians he admired, deepening his knowledge of their music through close observation. On nights when he wasn't playing, he and Isaac Smooth, a friend from the Waif's Home, checked out the scene: "We two silly kids would just go from one honky tonk to the other, and dig that jive . . . Also we would get a load of those whores, coming in signifying to one another about going with the same pimp . . . We wanted to learn all we could about life. Mostly music. We could always look forward to seeing and hearing some new piano player, with something new on the ball. Some guy who probably came from some levee camp, etc., sit on the piano stool and beat out some of the damndest blues you've ever heard in your life."

He was actually a little relieved when the job at Ponce's came to an end because he wasn't getting much sleep. A job delivering coal with the Karnofsky family took him into the Storyville district, otherwise off limits to an African-American child, which was bursting with musical excitement during the early 1910s. On one corner of Iberville and Marais streets Oliver's band was playing regularly at Pete Lala's, and on the opposite corner Manuel Perez was at Rice's Cafe. Down the block was Groshell's Dance Hall, and on Franklin Street, between Iberville and Bienville streets, were the lively 101 Ranch and Tuxedo Dance Hall. Armstrong wandered around deliv-

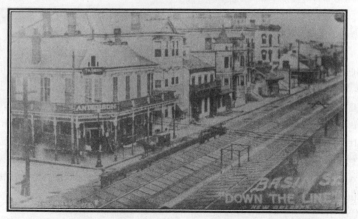

Basin Street in Storyville (New Orleans Public Library)

ering five-cent buckets of coal for prostitutes to use heating their small rooms. He usually started the fire for them. "I'd just stand there in that lady's crib listening to King Oliver . . . And I'm all in a daze," he wrote.

Four years older than Armstrong, Edmond Souchon was also sneaking into Storyville to listen to Oliver. Souchon grew up just a stone's throw away from Oliver's house, in a wealthy mansion on St. Charles Avenue. His nanny, Armotine, sometimes dressed him in his Little Lord Fauntleroy suit and walked him down to the grocery store on the corner of First and Dryades streets, where the two of them watched funeral processions sponsored by the Bull's Club. In this way Souchon got to know Oliver's music. As a young teenager, Souchon and his buddy disguised themselves as newsboys and hung out near the door of Pete Lala's, where Oliver played on Friday nights. Oliver wore a brown derby, tilted to the side to cover his bad eye, his collar open at the neck to expose a bright red undershirt (reminiscent of Bolden), and wide suspenders that, in the young Souchon's eyes, "held up an expanse of trousers of unbelievable width." Oliver was about six feet tall and heavy, an imposing figure.

Somehow, Armstrong came to Oliver's attention. Certainly he was keeping up his second-line activity behind the Onward Brass Band, begging Oliver to let him carry his horn. He was not shy

Pete Lala's (Historic New Orleans Collection,
Acc. No. 92–48-L MSS 520 f. 443, photo by William Russell)

about walking up to older musicians with his own cornet and asking for advice. Most of them brushed him away. Punch Miller said that "after a man retires he will show you almost anything, but as long as he's still playing, he doesn't want to show you his little tricks so you can catch up to him." For Armstrong, Oliver made an exception. Oliver started showing up at the honky tonk where Louis was playing after finishing his own job in Storyville—"fo' day" indeed— demonstrating little tricks for him right there in the tonk to the delight of the prostitutes and the gamblers.

Oliver remained the dominant musical influence on Armstrong until Oliver himself left New Orleans in 1918. "Everything I did, I tried to do it like Oliver," Louis said. He had found the perfect mentor and perfect model for imitation. No one was in a better position to show him what could be accomplished with an uptown background in church and blues, a little bit of legitimate training, and a good deal of ambition. The teenager began to make himself at home in the Oliver household, running out to get groceries for Oliver's wife, Stella, in exchange for cornet lessons. He ate meals with them and Stella began to think of him as her son. He started calling Oliver "Papa."

Oliver's Path

Oliver's biography is more obscure than Armstrong's, since he wrote little (a few letters survive, though there were certainly many more that may still turn up) and died early, in 1938, just before researchers were actively seeking out the early New Orleanian musicians. He was probably born in Abend, Louisiana, upriver from New Orleans, in 1885, which would make him approximately the same age as Louis's mother. His father is reported to have been a Baptist preacher who died when Joseph was young, and his mother died in 1900. After that he moved in with his sister Victoria in uptown New Orleans, working as a butler and gardener for wealthy white families. He learned to play cornet in a brass band for children organized by one Walter Kenchen, who was associated with the accomplished musician Dave Perkins. Perkins controlled the uptown market for renting instruments, a business that served as an extension of his teaching. Baby Dodds described him as a "straight man in music" who taught children of all colors, sometimes in classes that were quite large. Perhaps Oliver learned something from Perkins. Perkins had a strict reputation, and he would cut a lesson off if the student was not prepared.

When Oliver later decided to mentor Little Louis, he probably saw a good bit of himself in the boy. Both initially formed their musical sensibilities in church. Both showed an early skill in blues; Oliver was praised as a blues player even more highly than Armstrong was, and he must have been surrounded by the same kinds of blues inflections in speechlike music and musical speech, day in and day out, all through his childhood. His widow, Stella, said that he started out by learning to play songs he heard sung by railroad workers and dockworkers. Both Oliver and Armstrong had very dark skin. They both came from broken homes, with family origins outside of New Orleans, close to the plantations where the cultural and social legacies of slavery were strong. When Oliver decided to teach the only student he ever had, he must have recognized the multiple disadvantages Louis faced relative to the position of musically aspiring youngsters from Creole families downtown, and he must have decided to do whatever he could for the determined teenager with precocious talent.

Bunk Johnson claimed that Oliver was a slow learner when he first started out. Souchon remembered hearing Oliver playing "rough and rugged . . . [with] many bad chords," during the first decade of the century. "There were many fluffed notes, too." Johnson and his friend Walter Brundy got to know Oliver, and the two decided to work a little hustle on the young cornetist. Oliver later joked about how Brundy used to distract him while Johnson stole his sheet music, which was too difficult for Oliver to play anyway. In this way they introduced the teenager to the competitive realities of musical New Orleans. Later, as a bandleader, Oliver followed the standard practice of cutting off the titles from dance-band arrangements, thus preventing other bands from finding out the names of pieces and making it harder to add them to their own repertory.

Oliver enjoyed listening to the Eagle Band every Saturday night. This was the group that emerged out of Buddy Bolden's band after his demise, playing by ear in rough and ratty style. Pops Foster liked them too. "When I was with the Magnolia Band, sometimes they didn't play rough enough to suit me," Foster said. "So I'd lay off once in a while on Saturday night and go play with Frankie Dusen's Eagle Band. They were rough babies who drank a lot and really romped . . . They played hot all the time." After Bolden left in 1906 or so, the band went through a series of cornetists. Trying to ingratiate himself with the band, Oliver saved money from his butler job and started treating the musicians to drinks. He was still a novice, and the band had some fun at his expense: "Here comes so and so," they would say as he approached. Sometime in the year 1907 they invited him to sit in and play, though on his first job he played so poorly they had to send him home. Part of the problem was repertory; Eddie Dawson said that when he first met him, Oliver knew only brass-band music and had to turn down dance-band jobs.

Oliver eventually made his mark by building on the music of his youth, the heterophony he was probably brought up with in church. Heterophony (as explained in Chapter 2) is the texture produced when people simultaneously sing multiple versions of a single melody.

It is essentially a practice of making variations on the melody and singing them all at once. Oliver is said to have worked up some "variations" on the hymn *Sing On*; audiences liked it so much that the band brought him in to play regularly. Oliver could also match the Eagle Band with loud, rough playing. He kept his butler job, but during the next few years more and more musical opportunities opened up. Before long he was playing with the Magnolia Band, in direct competition with the up-and-coming Freddie Keppard, a Creole from downtown who had been the first brass player allowed to perform in Storyville.

Bunk Johnson summarized Oliver's career trajectory in a way that is full of social and cultural implication: "Now here is where Joe got well: when he crossed Canal Street and became a member of the Onward Brass Band with Manuel Perez, then he got real good and has been going ever since." Johnson's image of crossing Canal Street is surely to be taken in two ways. First, it should be taken literally: Oliver, from uptown, did indeed find his way into good-paying jobs in Storyville, on the downtown side of Canal Street. More suggestive is the metaphor of social movement, for to cross Canal Street meant to find one's way into Creole musical circles. For a relatively untutored uptown musician to move from Frankie Dusen's Eagle Band to Manuel Perez's Onward Brass Band was to cross over a complicated set of obstacles neatly symbolized by the historic boundary between the "American" and "French" sections of town. Souchon supplements Johnson when he says that Oliver had acquired, in the years between 1907 and the mid-1910s, a "technique that was much smoother . . . the band was adapting to white audiences."

Yet, even while Oliver was learning the Creole ways, he continued to advance in the uptown vernacular. This certainly included mastery of collective improvisation. If the amateur uptown brass bands were the likely sites where the heterophony of church came into wind ensembles, then Oliver was in a good position to become an expert. It is impossible to trace the history of collective improvisation with much precision, but a likely scenario would be this: one melody instrument—most likely the lead cornet in a marching band—memorized the tune, just as singers in church memorized hymns, and the other melody instruments contributed heterophonic embellishment of that tune. Out of this heterophonic ground grew the texture of collective improvisation, with its truly independent melodies. Percussion and bass (and sometimes trombone) performed the rhythmic foundation that is maintained by clapping in church. Like blues, collective improvisation was best learned by ear, for it involves nuances of phrasing like cross accents and the careful timing of surges and diminuendos. While pubescent Creoles were being trained to precisely render a written arrangement, non-reading uptown Negroes were hearing and practicing ways of adapting church heterophony to the emergent texture of collective improvisation.

Collective improvisation probably developed through *doublings* of the lead melody. During Armstrong's youth, dance bands regularly used two lead instruments—violin plus cornet, cornet plus clarinet, or cornet plus second cornet. Trombonist Eddie Summers described the violin as playing the lead straight while the cornet played a "modified lead" in order to "make all kinds of junk in there." A clarinet player could make the same kind of "junk," and so could a second cornetist, especially in brass bands, and especially, one must assume, in the amateur brass bands uptown.

Of vital importance for understanding both Oliver and Armstrong is some information about Oliver's role as second cornetist to Manuel Perez in the Onward Brass Band. Clarinetist Manny Gabriel remembered Perez playing "clean" and powerfully, stronger even than Oliver. But the band's success had more to do with division of labor than with simple loudness. Paul Barbarin said that Oliver was the "barrelhouse man" in this band. And Gabriel spoke about Oliver "making them monkeyshines while Perez was carrying that melody, you know." This can only mean that Oliver was improvising lively counterpoint against the lead melody; the resulting texture was perhaps located somewhere along the spectrum between heterophony and collective improvisation. Drummer Abby "Chinee" Foster used "monkeyshines" in the way I am interpreting it from Gabriel: "Your feet is time; your hands are what you make your foolishness with. See, in other words, I can play a 3/4 waltz time or a two-beat 2/4 time on the bass drum with my foot, yet I'm playing in groups of four with my hands. The hands, that's what you make your monkeyshines with, but I'd keep time with the bass drum."

During the early 1910s, when Armstrong's awareness of stylistic possibilities was growing, musicians were probably experimenting with ways of turning church heterophony into a texture in which the melody instruments are in productive tension with each other and with the rhythmic foundation. The innovation certainly originated uptown, where the venerable church practices were ubiquitous. Creole Perez and "them fellows played straight stuff . . . from what I can see, Oliver and them kind of fellows, they started to putting . . . more to the music," said Punch Miller. The story about Oliver making monkeyshines around Perez's lead is one of several indicators that he was the right person to teach Armstrong about the new advances in texture, which may have been his most important lesson.

Later, as a leader of his own band, Oliver was known to have strong opinions about texture. Albert Nicholas said that he "didn't want to hear any one person, wanted to hear the whole band. He wanted everyone to blend together . . . He had discipline in his band." Oliver abruptly introduced the classically trained pianist Lil Hardin (the future Mrs. Armstrong) to his textural vision just after she joined his band in Chicago. He interrupted her first tentative attempts at improvised figuration with a sneer: "We already got a clarinet in the band." Hardin was surprised by how organized the band sounded, even though there were no written arrangements. The texture Oliver desired was complicated and rich, but also clear thanks to his efforts in keeping the players out of each other's way. In the famous recordings of King Oliver's Creole Jazz Band in 1923, Armstrong brilliantly contributes to the total effect of the ensemble from his position at second-cornet. Perhaps these recordings document his thorough attention to the second-cornet work of his mentor, the monkeyshines and barrelhouse Oliver brought to Perez's lead, eight years earlier. "I was so wrapped up in him and lived his music that I could take second to his lead in a split second," Armstrong wrote.

Oliver also established himself as a great blues cornetist, perhaps the best since Bolden. He was especially admired for a subspecialty of blues known in New Orleans as "freak music." Freak music depended on the manipulation of the instrument's tone; in the classical tradition one would say manipulation of *timbre*. People flocked to hear Oliver using an array of objects to bend his cornet in imitation of the human voice. He was not the only player on the scene doing this, but in the mid-1910s he was one of the best. Beer buckets, toilet plungers, glasses, derby hats, coconuts, and kazoos combined with half valving, flutter tonguing, fake fingering, vibrato, growls, and subtle changes of tension in the lips to produce a creative array of vocalized effects. Punch Miller said Oliver was so strong, he "could do most anything."

The practice of timbral manipulation came ultimately from Africa, where it is most familiar to Westerners through the so-called talking drum. Because slave owners believed that messages could be sent in secret, African drumming was generally prohibited in the United States, though there were precise preservations of the practice in South America and the Caribbean. In New Orleans, Willie Hightower and Freddie Keppard worked up a routine of calling out names of people in the dance hall by manipulating beer buckets over the bells of their cornets. Oliver sometimes got angry with his musicians and refused to speak; he dished out comments on their playing through his "talking" cornet. Bottleneck guitar technique from Mississippi is another well-known example of the practice. The tip of a bottle is broken off and sanded down, slipped over a finger (a knife can be used too), and dragged across the strings to make them whine and moan. This was the technique described by W. C. Handy (Chapter 3) as the "weirdest music I had ever heard."

Uptown wind music from New Orleans is associated with the freakish and bizarre in an editorial on the "Dime Museum" from the *New Orleans Mascot* in 1890. A cartoon depicted an African-American wind band that had just been hired by the museum on Canal Street, near the corner of St. Charles (precisely where Armstrong would be picking up his newspapers twenty years later). For ten cents' admission, one could glimpse flying foxes, a dog circus, the Great Colony of Trained Rats, Lippert the Only Three-Legged Man, Tame South American Savages, the Elephant Boy,

Big Hannah the Mountain of Flesh, the Harris Quadruplets, and Professor Stendall and his electro-musical Thaumascope, which pulsated electric light through colored glass in synchrony with music. There were also pretend Zulus on display. "All the fashionable freaks of nature are visiting or will visit this place." The editorial objected not to the museum but to the band playing on its balcony. From the museum's point of view, the band provided just the right representation of the visual freakishness displayed inside. "The band has completely dazed the population," lamented the newspaper. African-American music—and thus the people making it—is framed as bizarre, comic, and primitive, put in the same freakish category as the pretend Zulu and the three-legged man. It was a common strategy, standardized long before, of course, in blackface minstrelsy and any number of institutions throughout the United States.

Less is known about the other side of the phenomenon—how freak music was heard by the people who made it and did not consider it bizarre. The virtuoso slide guitarist Robert Johnson, from Mississippi, once played *Come On in My Kitchen* for an audience in St. Louis. "His guitar seemed to talk—repeat and say words with him like no one else in the world could," said his traveling companion Johnny Shines. In the middle of the St. Louis performance Shines noticed that the room was totally quiet. He looked up to see everyone crying, men as well as women. The fact that vocalized effects on wind instruments became so widespread in African-American New Orleans suggests that the technique also struck deep emotions there. Uptown cornetist Mutt Carey alluded to this emotional intensity with a reference to church: "Joe could make his horn sound like a holy roller meeting; God, what that man could do with his horn." It is remarkable how easily the same musical practice shifted between the profound and the trivial, the passionate and the comic.

Oliver worked up a version of *Eccentric Rag* that became his specialty number, a vehicle for freak display. Large solo breaks gave space for his cornet to imitate a babbling baby. Later, in Chicago, his band built a skit into the piece. The routine was for Oliver to first imitate a white baby, to which bass player Bill Johnson responded, directly comforting the horn itself, "Don't cry, little baby." Then Oliver's cornet was said to imitate a colored baby, to which Johnson shouted, "Shut up you li'l so and soooo"; to this the house erupted in thunderous laughter and applause. Preston Jackson remembered white players from the New Orleans Rhythm Kings hanging around the bandstand at the Royal Gardens in Chicago, soaking up Oliver's technique and reproducing it in their recordings. The same effects carried the Original Dixieland Jazz Band a long way. Oliver's talking-cornet rendition of *I'm Not Rough* was so popular that it brought him the title "King" one night in 1919 at the Royal Gardens in Chicago. A paper crown was placed on his head and men threw their hats into the air. Today this kind of music is best known through the compositions of Duke Ellington, who kept at least one freak specialist in his band for its entire long-lived history. Ellington started down this road with Bubber Miley, who had learned by watching Oliver in the mid-1920s.

What Oliver Had to Offer

Through his talents in freak music and collective improvisation, Oliver had risen fairly high in the musical world of New Orleans by 1915. He was one of a handful of elite musicians who didn't have to keep a day job, in contrast to someone like Dave Perkins, who patched together a living by renting instruments, giving lessons, and taking whatever gigs came his way. Oliver could have ignored a teenage novice, as Bunk Johnson apparently did, but instead he decided to take Louis under his wing. His model for this largess may have been Manuel Perez, with whom he had been playing in the Onward Brass Band.

Perez was a successful product of the downtown Creole musical culture that was built on solid Eurocentric pedagogy, and he was also one of that culture's proudest advocates. Creoles admired him not just for his cornet playing but also for his generosity. He seems to have regarded musical mentoring of teenagers as a civic duty. Many Creoles gave lessons for a price; Lorenzo Tio Jr. charged fifty cents, for example. But Perez taught anyone he thought was deserving for free. "I'm going to make a cornet player out of you," he would say, and the offer could not be taken lightly; a boy who turned it down risked certain anger from his parents. Sidney Desvigne began taking two lessons per week with Perez in 1907, at age fourteen, and he continued for seven years. Another student, Natty Dominique, remembered how he ate many meals in the Perez home, even though, he emphasized, he was not a relative. "I loved him as a daddy," said Dominique, years after Perez had died. Getting to know Perez, Oliver must have realized how extensive and thorough was the clannish Creole support for music. He knew that he could not duplicate what the Creoles had to offer their young musicians—he simply did not have all the skills they taught. But he recognized what Armstrong was up against and the direction he needed to go if he was to become competitive.

The first step in the Creole pedagogy was to sing solfège; only after that could the student begin study of an instrument. Exercise books helped with breath control, fingering, precise intonation, crisp attack, and production of an attractive tone over the entire range of the instrument. The goal was to consistently produce a uniform sound. Arnold Metoyer had a carrot that he dangled in front of his students: he proposed that after week fourteen, there would be no charge for a lesson when it was played perfectly. Lessons could last as long as two hours, and the whole rigorous system severely tested the limits of adolescent impulsivity. Some of the Creole teachers, Perez, for example, were known to be patient. But even Perez could send a student home if he made just a brief flub, telling him to come back next week, better prepared. Baby Dodds had a hard time studying drums with Louis Cottrell, whom he described as a "nervous type of Creole fellow." "If you'd make one beat that he didn't tell you to make, he'd frown at you and snatch your sticks out of your hand," Dodds remembered. "I felt that was almost a whipping for me."

The best of the Creole musicians were ferociously precise readers of musical notation, which they drilled students on constantly. Vic Gaspard deliberately placed wrong notes in the solos he wrote out for his students to practice, thus exposing anyone who was relying on memory and ear rather than fluent reading. Students were taught to read ahead of the notes being played. They worked on breath control. They rehearsed brass-band parts before upcoming jobs. Gaspard taught his students to listen carefully to the other instruments, not to play too loudly, and to achieve proper balance. After the ability to sight-read was secure, the student was urged to increase his powers of memorization. On top of all this came advanced lessons in fancy tongue work, virtuoso speed, and agility.

This kind of training might have been available in some African-American neighborhoods on the uptown side of Canal Street, but it was certainly much harder to come by than it was downtown. More to the point, Oliver himself had little of this knowledge. So much Creole attention was placed on making a beautiful, round tone; Oliver's tone, in contrast, was inferior to that of other cornetists. It is unlikely that Oliver spent hours and hours on breath control, long tones, and other techniques for refining tone, unlikely that he was even introduced to these techniques. Instead, Oliver explored the creativity of freak music, thereby embracing every idiosyncrasy that the conservatory approach rejected.

Oliver may have worked on notation with Armstrong, but on a level far simpler than what the Creole teachers were aiming for. Oliver himself was never a fluent reader. He was probably never able to sight-read. New Orleanians from this period distinguished between "reading" musical notation (what is now usually called "sight-reading") and, more basically, being able to "spell." Spelling was the first, basic step of laboriously identifying one pitch at a time, as if sounding out letters as the first step toward reading a word. Oliver seems to have been a speller, not a reader. "I'm the slowest goddamned reader in the band," he said later, in Chicago. "You all better not laugh at my slow reading. If you do, I'll fire your goddamn asses." He had a visual handicap, which may have been part of the problem. But it was not at all unusual for uptown musicians (and, eventually, more than a few downtown musicians who found a place for themselves in early jazz) to be poor readers. Kid Ory and Johnny Dodds, for example, both had trouble finding work in Chicago because of their poor reading skills; neither one, most likely, could even spell very well.

Pops Foster summed up the uptown attitude: "A whole lot of guys back there couldn't read and didn't want to learn. They'd call the guys who could read 'cute guys.'" Rhythmic notation was even more challenging than pitch. The musicians struggled over "dividing," which meant counting out the precise durations for dotted, tied, long, and syncopated notes, then fitting them into the meter. Eddie Dawson said that Armstrong "didn't know division" when he knew him. It was so much easier just to hear the music and memorize it. From several sources it is clear that Armstrong learned to read music well only when he began spending a lot of time on the river-boats, in 1919. So it is doubtful that he did much reading with Oliver, and that would have made it difficult to use the exercise books that were so common downtown. There was certainly no training in solfège. Armstrong said that Oliver answered all of his questions, which may have included any number of basic details about the cornet. It probably did not include the intricacies of music theory, though there may have been some discussion of chords.

But what Oliver could not teach Armstrong turned out to be far less important than what he *could* teach him. This happened in the best combination: through direct instruction supported by the example of a successful performer. The knowledge Oliver had about the vernacular traditions that were passed on orally and aurally, by casual but timely remarks slipped in here and there, and by demonstration, was crucial for Armstrong's teenage development. Again, it is a struggle to see the traces of pedagogy in oral traditions. It would later seem to some jazz musicians that Armstrong had learned it all by himself: "Like Louis and all those guys . . . they're practically self-taught," said Dickey Wells. As with Larenzo the ragman's spell-binding talk, so it is with the mentoring relationship between Oliver and Armstrong: we need to make the most out of a few clues.

Armstrong wrote that Oliver taught him "the modern way of phrasing on the cornet and trumpet." In the following exchange with interviewer Richard Allen, Charlie DeVore, a white trumpeter who studied much later with Manuel Manetta and articulated technical detail well, helps us imagine what Armstrong might have meant by that:

ALLEN: But when you say "off the beat" do you mean 2 and 4 or do you mean like Bunk and holding back a little, or what?

DEVORE: Yeah, that's what I mean, holding back, phrasing, a whole phrase is off the beat. In other words, you could start ahead and you'd end up behind. Play behind, play ahead. Like Louis, on this tune *Once in a While*, he holds back. I mentioned that Louis thing because that little introduction always knocked me out. Louis perhaps, did it more than anybody, but Joe Oliver in some respects was even more subtle than Armstrong, more shading and stuff. So much of that was involved in how he phrased. Phrasing, attack, and tonality: that's the three things I keep in my mind whenever I play. No matter what, if I take some strange tunes, maybe some pop tune that might be popular right now that somebody'd request and we'd try and play it. You have to do that . . . to make it hot so it won't sound like some other square playing you gotta keep those three things in mind. Now when I say tonality . . . it's the vibrato, that is what gives a man a hot sound, as opposed to a legitimate man's straight tone . . . I tell [inexperienced players]: get it so it practically shakes your horn to pieces. Overemphasize it at first . . . that's what gives you a hot sound.

Recognizable here is the "way of hesitating" referred to in Chapter 3, a style of jazz phrasing that has been familiar for a long time but may well have been perceived as modern when Armstrong sat down at Oliver's kitchen table around 1915. Cornet players in New Orleans could not have been playing like this for very long, and cornet players in other parts of the country simply did not do it. DeVore also sheds light on Armstrong's comment that "no trumpet player had the fire that Oliver had. Man, he really could *punch* a number . . . Fire—that's the life of music, that's the way it should be." Oliver's musical combustion may have come from the three things DeVore recommended—phrasing, attack, and vibrato. When Armstrong arrived in Chicago in 1922, he was admired for his drive—"they called it 'attack' at that time," said clarinetist Buster Bailey. Yes, that's what it was, man. They got crazy for his feeling."

These uptown fundamentals were analogous to the conservatory-based pedagogy downtown. The best way for Armstrong to learn them would have been by imitating Oliver with the supplement of direct instruction. He learned solos Oliver played for *I'm Not Rough*, *High Society*, and *Panama*. Memorization of an admired solo is still a standard pedagogical technique in jazz, and here is an early, firmly documented example. It may seem hard to believe that Oliver's non-notated solos could be picked up by a young teenager as he heard them in a parade or on an advertising wagon. But the tendency at this time was to work up a solo and then repeat it. Repetitions from parade to parade and even over the course of a single day made it easy for a child with good ears to memorize applause-generating inventions as he walked alongside the band. To combine this with direct instruction from the person whose solos are being memorized is an excellent recipe for progress.

In later chapters I will reflect on higher-level teachings that Armstrong may have absorbed from Oliver, especially the texture of collective improvisation, standards of melodic design, and the topic of improvisation, generally. The imperative to study their relationship closely follows Armstrong's emphatic claims about his debt to Oliver, which he stated again and again and in various ways—"His style hypnotized me," for example.

Biographer James Lincoln Collier has argued that Armstrong overstated his musical debt to Oliver, and for a good reason: Oliver was the paternal figure he desperately needed during his teenage years. Other musicians commented on the relationship as one very much like father and son. With Armstrong addressing him as "Papa," Oliver occasionally teased that, indeed, he had actually fathered him. Armstrong returned the teasing when Oliver and May Ann finally met, whispering to Oliver as May Ann came up on the bandstand, " 'Well, Papa Joe, Mother's here. Shall I tell her what you've been saying?' Oh Gosh you should have seen Papa Joe blush all over the place." Oliver nurtured his student in many ways and on many occasions, helping him find jobs, giving him his old cornet, and advising him on what to do when he got into trouble. When Louis needed money to pay medical bills for his girlfriend, Oliver sent him as his replacement at Lala's cabaret and then paid him for the gig when the proprietor refused to. "I can [never] stop loving Joe Oliver," Armstrong wrote. "It seemed as though he would come to my rescue, every time I actually needed someone to come into me and sort of show me the way about life and its little intricate things."

Of the men Armstrong knew during his early teenage years, after his release from the Waif's Home, only his "stepfather" Gabe showed the same degree of kindness.

The musical differences between the mature Armstrong and Oliver are obvious: Oliver specialized in freak music, which Armstrong hardly ever played. In phonograph recordings from the 1920s, Oliver rarely goes above the middle range of his cornet, while Armstrong became a spectacular high-note player. And in improvisation, Armstrong was explosively creative, leaving Oliver's relative restraint far behind (more about this in the next chapter). That Oliver stayed in the middle range may be a distortion caused by our necessary reliance on recordings from the 1920s, for Armstrong said that in New Orleans, Oliver had been a high-note player. Johnny Wiggs insisted that "nobody will ever know what Joe Oliver really sounded like from listening to his records." In Chicago and maybe before, Oliver suffered from pyorrhea and attendant loss of strength in his gums, hampering his ability to play high. This physical problem was surely one reason why he brought Armstrong to Chicago in the first place, to help out. When he arrived, Armstrong was surprised to see that Oliver's teeth were so loose he could move them back and forth. "Joe wasn't in his prime, like he was before he sent for me," Armstrong wrote. By 1927 Oliver had lost all of his teeth.

Oliver's reliance on freak music may have been a compensating move, for his inability to play high handicapped the range of his improvisational invention. It is interesting indeed that Armstrong did not master freak music, but he was still trying to do so even after he arrived in Chicago. Oliver's solo on *Dippermouth Blues*, with its attractive wah-wah effects, was so popular that Louis went home with his new wife Lil and frustratingly tried to imitate it. Armstrong was surrounded by freak music during the 1910s, so the most interesting part of the story may be why he turned away from it.

That he went in a different direction may say less about his musical debt to Oliver than about his own interests and ability. The direction he chose turned out to be a good one, for by the end of the 1920s freak music was in decline. The African-American elite in Chicago scorned it as "hokum." The strong place for it in Ellington's orchestra says a lot about Ellington as a composer who was good at building pieces around contrasting styles. What was freakish and down-home in other contexts became for Ellington an exotic orchestral color that he could compositionally frame. But for most of the music that is now called jazz, timbral distortion came to be reserved for nuance, an effect to mix briefly into a solo, much like blues inflections, and not a kind of music that could stand as the main attraction. In order to become the kind of solo idiom that it ultimately did become, jazz had to turn away from freak music. By the mid-1920s, Armstrong presented the most influential solo model: one of fiercely precise (in the sense of harmonic syntax), polyrhythmically conceived, melodic sophistication. He understood how this conception was indebted to Oliver, but since he specialized in it exclusively (and for other reasons too), he was able to go several steps beyond his mentor.

Taken as a whole, all of the various things Armstrong seems to have learned from Oliver make him very much the central musical figure in his life. His sense of indebtedness grew as the decades wore on and he started to document his life story. He never tired of praising his mentor, and it is easy to agree with Collier when he imagines that without Oliver's sponsorship, Armstrong might have never left New Orleans. He could easily have turned into one of those legends talked about late at night by musicians. As Armstrong himself put it, "If it hadn't have been for Joe, you wouldn't have heard of me."

CHAPTER SEVEN

~~~~~~

Ragtime and Buddy Bolden

*There has been ragtime music in America ever
since the Negro race has been here.*
—*Scott Joplin*

*Bolden put 'em out and everybody came to lis-
ten. That's how we got jazz.*
—*Lawrence Duhé*

During the years around 1900, the elements of the music we now call jazz
could be found in many parts of the Deep South. Yet it has often
been claimed that jazz originated in New Orleans. Why did it happen there? Though it may never be possible to answer that question
to everyone's satisfaction, we can learn much about Armstrong—
and about the origins of this music—by considering it. Some historians regard the question itself as misconceived. Other places in the
country had traditions of African-American dance music that were
similar to those cultivated more famously in New Orleans, they say,
and the idea that jazz originated in New Orleans is a myth.
Certainly it is true that many of the ingredients in jazz were known
elsewhere. Dimensions such as the integration of music with body
motion, the production of vocal effects on instruments and the
favoring of an initial, percussive attack, the organization of music
according to two different perceptual functions, one foundational,
with fixed rhythmic patterns and the other supplemental, with variable rhythms, the use of timbral differentiation to distinguish layers
of a complex texture, and the use of cyclic forms—all of this (and
more) is found throughout the African diaspora.

This common base made it easy for African-American musicians arrived in large numbers after Reconstruction brought with them a kind of ragtime that was substantially different from the piano genre everyone knows today. To study their ragtime is to put ourselves in the middle of the higher-level lessons that Armstrong the young professional was trying to master as a teenager.

"Huddling for self-protection"

During the decades following Reconstruction, the tragic decades of retrenchment from the ideal of political equality and the increasingly violent decades of brutal racial terrorism, the freedmen and their families moved to New Orleans from the sharecropping plantations of Louisiana and Mississippi, an area that turned out to be stunningly fertile for music. Louis's mother came from Boutte, fifty miles to the west of New Orleans, and Mahalia Jackson's family came from a cotton plantation on the Atchafalaya River, about a hundred miles to the north. Joe Oliver's family came from Abend, near Donaldsonville, some sixty miles upriver, and bassist George "Pops" Foster from the McCall Plantation nearby. Henry Allen, whose son Henry "Red" Allen Jr. was a successful rival to Armstrong during the swing era, moved from Lockport in 1890 to work on the docks. Charlie Hamilton's father brought his family from Ama around 1910 so that his children would have a chance to go to school. Johnny and Baby Dodds's father Warren came from Alabama, where he had learned to play "quills," an African instrument made out of bamboo pipes. Cornetist Punch Miller grew up in Raceland, where he sang blues to himself while he worked the sugarcane fields. Trombonists Harrison Barnes and Sunny Henry moved to the city from the Magnolia Plantation, where they learned the ring shout and congregational heterophony. Cornetist Chris Kelly and trombonist Jim Robinson came from the Deer Range Plantation, also downriver. Louis Jones from Mississippi arrived after working in labor camps in Arkansas, Missouri, Illinois, and Tennessee. Clarinetist Louis James was from Thibodeaux, where African-American bands were suppressed in the wake of the bloody massacre of some fifty blacks in 1887, and where James worked in the fields for twenty-five cents a day.

to learn from each other when they moved around the country
part of the Great Migration. The particular stylistic formation th
emerged from New Orleans spread quickly because African Ame
cans brought up in vernacular traditions elsewhere could readily ma
sense of it. One can accept all of this, however, and still insist that tl
New Orleanian achievement was unique. For it is clear that musicia
from other places were stunned on first hearing the likes of Joe Olive
Freddie Keppard, Jelly Roll Morton, Johnny Dodds, Sidney Beche
and Louis Armstrong. They had enough in common with the Ne
Orleans style to find a way to imitate it, but most of them freel
acknowledged the captivating freshness that these musicians brough
with them as they traveled north, east, and west.

And yet the question—Why did jazz originate in New
Orleans?—is complicated from another direction as well. Armstrong
and other musicians tell us that in the early days they did not call
their music jazz. " 'Jazz,' that's a name the white people have given
to the music," explained Sidney Bechet. When asked what term
they did use, Armstrong and the musicians he knew said "ragtime"—or, as Armstrong typically wrote it, "rag time." The issue is
not simply one of interchangeable names. Ragtime was played in
many places, and it certainly did not originate in New Orleans. One
way to think about the situation is that in New Orleans there
evolved a unique way of *playing* ragtime; from this emerged a
unique ensemble style and solo style that ultimately became jazz. So
to rephrase the original question, Why did a unique way of playing
ragtime originate in New Orleans?

Exploring that question leads us more deeply into the musical
forces that shaped Armstrong during his teenage years. And anything we learn about the single most influential musician the city
ever produced will tell us something noteworthy about the complicated and multidimensional history of jazz. One distinguishing feature of New Orleans is obvious: its large population of people with
mixed ancestry, French and African, known as Creoles of color. The
Creoles were an important part of the story, and Armstrong's inter-
actions with them are explored in Chapter 8. Even more important
for Armstrong—and more important for the formation of jazz—
were the Creoles' new neighbors. The plantation immigrants who

Cornetist Willie Hightower came from Nashville. Kid Ory and clarinetist Lawrence Duhé came from the Woodland Plantation near LaPlace, where they learned how to rag tunes. Cornetist Oscar Celestin came from Napoleonville, cornetist Hypolite Charles from Parks, drummer Zutty Singleton from Bunkie, cornetist Jimmy Clayton from Jaspar County, Mississippi, and Professor James Humphrey from Sellers, upriver in St. Charles Parish. Trombonists Buddy and Yank Johnson came from McDonaldsville, cornetist Edward Clem and trombonist Kid Thomas Valentine from Reserve. Virtually all of these migrating musicians and their families relocated to one of the subsections of uptown New Orleans, to the Irish Channel, River Bend, Carrollton, Back of Town, the Battlefield, the neighborhoods described by Edmond Souchon, the wealthy doctor who learned as a child to enjoy Joe Oliver's music when his nanny took him to watch parades, as the "hotbed of dark, uneducated cornfield Negroes."

Disgusted with sharecropping and fearful of vigilante terrorism, African Americans came by the thousands—as many as forty thou-

Louisiana plantation, ca. 1900 (New Orleans Public Library,
photo by George François Mugnier)

sand arrived in the city between 1880 and 1910. Rural-to-urban migration was surging everywhere in the South during these decades; W. E. B. Du Bois called the phenomenon a "huddling for self-protection." Jazz history is often discussed in terms of migrations, but more typically with respect to the later Great Migration northward, to Chicago, New York, and elsewhere, beginning around 1910 and peaking during the 1920s. But here is the first crucial step, the one that brought jazz into its first full and variegated flowering. During these post-Reconstruction decades New Orleans gathered the musical energy of the plantations thanks to the independent efforts of thousands of families, a cumulative process akin to the Mississippi River building its mighty current through the joining of hundreds of small tributaries.

One thing that this migration of former slaves to uptown New Orleans created was a huge mass of patronage for the new music, an essential element of any artistic flowering. Working as a common laborer in New Orleans did not pay much, but it paid more than sharecropping, and people found themselves with a little bit of expendable income, which they happily spent on music. New Orleans during Armstrong's childhood was overflowing with African-American venues for music. By one count there were ten to fifteen dance halls uptown alone; between them they produced a function every night. A step or two below the dance halls were the ubiquitous honky tonks. Then there were the outdoor venues of lawn parties in the city and dancing pavilions at Lake Pontchartrain, where, on Sundays, up to twenty bands took position for daylong performances.

Jazz could not have grown without this abundant array of institutions. The immigrants were drawn to New Orleans as a safe place that offered better jobs, and they were delighted to find multiple spaces for the performance of their cherished vernacular culture. Surely every city in the Deep South had some venues for Negro entertainment, but it is hard to imagine any being as bountiful as New Orleans. Had this not been the case, had there not emerged steady, widespread patronage of the new music played by wind instruments, then this regional way of playing ragtime would not have been fired by the same degree of competition and striving toward sophistication and virtuosity, it would not have expanded creatively in dozens of different directions, and it would not have yielded soloists of the stature of Bolden, Oliver, and Armstrong. Twenty-five cents per dance-hall patron—that was enough, when spread through a population of some forty thousand immigrants, to nurture the new style.

The more complicated part of how the plantation immigration drove jazz has to do with the details of the musical culture the freedmen brought with them. They did not bring a uniform, homogeneous set of values and practices; the list of arrivals cited earlier gives notice of that. James Humphrey, for example, was one of the best-known uptown "professors" who taught many different instruments. Humphrey taught legitimate music; he had no particular skill in blues-tinged ragtime. He owned property in New Orleans and sold homegrown figs to pay his taxes. In his leisure he could be found sipping beer in uptown saloons, dressed up in black suit and derby. Shakespeare was his favorite author. Willie Hightower from Nashville was cut from a similar cloth. He reserved his highest praise for musicians who could negotiate the tricky melodies of Scott Joplin: "Any trumpet player could play *Cascades*, he was a musicianer of mine." Hightower had a knack for running businesses, first an ice cream shop, then a saloon. Humphrey and Hightower were not ratty people in anybody's classification, and it is important to realize that their interests in European-derived standards of musical taste and social practice were very much a part of the African-American cultural fabric.

But for every well-trained musicianer and upwardly mobile entrepreneur, there were hundreds more immigrants with gutbucket musical taste and common-laborer jobs. Like May Ann and the Saints, they had little or no interest in cultural assimilation. The culture they brought to the city featured a strong African legacy, among the strongest anywhere in the United States. One reason for that was that Louisiana held the largest plantations in the South, with Mississippi not far behind. Especially in the alluvial parishes along the river, the so-called black belt, Negroes far outnumbered whites. Simply by force of number, African-derived practices thrived. Furthermore, African slaves were brought to these plantations long after the overseas trade was criminalized, with New Orleans serving as a port of entry for the illegal slave trade all the way up to the Civil War. Frederick Law Olmsted claimed that 75 percent of enslaved people on the plantations of Louisiana and Mississippi were "thorough-bred Africans."

Vestiges of Congo culture and language (that is, the culture and language of the Bakongo people), for example, surface in Louisiana. The word "funky" may have come from the Ki-Kongo word *lu-fuki*, meaning bad body odor and also praise for artistic accomplishment, a flow of vital energy. Many words associated with voodoo come from the same linguistic zone. In Congo religion, time is conceived cyclically; in the slave culture of the Deep South, that conception was seen and heard in the circle dancing and singing of the ring shout. Crossroads are important in Congo religion, as a ritual space elaborated with a circle and discs, to the center of which sacred power flows upon the kneeling initiate; blues singer Robert Johnson from Mississippi sang about this symbol in the 1930s. Here and elsewhere throughout the African diaspora, music opens up pathways to the spiritual world. The African cultural legacy that shaped plantation life in late-nineteenth-century Louisiana and Mississippi also included dancing, gestures, verbal sparring, storytelling, linguistic patterns, architecture, textile designs, outdoor decoration (bottle trees, the raked dirt yard), crop cultivation, and diet.

The point here is not that the freedmen who moved to uptown New Orleans—and certainly not the musicians who created jazz—identified themselves as African. To emphasize, at considerable distance, the African legacy that shaped their expressive culture is to be out of step with the identity claims they seem to have been inclined to make—"They're all trying to take everybody to Africa, that's what they're doing," was the scorn Armstrong heaped on his bebop rivals in 1949—though one must acknowledge that very little evidence about this survives. My impression is that while uptown Negroes did not wish to abandon the expressive culture they had long cherished, they were also interested in finding a way to fit into an expanding national framework, in spite of the steady onslaught of oppression relentlessly directed toward them.

What is gained by recognizing this cultural legacy of Africa is, first of all, a sense of where the driving energy of jazz came from, both directly (the plantations) and remotely (Africa). Since jazz history has been highly contested, this is no small matter. Second, it is a useful way to educate our hearing. People hear in the way they have been trained to hear, and it is never easy to enter an unfamiliar sound world. In musicological literature it is striking, still, how often the cultural legacy of Africa is ignored in African-American music, as if it is a matter of no consequence or a matter that is not heard. At the same time that we learn to hear, we also gain a sense of how to think about music and its entanglement with a web of values and practices that may not be obvious. Highlighting an African legacy directs us toward the ways in which music serves various social agendas, how it is tied to physical gesture and movement, how music and speech mix with one another, how the aural arts relate to the visual arts, how music gives shape to emotions and how people think about and practice emotions, how time is conceived and how that is related to religion, and so on. Sometimes it is an achievement just to be able to bring issues like these into focus, since so much detail from the past is lost.

When they arrived in New Orleans, the plantation immigrants found a city that already had a place for an African cultural legacy. This was the city of voodoo, a presence aided by Catholic syncretism and sustained contact with the Caribbean. And it was the city of Place Congo, the most famous and vividly portrayed antebellum venue for the performance of African music in the United States. The performance of African music and dancing in this square was intensified or perhaps even caused by the immigration of some three thousand slaves around 1810 from Saint Domingue, as the Republic of Haiti was formerly known. Many of those slaves had originally come from the Congo, and their arrival doubled the slave population of New Orleans. At Place Congo one could hear drums, gourd rattles, sticks, *banjers*, woodblocks, jawbones, clapping, stamping, quill pipes, marimbas, singing, and whatever European instruments happened to be available. Benjamin Latrobe witnessed the scene in 1819 and wrote that he had never seen anything "more brutally savage"; he regarded the performance as a direct continuation of African practice. By the 1840s the African dances of the old days had yielded to

African-American hybrids, and by the 1850s performances in Place Congo had vanished.

It is difficult to know precisely where the balance stood, how much of early jazz, which foregrounded features that derived ultimately from Africa, was already in New Orleans and how much was brought from the plantations. City and country had never been totally isolated from one another, so it would be misleading to draw the boundary between the two too sharply. Certainly, however, the coincidence of the plantation immigrants arriving in New Orleans at the same time that jazz emerged was not accidental. There was also the ongoing presence in New Orleans of itinerant workers who kept musical innovations in constant circulation while they tended boats, loaded goods onto docks, and built miles and miles of levees. Larenzo, the rags-bottles-and-bones man, spread his tinhorn blues wherever his emaciated mule could haul his wagon, and these itinerant workers had long been doing the same thing, in and out of the delta regions as they traveled by boat, foot, wagon, and train. In doing so they brought vernacular music from the plantations to the river cities, especially the southernmost port. The long-term process may have resembled the earlier arrival of refugees from Saint Domingue, which both doubled the French population downtown, thus guaranteeing the survival of French culture, and doubled the slave population, thus bolstering African culture and sparking the public display of Place Congo.

Ratty Dancing

The freedmen brought to New Orleans their own love of dancing, and this was also a time when the entire nation was exploding with kinetic enthusiasm, stimulated by the syncopated vigor of a new musical genre—ragtime. This auspicious conflation of local, regional, and national interest made the situation right for the growth of a new kind of dance music. It was enough to launch the brief but spectacular career of the first famous musician associated with jazz, cornetist Charles "Buddy" Bolden.

For the uptown immigrants, the best ragtime in New Orleans was played by Bolden on his cornet. Armstrong heard him in 1906 at the tender age of five, just before Bolden's mental health dramatically deteriorated; in June of 1907 he was placed in an insane asylum where he remained for the rest of his life. Some believed that loud playing had damaged his brain, others that he was poisoned by a jealous lover. But in just a few years of brilliant, local glory, Bolden set the stage for all cornetists who followed, including Oliver a few years later and Armstrong just a few years after that. "Bolden put 'em out and everybody came to listen," said Lawrence Duhé. "That's how we got jazz." The legend of Bolden is misty and difficult to sift through. What follows is certainly not the only way to read the evidence, but it will draw us into the details of what was expected of Armstrong as a professional cornetist and why he called his music "rag time."

Bolden played for all types of dances, including the quadrille, schottische, waltz, polka, and mazurka ("mazooka" as Jelly Roll Morton called it). African Americans had plenty of opportunities, not only in New Orleans but on the plantations as well, to learn these traditional European dance steps. Bolden had to know how to accompany them just like dance-band musicians throughout the South. (Robert Johnson, the legendary blues guitarist from Mississippi, was described as a "polka hound" by one musician who performed with him.) Johnny St. Cyr and others said that tempos in New Orleans were much slower than they were in Chicago during the 1920s, which made it easy for patrons to dance all night without getting tired. "The schottische was a very beautiful dance," St. Cyr remembered. "On the old schottische, the couple were holding each other all the time, where in the promenade schottische they let go and moved from side to side, 1-2-3-4, formed a ring, and it was beautiful to look at."

It was easy to transform these traditional dances through an African-American vernacular sensibility. Armstrong wrote about Nicodeemus, a neighborhood buddy who "had a jazz way of doing a ballroom dance, . . . a sort of two-step, like." Pops Foster said that Ory's band "could play a waltz and make it hot." According to Baby Dodds, bands used to change waltz tunes by playing them with four rather than the traditional three beats to the measure; a preference for duple meter is common throughout the African diaspora. Yet it is also said that Bolden could play "sweet," which implies a degree of conformity to Eurocentric standards. He was probably versatile enough to vary his style to suit the dancers.

It is safe to assume that uptown dancers were both seen and heard. Their shoes touched the floor with the same percussive attack—the same *vitality*—that marked sound production on a cornet, clarinet, trombone, guitar, and bass and that often marks vocal and instrumental production throughout the African diaspora. Plantation slaves erected wooden platforms for their dance contests. They had no interest in dancing on the bare ground, Indian style; they wanted the percussive precision of foot against wood. Descriptions of Sanctified churches often mention the resonance caused by feet pounding on floorboards, an additional layer of percussion in the polyrhythmic web produced by singing, clapping, and the occasional instrument. There is threefold value in the percussion of shoe striking floor: the sonic participation of the dancer (or congregant) integrates sound with bodily motion; the sharp attack marks a rhythmic position in the flow of time; and, as Robert Farris Thompson observed in his study of West African religion, the percussive sound manifests the energy of life force.

Punch Miller said that the waltz and the two-step were danced for contests in New Orleans. After the prizes were awarded, the dance floor exploded into the creative vernacular. "There wasn't any such thing as jitterbug," he remembered, "but there was the two-step and guys squatting on the floor, coming up shaking, like they do at parades now." Pops Foster enjoyed dancing to the music of Frankie Dusen's Eagle Band: "I'd try to dance the quadrilles when they played; I'd run and jump and kick my leg out and have a big time." African-derived dances are typically uncoupled, thus freeing up different parts of the body to move independently in synthesized tension. "They dance by themselves or swing each other around. They didn't know nothing about these 'hugging' dance," said a former slave from Mississippi about the dances his African-born father had led on the plantation. When dancing to ragtime, "you could grab the chick and squeeze her anyway you wanted to," said Foster.

Dancing techniques common throughout the African diaspora included gliding, dragging, or shuffling the feet; assuming a crouching position instead of the stiffly erect posture of European dancing; mimicry of animals; improvisation; and the central importance of hip motion. Two and perhaps three of these are highlighted in a song titled *Don't Go 'Way Nobody* that Bolden is reported to have sung after midnight, thus launching a transition into a different style and mood:

> 'Way down, 'way down low
> So I can hear those whores
> Drag their feet across the floor
> Oh you bitches, shake your asses

Funky Butt Hall, where Bolden frequently played, got its nickname from a dance that threw many hips into vigorous syncopation. This is the hall at 1319 Perdido Street where young Louis peeked through cracks in the wall to see how "them chicks would get way down, shake everything, slapping themselves on the cheek of their behind." We may use the descriptions from Armstrong and Punch Miller—"guys squatting on the floor, coming up shaking"—to read Bolden's line, " 'way down, 'way down low," which perhaps describes a dance performed from a crouching position. The crouching position signifies vitality in Congo-derived culture. This is one possible source for the still-common slang "get down." There are a number of references to animal dances in New Orleans. Charlie Love danced the Eagle Rock at Bolden's dances; the Buzzard Lope is also mentioned. According to the *New Orleans Item* (1908), the Turkey Trot was "developed into its highest state of efficiency" in African-American neighborhoods of New Orleans, which were also the home of the Grizzly Bear and a "siege of erotic dances." There can be no doubt that improvised dance was commonplace.

"The older people loved the square dances but the younger generation wanted ragtime," said Bob Lyons. Nationwide, the new dance in the 1890s and the one most associated with ragtime was the two-step. Through a hugely expanding publishing industry and the sale of piano rolls, ragtime suddenly burst into public favor around 1897. The average American may not have known much about Scott Joplin, or even what color he was, but that American had probably heard the catchy melodies of *Maple Leaf Rag*, Joplin's

*Getting down (Courtesy of the Hogan Jazz Archive,
Tulane University, photo by Ralston Crawford)*

hit of 1899. John Philip Sousa, the most famous musician of the
day, was an enthusiast. Teddy Roosevelt listened to the Marine
Band play *Maple Leaf Rag* on the White House lawn. A journalist
estimated in 1915 that ten million Americans were fond of ragtime.
The driving energy behind this music flowed ultimately from vernacular music of the plantations, the same tradition that was behind
jazz in New Orleans. But the trajectories of the nation's ragtime—
the social, technological, and demographic trajectories—gave it a
shape very different from the new music in New Orleans.

National ragtime was molded by itinerant pianists who made
their living in a late-nineteenth-century version of "on the road,"
traveling by foot, on boats, and via rail lines up and down the lower
corridor of the Mississippi River. Again we see the river magnetiz-
ing plantation culture and channeling it into an urban center, but
now that center is located on the northern rather than the southern
edge of the lower corridor. It is St. Louis, to which pianists were
attracted because of the successful publishing of John Stark, who
promoted Joplin. New Orleans certainly had its share of ragtime
pianists, but their role in early jazz was marginal. Thus, in contrast
to the trajectories of jazz in New Orleans, the nationally known ver-

sion of ragtime flowed through St. Louis, through pianists (rather than through wind instruments), and through sheet music (rather than through the practices of musical illiterates).

The ragtime Sousa, Roosevelt, and the average American admired had multiple antecedents, but it was traceable by ear to the old-time music of the slaves. This was certainly how Joplin himself thought about it: "There has been ragtime music in America ever since the Negro race has been here," he told a reporter. When slaves performed familiar tunes in an African-American way, their practice was sometimes called "ragging" the tune; this usage is the main antecedent for the word "ragtime." Charles Ives heard an African-American minstrel troupe ragging simple songs with liberal sprinklings of syncopations in the early 1890s, and he later documented their technique in musical notation. Another way to rag was to leave the tune itself intact while recasting the accompaniment. Max Hoffman published several arrangements like this in 1896, and he called them "Negro 'Rag' Accompaniments."

In Hoffman's arrangements it is easy to see and hear a technique that has been used in many different kinds of African-American music. The technique depends on a division of musical labor: one group of instruments or voices (or just a single part) maintains a fixed rhythmic pattern; the other plays in variable rhythms, with the intention of creating a pleasing mix of agreement and disagreement with the foundational pattern. In Joplin's piano rags, the left hand marks the beat while the right hand dances along in variable rhythms. In a West African drum orchestra, the same underlying model is used to generate rhythmic layers of breathtaking complexity. Nevertheless, that complexity is always analyzable according to the basic distinction of fixed and variable. Not just analyzable; you can easily *hear* it. Distinct timbres help the ear distinguish the layers—cow bell, gourd rattle, voices, various sizes of drums in West Africa; stick, clapping, drum, voice, and fife in the rural ensembles from Mississippi recorded in the 1940s; clarinet, cornet, trombone, banjo, bass, and drums in early jazz from New Orleans. Also standard, to the point that exceptions are noteworthy, is the use of a simple binary pattern, a progression of twos or fours, as the basis for the fixed rhythmic group.

This model is one of the most durable features of music in the African diaspora, surfacing virtually everywhere that Africans were enslaved in the New World. Gerhard Kubik, who has spent a lifetime studying African music south of the Sahara, concludes that "in west Africa the superposition of two different, related pulse schemes is common and is like a grid in the mind." It is crucial to realize how foundational this grid was for Armstrong. It was transmitted, across the ocean and through the generations of slaves and their descendants, not via drum orchestras but through informal techniques of everyday music making such as clapping, foot tapping, dancing, singing, and "patting Juba."

Patting Juba was the pervasive plantation tradition by which a single performer tapped rhythms against parts of his or her body (thus achieving timbral diversity) to generate the mix of fixed and variable patterns. Drummer Chinee Foster (Chapter 6) made monkeyshines and foolishness with his hands against a foundational rhythm with his feet; he could just as easily have been patting Juba. Nineteenth-century observers did their best to describe what they were hearing. From 1880: "I have heard a Southern plantation 'hand,' in 'patting Juba' for a comrade to dance by, venture upon quite complex successions of rhythm, not hesitating to syncopate, to change the rhythmic accent for a moment, or to indulge in other highly-specialized variations of the current rhythmus." In an 1835 letter to Edgar Allan Poe, an observer compared patting Juba to poetry:

> I do not know to what to liken those occasional departures from regular metre which are so fascinating [in poetry]. They are more to my ear like that marvelous performance—"clapping Juba," than anything else. The beat is capriciously irregular; there is no attempt to keep time to *all* the notes, but then it comes so pat & so distinct that the cadence is never lost ... [Such irregularities] must be so managed as neither to hasten or retard the beat. The time of the bar must be the same, no matter how many notes are in it.

The writer seems to be describing the fixed-variable model when she mentions metric departures that somehow never lose the steady underlying form.

From more than a century later comes the following description, which bears an undeniable resemblance:

At the start of a recording session Louis Armstrong . . . stands in front of the mic and stamps out a steady rhythm. As the band picks it up, Armstrong's foot doubles the beat and starts tapping twice as fast. And as he sings and plays the trumpet he stresses accents *around and between* the taps of his foot.

Transmitting the fixed and variable model across the centuries required no verbal theory and no musical notation; it was learned through demonstration and imitation. The specific details of West African drum practice did not survive in the Deep South, in contrast to parts of the Caribbean and South America, where continuity is sometimes very precise. This model of fixed and variable, however, not only survived, but flourished. What made the model so durable was its flexibility. Slaves interested in performing European-American music—and there were, of course, huge incentives to do that—discovered many ways to adapt the basic grid. In doing so they and their descendants generated an infinite array of unforeseen transformations. The cyclic foundation merged with the concept in European-derived theory of the "measure" (or "bar"), a unit of time and a quantity of "beats" that replaced the drum ostinatos of Africa with no more effort than it took to adapt a Catholic saint in voodoo synthesis. Though the beats of a measure are far simpler than the ostinatos of a West African drum orchestra, the basic principle remained: the listener's delight comes from being able to follow, without effort, the regular flow of the fixed pattern, while the variable rhythms flow in and out of synchrony with this foundation.

Musicians all over the world intuitively seize upon the ear's ability to track multiple layers of sound. The musician learns how to have it both ways: the ear can identify distinct levels of musical activity at the same time that it can synthesize these levels into a coherent whole. The clever musician experiments with this basic principle, and out of that experimentation arise multiple techniques. What we are discussing here is a format favored throughout the

African diaspora for realizing this universal potential of human hearing. It is central to both ragtime and jazz, though in different manifestations and to different degrees, the details of which reveal much about the histories of these musics and their intersections in early-twentieth-century New Orleans.

Bolden

Bolden's ascent around 1900 was partly a matter of good timing in the sense that it coincided with the national ragtime craze. Today most people know ragtime through the polished piano pieces of Scott Joplin. The "ragtime era," roughly the late 1890s through 1917, knew a lot more music than that, of course. Songs for solo voice with piano accompaniment were called ragtime, and they out-numbered even the vast number of piano pieces written by countless composers, black and white, male and female. Bolden's repertory included the songs *Ida Sweet as Apple Cider* (1903) and *If the Man on the Moon Was a Coon* (1905), along with the instrumental pieces *Panama Rag* (1904) and *St. Louis Tickle* (1904). He and his band played the songs without a vocal part while women in the dance hall sang along. Bolden often brought a personal touch to the perform-ance of these pieces. One opportunity came in the "break," a one- or two-measure stretch at the end of a phrase for a brief, unaccompa-nied solo. Manuel Manetta remembered Frank Lewis, one of Bolden's clarinetists, "ripping" a vigorous break in the middle of *Ida Sweet as Apple Cider*. These little solos provided space to assert per-sonality and class values; the piece was locally claimed, in a sense.

Bolden had a good ragtime band, but the key to his success was his ability to tap into the emerging urban values of the Negro labor-ing class. In Isidore Barbarin's blunt assessment (Chapter 1), "He was famous with the ratty people." His performances included many low-class markers, some of them having nothing to do with sound and others central to the formation of jazz.

Manuel Manetta described how Frankie Dusen, a trombonist who eventually played with Bolden, made a name for himself in Algiers, directly across the river from Canal Street. Algiers supported two "colored" dance halls, the Odd Fellows Hall and the Sacred Heart of Mary's Hall. According to Manetta, "respectable people" went to Sacred Heart of Mary's, "ratty people" to Odd Fellows. Dusen rented out the latter hall and sold tickets to dances that featured his band. These evenings included ham-kicking contests: a ham tied to a rope was suspended from the ceiling, and any woman who could kick her leg high enough to touch the ham won it as a prize—providing that she was not wearing underwear. Odd Fellows Hall was full of practical jokes, including the bursting of paper bags that people mistook for gunshots. George Baquet, a Creole clarinetist from downtown New Orleans, was surprised when he first walked in and saw every man, including the band members, wearing a hat. This was poor manners, not something Baquet had seen in a dance hall before. Dusen and Lorenzo Staulz lowered their suspenders so that their pants drooped, anticipating current low-riding fashion by a century. Bolden himself wore a hat and went tie-less, with the buttons of his shirt undone to expose a red flannel undershirt. "The girls and women, how they did go for those red undershirts," remembered Jelly Roll Morton, with a trace of envy. Admission to Dusen's dances was fifteen cents.

Bolden heard about Dusen's success and the two formed a musical union of convenience: Bolden included Dusen in his jobs in New Orleans, and Dusen included Bolden at Odd Fellows Hall in Algiers. When Bolden's popularity really took off, Dusen moved across the river and found a place to live near Bolden's guitarist, Lorenzo Staulz, on Pitt Street. Staulz was clever about generating lewd songs; Manetta credited him with the words for *Brown Skin Who You For* and *Kiss My Funky Ass*, the latter taken up by Kid Ory as his victory song after advertising-wagon competitions. When the well-mannered Manetta performed with these men, they teased him about their obscene language, pretending to be careful not to offend him. Brock Mumford, another guitarist who played with Bolden, was the one who brought the shout "Oh Lord have mercy!" into dance halls, playfully imitating the mood of a Sanctified church. Staulz, Dusen, Bolden, and Mumford ran with rough women, on whom they depended for money—which is to say, they were pimping. Mumford's lady friend Edie overwhelmed him in fights: "the only way he could get away from her was to roll on the floor like a big fat frog," remembered Manetta.

The two venues most famously associated with Bolden were Odd Fellows and Masonic Hall, on Perdido near Rampart, and Funky Butt Hall, just down the block on Perdido Street, between Liberty and Franklin, and just around the corner from Armstrong's home. They were both rough places. Kid Ory played at Funky Butt Hall only once, and he claimed that it was absolutely necessary to have a razor or gun to enter. "You should see the place, how it looked," he said. "Regular big old barn, you know . . . forsaken place." At Odd Fellows and Masonic Hall the evening dances were "dicty" (that is, imitating whites), "nothing but waltzes," according to Pops Foster. "But after midnight then they would do the blues and quadrilles, slow drag and more. That was all honky tonk. You would see all them sporting women come in after they'd finished their work . . . That's about the time I would be in there. The quadrille people were the rough gang."

As the dances modulated down and dirty, those who drew a line at certain words and behavior cleared out. Couples did not always dance together but circulated around with different partners. When that happened, the erotic combination of blues and the slow drag could have dangerous consequences. Marking the spirit of the moment, Bolden is said to have sung *Don't Go 'Way Nobody*, with its reference to whores dragging their feet and shaking their asses. This was the time for full display of musical seduction. Legends grew around his power over women. Several fought over him with guns at a Mardi Gras celebration in 1907, and he is said to have lived with three or four women at a time.

The blues was another certain marker of low-class, African-American identity, and it became a featured part of Bolden's dance-hall repertory. There is no way to know if he was the first cornetist to feature blues; what can be said definitely is that he did it with spectacular success. Bud Scott witnessed this from his seat as guitarist in the rival Robichaux band: "Bolden was still a great man for the blues—no two questions about that. The closest thing to it was Oliver and he was better than Oliver. He was a great man for what

The Bolden band, ca. 1900, with (standing left to right) Frank Lewis, Willie Cornish, Bolden, and Jimmy Johnson, and (seated left to right) Willie Warner and Brock Mumford (Historic New Orleans Collection, Acc. No. 92-48-L MSS 520 f. 1691)

we call 'dirt music.'" Bolden took vernacular blues from the streets, the fields, and around the house and put it in the dance hall; the expressive inflections of everyday speech and everyday singing were now stylized by a powerful cornetist. The immigrants could not have heard *that* on the plantations, where dance bands were almost always limited to strings, especially violin, banjo, guitar, mandolin, and string bass. Blues were the place for Bolden to use ideas culled from the ragman, the levee camps, and church, the gestures that moaned and went all through you.

At this time, blues were always played at a slow tempo—a very, very slow tempo, as Baby Dodds explained: "We took our time and played the blues slow and draggy . . . it was so draggy, sometimes, people would say it sounded like a dead march." Slow blues accompanied the dance known as the "slow drag," with the dancers up close and sliding across the floor, "packed like sardines in there, sound like sandpaper," said Manetta. Pops Foster remembered "guys . . . doing nothing but shaking their butts very slow and dirty." Any piece, even the famous rags by Joplin, could be slowed down to "blues time" (compare with "rag time"). The Bolden band played *Ida Sweet as Apple Cider* in blues time, and *Make Me a Pallet on the Floor* became his signature blues. "That was his, nobody could play it like Bolden," said Manetta.

Recollections of Bolden are contradictory about his ability to read musical notation. That contradiction is, in itself, revealing. But several reliable witnesses say that he could read music, at least to a degree. Manetta said that the band had written parts for *Panama Rag*, a complete arrangement purchased from the local music store.

Where Bolden would not have been using written parts would have been in the blues, the only "ratty music" Manetta heard him play. Blues offered the challenge of exploring a new ensemble idiom that had no connection whatsoever to notated music but all kinds of connections to the vocal core of plantation culture that was nurturing early jazz. Here is one basis for the view that "blues is what cause the fellows to start jazzing." Papa John Joseph claimed that with "Buddy Bolden, nobody read in his band, and he used to kill Robichaux anywhere he went for colored." It was incorrect to say that nobody read, but it was probably true that the band's ear arrangements generated their greatest success with uptown African-American audiences.

With this arsenal of musical and nonmusical markers of the day-laboring class—ham kicking, profanity, gutbucket blues, ragtime music for ratty dancing, hats, exposed red underwear, and so forth—Bolden waged a kind of class warfare. At stake were the terms of expressive culture for the plantation immigrants who were looking for common ground in the dance halls. His most unmatchable weapon was loud playing, mentioned time and again in the oral histories. He scored his most famous musical victories outdoors, at Lincoln Park and Johnson Park, where he competed with John Robichaux's dance orchestra, a successful society band that played strictly by the notes. Each park held a band concert from two to six o'clock on Sunday afternoons, followed by a dance at eight. Buddy Bartley—several informants mixed up the names, Buddy Bolden and Buddy Bartley, in their recollections—impressed the crowd by floating to tremendous heights in his hot-air balloon. Bartley, like

Bolden, had a nasty reputation, "a pimp and notoriety as he could be," said Johnny St. Cyr. There is something poetic about the conflated memories of Bolden's horn and Bartley's balloon, the performance in each case extending audaciously through space, each beckoning people with the promise of vicarious participation in risk-taking adventure. Bartley once sailed too high and landed embarrassingly in the middle of Lake Pontchartrain. And we know what happened to Bolden.

The battles with Robichaux took on an epic quality. The rivalry was driven by the edge of profit making, for while Robichaux was playing at Lincoln Park, Bolden was in fact working at Johnson Park, four blocks away. The two segregated parks competed heavily, and Bolden liked to draw away Lincoln patrons by sticking his cornet through a hole in the fence and blasting in Robichaux's direction. He then turned and projected his call toward Armstrong's neighborhood, some three miles away, carrying the distance with such magnetism that people are said to have emerged from their houses and boarded the trolley, headed for Johnson Park. It became standard practice for cornetists to summon audiences in this way. Armstrong first did it in 1918 at a job in Houma: "I used to have to play my cornet out of the window while playing with the band . . . And sure 'nuff, the crowd would come rolling in."

The significance of Bolden's loud playing must extend beyond the obvious function of advertising a performance. Sociologist Pierre Bourdieu has observed that physical strength is one of the few reliable assets the working class has in its contest with the dominating classes. Thus, it surfaces as a value in cultural forms such as dietary preferences and passion for sports. Bolden's loud cornet may be understood in the same way. Johnny St. Cyr believed that "jazz musicians have to be a working class of man, out in the open all the time, healthy and strong . . . a working man have the *power* to play hot, whiskey or no whiskey." The musical idiom is analyzed here in terms of masculine identity and class identity; loud playing represented both.

When Bolden turned his cornet toward Armstrong's neighborhood to call his audience out to Johnson Park, he may also have been demonstrating symbolic transgression. For the sounds of his horn did not simply drop like a spotlight onto scattered African-American neighborhoods. His music *covered the city*, through the forbidden stretches and the alluring ones, from the wealthy mansions on St. Charles Avenue to the downtown Seventh Ward where the snooty Creoles of color lived. The sound crossed all physical and social boundaries. The cornet must have seemed to trump, at least for a moment, the latent violence in those places, violence that could materialize at any moment and did so most dramatically in the riotous destruction following Robert Charles's one-man insurrection in July 1900, only a few blocks from Bolden's house. Having been driven to the city by the urge to huddle together for protection, the immigrants witnessed the brutal annihilation of a single insurgent and the subsequent, random release of blood revenge throughout their neighborhoods. In these same neighborhoods they followed the call of Bolden's powerful cornet.

Bolden's musical audacity spread as wide and free in 1900 as the drums of Place Congo did in 1830. At least for some people, the reach and power of skillful sonic projection must have counted as a triumph over white exploitation of people of African descent. He was hardly the first musician to wrap political resistance into sound—think of the spirituals that work on two levels, religious and political, or the thinly veiled parodies and satires of plantation songs. But his music was definitely fresh and urban and perhaps unprecedentedly forceful, thoroughly matched to this time and place.

He became known as "King Bolden." No one doubted whose king he was. (It is impossible to tell if there was an ironic edge built into this title, as there certainly was with the Mardi Gras title "King Zulu.") Loud cornet playing became part of the uptown style. Whenever a Creole wished to distance himself from the immigrants and their vernacular music, he spoke about "loud" and "rough" sound production, the two code words that, along with "ratty" and "routine," automatically put low-class music in its proper place. Oliver was known as a loud player in New Orleans, and his student followed in step. When Armstrong made his first records with the Creole Jazz Band in Chicago in 1923, he had to be positioned in the back of the studio, as far from the recording horn as possible, in order to achieve a proper balance.

It is important to realize that Robichaux sometimes won his battles with Bolden. The competition was real—the result was not known in advance. In one recollection, Robichaux beat Bolden by adding to his orchestra Manuel Perez, who was not at all ratty but a legitimate player of strength and polish. Kid Ory admired Robichaux's orchestra second only to Bolden's, and he was certainly not alone. Remember that Bolden played a diverse repertory, including all the traditional dances as well as ragtime and the slow drag. The pull of legitimate music was very strong; certainly there were many pressures to turn in that direction.

A plurality of stylistic possibilities was always available in uptown African-American New Orleans. That plurality made it easy for styles to evolve, through constant adjustment and borrowing and experimenting that cannot be tracked in detail but was surely there. A localized class identity was being formed, not in an instant but over decades, as Bolden's music became a rallying point around which lower-class values gathered. The scale on which he accomplished this was probably unprecedented for African Americans in the United States. His success had everything to do with the immigrant search for a new urban identity that did not violate what they already treasured. It had something to do with the historic function of music as a practice for producing social cohesion for African Americans. And it had a lot to do with New Orleans, with its multiple spaces for gathering and performing vernacular culture and with its outdoor orientation, which led to a fondness for wind instruments. The immigrants voted with their feet by paying to attend the attractions that appealed to them and by investing so much in dance-hall culture.

Ragging the Tune

So far, I have been using the word "ragtime" in the straightforward, modern-day sense: ragtime is a *genre*, one crowned by the compositions of Scott Joplin, whose ultimate goal was to establish a kind of African-American music that could take its place alongside the great tradition of the European classics. In addition to piano rags, this kind of ragtime could be purchased in arrangements for bands, the most famous collection being the *Standard High Class Rags*, which New Orleanian musicians knew as the "Red Back Book."

In order to understand why uptown New Orleanians called early jazz "ragtime," however, the term needs to be opened up further, not along the lines of genre but as a set of *performance practices*. To complicate matters even further, the musicians often used "ragtime" in a stylistic sense, as a way to generalize about a repertory, especially as that repertory differs from music of the "jazz age," roughly the 1920s. Jelly Roll Morton used the word in this way when he pointed out that Bolden "didn't play jazz. He was a ragtime player." Here Morton is close to our modern way of thinking and in direct contradiction to other musicians who say that they called early jazz "ragtime."

The alternative usage of "ragtime" as a performance practice surfaces fairly often in interviews with musicians from Armstrong's circles. "Jazz was also called 'ragtime,'" said "Kid" Thomas Valentine. "The men in those bands could read but they usually played jazz." "Ragtime" here means music played without notation; if one is reading music, one is not playing ragtime. Manuel Manetta used the word in the same way: "Joe Howard didn't play nothing but his music, never played ragtime. Joe always had his music."

Sidney Bechet believed that ragtime was part of an oral tradition that originated with the slaves. "There's two kinds of music," Bechet said. "There's classic and there's ragtime. When I tell you ragtime, you can feel it, there's a spirit right in the word. It comes out of Negro spirituals." The vocal tradition of the spirituals was far indeed from the highly stylized piano rags transmitted through sheet music. Punch Miller used "ragtime" to describe a way of playing virtually any kind of music. At the Lyric Theater in the early 1920s, Miller remembered, "Robichaux would play the overture starting off like a march and about the middle of it they would start ragtime, jazzing it."

Lawrence Duhé provided an important comment that ties the New Orleanian usage to the plantations. "Ragtime . . . that's the onliest kind of music that was used at that time," he said. "We'd rag all pieces . . . *Turkey in the Straw* I can remember." On the plantation near LaPlace, Louisiana, where Duhé grew up, musicians ragged all pieces, including the classic minstrel tune *Turkey in the Straw*, also known as *Jump Jim Crow*. Like Valentine, Manetta, Bechet, and Miller, Duhé used "ragtime" not as a genre but to mean the practice of ragging the tune—any tune. This usage must have come from the plantations, even though most of these musicians first heard it in the city, where it must have been spoken of by more than a few of the forty thousand plantation immigrants. It circulated widely enough that it was understood by a Creole of color like Armand Piron, an entrepreneur, violinist, and bandleader who played society gigs. "Ragtime originated uptown," he said—and he was not thinking of piano music published by John Stark.

For Armstrong, ragtime was "hot" music, rhythmically exciting and emotionally charged. "They would make me carry the lead for them because they said, as far back as then, that they thought I had something on the ball, as a rag time singer . . . which matches the phrase, hot swing singing today," he said about his quartet experience. He remembered Peter Davis telling him at the Waif's Home that " 'a musician with a tone can play any kind of music, whether it's Classic or Rag Time.' That was the name of good hot music in those days." "I wouldn't say I know what jazz is, because I don't look at it from that angle," he said on another occasion. "I look at it from music—we never did worry about what it was in New Orleans, we just always tried to play good. And the public named it. It was ragtime, Dixieland, gut-bucket, jazz, swing—and it ain't nothin' but the same music." Duhé and others brought a musical practice from the plantations to the city, and Armstrong continued the practice until the end of his life.

In other words, the meaning of ragtime understood by these musicians is that which *preceded* the national fad for Ragtime (using an initial capital letter to refer, for now, to the genre, distinguished from the uptown New Orleans sense of ragging the tune), as composed by Scott Joplin and all the others. Both Ragtime, the popular genre, and ragtime, the uptown New Orleanian performance practice, derived from the plantation tradition of ragging a tune. But the connection to the plantations was much more direct for the New Orleanians. Among the implications of this line of analysis is this: early jazz in New Orleans may be the strongest, most vivid link we have to the plantation tradition of ragging the tune.

The uptown usage puts us in a time and at a place where music was conceived differently than what most of us are accustomed to. Blues, ragtime, jazz—our sense of these terms has been produced partly by the brittle one-dimensionality of marketing strategies, partly as a simplified way to parse the complicated history of popular music, a way of distinguishing Bessie Smith from Billy Holiday, Scott Joplin from Joe Oliver, and so on. Unlike "jazz" and "blues," terms that are still in play, our sense of "Ragtime" has become frozen. We still have continuous and evolving traditions of jazz and blues, and players in those idioms are aware of their relationship to the earliest players. Armstrong, Duhé, and the rest are telling us about a time when "ragtime," too, had a more open-ended meaning.

Moreover, these musicians are close to a time, perhaps even in the middle of it, when there was less difference than one might think between ragtime, blues, work songs, and religious music. They constantly associate early jazz with all of these idioms, and one sees evidence of the same fluidity elsewhere in the Deep South. On the plantations of Mississippi, blues was not at all limited to the lyric form people usually think of today; more often than not, it was music for dancing. When the uptown New Orleanians speak of "blues time" to mean a slow tempo distinguished from the faster-tempo "rag time," they reveal a way of thinking that has little to do with stylistic differentiation. Blues was beginning to take on strong associations of vocality, even when played on instruments—this was part of what Bolden offered. Yet ear pianists who played blues and nothing else were certainly not playing the piano in a vocalized way; the contemporary conception of the idiom was broader than that. Ragging the tune, a way of transforming *any* kind of music, undoubtedly included many of the gestures associated with blues— bending pitch, subtle details of phrasing, and vocalized timbre, whenever appropriate. Certainly it did for Louis Armstrong.

One might be tempted to give up on this terminological puzzle, but it should be remembered that it did not cause problems for the people who made the music or for those who enjoyed it. The puzzle is caused mainly by later trajectories that flowed from that music, and by complicated, multidimensional forces of history that must be cleared away in order to enter their world. The most difficult historical claim to work through, one commonly invoked in the literature on jazz, is that Ragtime and blues were the antecedents to early jazz. When taken as a starting point, this claim only spins confusion. It is better to see the music that would eventually be called jazz as coming into focus at the same time that Ragtime and blues were beginning to mark out distinct arenas of practice, one an idiom crafted by composers and distributed through sheet music, the other dominated by singers and featuring a standard poetic form. Early jazz embraced all the good that Joplin and his popular colleagues had to offer: their harmonic ideas, melodic contours, arpeggiations, and different forms of syncopation. And it also benefited from the energy that was coalescing around blues. The point to emphasize is that it belonged to a tradition that had always been open to different kinds of music. In its own time and place, *Turkey in the Straw* was as important to the ragging musician as *Maple Leaf Rag* was in New Orleans around 1900.

The important thing for a musician, when ragging a tune, was what he added to it. "He's supposed to be playing different from the straight lead and getting off on his own ideas," was Punch Miller's assessment of uptown practice. The technique was learned by listening, by imitating and experimenting, by soliciting a few timely words of advice, by sitting in with more experienced musicians, perhaps by lessons—by all the ways that Armstrong was learning during his middle teenage years. When ragging a tune, the musician used the familiar melody to draw the listener into his own field of creativity. The strategy was dictated by necessity, an example of the old African-American saying "Take advantage of the disadvantages." The slave-musician had no recourse to copyright, no way to reap the benefits of distributing his own *composition*—this was the historical injustice that Joplin wanted to overcome. Instead the slave had his techniques for transforming what was already known and with this he could do a lot, perhaps acquire privilege, status, or even a little bit of cash. This tradition found fertile ground in post-Reconstruction New Orleans.

It is easy to see how, in this conception, the emphasis is not on a musical object—that is, a *piece* of music—but on music as an activity, as it was in the Sanctified Church (Chapter 2). The compelling energy of the performance flows not from a faithful rendition of a unique tune but from the practices and inventions that are brought to it. Beginning and ending are not of great importance. W. C. Handy heard a plantation string band in Cleveland, Mississippi, in 1903 that was probably ragging a tune in just this way:

> Their band consisted of just three pieces, a battered guitar, a man-dolin and a worn-out bass. The music they made was pretty well in keeping with their looks. They struck up one of those over-and-over strains that seem to have no very clear beginning and certainly no ending at all. The strumming attained a disturbing monotony, but on and on it went, a kind of stuff that has long been associated with cane rows and levee camps . . . Their eyes rolled. Their shoulders swayed. And through it all that little agonizing strain persisted . . . A rain of silver dollars began to fall around the outlandish, stomping feet. The dancers went wild.

When Handy witnessed "monotony" being rewarded with a rain of silver dollars, he began to understand the popular appeal of vernacular music.

In uptown New Orleans, marches, blues, and popular tunes were performed in this same over-and-over way. Nonreading bands often learned only the familiar strain or chorus, which they repeated to the delight of equally outlandish, stomping dancers. The ideal of a continuous, powerful flow of sound, with no beginning and no ending, occasionally proved a bit too seductively impractical for improvising musicians. One Johnny Brown, a clarinetist, "just couldn't make no ending," said Pops Foster. "When you got to the end of a number, you'd reach over and pull the clarinet out of his mouth so he'd stop." Oliver gauged the dancers' reception of a piece to determine its length. He kept a brick near to hand, and when he wanted a piece to end, he signaled the band by slamming it on the floor.

Ragging a tune may be conceived as a style of melodic ornamentation. Zora Neale Hurston reflects on ornamentation as a basic concern of African-American culture:

> The will to adorn is the second most notable characteristic in Negro expression . . . The stark trimmed phrases of the Occident seem too

bare for the voluptuous child of the sun, hence the adornment. It arises out of the same impulse as the wearing of jewelry and the making of sculpture—the urge to adorn. On the walls of the homes of the average Negro one always finds a glut of gaudy calendars, wall pockets and advertising lithographs. The sophisticated white man or Negro would tolerate none of these . . . I saw in Mobile a room in which . . . the walls were gaily papered with Sunday supplements of the *Mobile Register*. There were seven calendars and three wall pockets . . . The mantel-shelf was covered with a scarf of deep homemade lace, looped up with a huge bow of pink crepe paper. Over the door was a huge lithograph showing the treaty of Versailles . . . decorating a decoration . . . did not seem out of place to the hostess . . . The feeling back of such an act is that there can never be enough of beauty, let alone too much . . . Whatever the Negro does of his own volition he embellishes.

Armstrong himself made visual collages in the tradition described here when he decorated hundreds of reel-to-reel tape boxes, yielding an idiosyncratic musical and visual diary.

Musically speaking, Armstrong and his colleagues used three simple terms to describe the ragtime approach to ornamentation— "making variations," "adding," and "filling in." Since the terms "variations" and "ragtime" each have their place in literate traditions, it has been easy to miss the point that, for the New Orleanians, making variations was the direct continuation of the plantation tradition of ragging the tune. Perhaps they knew about the classical tradition; that is certainly possible, but it is more important to realize that African Americans had a longstanding tradition of their own to build upon. What was heard from the dance bands that continued the plantation tradition was certainly close to the crooks, turns, slurs, and appoggiaturas, the common stock of church heterophony that the observer of congregational singing heard in 1863 (Chapter 2). "Filling in" and "adding" have obvious meanings, terms coined as direct descriptions of practice.

When filling in and adding take over, and when allegiance to the preexistent tune recedes, then the musician stands as an inventor. "Invent" is the verb the New Orleanians typically used to describe what is now called "improvisation." More than a few were good at both ragging a tune and inventing. Inventing probably dates all the way back through slavery, as hinted in reports like this: "I have heard Negroes change a well-known melody by adroitly syncopating it . . . so as to give it a *bizarre* effect scarcely imaginable; and nothing illustrates the Negro's natural gifts in the way of keeping a difficult *tempo* more clearly than his perfect execution of airs thus transformed from simple to complex accentuations." So much is said in the word "bizarre" here. It must have included a sense that the creative contribution of the musician commanded attention at the expense of the simple air. The effect was, indeed, scarcely imaginable until it issued from the imagination of the slave musician.

When a group of musicians makes variations, adds, and fills in, they produce collective improvisation. One model for that technique was sung heterophony, as we saw in Chapter 2, which was almost certainly used in instrumental ensembles too. Once wind instruments were brought into the ragging tradition, which on the plantations had largely been limited to strings, there was more incentive to extend heterophony in the direction of polyphony. With the cornet, clarinet, and violin each able to command the melodic spotlight, there must have been some pressure to highlight their individuality. The winds also added timbral diversity, with each instrument easily distinguishable from one another as they veer off and articulate their independent layers.

During the post-Reconstruction decades, the plantation tradition of ragging the tune gathered momentum around the river corridor and diverged in two directions, each associated with a city. One was located just beyond the northern tip of the South, the other at its southern tip. St. Louis became a publication center for compositions created by pianists, while New Orleans gained distinction for group improvisation on wind instruments. The piano offers complete control of harmony, thus facilitating composition, just as it always has in the European classical tradition. Wind instruments, with their ability to create vocal effects and with enhanced possibilities for timbral distinction, offered new possibilities for the practice of ragging the tune, now mixed into a diverse professional scene.

Through sheet music and piano rolls, the compositional tradition reached national popularity, which touched New Orleans as much

ugh that there was
ultural practices that
ny whites must have
elonged in the base-
confirmation of the
the New Orleans of
hurches, dance halls,
nd the public streets
s, others marched in
vided bursts of lively
trong's early musical
ommunity, gave him
of vernacular culture.
y African Americans,

n South, W. E. B. Du
ontact between whites
h to take a man by the
his eyes and feel his
a social cigar or a cup
lls and magazine arti-
equences of the almost
ween estranged races,
street cars." But the
exceptional? Du Bois
t hold uniformly, that
rmstrong this does not
ere were certainly no
rsal brotherhood. As a
some white playmates
t of the whites he knew
, Italians, and Jews.
s with whites was sub-
ription of the southern
y one public relation of
bitrarily and unlawfully
e attitude of an alien, a

as anywhere. Musicians now regarded *Maple Leaf Rag* and other popular hits of the day just as ragging musicians always had—as material to rag. The New Orleanian approach to ragging the tune, having nothing to do with sheet music and everything to do with performers who assert control through a set of performance practices, gained national popularity much later, when phonograph companies decided to explore the vernacular market. Armstrong soaked up the practice during his years of apprenticeship and he never abandoned it. He was still ragging tunes some fifty years later, in his famous rendition of the song *Hello Dolly*.

There is a bit of overgeneralization in this north-south portrayal, but it clarifies the most salient dynamics of the period. Buddy Bolden rode the crest of several waves at once. He and his uptown colleagues brought wind instruments to the plantation traditions of blues and ragging the tune. He was probably good at integrating the national style of Ragtime with the plantation practice of ragging. And he skillfully infused that mix with a potent array of class markers. As Kid Ory said, "You have to give [Bolden] credit for starting the ball rolling."

❧ A lot happened in the ten years or so between Bolden's exit from the scene and Armstrong's first professional efforts. There was still much more of the vernacular tradition to bring into dance music. Practices were developed, refined, combined, redirected, and invented, under pressure from an array of social determinants— plantation ancestry, migratory optimism, urban sophistication, class differentiation, and more. There was also more to learn of Eurocentric practices, which were in the hands of people of color and thus constantly within earshot of Armstrong. Not just any people of color, but a group who considered themselves special and distinct. The Creoles loomed large on the scene, not least because they held advantages in the market of professional music making. If Armstrong was going to be a professional musician, he could not avoid them. One of the main tasks of his teenage years would be to learn some of their ways and learn how to deal with them.

CHAPTER EIGHT

"Most of the musicia
were Creoles"

Most of the musicians were Creoles. Most of
them could pass for white easily—They mostly
lived in the Down Town part of New
Orleans, called the Creole Section. Most of
them were also good Sight Readers. They had
Small Bands. The same as we call Combos'
today. They went a lot of places with ease,
because of their light skin. Places we Dark
Skinned Cats wouldn't Dare to peep in.
                                    —Louis Armstrong

The Downtown boys, the Creoles, thought
they were better than anybody else and
wouldn't hire the Uptown boys.
                                    —Pops Foster

From where Armstrong stood, it looked like the Creoles, livin
the other side of Canal Street and mostly in the di
Ward, dominated the musical scene. Pops Foster expl:
were able to sustain their musical domination by e:
Uptown boys," by which he meant Negroes like
Armstrong who lived on the uptown side of Canal S
situation was not hopeless. Oliver, for one, showed wh
ble when he started playing with the Creoles and b
well," as Bunk Johnson phrased it.

Armstrong thought of New Orleans as made up o:
social groups—whites, Creoles, and Negroes. This trip

In fact, the strategy was working well en
really no reason to regulate African-American c
flourished independently of white control. Ma
heard "rough" vernacular music—music that b
ment of the "mansion of the muses"—as soni
inferior status of blacks. Our journey through
Armstrong's youth has taken us to storefront c
honky tonks, a home for juvenile delinquents,
where men collected scraps and blew tinhorr
parades and funeral rituals, and still others pr
entertainment on advertising wagons. Arms
experiences, largely shaped within his own c
concentrated exposure to the entire spectrum
For the most part, this activity was controlled l
and whites had little to do with it.

On his tour through the post-Reconstructic
Bois found a disheartening retreat in social c
and blacks: "In a world where it means so mud
hand and sit beside him, to look frankly int
heart beating with red blood; in a world where
of tea together means more than legislative h
cles and speeches,—one can imagine the cons
utter absence of such social amenities bet
whose separation extends even to parks an
legend begs to differ: wasn't New Orleans
acknowledged that his sad picture might no
there could be pockets of interaction. For A
appear to have been the case. For him th
friendly cigars, no relaxed celebrations of univ
child he did play cowboys and Indians with
("We were the Indians," he dryly noted). Mo
belonged to the despised groups, the Chinese

The main quality of Armstrong's relation
servience. George Washington Cable's desc
situation in 1885 still held: "There is scarce
life in the South where the [black] is not a:
compelled to hold toward the white man th

menial, and a probably reprobate, by reason of his race and color."
Social distance was encoded in various ways, some obvious and
some subtle. His mother worked as a domestic for Henry Matranga
("an Italian white boy," Armstrong called him), who owned a honky
tonk. She sometimes fed Louis spaghetti in the kitchen, and he
remembered how the family "enjoyed seeing me eat." Matranga
hired an African American to manage his honky tonk. "Knowing
how sensitive my people are, especially when a white person shout
at them, he just left everything up to 'Slippers,' the manager of the
joint," wrote Armstrong, "which made it operate much better." That
kind of alliance worked both ways. Slippers gave Armstrong some
advice that he liked to recall as a colorful, homespun anecdote late
in life: "Always have a *White Man* who likes you and can and will
put his Hand on your shoulder and say—'*This is My Nigger*' and,
Can't Nobody Harm Ya."

Armstrong's manager Joe Glaser with hand on Armstrong's
shoulder (Courtesy of the Louis Armstrong House and Archives
at Queens College/CUNY)

Such an alliance, formed between his father and his father's white boss, was enough to get Louis out of the Colored Waif's Home for Boys, but it was not there when his mother's side of the family needed it a few years later. His cousin Flora Miles gave birth as a young teenager to a baby whose father was "an old white fellow by the name of Hatfield." Flora died shortly after the birth, Hatfield disappeared, and within a couple of years Armstrong himself was taking care of the child with his wife Daisy. "Everybody was telling old man Ike Miles, Flora's father, to have Hatfield arrested," Armstrong wrote. "But that did not make sense at all . . . Hatfield was a white man, and the judge would have thrown us all out in the streets, including Clarence the baby." Clarence suffered brain damage from an accident and required special care. He took the last name Armstrong and Louis supported him for the rest of his life.

In the large context, New Orleans may have been exceptional in the degree of relaxation that characterized relations between "races," but the large-context view was not Armstrong's. He grew up in the wake of one of the bloodiest race riots against blacks in the history of the country, in the face of violent threats and intimidation, and with the burden of taking care of a child who was the product of a white man's statutory rape of his cousin. He learned how to act in a way that confirmed his role as social inferior, how to perform that role daily through "yes sirs" and "yes ma'ms," stepping aside on the sidewalk, and avoiding eye contact. Survival meant understanding what whites were willing to do to defend, as Danny Barker put it, the "Great White South's Perpetual Proclamation: 'Ouah Way of Life.'" Armstrong made his peace with the situation and used his psychological nimbleness—the same nimbleness that so beautifully shapes his music and stage gestures—to negotiate a dangerous world. These skills served him well, both on stage and off, for his entire life.

Of course, whites routinely patronized black bands. Willie Hightower remembered getting hired for a house party near Audubon Park. He proudly dressed his band in new white uniforms, with white duck pants, cap, and canvas shoes, topped by the splendor of a blue blazer. He was stunned when the band's sartorial dignity was not received positively. "I'll tell you, what got the most of the white people," he said. "The most of the white people in New Orleans they had never seen Negroes dress up in white." Pops Foster said that whites didn't care what the musicians played, and the implication is that they regarded music as a dash of atmosphere, with appearance mattering more than sound. Several musicians explained that whites preferred to hire black musicians for parties because they knew how to disappear during breaks, in contrast to white musicians, who liked to mingle with the guests. For Armstrong, steady exposure to white audiences came only with his jobs on the riverboats, beginning in 1918. He certainly did not know any white musicians in New Orleans, and he rarely heard them play.

His eventual turn to white audiences had an impact, but for the most part whites were irrelevant to his musical upbringing until those last few years. There is no evidence that the ideological program that placed black vernacular music in the basement of the mansion of the muses had any direct impact on him. He was eventually motivated to master music marked as white because he recognized that doing so would open up better opportunities. But until then, he seems to have been happily situated within the vernacular tradition where white values and opinions did not matter.

The Creoles, however, were hardly irrelevant. To the contrary, they were unavoidable. To understand who they were and why they acted as they did, it is necessary to go back a bit into their unusual history.

Gens de Couleur Libres

That history began from the moment African slaves arrived in Louisiana. As is well known, the early French settlers were not troubled by the idea of partnering up with "other" types of women. They had before them the example of the French Canadians, who, according to the "one blood" theory advanced by the government as an extension of French mercantile policy, were encouraged to select women from the native population. The settlers were advised to intermarry with the heathens and "gently polish" them, gradually turning them into French people. The goal was to bring the colonized population into French culture rather than push them away, as the English tended to do.

And so it was that the first presiding cleric in Louisiana, newly arrived from the Canadian settlements, could proclaim, "The blood of the savages does no harm to the blood of the French." The isolated settlers in Louisiana found it pleasing to agree. This miscegenational impulse eventually led to the institution of *plaçage*, a contractualized form of adultery between Frenchmen and women of French and African ancestry that would inspire great flights of eroticized imagination throughout the nation. From antebellum *plaçage* it was but a short step to the legendary Storyville, the greatest prostitution district in the world outside of Paris, in Jelly Roll Morton's estimation, where women of mixed ancestry, French and African, were highly prized—"first class Octoroons," ran the advertisements—and where many musicians earned a lot of money.

When Frenchmen granted or bought freedom for their offspring of slave mistresses, those offspring were classified as neither white nor slaves but as *gens de couleur libres*. The category was a legal one. It granted rights to own property, slaves, and weapons, and it determined the field of marriage possibilities—that is, with other *gens de couleur libres*. It was possible for a full-blooded African to gain this legal status, but in social parlance it came to designate people of mixed ancestry, French and African. Many of the Creole musicians Armstrong knew could trace their ancestry back to the *gens de couleur libres*. As the Louisiana colony was transferred to Spain and then back to France during the years 1768 through 1803, the pattern continued: French and Spanish mixed easily together, and both mixed with slaves and with the *gens de couleur libres*.

These arrangements were interrupted by the American purchase of the Louisiana Territory in 1803. Signs of French-American tension surfaced quickly. In 1804, for example, the manager of an opera house admonished patrons that the orchestra would make every effort to play the various national anthems whenever possible and that it was not necessary to holler and fight about the matter. In the decades after the American purchase, the capitalized Americans, expanding on the uptown side of Canal Street, enjoyed extensive and visible prosperity, their material success creating a glaring contrast with downtown stagnation and adding fuel to the cultural tensions already in place. Tension rose to such a degree that the city was partitioned between 1836 and 1852 into three districts, each with its own mayor, two on the downriver side of Canal Street and one on the upriver side.

It was during this period that the term "Creole" became important. Earlier the word had been used casually and not very often as a category for native-born people of foreign ancestry. Now it symbolized precedence, a sense of belonging, a historic claim to the city long predating the money-grubbing, poorly mannered Americans. Without hesitation, "Creole" included both whites and *gens de couleur libres* during this period. The Creoles, white and free colored, had every incentive to stick together, cousin with cousin, Frenchman with Frenchman, opera lover with opera lover, as a proud group slipping in political strength. The phrase "Creole of color" belongs mainly to a later period; in antebellum New Orleans, they were all simply Creoles. The population of *gens de couleur libres* in the 1860 census, the last that would ever include the category, counted out to 10,689.

After the Civil War the *gens de couleur libres* found themselves in a strong position. Their qualifications for leadership were obvious: 88 percent of Negro voters (76,000 out of 86,000) in Louisiana were illiterate (by an 1870 count); in contrast, 90 percent of the free colored population in New Orleans were literate (by an 1860 count). Some of them articulated a political vision of broad inclusiveness, a sense that actions were being taken on behalf of the freedmen on the plantations as much as the colored property owners downtown. The famous court case *Plessy vs. Ferguson*, adjudicated by the Supreme Court in 1896, is an example of this inclusive vision. Homer Plessy, a Creole of color, did not need to force the issue of whether or not Jim Crow could regulate where he sat on the train. Since he easily passed for white, he could sit anywhere he wanted to. The whole point of the action was that he had to proclaim his identity to the conductor, who would not have noticed him otherwise; the absurdity of the law would then be apparent to everyone in court. Plessy and his group could not have imagined that the momentum behind Jim Crow would be strong enough to sustain it for a good seventy years.

The fierce southern backlash against Reconstruction included a direct attack on the historic position of the *gens de couleur libres*. Uptown Americans had long been stirring mischief by observing that more than a few Creoles—perhaps *all* of them, came the occasional uptown sling—were tainted by a "touch of the tarbrush." There they were, on the other side of Canal Street, sharing last names and so much else. With the collapse of Reconstruction, the accusation was potent enough to inspire white Creoles to align themselves with white Americans. White Creoles began to move from their historic downtown wards into distant uptown neighborhoods that were securely white. During the post-Reconstruction decades, the legal vestiges of the tripartite social structure were steadily eroding and being replaced with all-American, black-and-white duality.

It is in this context that we should read what seems to be a pattern of dissemblance about racial identity from the Creole musicians Armstrong knew. Isidore Barbarin (b. 1872) explained to an interviewer, "I didn't know I was colored until, I mean, well later years— I didn't know I was colored." Don Albert (b. Albert Dominique in 1909) was asked what a Creole is. He thought that "it is debatable," but, in his view, it is a "mixture of races, Indian, Philippino, Turk, Italian." Or listen to easygoing Barney Bigard (b. 1906) who, after acknowledging that both of his parents were Creoles of color, defined the term: "Creole of color . . . was essentially a mixture of Spanish and French." And then there is the infamous insistence of Jelly Roll Morton (b. Ferdinand Joseph Lamothe in 1890) that he had no African ancestry. Morton's denial has usually been read as a personal weakness for false self-representation. But even though Morton was incorrect, it is hard to be sure that he was lying. He could easily have been raised with the idea that he was French and only French.

Since Creole identity was a matter of trying to gain advantage in a turbulent and dangerous political world, it is easy to believe that Creole musicians might have grown up with no awareness of African ancestry. If you were Creole, you could not be colored; the fierce momentum was all in favor of making a clean distinction between the two. To be placed on the wrong side of the color line— in the wrong railroad car beginning in 1890, on the wrong side of voting rights beginning in 1898, in the wrong school, saloon, or mental institution beginning around 1900—was to be placed with people who had suffered severely under past structures of white supremacy. In 1938, a Creole of color framed the options this way: "When one brother could pass in olden times, he did; the other one, who could not, remained a Negro."

Yet, even though the Creoles of color found themselves on the wrong side of the color line, they still enjoyed pockets of special status. An older woman interviewed in the 1970s remembered filling out job applications that directed her to check one of three boxes labeled "W," "B," and "C." She could not bring herself to acknowledge the painful reality that "C" was an abbreviation for "colored," a vestige of the antebellum legal category *gens de couleur libres*. To the laughter of her son, who, like everyone else, knew exactly what it meant, she guessed that it stood for "Caucasian," or maybe "Creole." It is difficult to know how often Creoles of color like Morton, Barbarin, and Albert were trapped in similar self-delusion and how often they were simply brought up with a bleached narrative of their family history. This history of identity demonstrates why one does not want to fall into the present-day trap (more than one writer has so fallen) of calling the Creoles of color "African American": those are exactly the two things they were willfully not—African and American. The narrative of French descent formed the core of Creole identity, and it was powerfully reinforced by language, religion, and a whole array of cultural practices played out in the mundane worlds of home, work, and social relaxation.

The Creoles who dominated the music profession during Armstrong's youth were not the land-holding, well-educated artists and intellectuals, reading their plays and attending operas, in the manner of some of the more illustrious *gens de couleur libres* of the early nineteenth century. Most of the Creoles Armstrong knew had only a fifth-grade education. They may best be described as belonging to an artisan class. Many worked in trades that had been associated with the *gens de couleur libres*. For much of the nineteenth century, when the city was expanding in all directions, Creoles of color enjoyed good employment as carpenters, plasterers, bricklayers, and tinsmiths; in 1860, only 10 percent of the *gens de couleur libres* worked as common laborers. Of the Creoles Armstrong knew, Isidore Barbarin was a plasterer, Alphonse Picou and Manuel Perez were tinsmiths. Perez, George Fihle, and Barney Bigard rolled cigars, another occupation associated with the *gens de couleur libres*. The Creole-of-color sense of class position was very much tied to this profile of skilled labor, which distinguished them from the common-laboring Negroes uptown, just as their ancestors had been distinguished from slaves by caste position and type of work.

Music fit right in with this artisan-class position. The strong pedagogical program favored by the Creoles of color has already been described—the years of training in solfège, in the production of a uniform, attractive tone quality, in basic and advanced skills of instrumental technique, in music theory, and in flawless sight-reading. These skills could only be learned through years of tutorials, which were available only to those with the proper connections and family support. The results were widely noticed. "New Orleans is probably the only city in the United States that can boast of an orchestra, complete in all its details, composed entirely of colored men," was the claim of the *Weekly Louisianian* in 1877.

The history of the Tio family demonstrates these social-cultural patterns from the colonial period through early jazz. Armstrong may have played with Lorenzo Tio Jr. (1893–1933), a clarinetist who performed regularly with the premiere units in the city, including the Excelsior Brass Band, John Robichaux's orchestra, the Tuxedo Brass Band, and Armand Piron's orchestra, where his featured number was an arrangement of Liszt's *Liebestraum*.

Lorenzo Tio Jr. could trace his ancestry back to Marcos Tio, who was born in Catalonia and owned, in the 1790s, a tavern and importing business on what is now Decatur Street. Marcos Tio entered into a *plaçage* relationship with Victoire Wiltz, a free woman of color. Their progeny married other *gens de couleur libres* and settled into the expanding downtown community. Among the extended family was Louis Hazeur, a carpenter who played in a *gens de couleurs libres* militia band at the Battle of New Orleans. Marcos Tio's grandson Thomas Tio (1828–1881) played clarinet when he wasn't rolling cigars, and he was well connected within a strong musical network of *gens de couleur libres*.

Two of Thomas Tio's sons, Louis (1862–1922) and Lorenzo (1867–1908), became prominent clarinetists. By the late 1880s they were playing in the Excelsior Brass Band for dances, concerts, parades, picnics, and sporting events, dressed in uniforms resembling those of the Prussian military. Notice again the traditional trades: when they weren't making music, Louis rolled cigars and Lorenzo worked as a bricklayer. In 1887 Louis set his bricks aside and took off on a national tour with the Georgia Minstrels, headlined by the famous Billy Kersands. In 1889 the two brothers helped form the Lyre Musical Society, a Creole orchestra that met in members' homes and performed public concerts to raise money for scholarships. The society included George Baquet and Alphonse Picou. Louis and Lorenzo each gave lessons, and Lorenzo arranged and composed marches and dance music.

When, in the early years of the twentieth century, Louis Tio heard uptown ragtime approaching, he made a show of running into whatever house happened to be nearby: "Let me get under the bed. Listen to that, those fools just messing up good music." He gradually faded from the music profession and settled on rolling cigars, earning eight dollars per thousand. This piecework was not as bad as it might seem. You could work as hard and as long as you wanted to while hanging out with your buddies, smoking constantly and sipping whisky.

Lorenzo's son, Lorenzo Jr., received solfège lessons around the parlor piano at a young age and then took up clarinet. Each lesson had to be played perfectly before progressing to the next one. Family entertainment consisted of pulling out a piece of sheet music and playing through it together. As soon as he was old enough, Lorenzo's father and uncle brought him into their bands, where he impressed the other musicians with his sight-reading and sense of phrasing. Music was not always enough, however: in 1916, Lorenzo Jr. was listed in the city directory as a painter.

Several musicians who regularly played with the Tios were able to "pass" and play with white bands. Arnold Metoyer, Achille Baquet, and George Moret each had the right combination of appearance and skill. When Metoyer and Moret passed—and that is the word used in the oral histories—they did so only in a temporary sense, for a specific musical performance. After the performance, they returned to their Creole communities on the downtown side of Canal Street. Why were they recruited into white bands? There was only one reason: they were excellent musicians, far superior to the white musicians who recruited them and knew all about their solid grounding in European standards of musicianship. By passing, the Creole-of-color musicians were not trying to acquire a culture that they lacked. No, they were offering on a professional basis something that they were already good at and claimed as their own.

European standards of musicianship had been solidly part of the identity of Creoles of color for a long time. Now, in the repressive years of early Jim Crow, their control of this musical tradition received a special charge. Through musical technique everyone could hear that *they were not black*. Music was the most powerful form of cultural capital within reach of these painters, tinsmiths, plasterers, and cigar rollers. The attitude of the social group from which the musician temporarily passes would not have been hostility—the typical reaction toward *passé blanc*. It would have been pride, a matter of recognizing the status of the whole group, which excels in its skillful, craftsmanlike, Eurocentric work.

Clarinetist Achille Baquet went a step further and tried to "cross over" entirely. In the census of 1900 he and his brother George, also a clarinetist, were living in their father's house. By 1910 they were at separate addresses, and the census identified George as black, Achille as white. George always played in the traditional Creole-of-color bands, where Armstrong heard and admired him, but Achille ended up playing only in white bands, even though the white musicians "knew he was very bright," as Louis Keppard phrased it. The story took a dangerous turn when Achille demonstrated crying and whining freak techniques, apparently exposing his colored identity. "He went too far, I guess," was Keppard's view, in only partial sympathy.

Crossing Canal Street

"The lines between the separate sections of colored Society here, are distinctly marked," wrote an observer in 1864. "Very few French live above Canal St., very few Americans below it, and save politi-

*Canal Street, ca. 1900 (New Orleans Public Library,
photo by George François Mugnier)*

cally, they seldom affiliate." During Reconstruction, Creoles of color
who promoted a vision of political integration were working against
the traditional sense of separation from the lower caste that was
long ingrained in the *gens de couleur libres*. This was, of course, what
the caste system was all about, the definition of distinct social
spaces. It is easy to understand how, in New Orleans or anywhere
else, the middle caste feels the matter acutely.

The historic sense of middle-caste superiority continued long into
the Jim Crow era, when it was challenged from one direction by Jim
Crow legislation, which drew the color line badly for the Creoles
of color, and from another by the rush of impoverished freedmen
into the city. For more than a few people these were reasons
enough to heighten, not diminish, their distance from the former
slaves. Everyone knew how severely the plantation slaves had suffered. French New Orleans had its circumscribed traditions of tolerance and opportunity, but nothing like that was possible for the field
laborers on the huge and ruthless sugar and cotton plantations—or
at least that was how it seemed. The plantation slaves took the worst
that slavery had to offer, and now they were sitting next to Creoles of
color on the wrong side of the movable screen in trolley cars.

Manuel Manetta told a story about trombonist George Fihle that reveals the first thought many Creoles must have had about uptown Negroes. Manetta was versatile enough, both musically and socially, to work in both uptown and downtown circles. On a job at the new Tuxedo Dance Hall around 1913 with Fihle and several other Creoles, the band needed a substitute cornetist one day. Manetta suggested uptowner Oscar Celestin, but Fihle immediately objected, "We don't want the out of towners." Fihle says not uptown but *out* of town to put the worst possible spin on the situation. When Fihle thinks of uptown Negroes, he thinks of the recent immigrants and he does not like to think about having them in his band.

Understandably, some uptown Negroes—probably more than a few—returned the Creole disdain. Baby Dodds remembered how his mother forbade him when he was young to play with a Creole of color who happened to move into their uptown neighborhood: "Didn't want to have any parts of them. Now my people we were mixed with Indian, but we didn't want no parts of Creole talk . . . If our mother would catch us doing that she'd slap us in the mouth. Anytime we'd be caught playing with any Creole children, 'Come in here!' That's the way it was." Dodds eventually befriended a Creole who invited him to the downtown dance hall Francs Amis, where Dodds got a sense of what was driving his mother's irritation. The friend's skin was darker than Dodds's, but he was able to gain admission for both of them by speaking French. The girls refused to dance with Dodds until, once again, his friend spoke to them in French and asked them to be nice. The differences between uptown Negroes and downtown Creoles were in some ways, at some times, as marked as those between Negroes and whites. Frank Dusen, the rough trombonist who played with Bolden, got the nickname "Frenchman." The humor of this—on the same pitch that Jelly Roll Morton found when he teased the dark-skinned Oliver by calling him "Blondie"— derived from the fact that Dusen was so obviously not French.

It may seem natural to think of the distinction between uptown Negroes and downtown Creoles of color in terms of ethnicity, since some of the traditional markers that we consider ethnic were vividly in play. The incense burning at the baptism of Sidney Bechet, at

Saint Augustine's Church, certainly articulated the difference between Creoles and Negroes as much as anything. An ethnic analysis of the situation falters when we turn to music, however, for French music was not a terribly important part of the scene out of which jazz emerged. When Creole families met on Sunday afternoons at the invitation-only Autocrat Club, for example, they played symphonies for themselves, but it did not matter too much if the repertory was French or American. Cornetist Don Albert remembered the twenty-five to thirty musicians there playing "high-powered symphony numbers," by which he meant light classics such as overtures by Rossini and Donizetti. When Albert was eight years old, he made his singing debut at the Autocrat Club with the 1916 hit *Roses of Picardy*. The orchestra accompanying him included Lorenzo Tio Jr. Membership in the Autocrat Club was strictly "light complexion," Albert tells us. What these lightly complected Creoles of color were working hard to define with their music was not ethnic identity but something else. What was important was how the components of ethnicity hooked up with race, vestigial caste, class, and what is sometimes known as "color caste" or "pigmentocracy"—identifying people according to relative darkness and lightness of skin.

The vestiges of the tripartite, antebellum caste system created an ongoing social space of advantage for light-skinned descendants of the *gens de couleur libres*. It gave them access to a layer of service-based employment that was relatively lucrative and not usually available to Negroes. For example, it was directly responsible for the employment enjoyed by someone like Armand Piron, whose orchestra played regularly at the New Orleans Country Club, and by John Robichaux's orchestra too. Light-skinned Creole musicians enjoyed something of the same desirability that was directed toward the famous octoroon prostitutes. When brass instruments were first allowed to play in the Storyville district, around 1905, light-skinned Freddie Keppard and his Creole friends were in an excellent position to dominate the new and good-paying market. The situation was certainly not unique to New Orleans. But light-skinned hiring biases there had an elaborate social history that was active on the musical scene in ways that are probably not yet fully understood.

Vestiges of tripartite caste were entangled with distinctions of class, as defined by occupation. Most uptown Negroes worked as unskilled laborers in jobs ranging from dock work to shoveling coal—both jobs held by Armstrong in his teens. Women did domestic work, cooking, cleaning, and laundering. Pimping and prostitution offered a way out of the cycle of drudgery and low wages. Creoles of color preferred not to have their women work; if they did work, they usually did so secretly, in the home. Creole men followed the traditional trades of the *gens de couleur libres*. The boundary between skilled artisan and unskilled laborer had, in ante-bellum days, marked the difference between freedom and slavery, and it did not disappear after the Civil War. With the stability of the old caste system gone and with legal structures and social positions shifting, this boundary was still important; it is interesting to think about how it played out musically.

The descendants of the *gens de couleur libres*, alerted from their cozy neighborhoods of security to the news that they were now colored in a dangerous way, must have keenly felt the potential of using cultural practices to support some social advantage. In his class-based study of cultural distinctions in France, Pierre Bourdieu identifies music used in this way as a matter of repertories. Perhaps the Creoles sang French songs with a sense that they were performing a cultural legacy that could not possibly be matched by the immigrants on the other side of Canal Street. They may have listened to a French opera now and then, but opera is rarely mentioned in the oral histories, and it is likely that most of the cigar-rolling and plastering musicians Armstrong knew from downtown never heard one. No, Creoles like Barbarin and Perez were happy playing *Roses of Picardy* or the latest Sousa march.

I doubt that they found any sense of social superiority in the march, per se. Cultural capital did not accrue from a given set of pieces but rather from a set of *techniques*—skillful command of the instrument, a big round tone, precise intonation and ensemble work, fluency in musical notation, and so forth. To play with polished technique was very much like working a trade, and it must have positioned the Creoles relative to the uptown roughians in just the same way that their trade skills positioned them relative to unskilled labor. The "profits" yielded by musical technique are social distinction, the confirmation of one's legitimate (that is, sought-after) place in society, surely a serious matter for the Creoles, under siege as they were by the Jim Crow laws that were moving toward them like flood waters.

Their artisan-class position explains the high Creole regard for uniformity and precision as well as their intense preoccupation with the transmission of craft to each new generation. Class identity is defined not through a repertory but through the *production* of sound. And thus one finds the repeated Creole complaints about the uptown musicians: their lack of technique, their lack of note-reading ability, their rough sound. If the unskilled laborers took pride in playing loudly as a manifestation of physical strength, that class distinction simply confirmed the difference that was, in turn, the primary concern of the Creoles.

"Listen to that, those fools just messing up good music," said Louis Tio when he heard uptown ragtime. They messed it up by playing forceful, random dissonances—the dissonances that are not to be ironed out, according to Zora Neale Hurston. By deviating from standardized intonation in order to bend pitch and create blue notes—the strongest notes you can play, according to Pops Foster. By manipulating timbre to create a freakish array of vocalizing effects—the effects that made Joe Oliver's cornet sound like a Holy Roller meeting, according to Mutt Carey. And by adding to and filling in around the given melody in order to create rhythmic vigor and the polyphony of collective improvisation, thus energizing the second line, which brought the ring shout into the streets.

The Creoles were not interested in adding to a given musical text. No, the job of the artisan musician was to perform that text as precisely as a bricklayer follows the dimensions of a house. Louis Tio had a nasty way of embarrassing musicians who played wrong notes. "And he'd say to the guy, 'What's the matter? You keep making the same damn bad note," remembered Barney Bigard. "Can't you see it?'" How different the attitude was from the relaxed sense of accommodation, the value placed on *willingness* (Armstrong, Chapter 2) to engage passionately within a space where you can play "just whatever come in your head." All those lessons in solfège were designed not simply to improve the student's hearing; they *trained* the ear to follow a rigid system of Eurocentric musical syntax. Bent blue notes and stray dissonance were simply mistakes. Uniformity in timbre, in intonation, in ensemble, and in the syntax of pitch was the way toward craftsmanlike perfection.

When Tio and the Creoles heard rough uptown musicians, they heard lack of skill, which they took as a marker of a downtrodden class, the ratty people. They heard an inability to control passion and aggression, which also manifested through promiscuity and problems with the law. An artisan-class Creole took charge of his instrument, not the other way around. The uninhibited rituals of the uptown Saints, which brought emotions out to the moving surface of life, were incomprehensible from this perspective.

Even passive resistance to Jim Crow could mark the boundary of Canal Street. The seating screen on trolley cars was supposed to be moved up and back, depending on how full the white and black sections were. That simple practicality opened the door to passive resistance. A light-skinned Creole boy told of sitting two rows back, with an empty row between him and the screen and then another empty row behind him. As the white section filled, whites boarding the car asked him to move back a row in order to open up their section, but he pretended not to hear, leaving them to surmise that he was either deaf or stupid. Armstrong remembered how the "colored people used to get their real kicks out of those cars whenever a whole flock of them get on at the picnic grounds, or at Canal Street, some Sunday evenings, and the colored folks would outnumber the white folks . . . the colored folks automatically takes the car over . . . My, my, it certainly would feel good to sit up there once and a while." Moments like this brought the resisting community together. Yet they were also moments that articulated division within that community, for this kind of behavior was a bit aggressive, something only lower-class dark-skinned people would do, according to one Creole of color.

Did their dark skin also make it difficult for Oliver and Armstrong to cross Canal Street and make good with the Creoles? The evidence for social hierarchies based on relative lightness and darkness of skin is sketchy and sometimes contradictory. It is not a topic that is usually discussed freely, yet it has a pervasive history in the United States. The end result of our story was that the dark-skinned Oliver *did* eventually play with Perez, who could pass as white and whom Armstrong described as "a waltz and schottische king from downtown 7th ward, known as a *Stompdown Creole* (meaning) a *full blooded* Creole—better than black." ("Full blooded Creole" is a fascinating concept, a contradiction of terms yet completely appropriate to the situation.) Yet, it is impossible to dismiss the significance of color from the dynamics of a period when color could be a matter of life or death.

A fifteen-year-old girl, interviewed in 1938, explained that "there are some nice dark people but most of them are low-down, mean, and rough." Many Creoles discouraged their children from dating people with darker skin, since a marriage meant dragging the whole family more deeply onto the wrong side of the color line. Parents regulated the mating of their children at light-skinned venues like the Francs Amis dance hall, where dark-skinned musicians were usually forbidden to play; if they did manage to get hired, they had to stay on the bandstand during intermission while their lighter-skinned colleagues went to fetch drinks. The fear of dark-skinned

Francs Amis Hall (Historic New Orleans Collection,
Acc. No. 92–48–L MSS 520 f. 902, photo by William Russell)

contamination of the gene pool that so obviously surfaced at a place like this was simply an extension of the bedrock legal principle of the old tripartite caste system: do not marry outside of your caste.

It was always possible to construct a situational pigmentocracy on the spot. Dark skin was taken as a signifier of poverty, inferiority, criminality, illiteracy, and all the projections habitually associated with caste, class, race, and a different social history. When the Creoles saw scruffy Little Louis carrying his beat-up cornet in a paper bag and stepping up as a called-in substitute, this is what they saw. Even if you were a Creole who spoke fluent French and had a good business, dark skin could be a lethal liability. In the rioting and destruction that followed the Robert Charles shootout, Louis Keppard's father did not have a problem because he was "kind of bright." Less lucky was Big Eye Louis Nelson's father, who was murdered on his nightly trip out to buy meat for his butcher stall at the French Market. Nelson, born Louis Delisle, had relatively dark skin and his father did too, presumably. Nelson's father was simply in the wrong place at the wrong time with the wrong color of skin. Being an integrated member of downtown Creole society, being fluent in French, having an established business—none of that could help when it came to "Nigger hunting time" and his entire existence was categorized and destroyed on the basis of pigmentation.

The nonlethal liabilities of dark skin could be subtler and therefore difficult to detect from the distance of a century. Jelly Roll Morton, who, with his fascinating mix of braggadocio, keen observation, and high musicality, is always someone to pay attention to, said that Armstrong was never in Keppard's class. Outside of Morton's range of hearing, Johnny St. Cyr tells us that "when you come darker than Keppard, you didn't score with the mulattos at all," while Morton's wife Mabel reports that "Jelly didn't like Negroes—he always said they would mess up your business." Yet Morton admired Oliver's music, even while teasing him with the nickname "Blondie," as if to make clear where everyone stood.

Emile Barnes acknowledged that musicians on the two sides of Canal Street would "be friends and all, but you know like distant friends." Jazz musicians for years to come were often ahead on the path toward integration, so it is not surprising, ultimately, that there was strategic mixing across Canal Street. But the distance Barnes noticed was part of the social-musical equation. Danny Barker idolized cornetist Chris Kelly and wanted desperately to play in his band, but in his case the barrier of Canal Street—now working in the opposite direction—was a brick wall: "the cats in his band would say, 'He shouldn't play with us. He's from another caste.'" Conversely, George Lewis found that some "Creole bands wouldn't hire a man whose hair wasn't silky."

The social-musical rivalry between Creoles and Negroes was not one-dimensional, it was not universal, and it was not inescapable. Nevertheless, at any given moment it could *seem* all of these things. All the different dimensions of the conflict between the two groups could reduce to a single, unalterable marker—relative lightness and darkness of skin. From where Preston Jackson stood, in the Twelfth Ward in the Garden district where there was a mix of people, light and dark, it looked like the downtown Creoles were all light-skinned; in his experience, they let darker people know that they felt superior. The point of the reduction was to revive the tripartite caste system: you could learn a new kind of music, you could learn French, but you could not change the color of your skin. Joe Oliver could play everything from waltzes to marches to schottisches, and he even spoke a bit of French. He himself made fun of his dark skin, but he could also fall into despair about it. Clyde Bernhardt believed that Oliver "had an inferiority complex." He remembered Oliver saying, "Goddamn, they only invite this black, ugly nigger to parties 'cause they know they get the whole damn band to come."

When Armstrong moved to New York City in the mid-1920s, he was not surprised to notice favored "pets" in the Fletcher Henderson band, which he related to his experience with color bias in New Orleans. "That shit would always come out when I was in school," he said. "I'd see the teachers going wild over some dogass stupid child don't even want to study his lesson—if you got straight hair or something." As a child he had a crush on Mrs. Martin's daughter Wilhelmenia, "real light skinned, on the same order as the Creole type," but he couldn't talk to her: "I had a sort of inferiority complex . . . I felt that I wasn't good enough for her." In a late memoir he wrote bitterly about Jelly Roll Morton and the advantages light skin opened up for him with jobs in the best-paying houses of prostitution. "They did not want a Black piano player for the job," he wrote, and even though he would have been too young to have any first-hand knowledge, one can sense the emotional truth that defined his position. There were exceptions to that rule, but when you saw things from the other side of Canal Street, from the perspective of living out the disadvantages and dangers of having dark skin, the stray exception did not matter much.

Crossing without Assimilating

The first essential social movement that led to early jazz was the immigration of some forty thousand freedmen from the plantations into New Orleans. The second involved a handful of musicians from within that group, Oliver and Armstrong being the most famous, who found a way to cross Canal Street and play with the Creoles. Before 1900, Creole and Negro musicians rarely played together. By 1920, not only Oliver and Armstrong but also Pops Foster and a good number of other uptowners had played in bands with Creoles. As Hypolite Charles bluntly commented, "Sometimes we used to mix the Protestants in . . . sometimes we couldn't get musicians and we used anybody we could get." Baby Dodds has already identified for us the main qualification for crossing Canal Street on a more regular basis: "the [uptown and downtown] musicians mixed only if you were good enough."

The Creoles had cherished Eurocentric assimilation for more than a century within the social structure of a powerful caste system and its vestigial effects. Given that situation, it seems unlikely that they could have done much to create jazz. The sense of categorical identity—a learned definition of one's social group that extends beyond the boundaries of any single person's experience—was so strong, and the cultural trappings that served that identity so entrenched, that cultural innovation was difficult. They worked hard to give the impression of a static, tradition-bound culture: they had to socially exclude, to make false claims of ancestry, to ignore similarities and exaggerate differences, and to intensively train their children in traditional pedagogy.

With the class-based values of Eurocentric technique and the racialized values of white cultural assimilation working together, there could not have been much incentive to break open the seams of musical style and explore new possibilities. The momentum worked in the other direction, toward acquisition of the status quo and being able to play it better than anyone else. The arguments for a substantial contribution from the Creoles in the creation of jazz are based partly on mistaken notions about the role of Latin dance rhythms that found their way into Creole circles and partly on the role that many Creoles eventually did play jazz. But it must have been difficult, initially, for Creoles to learn black vernacular music. Many of them were even forbidden to second line or to buy tickets into Lincoln and Johnson parks, where Bolden played; "Creoles didn't want their children in such places," drummer Joe René said. And they obviously did not grow up in the Sanctified Church or on the streets with the ragmen, surrounded by blues.

Oliver and Armstrong *crossed* Canal Street to play with the Creoles, and some Creoles *passed* into white society, temporarily, for a musical gig, or permanently, leaving friends and family behind. Crossing and passing have something in common—the aim of the musician to join a socially advantaged group. The differences, however, are more important. Creoles who passed could do so first of all because they looked white, second because they already possessed the culture of the advantaged group. Before they tried to cross Canal Street, Oliver and Armstrong were immersed in uptown vernacular values, the music of church and blues and plantation ragging, and they had to work long and hard to put themselves in a position where they could even think about playing with the Creoles. Were they trying to *become* Creoles culturally when they did that? It is an important question to address, even if there is no way to get inside the minds of those who lived a century ago.

My sense is that they were not trying to do that at all. While Creoles were trying to use the cultural capital of Eurocentric music to rescue a social position that was slipping away, the situation for uptown Negroes was very different. Yes, there were assimilative Negroes who accepted the idea that vernacular music belonged in the social-cultural basement where they had no intention of residing.

But in New Orleans they were outnumbered. A critical mass of people who stubbornly asserted vernacular practice found in the new music expressive depth, communal nurturing, and symbolic resistance to the system of social subordination—a public, aural statement that they were just fine as they were, that they were not inferior. "Nice lesson for them," Armstrong said to Ory (Chapter 1) when the two of them showed John Robichaux and his Creole hires how to swing, and it must have been a very satisfying moment indeed.

The relaxed space of inclusiveness that characterized early jazz allowed it to be a music that, in historian Eric Hobsbawm's words, "speaks directly from and to the ordinary untrained man or woman . . . and which, by virtue of this directness is a standing protest against the cultural and social orthodoxies from which it is so sharply distinct." The long-distance blasts of Bolden's cornet, the in-your-face shaking by the kitchen mechanics to Chris Kelly's blues that so irritated the Creoles, the second-line antics in parades that drove Manuel Perez out of town—these gestures proclaimed who the music belonged to, how different it was, and how it could be used symbolically in social conflicts. If Sanctified religion was a political act as much as it was a religious act (Chapter 2), then how much more true that was for the second-line parades, which took the ring shout into the streets. Here was the musical equivalent of a boxing victory by Jack Johnson over the "Great White Hope" or a passive takeover of a trolley car, a victory over the artisan Creoles, the French-speaking light-skins who could read music fluently and had the best jobs sewn up.

To cross Canal Street required tremendous determination. But that energy was conditioned by the economic drive to make more money in a layered marketplace, not by the ideological drive of cultural assimilation. In order to get the best jobs there were certain things that had to be done. With less ideological engagement, the approach to Eurocentric musical material was less rigid and more flexible, thus opening the door to innovation.

Had it been otherwise—had Armstrong been told from birth to speak proper English, to bleach his skin and straighten his hair, to sit still in church rather than to move around, to look and act like a white person and turn his back on the music of the vernacular basement—his music would have turned out very differently. He saw from Oliver what could be gained by crossing Canal Street. But it took him a long time to adapt, probably because he refused to let go of the vernacular values he had learned during childhood. The identity Armstrong was after was not white or Creole but that of the black, professional, uptown musician, exemplified by Oliver, and this meant being able to master more than one style. There is always this puzzle at the core of analyzing music and its social context: on the one hand, music does a lot of work forming social identity; on the other, musicians learn how to convincingly perform a variety of musical identities, giving up one for the other with ease. This is especially true for popular musicians in the United States, and even truer for African-American musicians. The musician learns to be an identity magician, pulling social signifiers out of his or her horn and energizing them with emotional power. Armstrong learned to do this without buying into the alternative project of using music as a form of cultural capital.

Creole Rebels

The Creoles were led into uptown ragtime by a few stray rebels. Big Eye Louis Nelson (b. 1885) may well have been the first. Uptowners like Armstrong and Foster thought of the musical scene in dualistic terms—uptown and downtown, Protestants and Catholics, dark skin and light skin, former slaves and former *gens de couleur libres*. But Creole society was not quite so monolithic. In 1900 it included, for example, people who had been enslaved downtown and simply stayed right where they were after emancipation. They were Catholic, knew French, and in many cases were related to the *gens de couleur libres*, so it was not that difficult for them to blend in and, after several generations, count themselves as Creoles. The downtown population was not homogeneously *ancien* either. Nelson's father moved to the Seventh Ward immediately after emancipation, in the first wave of fifteen thousand plantation-to-city immigrants. His son Louis started out musically on his father's accordion and then took lessons on the violin. But he did not have the temperament for the slow-moving pedagogy of his teacher. "After four or five months, I got disgusted," Nelson remembered. "He just had me *holding* the violin, hadn't let me pull the bow across the strings one time!"

Where was a Creole boy to go if he didn't have patience for the long, systematic lessons his teacher put in front of him? If he was fifteen-year-old Louis Nelson, he wandered toward Canal Street, to the edge of the American section, and hung out at the Big 25, a gambling house for Negroes that was also becoming a hangout for musicians. He brought along his violin, and Charley Payton, leader of the house band, invited him to sit in. Payton was an accordion and string player from Alabama. He is remembered as having the premier ragtime band at the time, with a specialty in blues; Jelly Roll Morton said that he played "a very lowdown type of quadrille for the low class dance halls." Frustrated with the legitimate route of the Creoles, young Big Eye Louis took a jump-in-and-learn-to-swim tour of the plantation tradition of ragging the tune. He found uptowners to be more relaxed than the Creoles, more sociable and inclusive.

The Seventh Ward Creole neighborhood where Nelson lived was chock full of clarinetists; Picou and the Tios all lived close by. Nelson eventually took up the clarinet, had some lessons with Lorenzo Tio Sr., and learned enough technique—though not chord formation or reading skills—to become a sought-after player in the emerging ragtime market. He was good at freak music. And he was good at playing fast and making variations; he often played the lead melody on his *C* clarinet. He was improvisationally inventive. "Big Eye Louis Nelson was the best ragtime clarinet player we had down there. He was strictly a jazz clarinet player . . . the greatest clarinet player I ever played with," said Pops Foster.

Following Nelson's footsteps was the slightly younger Freddie Keppard (b. 1889). Like Nelson, Keppard started out on violin; he then changed to cornet in the wake of Bolden's success. And like Nelson, Keppard bucked the Creole tradition and refused to learn musical notation, relying on his excellent ear instead. His brother Louis framed in an interesting way the connection between Big Eye Louis and Freddie, both of whom performed a kind of reverse crossing of Canal Street: "When he [Freddie] went away, like Louis [Nelson], he learned more ways . . . Freddie never did learn the music here." There are some indications that Keppard was particularly obnoxious to uptown Negroes, even though—or perhaps because—he was obviously indebted to their music. He became the leading Creole cornetist of his generation to participate in the uptown excitement, which the Creoles could appreciate more easily when it was performed by a musician with lighter skin (St. Cyr: "when you come darker than Keppard, you didn't score with the mulattos at all"), and with adjustments of style and technique that were clear to everyone at the time yet difficult to identify precisely a century later.

An interesting witness to Keppard's style is white cornetist Johnny Wiggs, who described two different cornet styles during the 1910s, one associated with Keppard, the other with Oliver. Keppard's playing was "ricky-tick," a "corny" kind of "imitation jazz." Oliver, on the other hand, had a "hot, lush style" that reminded Wiggs of the rags-bones-and-bottle men playing their tinhorns on the streets. Oliver routinely bent pitches one-half tone or more. Keppard probably played in a clipped melodic idiom, in 2/4 rather than the less restrictive 4/4 Oliver was building on. What could be read on the downtown side of Canal Street as a Creole adaptation of the uptown style—a civilization of it, they might have thought—was necessarily a move away from the deep blues tradition.

Louis Keppard offered a Creole perspective: Oliver was "too big" to play cornet, he said, which caused him to play out of tune. Oliver would have been more successful as a tuba player, Louis believed. Baby Dodds said that Keppard "had a style that most of the Creole fellows played in New Orleans," which may be an indication of how widely he was imitated. Wiggs first heard Oliver at Tulane gymnasium dances in 1917, with his uptown band of Ory, Johnny Dodds, and Red Happy Bolton. "It sounded like heaven" to the open-eared teenager. What is clear from these reports is that the distinction between uptown and downtown was still audible even after downtown musicians caught on to improvising, which, lest one forget, can be practiced in many different styles. Zutty Singleton talked about the downtown-uptown comparison, describing the uptown style as "bigger." "All the white boys were influenced by the downtown gang," said Singleton. Armstrong was once asked about uptown-downtown differences and he diplomatically answered,

"Little differences—tone, phrasing and imaginations," which may well have been his way of saying that the differences were *more* than little.

Big Eye Louis Nelson was followed even more directly by Sidney Bechet (b. 1897) in the sense that Nelson was Bechet's stylistic model and even gave him a few lessons. Bechet grew up in the same Seventh Ward neighborhood, within blocks of Nelson, Keppard, Picou, and the Tios. Reminiscing in 1944, Bechet and Nelson

Armstrong (standing) and Joe Oliver, ca. 1923
(Historic New Orleans Collection, Acc. No. 92–48–L MSS 520 f. 1021)

Sidney Bechet (standing) and Freddie Keppard, ca. 1918
(© Frank Driggs Collection)

remembered Bechet coming to Nelson's house for a lesson and bringing along a solfège book. But he left it there and "went running"; the image of Bechet running away from solfège made them laugh. His first band, organized by his older brother Leonard, was called the Silver Leaf, and it irritated him how they "used to rehearse, and rehearse, and rehearse." By his mid-teens he was playing with the Eagle Band, "rough babies who drank a lot and really romped" in Pops Foster's description and characterized by Bechet as a "real gut-bucket band, a real low band that really played blues and things, and those real slow tempos." Bechet was soon playing with Oliver. Just a couple of years earlier, a Creole boy like Bechet would have drifted off and left the wind instruments altogether. Now there was a place for him, a place where he did not have to practice solfège and play with a band that rehearsed and rehearsed and rehearsed.

No one has ever suggested that Sidney Bechet sounded ricky-tick. He became a great blues soloist and master of collective improvisation, one of the strongest representatives of the New Orleans style during the 1920s and a fierce rival to Armstrong. His thorough absorption of uptown ragtime, surely much stronger than Keppard's, reflects his younger age and the advantage of having the example of and direct instruction from Nelson. Bechet was truly rebellious. He has been portrayed as coming from a bourgeois, middle-class background, but his family was really right in step with all the other artisan Creoles. He quit school at age twelve or thirteen, left home, slept in the streets, picked fights routinely, and bummed money to support his incipient alcoholism. Leonard tried to have him placed in the Colored Waif's Home for Boys. New Orleans was a "bad luck place" for Bechet, said Emile Barnes.

Yet the musicians recognized his enormous talent. Even though he was unreliable and difficult to get along with, they made a place for him on the uptown scene. With his great ear, there was no need to learn how to read music: "He didn't know what key he was playing in, but you couldn't lose him . . . Never saw anything like it," said Peter Bocage. He invented his own fingerings. He studied briefly with both Louis Tio and Lorenzo Tio Jr., who, as noted already, taught his students an exercise in which they held out a note for a long time without varying it in timbre or in pitch; the idea was to acquire uniform tone and precise intonation. In their few lessons together Bechet must have exposed his interest in freak timbres, for he remembered Tio scolding him, " No, no, no, we don't bark like a dog." Many years later, Bechet gave lessons himself and decided to turn Tio's Creole exercise on its head by asking his student to play one note and vary it in pitch and timbre as much as possible. "See how many ways you can play that note—growl it, smear it, flat it, sharp it, do anything you want to it," his student remembered him saying. "That's how you express your feelings in music. It's like talking."

It is hard to put too much cultural and social weight on the decisions of a few teenage boys to bolt from the Seventh Ward and start hanging out with the relaxed uptown musicians who taught them how to play blues and rag tunes. Of broader significance was the expanding taste for blues-based ragtime among different social groups in New Orleans. The phenomenon is not well documented, and to explore it here would take us too far afield. It seems clear that the new fashion tempered but did not dismantle the Creole use of Eurocentric musical technique as a form of cultural capital. One should not imagine a situation that was moving steadily toward jazz; the multiplicity of tastes—even for a single person—was too complicated to produce that. The Creole advantage continued long after the initial shock of Bolden's vernacular had touched dance music for not only Negroes but also some Creoles and even, perhaps without fully noticing, a few whites.

In 1913, when Manuel Manetta was asked to put together a band filled with the "greatest musicians in this town" for the new Tuxedo Dance Hall in the Storyville district, he recruited the old-line Creoles—George Fihle on trombone, Peter Bocage on violin ("real Creole people" said Manetta about Bocage), Arnold Metoyer on cornet, "Old Man Papa" Louis Tio on clarinet, Louis Cottrell on drums, and Nookie Johnson as singer and "entertainer." The greatest musicians in town earned $1.25 per night per man from the house plus generous tips, and the Creole advantage was confirmed. "We don't want the out of towners," said Fihle when it came time to find a substitute, and the borderline of Canal Street was drawn in the musical air once again.

A few years later, in 1918, when Armstrong and Ory subbed on their parade gig with John Robichaux and his Creoles, the regulars felt superior and were surprised, still at this late date, at the second-line applause showered on the nonreading uptown musicians. The situation throughout Armstrong's youth was one of ongoing creative and social tension, a continuing pattern of give-and-take that yielded a fertile field for innovation in spite of the clannish downtown exclusion. It was all part of the competitive scene Armstrong was learning to negotiate as he kept his eyes and ears open and kept Oliver's example in mind.

꿍 Social tension was also being generated from a different direction, one that may have actually helped to cut across all the varied distinctions associated with Canal Street. It came from the mapping of masculinity onto a set of practices and institutions that imparted a gendered edge to this vibrant musical scene. This too was set out plainly for Armstrong during his early teenage years, as a prominent part of the music he was aspiring to master. For him, growing up to be a successful musician and to be a man would largely amount to one and the same thing.

CHAPTER NINE

Musicians as Men

Under the present order of things, our man-
hood is sacrificed. The broad stamp of infe-
riority is put on us.
—New Orleans Tribune, *February 7, 1869*

The trumpet is an instrument full of tempta-
tion. All the young cats want to kill papa.
 —Louis Armstrong

During the turbulent years between emancipation and fully implemented
Jim Crow laws, African Americans regularly discussed their political fate in terms of manliness. In 1865, an assembly of freedmen in
Alabama inflected the heady optimism of their newfound liberty in
just this way: "We claim exactly *the same rights, privileges and*
immunities as are enjoyed by white men, [because] . . . the law no
longer knows white or black, but simply men." The optimism of
1865 was bound to deteriorate, but this masculine inflection did
not. The *New Orleans Tribune* (quoted above) conceived the resur-
gence of white supremacy as a sacrifice of manhood. In 1906, after
voting rights had been stripped away and the keystone of Jim Crow
disfranchisement was put in place, W. E. B. Du Bois turned to the
familiar theme in order to inject a dash of hope: "With the right to
vote goes everything: freedom, manhood, the honor of your wives,
the chastity of your daughters, the right to work, and the chance to
rise . . . we are men; we will be treated as men." The rhetorical conflation of political empowerment with manliness seemed like a natural way to articulate the goal of moving away from dependent
status, bound in identity to a slave owner, and toward the status of
full and equal citizen.

So the question must be raised, What did the loss of political freedom and its attendant blow to masculinity have to do with early jazz? The fact is that the emergence of this music coincides precisely with the oppressive march of Jim Crow legislation. And one does not have to look very hard to discover how the musical scene in New Orleans was bound up with masculinity at many different turns. The musicians were not as articulate about this as were the politically inclined writers just cited—or, rather, they lacked forums to record their thoughts for history. But Johnny St. Cyr certainly came close to the matter when he said (Chapter 7) that jazz musicians "have to be a working class of man . . . a working man have the *power* to play hot." Armstrong, with his talk of young cats symbolically killing papa (on one level, read "Pops," his nickname) with their trumpets, alludes to another way of thinking about jazz in masculine terms. He knew all about that kind of competitive ritual, which surrounded him on a daily basis during his teenage years. Assertions of masculinity were very much part of what he was learning after his release from the Colored Waif's Home for Boys, as he found his way into the fraternal world of musicians.

And it was, indeed, a *fraternal* world. Women were almost completely excluded from the scene of professional musicians. Women obviously had a place on the dance floor and as spectators who moved in time to the music of parades, funerals, and advertising wagons. But the typical place for female music making in African-American uptown New Orleans was in the storefront churches, where women sang and sang and sang. Occasionally, a woman like Betsy Cole could make her mark as an entrepreneur who sponsored lawn parties. There were even a few women who played piano professionally in Armstrong's circles, but this was rare. The vast male dominance of the musical environment that shaped him during his teenage years indicates he was learning not just how to play music professionally. He was also learning how to play music as a man.

We have seen how early jazz was a public kind of music far removed from Eurocentric notions of a privately governed sphere of art. It was not music for the parlor but for places that invited open interaction. This orientation opened the door for the use of music as a vehicle for status and respect, which were often articulated in masculine terms.

Sexual seduction provided one obvious way for a musician to articulate masculinity. Bolden's cornet manifested not just the power of the
working class but also his own ability to attract women. This was
especially true with blues. When we find young Louis just out of the
Colored Waif's Home for Boys, playing late into the night at the
neighborhood honky tonk and being teased by the prostitutes about
his precocious ability, we may identify a coming of age, a recognition
of emerging sexuality and also blues talent, as if the two were one and
the same. The image of the teenager sitting on a prostitute's lap, geni-
tals in near contact, makes clear the reward that waits for him when
he reaches sexual and musical maturity. Within a couple of years he
had figured out how to make arrangements with a hotel clerk to keep
a room open for him, so he could enjoy his evening prize after gigs.
He believed that his skill in blues was what did it for him.

Promiscuity was part of the successful musician's life. Armstrong
recalled some advice Black Benny Williams had given him as he
was about to leave New Orleans for Chicago in 1922: "He said to
me, 'You're going out into this wide, wide world. Always remember,
no matter how many times you get married—always have another
woman for a sweetheart on the outside.'" And it is easy to see how,
for musicians, promiscuity could merge with pimping, which is frequently mentioned in the oral histories and autobiographies. Pops
Foster summarized the situation succinctly enough: "All the musicians back in New Orleans wanted to be pimps."

Armstrong acknowledged his own early efforts, which probably
began around age fifteen with a girl named Nootsy. "She wasn't very
much to look at, but she made good money," he wrote. "I would
notice the youngsters whom I ran with, they all had a woman who
were prostitutes. They did not get much money from them. But the
notoriety among them were great." Foster, Armstrong, and other
musicians talk about pimping straightforwardly, without apology
and without sensationalizing it. They leave it to us to observe and
understand it, looking without judgment from the security of our
patch of twenty-first-century middle-class respectability to see how
it was woven into a web of cultural practices. We are not asked to
extend respect, only to see how respect was part of a formula that
was alive with the energy of music.

Pimping brought "notoriety," a kind of status. It showed an ability to get over, and an understanding of how to take advantage of the disadvantages through interpersonal skill, intimidation, and daring. The most spectacular funerals in New Orleans are usually remembered as those for pimps. There was the huge funeral for Clerk Wade, for example, "the sharpest pimp that New Orleans ever had," according to Armstrong. Musicians who pimped on a smaller scale found a little bit of the same status. Their gigs brought them into constant contact with the city's many prostitutes—over two thousand were legally registered—and their late-night connections made pimping seem like a natural supplement. The big-time pimps had their own social club and sponsored popular parades and a dance known as the Pimp's Ball at Economy Hall. Some of them were fine dancers, "waltzes and everything," said Manuel Manetta, complete with holster pistols on display.

Bold clothing was part of the image of the hustler, a social designation that conflated pimping and gambling. Assertive clothes symbolically contradicted Jim Crow subservience, marking the hustler as a man who did not play by the common rules, an outsider immune to the normal racial, domestic, and economic pressures. The hustler was someone who had escaped the curse of endless unskilled drudgery and poverty. Baby Dodds said that in 1918 Armstrong dressed like a "low class hustler" because "that's what Louis wanted to be in those days." He wore a tight collar that kept popping when his neck swelled from the pressure of playing the cornet. All of his earnings disappeared through gambling. Hustlers liked tight trousers, tailored, if possible, by Burtenard and Wager's— "They knowed how they wanted their clothes and they'd fit em that way," said Jelly Roll Morton. Gold belt buckles and gold initialing flashed alongside diamonds inserted in teeth, ties, garters, and socks. As a special attraction, a little light bulb, energized by a pocket battery, flashed in the toe of a shoe. The hustler's walk, known as "shooting the agate," advanced at a slow tempo, one suspender lifted off the shoulder, arms stiffly out to the side and index fingers pointing down; this was the look that helped keep a "fifth class whore" under control. Flashy visual display was an integral part of the musical scene surrounding early jazz, which was an extro-

verted, ostentatious kind of music—"brassy, broad and aggressively dramatic," as poet and critic Amiri Baraka has described Armstrong's playing of the 1920s and 1930s.

Some pianists were exceptions to this profile. A few—Jelly Roll Morton, for example—did indeed pimp and cultivate the image. But others were outsiders to the large group of dance-band and brass-band musicians. Morton is said to have rarely left his lucrative jobs in the brothels of Storyville. Most of them had pianos, but dance halls usually did not, so the dance tradition evolved without them. Pianists made extremely good money in the brothels, and they spent it in highly visible ways. For example, while heavy use of alcohol was common among the dance-band musicians, the hip flask being a standard accoutrement, some of the pianists visited hop houses in Chinatown on Tulane Avenue to smoke opium, which they could afford along with cocaine, heroin, and morphine.

And more than a few pianists, apparently, were homosexual. Best known of all was the great Tony Jackson, whose playing had an impact on Morton. Jackson regularly held court at The Frenchman's, a small place on the corner of Bienville and Villere where pianists congregated after hours. African-American vaudeville entertainers also liked to go there when they were in town. The Frenchman's was known as a hangout for cross-dressers. "Them freaky people used to bum [there]," said Manetta. "Tony's bunch . . . they was all cooks and everything like that . . . for the big white people and they go there and that's where they have their pleasure. That was their headquarters. They dress just like ladies, yes sir!"

In addition to his strong piano playing, part of Jackson's act was to sing in a feminine register. His specialty number was a blues that went "I've got Elgin movements in my hips with 20 years' guarantee." "The band musicians thought piano was for women . . . We'd call them 'Sissies' or say 'look at that faggot up there,'" said Pops Foster. The sexualized hierarchy of masculine musicality did not have room for homosexuals, or at least it did not make room easily. The band musicians must have felt that homosexual pianists put the whole equation of music and masculine power at risk. Morton once claimed that he himself got into pimping so that no one would be confused about his sexual identity.

Cutting and Inventing

Masculinity was also articulated musically through public competition with other musicians. Musicians thus worked with a twofold approach to manly power, with one vector directed toward the sexual seduction of women, another toward the symbolic conquering of men. In these competitive practices, music stood close to traditions of verbal performance. Both musical and verbal competition surface throughout the African diaspora and are documented in southern slavery, so it is not surprising to see them manifesting so prominently in early-twentieth-century New Orleans.

Musical competitions were known as "cutting" or "bucking" contests. "Bucking" obviously refers to horses, and in fact it was common to tie together two horse-drawn advertising wagons as they happened to meet on the streets and settle in for a little musical exchange. One of Black Benny Williams's several responsibilities, along with beating a drum and wielding a blackjack, was to carry the rope that knotted the wagons together, thus eliminating the possibility of escape from potential humiliation.

The etymology of "cutting" is easy to misconstrue. Although it has often been associated with knife violence, a more likely history involves dancing, as can be seen in references from slavery, for example: "Master and mistress would be there, one of whom would award the prize for the best 'cuttin' of figgers.'" This usage has been traced to Africa, where it has the sense of taking turns leading an ensemble. It occurs in an early-nineteenth-century description of dancing in Place Congo: "One will continue the rapid *jig* till nature is exhausted; then a fresh disciple leaps before him or her and 'cuts out' the fatigued one, who sinks down gracefully on the grass, out of the way." This usage is certainly the source of cutting in jazz, meaning to win a musical contest. "If we said that a band cut you on the street, that meant they outplayed you," said Baby Dodds.

The best-known verbal manifestation of this competitive spirit is the game of trading insults known as "the dozens." Civil rights activist H. Rap Brown wrote that in his youth "we played dozens for recreation, like white folks play scrabble." In their study of New

Orleans from the 1930s, sociologists Allison Davis and John Dollard described the dozens as "free aggressive expression . . . [In] its dirtiest and most aggressive forms [it] is the province of lower-lower-class people."

In New Orleans, guitarist Lorenzo Staulz made his reputation through imaginative dozens play and the invention of many song lyrics, some referencing current political events. Joe Oliver was also known as a fierce competitor. The most complete description of Oliver's ability comes from Clyde Bernhardt: "He just loved to play the dirty dozens . . . The more insults tossed back and forth, the better he like it. Herman Elkins and Walter Dennis always try to dozens him back but they didn't stand a chance. He tell them something bad about their mother or sister, about sleeping with them and what they did and how they did it and what they said about it and things like that . . . He was no contest. His dozens won every time." Barney Bigard teased Oliver one day and was surprised to see Oliver quickly turn moody and eventually tell Bigard, "Don't kid me no more. I had a dream and my mother told me not to tell the dozens ever again."

Verbal skill—demonstrated improvisationally, dialogically, and competitively—helped establish interpersonal power and could lead to positions of musical leadership. George Jones was a weak bass player, yet through verbal wit he established himself as an important figure on the scene. "Jones got a lot of work; he could make up on-the-spot rhymes to anything, so he was popular," remembered Eddie Dawson. One Poydras Market Dan "couldn't sing, but he could talk and rhyme," according to Earl Humphrey. "Dan had connections with some good people, who would give him jobs." This association of verbal invention with leadership was documented during slavery, when men gained the position of "captain" in corn-shucking celebrations by being good at inventing rhymes. Joe Oliver fits the pattern well, since he was known both as a competitor in the dozens and as a strong musical leader. No one ever talks about Armstrong and the dozens, but he was admired for his creative slang, contributing, it has been claimed, innovative usage of "terrible," "crazy," "cats," "Pops," "jive," and "scat."

It must be common throughout the world to test improvisational skill in competitive settings. In the New Orleans of Armstrong's youth, the ferociousness of the dozens was easily matched in the musical cutting contests, which could be set either individually, soloist against soloist, or collectively, band against band. "It seemed as though all the bands were shooting at each other with those hot riffs," wrote Armstrong. When two bands met on the streets, a single player might step out and challenge his counterpart in the other band. Apparently it was not unusual for the bands to play at each other *simultaneously*, which must have been quite a cacophonous thrill for everyone. Or they exchanged numbers back and forth until one band acknowledged defeat by failing to return the musical volley. Buddy Petit once faked drunkenness and frailty in an attempt to lure in the competition; after the wagons were tied together, he jumped up to join battle in vigorous sobriety. Oliver instructed Louis to stand up and signal when he was in an approaching wagon so that Oliver could direct his own band's wagon off in another direction. Spontaneous battles like these could last as long as two hours.

Sometimes two bands would be called to compete for a job, the winner being directly awarded the paying gig. Unemployed bands roamed around, on the lookout for any chance to embarrass another band and steal its job. Jack Carey's Crescent Band once showed up at a dance hall where Kid Ory's band was playing. From the front door Carey sent word up to the stage suggesting that Ory should play a march to accompany the Crescent's entry into the hall. Ory was indignant: "I ain't gonna stop the people from dancing, I ain't gonna play especially for them." Though this little bit of gamesmanship did not work, Carey and his band did eventually get on stage for a little contest.

Ory certainly had it coming to him, for he too was known to hunt down competition aggressively. He was the first to purchase a truck for advertising gigs, which allowed him to chase the slower horse-drawn wagons; "They couldn't get out of the way," he gleefully remembered. He liked to pour salt on the wound by pursuing a losing band in its retreat and singing, "If you don't like the way I play, then kiss my funky ass." A substantial public was devoted to these events, watching closely and adjusting their allegiances. Food and drink was immediately offered to the winner and an encore was expected. Losing musicians were greeted with subtle and not-so-subtle put-downs when they entered bars. In Jelly Roll Morton's poetic phrase, carrying just the right touch of masculine bravado, "It was a terrible thing when the feathers had been plucked from the peacock's tail." More than a few musicians lacked the temperament for this kind of public humiliation. Clarinetist Jimmie Noone is said to have run away from cutting contests and even to have jumped off a wagon in the middle of one, and he was certainly a fine musician.

"The Creoles would hate to see that" (Courtesy of the Hogan Jazz Archive, Tulane University, photo by Ralston Crawford)

Not surprisingly, some stories about cutting contests set uptown bands against downtown, replaying the classic rivalry, or, with less ethnic articulation, they set readers against nonreaders. The Creoles, with their traditional polish and command of a large repertory, had real advantages: "They could play anything that was wanted . . . they'd be the ones, their band, who'd win," said Sidney Bechet. But uptown musicians aggressively met the challenge, especially when they were able to do battle on friendly turf. "Get out of that neighborhood if you see the Eagle Band coming," said one Creole.

Creole Freddie Keppard had been the first cornetist allowed to play in the Storyville district, with Oliver following shortly after. At one point the two were playing on the same block, and Oliver decided to issue a challenge. "Get in *B*-flat," he barked, and that was all that pianist Richard Jones needed to know to start a blues accompaniment. Oliver walked out to the sidewalk and pointed his cornet toward Keppard. The ensuing competition drew a large and delighted crowd, which, by legend, proclaimed Oliver victor. Oliver remembered how he and Keppard sometimes competed for hours, with no one willing to surrender. The likely places for that kind of extended engagement would have been the two main hangouts for musicians in Storyville, Big 25 and Pete Lala's cabaret, where cut-

The Big 25, Franklin Street near Iberville (Historic New Orleans Collection, Acc. No. 92–48–L MSS 520 f. 762, photo by William Russell)

ting contests often took place after closing, the musicians playing until the break of day while their prostitutes waited for them.

Armstrong, when challenged by another musician, responded by playing with an angry intensity, as musicians outside of New Orleans were shocked to discover. In the mid-1920s in New York he thoroughly embarrassed a confident Jabbo Smith. Johnny Dunn from Memphis challenged him when he was still second cornetist in Oliver's band. Papa Joe turned to his protégé and said with his familiar authority, "Go get him." By the time Armstrong finished playing, the astonished Dunn had disappeared. Danny Barker described him on another occasion with red eyes, expanded nostrils, quickened breath, and blasting "one or two hundred choruses of *Chinatown*"—an exaggeration designed to convey the intensity of the moment. Oliver was his model, as he was in so many ways. Without this kind of competitive drive—the same quality, of course, that has always propelled the great popular musicians onto the national stage— neither one of them would have been able to overcome the obstacles against crossing Canal Street. Cutting contests were not unique to New Orleans, but the institutional attention to them there, which was daily and highly public, ensured that competition stood as a routine dimension of expressive culture.

The style of social engagement in a cutting contest was quite different from that typical of church. Religions of all kinds hold transcendence of personal rivalry as an ideal that is not necessarily reached in practice. The contradiction of trying to outdo one's neighbor while reciting the commandment to love her or him must have blemished, at least occasionally, even the Sanctified Saints of New Orleans. Nevertheless, those churches also reaffirmed the ideal of social bonding as a path toward spiritual depth. It was through intra-male competition in the cutting contests, the use of music as a vehicle for gaining status, economic success, and sexual dominance, that jazz moved away from the communally inspired practices of church. The brash energy of competition helped open up a diversity of solo styles. Communal and mutually nourishing musical values had been so strong during slavery that there was limited room for a more individualist ideology. But individualism was instantly rewarded in the competitive atmosphere of early jazz, making diversification of style inevitable. Quickness, extended-range playing, speed of execution, fresh ideas, harmonic experimentation—all were sources of reward and prestige in the manly musical world of New Orleans.

So was the ability to "invent." It is interesting to think of competition for status as a driving force behind improvisation. Musicians did not *have* to improvise in cutting contests. The modern-day insistence, derived from bebop, on spontaneous creation as a primary standard for evaluating jazz was foreign to this setting. To the contrary, it was standard practice to trot out one's store of preworked musical tricks. Jelly Roll Morton pointed out that this was why a lot of musicians refused to record or publish, so that they could protect their ideas and reuse them whenever a competitive situation arose. The most famous example is Freddie Keppard, who covered his fingers with a handkerchief so that rivals could not steal from him, and refused to record for the same reason. The standard practice in New Orleans was to stick with a successful solo. Why give it up if it worked? "Once you got a certain solo that fit in the tune, and that's it, you keep it," said Armstrong.

Yet it is also clear that improvisation gave the uptown musicians an advantage over their downtown rivals. "Inspired improvising," said Bechet, was a sure way to win a cutting contest. Bebé Ridgley said that Jack Carey and other nonreading trombonists "could raise so much sand on a trombone, they'd really give the reading fellows a good time, especially out on the street and different things like that . . . Jack Carey wasn't a good reader, but could really 'catch.' Those are the guys that wear you out. He could take a piece and add to it or take away." This comment highlights a central problem in understanding improvisation in early jazz. To "catch" a tune means to pick it up by ear, which is not the same thing as improvisation. But to add to or take away from the caught tune is an act of creation clearly related to improvisation. The problem is important for understanding the environment that nurtured Louis Armstrong, who became, by universal acclamation, one of the greatest and most influential improvisers ever.

In African-American vernacular culture in New Orleans around this time, all performances—verbal, musical, and kinetic—were expected to include a degree of improvisation. That expectation came from Africa, and it followed the mandate that social interaction was part of what music was all about. In the ring shout, for example, rotating leaders generated new musical material, which was anchored by the repetitive "basing" of the group. The same format was used in corn-shucking celebrations, which we know through descriptions like this: "Selecting one of their number—usually the most original and amusing, and possessed of the loudest voice—they called him 'captain.' " The captain "seated himself on top of the pile—a large lightwood torch burning in front of him, and while he shucked, improvised words and music to a wild 'recitative,' the chorus of which was caught up by the army of shuckers around." Zora Neale Hurston was impressed by how much improvisation there was in the early years of the Sanctified Church: "Moreover, each singing of the piece is a new creation. The congregation is bound by no rules. No two times singing is alike, so that we must consider the rendition of a song not as a final thing, but as a mood."

The twin pressures of commercial reward and the climb toward urban sophistication helped stimulate improvisation. There was no American precedent for the situation. This urban, individualistic adaptation of traditional group practices created an environment in which an improviser of Armstrong's stature could blossom. His model, once again, was Oliver, who reached high status in New Orleans not only through skill in the dozens, loud playing, and freak music but also through his ability to invent. Armstrong makes this clear again and again. "The way I see it, the greatest musical creations came from his horn—and I've heard a lot of them play," he wrote. "[Bunk Johnson] didn't have the get-up-and-go that Oliver did; he didn't create a phrase that stays with you. But Joe Oliver *created* things." Band leader Fess Williams remembered a night in Chicago when a few white musicians offered Oliver a dollar for every new break that he could play. "Joe broke them that night; took all their money, and was still playing breaks afterwards," said Williams.

What is different about early New Orleans, compared to more recent jazz, is that improvisation was not built into the commercial product in the same way. Before the advent of paid jam sessions in the 1940s, jazz usually included a degree of creative tension between the "arranged" parts of the music and improvisation. Fletcher

Henderson and Duke Ellington sprinkled "hot solos" into rehearsed ensemble pieces. In uptown New Orleans this was not an option, due to the high value placed on the lead melody, which, as we know already from Baby Dodds (Chapter 1), "is supposed to be heard distinctly from some instrument—the trumpet, trombone, clarinet or violin. At all times." But in the cutting contests, improvisation sometimes took center stage, with virtuosos like Oliver and Keppard spinning out ideas for a long time without drying up or giving in. "Lack of closure is highly desirable; the performer wants precisely to give the impression that she could go on forever, that . . . her own powers to invoke . . . are limitless." Those words describe women oríkì singers among the Yoruba people of Africa, but they apply equally well to the masculine situation in New Orleans. Armstrong described Oliver in similar terms: "Nobody could touch him. He had the power, no one had the nerves to attack."

In commercial settings, one small opportunity for solo improvisation came in the "break," a brief pause at the end of a phrase that can be inserted in many different kinds of music. Jelly Roll Morton insisted that the break was integral to jazz in a way that is difficult to appreciate today. But the best opportunity for solo improvisation was in blues. In order to play blues for an extended time—and in honky tonks blues were played all night long—a soloist needed considerable skill in melodic invention, since the repertory of preexistent blues melodies was small. To regard blues as the main opportunity for demonstrating improvisational prowess gives us one more way to think about the provocative opinion (Chapter 3) that "blues is what cause the fellows to start jazzing."

The other ubiquitous outlet for improvisation was collective improvisation, which required invention not of the leading melody but of the texture surrounding it. "The band often repeated the same selection, but never played it the same way twice" was how a reporter from *Variety* condemned the African-American music he heard in the "heart of the New Orleans' 'Tenderloin' " in 1911. Though whites were puzzled by the continuous transformation of familiar musical material, uptown African Americans obviously held that kind of transformation in high regard. Armstrong excelled at creating the texture of collective improvisation, just as he excelled in blues. Thus, his gift of musical creativity found the proper nurturing in his hometown. He once recalled examples of other musicians taking credit for his musical inventions, but then shrugged and put the best face on the matter. "But there will be other tunes," he said. "There's always another one coming along—like a streetcar."

The Insurance of Dignity

Musicians were not the only men who found music to be a useful vehicle for asserting status. To realize how thoroughly men's social clubs were involved with the sponsorship of dances, parades, and funerals is to begin to understand the extent to which these institutions helped define the music in masculine terms. In funerals especially, music was counted on to produce a public moment of manly dignity. This famous ritual, such an enduring icon of New Orleans and early jazz, was completely controlled by the fraternal clubs.

African-American fraternal organizations in New Orleans had their origins in the antebellum period as "aid societies" that provided insurance for medical bills and funerals. Such societies grew in number and strength during the last decades of the nineteenth century, part of what historian Steven Hahn calls a "remarkable 'thickening' of African-American civic and associational life." Civic organization was turning away from political parties and into less overtly political groups, an understandable response to the intensification of disfranchisement. In New Orleans, the dramatic expansion of aid societies was spurred by the arrival of the plantation immigrants. "Everybody in the city of New Orleans was always organization minded," observed Jelly Roll Morton.

"Pleasure clubs" grew alongside the aid societies. As their names imply, the two kinds of groups had different functions. Nevertheless, the trend during this period was for each type to expand and include the activities of the other—for example, the Zulu Aid and Pleasure Club, which began in 1909 in Armstrong's neighborhood. Some of the clubs were labor-based; workers who laid sewer lines called themselves, with a dash of humor, the Turtles. Others were nationally chartered clubs like the Odd Fellows and the Masons. Armstrong joined both the Knights of Pythias and the Tammany Social Aid and Pleasure Club.

Membership could cost as little as fifteen cents per month. There was a degree of fluidity, and men commonly belonged to more than one club. Nicknames were routinely assigned and they could multiply, a phenomenon that reflects a fluid and relaxed identity rather than a rigid, centralized one. In New Orleans Armstrong was known as Boat Nose, Hammock Face, Rhythm Jaws, Slow Foot, Dippermouth, Gatemouth, and Satchelmouth.

Savvy musicians used the clubs to further their careers. Oscar Celestin shrewdly joined the Masons, the Odd Fellows, and the Pythians, which set him up with jobs for his Tuxedo band. The fact that Celestin was an uptowner may also have helped him, for his uptown band could match the old-line Creole brass bands that were often used by the uptown clubs; this made it possible to hire within the community without sacrificing quality. "Tuxedo, Onward, Eureka—they were the standard bands that used to play for funerals," said Hypolite Charles, the latter two based downtown. Over in Algiers, Henry Allen had a similar web of connections that established him as a bandleader in spite of limited musical ability. Once connected to a club, a band could count on continuing patronage for their dances, parades, and funerals. Isidore Barbarin remembered the Odd Fellows having a funeral with music everyday, which is possible since the thirteen African-American lodges in the 1880s had more than a thousand members.

The clubs were often neighborhood-based, and they found various ways of distinguishing themselves. Most had annual parades, sometimes at night with torches. The pimps' club flaunted guards riding horseback. Armstrong remembered the last parade he saw in New Orleans. It featured the Bulls (based at Eighth and Daneel streets), the Hobgoblins (from the Battlefield), the Zulus ("the neighborhood that I was reared"), the Tammanys, the Young Men Twenties ("Zutty Singleton's club"), the Merry-Go-Rounds, the Jolly Boys, the Turtles, the Original Swells (on Claiborne Street), the San Jacintos, the Autocrats, the Francs Amis Club, the Cooperatives, the Economys, the Odd Fellows, the Masons, the

Knights of Pythias ("my lodge"), and the Diamond Swells ("from out in the Irish Channel"), all trying "to outdo each other and they certainly looked swell." Jelly Roll Morton ranked clubs according to subtle gradations in class, in the same way that many people thought about the Protestant denominations, from the elite Orleans Eight all the way down to the Charcoal Schooners, whose membership included Black Benny Williams.

The Masons were prohibited by their national charter to march with any other club, so a Masonic funeral never had more than one band. Otherwise, a popular man who could afford to join several clubs could count on a colorful and grand display at his funeral, with multiple societies marching behind multiple bands and attracting lots of people (Chapter 4). A musician's funeral might be special. At Black Benny's funeral in 1924 his bass drum was draped in black cloth and carried behind the hearse. When Henry Zeno died, a substitute carried his drum silently to the cemetery; on the celebratory return, after the body had been "turned loose," the substitute played the instrument as if it too had been released from its previous earthly ties.

A grand marshal, 1950s (Courtesy of the Hogan Jazz Archive,
Tulane University, photo by Ralston Crawford)

But the funeral with music was not mainly about religion. African antecedents for the practice may have included the idea that a proper burial was necessary for establishing the deceased as an ancestor worthy of worship. It is easy to imagine how such a ritual could have been transformed, within a more secular context, into a public display of status. There were strong white models for this in New Orleans. One came from England, where military bands accompanied processions both to and from the cemetery. The practice of playing "lively airs" and "cheerful music" on the return, tunes such as *We Can Very Well Do Without Him*, is documented and decried in New Orleans beginning in the 1850s. African-American aid societies eventually adopted this practice—the earliest reference is from 1886—and kept it going long after its abandonment by whites.

Benjamin Latrobe described an African-American funeral from 1819 with priests, candles, and alter boys; by 1900 these were nowhere near the funeral with music. Preachers were hired to say the appropriate things. Or they might say more: Pops Foster told a story of one preacher at the grave site scolding the musician friends of deceased cornetist Joe Johnson; he blamed them for "pulling [Johnson] out of church." Even Mahalia Jackson, who had strong opinions about religion and did not hesitate to criticize the secular shortcomings of New Orleans, could approve of the ragtime return from the cemetery. She justified it by quoting the Bible—"Rejoice at the outgoing!" The phrase is nowhere to be found in the Bible, however, and Mahalia may not have realized how secular the practice actually was.

The funeral with music was more about masculine dignity than anything else. There are several signs of hostility toward the practice from organized religions. Three groups of people were never buried with music—women, preachers, and Catholics. The self-exclusion of preachers and Catholics indicates suspicion of the practice by official religion, while the exclusion of women frames it as a matter of manhood. When, as often happened, the procession picked up the deceased at his house, where the wake had been held, the funeral did not involve a church at all. Eddie Dawson said that he left the Catholic Church when he joined a fraternal organization. This appears to have been a common choice to have to make, stemming, most likely, from opposition to the clubs from the church hierarchy. It is not clear how many ex-Catholic Creoles of color participated in clubs that sponsored funerals with music; certainly all the religious songs that were remembered from the processions were Protestant. Betsy Cole, a longtime sponsor of lawn parties where Ory and Oliver frequently played, emerges from the oral histories as the lone exception to the exclusion of women from the funeral with music.

The fraternal clubs were for many men what church was for many women, so it is not surprising that they took the funeral ritual into their own hands. The funeral with music was part of the proliferation of autonomous spaces for black culture in New Orleans. It was another opportunity for the open-air performance of cultural autonomy for all to hear and see, and rather audaciously at that, since, as we have seen (Chapter 1), the ritual included military gestures such as uniforms, plumed hats, the parade stance, the muffled snare imitating a military kettledrum, and sabers. These dignifying ornaments were charitably extended to men who died without club membership, and hence without the insurance that would pay for a funeral with music. Cash to pay for a band and refreshments was raised in a cigar box or saucer put on the corpse's chest as it lay in the front room. In this way, the community's resources were shared with the impoverished and socially isolated. Kid Ory said that people wouldn't give a dollar to a desperate man if he was hungry, but they would unhesitatingly put up five dollars to bury him.

Though manly dignity was under daily attack in life—*because* it was under attack—it could be ensured at the moment of death via club membership and a grand, public display. The first documentation of the performance for an African-American funeral of up-tempo music on the return from burial is dated 1886, and the practice continued to flourish in the black community through circa 1965. The beginning of the African-American embrace of this ritual thus coincided with the beginnings of harsh post-Reconstruction retrenchment from political rights, and the practice ended—not totally, but as an organic dimension of civic life—when civil rights came to fruition, as if to make clear the political nature of the ritual.

Music drove the procession of emotions, from mourning on the way to the cemetery, climaxing at the moment of burial, to rejoicing

The funeral procession approaches, 1946 (Historic New Orleans Collection, Acc. No. 92-48-L MSS 520 f. 369, photo by William Russell)

after the body was turned loose. Music called the community together, following the traditional African-American interest in music as a tool for producing social cohesion. At the same time, musical skill generated dignity, a compelling assertion of symbolic power in a way that was very much a part of the post-Reconstruction South. These benefits were shared; they did not simply accrue to the memory of the deceased man. For the aid and pleasure societies were built on a collective vision of mutual support. The dignity being performed and processed through the streets extended from the dead man to each marching club, to the family, and to the entire participating community.

The *New Orleans Tribune* lamented in 1869 that "the broad stamp of inferiority is put on us." A century later, Armstrong told friends in the privacy of his living room that the musicians he knew from New Orleans were plagued by feelings of inferiority so crippling that they could not succeed professionally. He recorded this and many other conversations expressly for the purpose of revealing the life and thoughts behind his public mask; "I'm putting it on tape for my posterity," he says at one point. The musicians he knew couldn't make it elsewhere because they got homesick and gave up, returning in defeat to the city to "fight them mosquitoes and everything." He cited the paranoid example of Freddie Keppard covering his fingers with a handkerchief and refusing to make phonograph records ("then here comes ODJB [Original Dixieland Jazz Band]— should have been Freddie's"). Problems with alcohol, mistrusting white managers, turning down opportunities, lacking the confidence to stand in front of an audience and command attention— these were all signs of the same problem, "an inferiority complex most all of the great musicians had in New Orleans."

Perhaps he thought of Joe Oliver as an exception, for Oliver did indeed successfully leave New Orleans, forge a career, record plentifully, and shun alcohol. Pops Foster felt that Oliver "was very confident in himself, didn't look up to anybody." Nevertheless, Clyde Bernhardt (Chapter 8) insisted that Oliver had an inferiority complex associated with his dark skin. Businessman Walter Melrose described Oliver as "the old Southern-type nigger . . . Didn't want any trouble with anybody." The idea that performing artists are driven by deep feelings of insecurity is hardly new and hardly specific to African-American musicians from New Orleans. But, as argued in the previous chapter, it could not have been easy for Armstrong to escape the crippling psychology of color prejudice, which was designed, of course, to keep dark-skinned people in their place—the place of complete subordination, mimicking as thoroughly as possible the hegemony of slavery. For hundreds of years, dark skin had been conflated with dependency, and the darkest skin implied the greatest involvement with the historic horrors of such dependency. When Armstrong said that musicians from New Orleans suffered from an inferiority complex, it is difficult not to think that he silently and unconsciously included himself.

I have speculated about the politics of the Saints and their turn away from assimilative Baptist pressures (Chapter 2) and about the political implications of working-class music blasting out from a segregated park for miles across the city (Chapter 7). Was there also a political dimension in the swirl of competitive energy that flowed through the cutting contests? These improvisational battles took place exclusively within the African-American community, and the only stakes were the victory of one African-American musician over another. Yet the dignity being gained is identical to the dignity being denied by the white world of Jim Crow; it is the same dignity, attacked and dragged down in one setting or glorified in the ascent in another. "It is probably not too much to say that the language of the performance of masculinity *was* the language of honor, for blacks as well as whites," writes historian Jane Dailey about late-nineteenth-century Virginia. In the New Orleans of Armstrong's youth, the language of music was part of that same equation.

The sounds of early jazz thus carried masculine honor just as well and just as clearly as the saber, plume, and strut of a grand marshal. Once while Louis was playing baseball, a brass band led by Oliver came within earshot. Oliver was playing lead on *It's a Long Way to Tipperary*, the big hit of 1914–1915, and the boys abruptly stopped their game and ran to follow. Armstrong was a young adolescent growing up fast, and the choice he made marks a developmental moment: baseball, the pastime of boys, yielded to the masculine, musical procession of men. He remembered Oliver going "way up there" with his cornet on the last chorus. His hero demonstrated with his ascent into the higher range of his instrument the flash of masculine power—a symbolic weapon to be sure. Freddie Keppard added a visual dimension: he always played with his cornet pointed up in the air, a pose that may be read as mimicking erection. A great deal was packed into this music, and as Oliver's young admirer memorized his solos, he did so for more reasons than might be obvious at first.

CHAPTER TEN

"Rough and beautiful"

*[Joe Johnson] played the middle range and
played it rough and beautiful.* —Pops Foster

*Some people like music very rough. Some peo-
ple like music very nice.* —Hypolite Charles

After Oliver got Louis headed in the right direction, it took several years
until he was good enough to play full-time. His break came in the
summer of 1918, when Oliver left the city and Armstrong took his
place in Kid Ory's band. Soon after that he started to play on the
riverboats, and that job eventually opened up for him a much bigger
stylistic and professional range. But until Ory hired him, music was
a part-time affair, limited to entry-level jobs.

Viewed from a distance, a positive side of the situation comes
into focus: his limitations kept him in the thick of the kind of music
Pops Foster described as "rough and beautiful." His mid-teen years
were spent hanging out uptown, singing with the vocal quartet,
pimping and hustling women, playing in the honky tonks and on
advertising wagons, substituting in dance bands, and trying to be
one of the guys. It was a critical period during which he continued
to build on the foundations of church, blues, and ragging the tune.
During these mid-teen years of apprenticeship, his aim was to
become a professional with a broader range as well as a master of the
orally based vernacular tradition.

Little Routine Bands

Honky tonks and advertising wagons were an important part of the scene because they provided points of entry into the musical market. The humble institution of the advertising wagon may seem like a quaint, regional novelty, but many uptown musicians found steady work there. "All them little routine fellows would play [advertising jobs] and they'd live off it," said Manuel Manetta. "Routine"—most likely from the French *routiner*, "to memorize"—meant an untutored musician who played by ear, which is certainly what Armstrong was doing around 1915–1918. Creoles used the term as a put-down. Manetta, however, appreciated the contribution routine musicians made to daily life: "Lots more music back then than today, more livelier—funerals, parades, saloons, every little advertisement, things, grand openings of a place. They was playing regular. All them had players like them ear players, they made a living off of it. Every day."

Advertising jobs were perfectly suited to a beginner who had a very small repertory in his bag. A band really only needed to know one or two tunes that could then be played over and over as the wagon circulated. When a better gig came up for one of the players, it was standard practice to send in a substitute, even a child. A little experience with a brass band was more than enough. "Professor" Paul Chaligny had a brass band of thirty children and he regularly took every single one of them out for advertising jobs on a big flat bed. With smaller bands, the bass player and the trombonist sat near the tailgate (hence the term "tailgate trombone"). A large sign was tacked to the side of the wagon, announcing the furniture sale, boxing match, or whatever was being advertised. Any band that had a dance gig was required to promote it during the day. So on a busy dance night many bands were out during the afternoon.

Armstrong once played an advertising job with Bechet, just the two of them plus a drummer, and he got paid fifty cents. Richard Jones remembered watching them play, and he remembered the holes in their pants, which, unlike today, were not part of teenage fashion. Sometimes Armstrong encountered Buddy Petit, who, a few years older, was leading the way for a new generation of cornet players. "We both would meet on a corner, play our tune, or a couple of tunes, and we would cut out into different directions and give a big wave, playing our cornets with admirations of each other's blowing," he wrote. "That alone cheered both of us up." All that was required of most advertising bands was that they attract attention, which was inevitable. Bands typically advertised from one to six o'clock in the afternoon and then played at a dance from eight at night until four in the morning, a long workday by anyone's standards. The public response helped energize the musicians. The wagons were really the centerpiece of the steady stream of outdoor music that came from the rag men, strolling vocal quartets, street corner guitarists, brass bands, serenading bands, lawn parties, and Sunday gigs at Lake Pontchartrain. "All day Sunday the streets would be jammed with people," said Punch Miller. "Wasn't nothing but fun."

The elite Creole bands like the Excelsior and the Onward loomed large on the parade and funeral scene, but there were also "a lot of ratty brass bands that would play tonk music in the streets," as Emile Barnes put it. Most of these were "jump up" bands, assembled ad hoc. Two established uptown routine bands were Jack Carey's Crescent Band and Frankie Dusen's Eagle Band. When Carey or Dusen got a parade job—which they were eager to take for the publicity—they expanded their dance bands by taking on a few additional musicians. Fifteen-year-old Baby Dodds played with the parade version of the Eagle Band in just this way. A parade band could get by knowing only two numbers, and simply the main parts of those two numbers, at that. As discussed in Chapter 2, these uptown, jump-up brass bands were a likely site for bringing the heterophony of church into the world of the wind instruments and for working out the techniques of collective improvisation; the constant playing and replaying of the same small set of tunes would have facilitated the innovation. Cornetist Kid Howard said (in 1963) that the jump-up bands Chris Kelly put together played "in the rough style associated with the New Orleans brass bands of the present. The kind of music he would play for funerals would put 'em in the alley when coming back from the burials."

The case can be made that outdoors was in fact the place where musical innovation was most likely to occur. Since there was little or no overhead—both literally and figuratively: no building, no roof, and hence no need for capital investment in a venue—the whole outdoor enterprise was monitored loosely or not at all. Wind instruments carried well in the open air, and the low pay and low status of these jobs created a demand for unskilled players. This is precisely where we find Armstrong around age sixteen, as one of the many "little routine fellows" playing wind instruments outdoors. Outdoors was where uptown African Americans "could express themselves loudly and without restraint or caution," as Danny Barker observed. Music in the full air was the most fluid, the most open socially, the least restricted because of any expectations from patrons, the place for experiments. The daily work of advertising jobs and ratty parade bands was driven by enough patronage to sustain participation, yet not enough to smother it with demands. The climate made New Orleans perfect for outdoor music and thus a fertile ground for musical innovation.

Two types of venues, lawn parties in the city and picnics at Lake Pontchartrain, straddled the distinction between outdoors and indoors and hence lay in the middle of this spectrum. Lawn parties and picnics required minimal shelter or no shelter at all, so they had low admission prices (or admission by invitation at the lake, when a party was sponsored by a club). Anyone who could put up the money to rent a lawn, buy a keg of beer at Jackson Brewery, and get some fish cooked could put on a lawn party. When there was more than one, the crowd went with the best band. Mrs. Betsy Cole had a little business turning these parties out every weekend for as many as two hundred customers, her favorite band being Kid Ory's. Her lawn, surrounded by a wooden fence, had a wooden platform for dancing. A little porch over the front steps of her house sheltered the band from rain.

The shores of Lake Pontchartrain on warm-weather Sundays were jammed with people and music. When Protestant Americans began moving to New Orleans in large numbers after the Louisiana Purchase of 1803, they were shocked to discover how the French and Spanish Catholics behaved on Sundays: it was not a day of contemplation and remorse but rather one of gambling, picnicking, dancing, and drinking. (This was precisely how Place Congo had fit into the local scene, as the weekly slave version of Sunday celebration.) Well before 1900, the Sunday party had moved to Lake Pontchartrain. Sometimes when a club hired a band to play out at the lake, the band would meet the club members in the city, at club headquarters, and play a march as the membership proceeded to the train station. The train delivered them all to the western end of the line, a spot known simply as "West End" and later immortalized in Armstrong's famous recording *West End Blues*, from 1927. Whites disembarked on one side, African Americans on the other. Bands still looking for work that day auditioned on the boardwalk, right at the train stop, trying to catch the attention of disembarking passengers.

At the lake, bands routinely set up early in the morning and continued playing, with frequent breaks, until six in the evening. Musicians speak of up to thirty bands altogether on Sundays. Clubs owned or rented little "camps," shacks painted yellow, red, green, or blue and built at the ends of docks that extended into the lake to take advantage of the cooling effect of the water. The camps were close together and provided yet another opportunity for musical competition. Adjacent camps commonly had their hired bands alternate with one another; people in each camp could then choose whether they wanted to dance to their own band or to the one next door. There were even a few white bands at the lake, and this was a chance for the Negro and Creole musicians to hear them. The lively racial mix was sometimes hazardous, however. Barney Bigard's band played so well at the Spanish Fort resort that a jealous white band planted stink bombs to scare away the public; apparently the sabotage worked.

The situation put within earshot many different styles, which were therefore imitable and transformable. And all of these low-paying outdoor and quasi-outdoor venues brought together musicians of different levels. The same thing could happen in indoor jobs too, many of which, after all, did not pay very well. These circumstances produced a musical marketplace where amateurs brushed alongside semiprofessionals, semiprofessionals alongside professionals. An ambitious musician could move up from honky tonks and advertising wagons into the parade scene, then to the lakes and lawn parties, after which he might play in the dance halls and then in cabarets and white society jobs. This movement created a flow of styles and techniques, a spread of ideas up and down the social spectrum. The ratty brass bands experimented with the texture of collective improvisation, and in due time their innovations were taken up by the lofty Onward Brass Band, where Oliver spun monkeyshines around Perez's lead. When the second-line marchers demanded an encore, they were perhaps recognizing the kind of musical-social fluidity I am imagining. To be sure, a cabaret in Storyville was not as open to the latest twist on vernacular blues and ragtime as an advertising wagon was. But the idea that came from someone's clever attempt to better a rival in a bucking contest might undergo any number of modifications as it moved through this sprawling network.

It has been claimed that cultural innovation often comes from the margins of society. New Orleans had lots of margins, and they were all connected in some slippery way to every other venue along any number of musical-social tangents. From the high aerial view the scene was a huge indoor-outdoor loop, with some musicians anchored on one end of the spectrum or the other, some moving up, from outdoors to the better-paying indoor jobs, and most aware of what the others were doing. Uptown bands were more fluid than the downtown bands, which tended to be "organized" with steady personnel, almost like a club or an extended family unit. As Punch Miller remembered the situation, "The organized bands had their number of men; they didn't want anybody else." Big Eye Louis Nelson, the clarinetist who bucked against Creole pedagogy and apprenticed with a ragging string band, found uptown musicians to be more sociable and relaxed than downtown musicians. These were some of the ingredients of the environment that fostered the stylistic innovations of early jazz: a constant flow of low-paying, unmonitored performances, steady movement between social levels, and a relaxed attitude.

A Song Writer and Entertainer

During his mid-teenage years Armstrong worked common-labor jobs and took musical work when he could get it, just like most of the uptown musicians he knew. There was high turnover in common labor; if you made the right connections and a regular musical job turned up, you simply walked away from your day job. Richard Jones described a lot of hanging out and checker playing, a slow-moving life, "not like New York, where they went to school—no schools, nothing enforced. If they wanted to take up an instrument, [they] had all the time in the world to perfect their playing." But when they had to, the musicians found work in the rice mill (Johnny Dodds), the bag factory (Baby Dodds), or on the docks (Pops Foster).

Louis worked the junk wagon with Alex Karnofsky and played a tinhorn to call kids with their bottles and rags, just like Larenzo. When (probably in 1915 and 1916) the Karnofskys started to sell coal in Storyville, the job brought Armstrong into listening range of Oliver, Keppard, Perez, Bunk Johnson, Petit, and Joe Johnson playing in the cabarets and dance halls. Later he drove a coal cart for the Tennessee Coal Company while Pops Foster was doing the same thing for the Pittsburgh Coal Company. The two passed each other on their routes every morning and took turns buying a "big bottle of

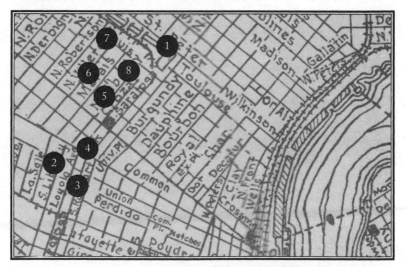

New Orleans, 1924 (New Orleans Public Library)
1) Site of Place Congo   2) Funky Butt Hall
3) Odd Fellows and Masonic Hall   4) Pelican Dance Hall   5) Big 25
6) Pete Lala's   7) The Frenchman's   8) Tuxedo Dance Hall

10 cent Southern Whiskey" to help them through the day. Since musical jobs often went late into the night, it was tough to keep a day job going. Foster remembered playing late, getting up early to hitch his mule, and sleeping on the wagon while the mule slowly followed the one directly ahead. Armstrong recalled finishing his musical gig at four in the morning, sleeping for a couple of hours, then fetching his load of coal, which he hauled from seven until five in the evening. Physical demands like these kept the music business young.

Armstrong moved up slowly; no one was talking about him as a budding genius that they simply had to have in their band. The musicians started to use him as a substitute on dance gigs and worked around his limitations, as we have already learned from Pops Foster. Several stories have a negative edge and make clear that he still had some distance to go. Bill Matthews recalled the Excelsior band needing an extra cornetist, so Matthews suggested Armstrong. The others pointed out that Armstrong could not read music, but Matthews won out and went to find him. The next day, however, when it was time to begin the job, Armstrong was so nervous that he drank himself sick on cheap wine. Bechet once explained why it was difficult for jump-up bands to compete with the organized bands: "The musicianers from the other bands, bands that had just been gotten up for that day—they were just a bunch of men who was going to play and that was a difference; they wouldn't have that sure feeling inside." During his mid-teens, Armstrong definitely lacked "that sure feeling inside." Around 1918 he showed up as a substitute with the Silver Leaf Band. Clarinetist Sam Dutrey walked in, said hello to the other musicians, saw Armstrong, and barked out "WHAT THE HELL IS THIS? GET OFF OF HERE BOY." It was a half-joke, the humor of which Armstrong missed entirely. For the entire evening he had trouble relaxing into the gig. "Louis would get nervous, Louis get on the stand," said Manetta. "[Dutrey] didn't give Louis no credit, nothing like that. 'Oh no, Oh no, Not that way, not that way,' that's how he'd talk."

He was still physically small, something most people have trouble imagining since they have seen him only on television and in movies, where he fills up the screen. It may be hard to believe, but according to Ory, Black Benny sometimes tied Louis to his own wrist so that he didn't get lost in crowds while Benny escorted him, dressed in his short pants, to jobs where he substituted for Mutt Carey. This probably happened in 1916. Oliver had worked up a solo for W. C. Handy's *Ole Miss* (published in 1916), and Armstrong learned it too, no doubt in imitation of his mentor. Ory said that when Louis filled in for Carey, he only knew three numbers, *Ole Miss*, *Keep Off Katie's Head*, "and blues." The song about Katie was Armstrong's own composition, and it was a bit naughty:

> Why don't you keep off Katie's head?
> Why don't you keep out (of) Katie's bed?
> It's a shame to say this very day,
> She's like a little child at play.
> It's a shame how you're lying on her head.
> I thought sure you would kill her dead.
> Why don't you be nice, boy, and take my advice,
> Keep off Katie's head, I mean, get out (of) Katie's bed.

Manetta, playing in a band led by Oliver, described a similar situation. He remembered how "there were always poor boys coming around to get in the place," including Armstrong and Red Happy Bolton. Oliver liked to send them on little errands to make them feel part of the scene, and he let Louis and Red Happy sit in briefly with the band. Bolton was a few years older than Louis; the two had sung together in the vocal quartet and Bolton also spent time at the Waif's Home. He eventually became a popular drummer in the Oliver-Ory band. "If you had a 100-thing-set-up for him he could hit them all at the same time. He was just that fast," said Hypolite Charles. "Red Happy was bad, man," said Punch Miller, meaning that he was exceptionally good. Paul Barbarin said that the first time he ever heard flat 4/4 drumming was when Bolton was playing blues with Oliver and Ory in Economy Hall, and Johnny Wiggs said that the success of that band was due mainly to Oliver and Bolton. Red Happy was also good at scat singing, which he mixed into a dirty song. Wiggs insisted that Bolton had an influence on Armstrong's own vocal style. Armstrong described Bolton as "the greatest showman of them all."

Manetta, like Ory, remembered Armstrong knowing only three
tunes when he started sitting in, but he named them slightly differently—*Wind and Grind, Take Your Feet off Katie's Head*, and "the
blues." "He played them nice," Manetta said. Manetta played
piano to accompany Louis singing *Take Your Feet off Katie's Head*
while the regular band members took a break. The audience
enjoyed the humor of having an obscene song sung by a child, but
his budding talent was also evident. "Well, you believed in him a
little bit, you see," said Manetta. Given the limitations mentioned
elsewhere, this seems to strike the right note—detectable talent
not yet in full bloom. The dance patrons once demanded an
encore, which caused the jealous Bolton to pick a fight with Louis.
Manetta had to separate them; "Louis know how to fight, too,
around the Battlefield," he said.

It is indeed interesting that Armstrong had, by age sixteen or so,
composed a piece of music. And not just any piece: his naughty *Take
Your Feet off Katie's Head* was tweaked by Clarence Williams and
Armand Piron into the 1919 best seller *I Wish That I Could Shimmy
Like My Sister Kate*. Williams and Piron started a publishing house
at 1315 Tulane Avenue in February of 1916, in the wake of
Williams's successful *Brown Skin Who You For*. "Hey brown skin,
who you for?" was a pickup line used by men on Rampart Street, to
which women would sometimes respond, "I'm for you, baby," and
other times, "I'm for your daddy when your mother ain't home."
Williams's intention was to capture a vernacular atmosphere and market the song "for people of color," as the advertisement said, something along the lines of W. C. Handy's big hit *Memphis Blues* from
three years earlier.

Though he didn't match Handy, Williams did achieve local success. In February 1916 the New Orleans police sang the song at
their annual minstrel show, and by March many bands were playing
it in the Mardi Gras parade while people along the streets wore
brown leather and sang along. "It was the biggest day of my life,"
remembered Williams. Members of a white band who immodestly
called themselves the Original Dixieland Jazz Band left the city five
days before Mardi Gras, and when they arrived in Chicago they
immediately made the song the "house ditty" at the Schiller Café.

They tweaked the lyrics slightly so that "Who you for brown skin?" was answered with "I'm for you, white folks"—"stuff like that, that would appeal to the northern man," explained cornetist Nick LaRocca. The ODJB took credit for the song, just as it later took credit for having created jazz, bringing the final twist to this little story, packed as it is with so much representation of the social dynamics that routinely touched African-American music during this period.

Musically rich New Orleans was a good place for Williams and Piron to run a publishing company. They hired Steve Lewis, who was musically illiterate but compositionally talented, and also Johnny St. Cyr, who was credited as co-composer with Piron for *Mama's Baby Boy* (1917), though he claimed never to have received any money for it. Armstrong sold his song to them for fifty dollars, though he too said (on one occasion—the story changed in different tellings of it) that he never got paid. Composer credit went to Piron, with no mention of Armstrong. The theft was not isolated; in 1930, for example, Williams and Piron published and claimed credit for *High Society*, which had been composed by Porter Steele in 1901. Piron insisted, surely with a bit of self-interest, that Armstrong had taken commonly known material to make his song. There was certainly a lot of that going on. Bolden was using the tunes of the rag-bottles-and-bones men in his blues, and composers W. C. Handy and William Grant Still both acknowledged their own use of what they considered common-practice blues material. If Armstrong was working with a song that had been circulating in oral tradition, he probably also adjusted it enough to believe that it was his own creation. In any event, it was precocious of him to pick up on these possibilities at such a young age.

When Armstrong sold his song to Williams and Piron, he was stepping into a relationship marked heavily by social class. Piron was a light-skinned Creole who would soon be performing with his dance orchestra for debutante balls on St. Charles Avenue and afternoon tea dances at the New Orleans Country Club. Here was the Creole advantage in action, and the same advantage undoubtedly operated on some level in the publishing house. A musically illiterate composer had to rely on someone who could notate the

piece and make business arrangements. "I wasn't brought up to educate myself in that kind of business, like some other cats were,"
Armstrong acknowledged. Someone in his position lacked not only
capital but also the sense of how to fit into a market structure, how
to make connections for distribution, advertising, production, and
management. He had nothing to lose by offering his song to
Williams and Piron, because he had nowhere else to go with it.

Thus, the reach for the next big popular hit through published
sheet music was part of the early jazz scene. It is common to think of
improvisation and the composition of popular songs as two necessary
but independent parts of jazz, two types of musical creativity that
move in parallel without overlapping. The jazz musician takes sheet
music and uses it to create something new, in the time-honored tradition of ragging the tune; song writing is something else altogether. In
New Orleans, the two creative acts were closer to one another than
that. In fact, the musicians were tinkering with melodies all the time.
Alphonse Picou made a name for himself by simply adapting the piccolo part for *High Society* to his clarinet. (The solo became so well
known that Charlie Parker was still quoting it in the mid-1940s.)
Others created breaks: Perez, for example, added a little run to a tune
that people in Francs Amis Hall waited for. Big Eye Louis Nelson
made up a special chorus for *St. Louis Blues* that other clarinet players
then copied, and Manetta did something similar for *Panama*. Freddie
Keppard made up an obbligato part to go along with the melody
Sweetie Dear that became popular, and so on.

When they moved to Chicago and got familiar with a larger
industry, the New Orleanians chased the dream of publishing the
next big hit even harder. Tony Jackson, the pianist and entertainer,
hit pay dirt in 1916 with *Pretty Baby*. Soon after arriving in
Chicago, Oliver hired pianist Lillian Hardin away from her job
demonstrating sheet music and set her to notating his own lead
sheets, which were then filed for copyright in Washington, D.C. A
few years later he wrote to Buddy Petit, "If you've got a real good
blues, have someone to write it just as you play them and send them
to me, we can make some jack on them. Now, have the blues wrote
down just as you can play them, it's the originality that counts."
After Armstrong hooked up with Lil in Chicago, the two of them

sometimes sat on the back steps of their apartment sketching out tunes with the same rewards in mind. In August 1923, for example, they submitted for copyright a song called *When You Leave Me Alone to Pine*, "music by Louis Armstrong, words by Lillian Hardin."

The other dimension signaled in these stories about the teenage Armstrong is showmanship. The Satchmo who filled the stage and movie screen got his start in his mid-teens, or even earlier. In a late memoir, he casually mentioned winning an "amateur contest" at the Iroquois Theater; his act was to cover his face in flour, thus inverting the traditional minstrel mask and putting on "white face." Bebé Ridgley recalled how Armstrong "used to dance, shadow box, every-thing" during his teens. Armstrong himself said that he had a "jive routine" with tap dancing. He and others admired his friend Nicodemus's ability to "mug and make some of the funniest expres-sions, especially when he was dancing with a sharp chick." Jazz in New Orleans was entwined with minstrel-style showmanship from the beginning, and this dimension would be intensified when musi-cians left the city to perform with vaudeville tours. Oliver and his band dressed in plantation outfits for a show that traveled to California, for example. Clarence Williams was a "character man" in Benbow's Old Plantation Minstrels, and Jelly Roll Morton dressed in blackface makeup to perform comedy—"as a comedian, Morton is grotesque in his makeup," was one reviewer's opinion.

There were ample opportunities for Armstrong the showman to absorb the entertainment styles of his day, either at the Iroquois Theater or at the Lyric Theater. The degree to which minstrel styles were saturated with racism and social exploitation was overlooked, simply because of the opportunities for performance that minstrelsy provided. Through his mugging technique, Armstrong perfected a style of shifting quickly between the comic and the serious, a stage sensitivity that says a lot about his approach to entertainment, including his interpretation of popular songs. He was often able to convey the emotions of a schmaltzy song while also recasting it through the intellectual intensity of what he adds. Part of his stage appeal lay in this ability to have things both ways. "What did I do, to be so black and blue," he would sing much later, with both a tragic and a comic touch, simultaneously.

Scat, which Armstrong may have first heard from comedians as an exaggeration of minstrel malapropism, offered the same possibility. In minstrel settings, scat was typically banal and humorous. For Armstrong in his musical maturity it became a way of using low humor to create dazzling artistry. It is the typical Armstrong combination taken to an extreme: the text speaks comedy or racism or sappy sentimentality, while the intensity of his melodic spin elevates the African-American vernacular to one of its greatest heights. Different audiences could hear him differently. But even those who were reassured by the old minstrel stereotypes knew, even if they may not have acknowledged it, that they were listening as much to the virtuoso ragging as to the tunes themselves.

Playing by Ear

Around 1917 Armstrong formed a six-piece band, with Joe Lindsay on drums, Louis Prevost (sometimes cited as Louis Privo) on clarinet, Maurice French on trombone, Eddie Green on bass violin, and Keebo Remee playing guitar. Their model was the famous band led by Ory and Oliver. "We were (for youngsters) the closest thing to the Ory band," according to Armstrong. The band broke up when Lindsay managed it dishonestly and made a mess out of the deposits. "That is one reason why I never cared to be a band leader," said Armstrong. "Too much small pittance and catty things went on. I just wanted to blow my horn peacefully, the same as I am doing now." This band may have played once or twice for frat dances at Tulane University. Souchon remembered Armstrong filling in there on occasion, with Armstrong himself playing too loudly. He was "perhaps not good then," said Souchon.

The Lindsay band, like the Ory and Oliver band, Frank Dusen's Eagle Band, and Jack Carey's band, was not a reading band. I doubt that any of Armstrong's friends could read music. Several things made it possible for bands like this to be active professionally. First was the fact that they only needed to know a small number of tunes. The "popular music" scene was nothing like it is today, with repertory pushed rapidly in and out of public awareness by radio, television, and intensive marketing. One musician recalled how his band learned *If the Man on the Moon* and played it for two years before people began to like it. Louis James's band worked up a set of two waltzes, two two-steps, two schottisches, and two mazurkas, finishing with the five-part quadrille; after a break they simply reversed the order within each set, disguising the repetition from the dancers. "It was like having beans and rice one day, then rice and beans the next day," quipped James. There was a relatively small repertory that every routine musician tried to learn so that he could move in and out of bands when called. Not everyone was nimble enough to do that, however. Johnny Dodds told Pops Foster how frustrated he was by his own limitations: "That's what I did wrong. I got wrapped up around one band and I sounded funny with anybody else." According to Foster, Dodds was not unique. "There were a lot of players around New Orleans who would only play with their own band," he remembered. "Some of the guys were Ory, Frankie Dusen, Albert Nicholas, and George Brunies. Those guys couldn't read so good or couldn't read at all, and they couldn't go into other bands and start playing."

One way to learn new tunes was to listen to other bands and memorize what they played. At Lake Pontchartrain, where the bands were in close proximity to one another, band members were sometimes assigned to memorize the part played by their counterparts in another band, thus generating an entire arrangement if everyone was successful. Jack Carey sent out Punch Miller with assignments to try and "catch" sections of pieces his band was having trouble with. It was not unusual to combine sections from different pieces to make a new piece. Clarence Williams was known to respond to audience requests by asking the patron to come back the next day; in the meantime, he trotted down to the five-and-ten-cent store, pulled out the song for the piano player to demonstrate, and memorized it on the spot. Similar service could be procured at the Big 25 club, a hangout for musicians that had a piano. This way of learning music fostered memorization skills, and there are many stories about how rapidly and completely the stronger musicians could absorb a tune.

Nevertheless, the more successful routine bands often found it useful to bring in one reading musician who played the lead melody in performance and taught it to the others. More often than not this was a violinist. The role of the violin in early jazz has often been ignored, but it was very common in the uptown bands to have a violinist who played a straight lead while the other melody instruments filled in, added, or doubled the lead heterophonically. "For a long time the violin was the top instrument around New Orleans," said Pops Foster. It receded in importance during the late 1910s, and in the recordings of Oliver, Ory, Keppard, and Morton from the early 1920s the violin has disappeared.

But the bands Armstrong admired in 1917 had plenty of violin. The Eagle Band hired Peter Bocage and then Manetta. Ory hired Emile Bigard, and Oliver hired Manetta. Keppard's band, downtown, had Jimmy Palao and then Armand Piron. Baby Dodds thought that violin players had the advantage of not needing to pause for breath; compared to a clarinetist and cornetist, a violinist could play continuously. Foster liked its versatility: the violin could "play a whole lot of melody that the trumpet couldn't play." Uptown bands typically learned only the chorus or main section of a new tune, added a brief introduction, and played the chorus three times. Eventually they came upon a formula of alternating soft and loud on these repetitions, though "they never got so loud as to drown out the violin," said St. Cyr. On the last, loud chorus, the violinist played the melody an octave higher so that he could be heard amid the loud winds. Manetta thought that the reason modern bands (he was speaking around 1960) played loud all the time was that "they are no longer string bands," by which he meant that they no longer had violin, guitar, and string bass. "The way we used to play a long time ago sounded awful sweet," said Baby Dodds. Ory's band was nicknamed "the sweet and soft" because of its effective use of dynamic contrast.

With all of these strategies for dealing with their limitations, routine musicians were content with basic "spelling" or with no reading at all. More than a few believed that it was *better* not to read music. Chinee Foster noted a preference for nonreading drummers because of what they brought to a band: "He's got so much faking to do in order to swing the band." Cornetists Bocage, Perez, and Metoyer were all "musical men, but they couldn't get rid of that exercise book," said Foster, by which he meant that their improvisational invention was unimaginative and stiff. Johnny Wiggs believed that too much reading "slows down your improvisational wits." For Barney Bigard, written arrangements interfere with the expression of emotions: "With those heavy arrangements you are not free to express your feelings; you are just too busy fighting the damned notes."

It is easy to see how, in a situation as heavily loaded with issues of social distinction and control as New Orleans was in the 1910s, a group of disadvantaged people might become defensive about their own musical illiteracy and develop the counterargument that their limitation is actually an asset. Baby Dodds observed that a musician cannot play well unless he is relaxed, and there is no doubt that a printed page causes anxiety in anyone with shaky reading skills. We owe the insider's point of view about the advantages of aurality more serious consideration, however, especially since it finds support from several outside directions. Robert Palmer suggested (Chapter 3) that "deep blues" were possible only in a nonliterate environment. But the potential range of the discussion is much broader than that. When, for example, we discover Plato in ancient Greece worrying about the trade-off between orality and literacy, warning that the latter is mechanical, incapable of living dialogue, and a cause of weakened memory, then we should notice the similar concerns articulated by the New Orleanians and reflect upon a panhuman condition that may have unexpected implications.

Walter Ong, the most famous writer on "orality," offers sustained reflections on this topic, working mainly with remote cultures that had no knowledge of writing—remote until we remind ourselves that slaves were fiercely forbidden to read and write, and that many people who moved from the plantations to New Orleans in the late nineteenth century were completely illiterate. "Narrative originality lodges not in making up new stories but in managing a particular interaction with this audience at this time—at every telling the story has to be introduced uniquely into a unique situation, for in oral cultures an audience must be brought to respond, often vigorously," writes Ong, and one cannot help thinking of the interaction between a ragging routine band and the second line. And when Ong analyzes the "pre-emptiveness" of literacy, the way it takes over verbal functioning and makes it difficult to engage with habits of orality common throughout most of human history, we may begin to understand the New Orleanian attitude that it was better not to read music.

The topic has special relevance for early jazz, which developed a relationship with written texts distinct from Ragtime on the one hand and blues on the other. Ragtime became a thoroughly literate music, an idiom that took inspiration from the vernacular while making clear its distance. Joplin aimed to rival the permanent and sophisticated designs of classical music. He was apparently unable to play some of the piano rags he composed at his desk; in other words, his break with aurality was complete, and he was as far from the ragging improvisers of New Orleans as he could be. Blues musicians happily staked out territory on the other end of the spectrum. The idiom has flourished for its entire history with practically no trace of literate impact. What is interesting about jazz, the coeval cousin to Ragtime and blues, is the *interaction* between aurality and literacy that was built into the tradition early on. That interactive dynamic touched Armstrong in his late teens, and it became even more important after he left New Orleans in 1922 for Chicago, where he had to negotiate his way through a musical world in which literacy held even greater sway.

It seemed to the uptown routiners that aurality had its own set of advantages, and in the absence of strong evidence to the contrary it is hard to argue against them. What can definitely be said is that jazz could only have arisen within a musical culture that specialized in aurality. It obviously takes years of intensive training to perform at a high level in any artistic medium, and the uptown routiners believed that you could not have it both ways. Certainly Armstrong would not have developed in the same way if he had divided his time during his formative years between the vernacular and literate traditions. He was intensively trained in the unnotatable nuances of blues and ragging the tune and in the conversational sensitivities of collective improvisation. The routine bands learned their way of playing together by doing it constantly in public. Theirs was not the road of practicing in isolation, such as downtown musicians were known to do. Many routiners played only when they were together as a group, the entire range of their musical activity taking place in an environment of musical dialogue. Jazz is famous for this kind of exchange, and it could not have come about in any other way.

A well-articulated binary opposition was in place, oral/aural versus literate—or, as commonly phrased, "routiners" versus "musicianers." However much one might like to soften the opposition, for the participants it was a basic part of the social situation and loaded with implications. "The downtown bands always had better reading musicians than the uptown bands," said Bebé Ridgley. "Most of the faking was done by the uptown bands." The binary split between routiners and musicianers did not map onto the social geography of New Orleans quite as precisely as Ridgley implies, but it was definitely sustained by the historical trajectories associated with that geography. And it carried with it many of the associations of race, caste, and class discussed earlier (Chapter 8). To hire a musicianer usually meant looking downtown, especially if a violinist was desired. Manetta, from Algiers, across the river, was a favorite since he had all the Eurocentric skills but none of the Creole haughtiness.

The traditional downtown bands used their Eurocentric skills to advantage when they battled against routine bands in cutting contests. Their weapon of choice was any number from the "Red Back Book." Published in 1912 by John Stark in St. Louis, the "book" was actually a set of part books, arrangements of rags by Joplin—*The Cascades, Maple Leaf Rag, The Entertainer, Ophelia Rag*, and so on— plus a handful of others, including *Grace and Beauty* by James Scott and *African Pas* by Maurice Kirwin. Manetta's own copy is preserved today at the Williams Research Center in New Orleans; penciled-in marks in some of the cornet parts help the player (was it Oliver?) negotiate the rhythmic divisions. "I used to play Scott Joplin numbers by heart, man," said Manetta. "I used to play them on the violin plenty. That was popular music, but certain bands couldn't get after it. Bands uptown never fooled with that. Only bands downtown."

Yet, as dazzling as a fully arranged, perfectly executed rag by Joplin could be, the routine bands had an advantage that the Creoles increasingly had to pay attention to during the 1910s. As Armstrong summed it up, "Any learned musician can read music, but they all can't swing." We can be certain that Oliver did not get into Perez's Onward Brass Band because of family connections, strong reading skills, or tone. He got in because he could play barrelhouse and make monkeyshines that were well received on the streets. It is often difficult to study the public reception of art, and that is certainly the case with our subject. A taste for vernacular music was apparently spreading to dance halls very different from Funky Butt Hall, where Bolden had found success. "Way late around New Orleans the dicty people got tired of hearing that violin scratchin' all night and started to hire some bands who'd play some rough music for them," said Pops Foster. "The bands that couldn't read made the most money and were the biggest talk of the town. They were gutbucket bands like Ory's and for a while Dusen's Eagle Band. They played hot all the time." A sweeping statement like that covers up as much as it reveals, but the general trend is clear: the bluesy vernacular was on the rise. Bands on both sides of Canal Street came to recognize the advantages of having a diverse repertory. The uptown vernacular was gradually being imposed on the downtown Creoles, against the grain of their literate, Eurocentric values. Eventually even Jimmy Palao, born from "society people," learned to fake and play blues on his violin, though he was one of the few violinists to do so.

War and an Epidemic

After the Joe Lindsay band fell apart, Armstrong kept playing in honky tonks and on advertising wagons, gradually expanding his repertory. Oliver sent him to substitute at Pete Lala's, but he was turned away because he couldn't play the freak music Lala was expecting. Bebé Ridgley once needed a cornetist for a job out at Lake Pontchartrain and he tried to get Oliver, who was busy and recommended Louis. Ridgley and his musicians knew nothing about him, and they started to worry when they saw a boy walking toward them dressed in an undersized, worn-out blue coat and police cap, his cornet in a dirty bag under his arm. Ridgley took Louis aside and ran through some song titles, asking him if he could play them. The band was playing for a club that had a habit of making specific requests, songs like *Old Kentucky*. There was no piano out at the lake, so they could not rely on a sheet-reading pianist to lead them along while they faked a requested song. It turned out that Louis knew more tunes than most musicians in the band, and Ridgley did not hesitate to use him again when he needed a substitute.

But he was still a kid, working lots of odd jobs and pursuing music on the side. One observer claimed that he was still tagging along in short pants behind Oliver in parades during World War I, and another saw him in 1918 "with a big broomstick, second lining behind us, pitching it up in the air drum-major-like." He washed dishes at a restaurant on the corner of Canal and Rampart streets and was allowed to eat as many doughnuts, cream puffs, and bowls of ice cream as he wished. He overdosed on the sweets, got tired of handling the delicate "high class dishes," and quit after two weeks. That brought him back to his coal cart. While driving "Lady," his mule, he composed a song that he named *Coal Cart Blues*. For lunch he ate poor-boy sandwiches, washed down with a ten-cent can of beer at Joe Segretta's Saloon on the corner of Liberty and Perdido streets, and loved listening to the men talk. He also kept his prostitute Nootsy going, though that soured when she stabbed him in the shoulder with a knife. He ran home to show the wound to May Ann, who hunted down Nootsy and nearly choked her to death, warning her never to bother her son again.

The closing of Storyville in November 1917—an indirect consequence of World War I—made things difficult for musicians. The worldwide flu epidemic of that year further handicapped the professional scene when dance halls were closed in an effort to check its spread. "Everybody was down with [the flu] except me," Armstrong wrote, with gratitude for his purging laxatives. "That's because I was always physic minded, and kept myself open at all times." The mortality rate from the flu kept musicians busy playing funerals, but the combination of the dance-hall closings and the closing of Storyville created a significant drop in opportunities. Armstrong took a job for a few weeks in Houma, Louisiana, playing for "country dances." Back in New Orleans, he played "a lot of blues for those cheap prostitutes, hustlers, etc." at Henry Matranga's tonk, in a small band with one Boogus on piano and Garbee on drums. But in a short time, the forced closings designed to check the spread of the flu epidemic touched even this small-time tonk, which was shut down by city order.

Another consequence of the war were the so-called work-or-fight laws. Any man of eligible age not engaged in a job that aided the war effort was required to enlist; in practice the laws were used to force labor on younger men like Armstrong as well. Southern states took advantage of the situation to flood the market with cheap African-American labor. Armstrong worked as a stevedore until he saw a huge rat and ran off. He and Kid Ory helped build a port of embarkation for soldiers. A little later he was forced by the work-or-fight laws to haul coal again. Relief came at 11:00 a.m. on November 11, 1918, when he heard the news of the Armistice and said to himself, "The war is over. And here I am monkeyin' around with this mule." With that he dropped his shovel, looked at his mule, and said, "So long, my dear. I don't think I'll ever see you again." No more coal hauling, stevedoring, or carpentry. "Now I can play my music, the way I want to and when I want to," he told his mother when he got home.

The drying up of musical jobs prompted more than a few departures, including Oliver's. "When the law commenced closing Storyville down on Saturday nights, the best nights anywhere in the world, it was time for Papa Joe to start looking for new fields," Armstrong wrote. Oliver left for Chicago with clarinetist Jimmie Noone in the summer of 1918. He had been the featured attraction in Kid Ory's band, and after some deliberation Ory offered the position to Armstrong. Ory at first had his doubts, but the other band members convinced him that Armstrong was the best choice. After all, he knew Oliver's solos by heart, and the band he had with Lindsay was a direct copy of Ory and Oliver's band. Armstrong even opened up his collar and draped a towel around his neck in imitation of his mentor. "I lived Joe Oliver from the word say go," he wrote.

It was a heady moment, a dream come true. He was now directly following in the footsteps of his mentor and playing steadily with a group of mature musicians. In 1951 he was asked to comment on his famous recordings from the 1920s, including the renowned

*The bandstand at Artisan Hall (Historic New Orleans Collection,
Acc. No. 92-48-L MSS 520 f. 634, photo by William Russell)*

Potato Head Blues. When he had made the recording in 1927, he
remembered, he "could look direct into the Pelican Dance Hall, at
Gravier and Rampart Streets in New Orleans," and see Oliver, Ory,
and Dodds playing the piece from the bandstand. They stood in the
left corner of the room, up above the dancers' heads—"in order to say
hello to any member of the band, you had to look up." "All of that
good music was pouring out of those instruments—making you want
to just dance and listen and wishing they'd never stop . . . Every note
that I blew in this recording, I thought of Papa Joe." The emotional
charge of the moment was still vivid more than thirty years later. It
was, perhaps, a moment when his teenage identity crystallized.

Ory's Band

In 1918 Kid Ory loomed fairly large on the uptown musical scene.
A musician of limited talent, he had a good knack for business and
was able to do well for himself during the nine years or so that he
lived in the city. History books routinely misrepresent him as a
Creole, as if he were part of the downtown scene. For anyone interested in the social complexities of New Orleans, this is exactly the
kind of haunting problem that seems to lurk around every corner.

The light-skinned Ory may have been Creole in the broadest
usage of the term in Louisiana, but he was almost as far removed

from the downtown Creoles as Armstrong was. He never learned to read music and covered up his weak command of the trombone by smearing over missed notes with glissandi. He was born around 1886 on a sugar plantation near LaPlace, Louisiana, some thirty miles upriver, to a white Frenchman and a mother of mixed ancestry—native American, African American, and white. He moved to the city when he turned twenty-one, and though he did speak a bit of French, no one mistook him for a downtown Creole of color. Ory told Sidney Bechet one day in the mid-1910s that he himself was a Creole and Bechet did not believe him. Ory spoke the dialect right then and there, but for years Bechet was convinced that he was pulling a joke. As downtown Creole Paul Dominguez once observed, "Speak French, but what does that prove? If you learn Italian, it don't make no Italian out of you."

After he arrived in the city, Ory soon put together a band that was popular enough, he later claimed, to draw patrons away from John Robichaux, the leader who had competed with Bolden at Lincoln and Johnson parks. As Ory told the story, Robichaux responded by trying to hire him. Ory answered that with a bit of signifying: "I said, 'Thank you Mr. Robichaux, I'm doing all right.' Called him 'Mr. Robichaux.'" In other words, he mocked the dicty Robichaux by addressing him as if he were white, thereby exagger-

Kid Ory's band, LaPlace, Louisiana, ca. 1907
(Historic New Orleans Collection, Acc. No. 92–48–L MSS 520 f. 2313)

ating the social distance between them. The offer must have roused Ory's competitive spirits. He had his sights set much higher than playing trombone in somebody else's band.

Ory had on his side a family history of entrepreneurship and perhaps even a little bit of cash. His father's cousin owned the grocery store on the plantation, and his brother Johnny eventually owned a saloon in New Orleans at the corner of Conti and Claiborne streets, two blocks from the Storyville district. Already as a teenager on the plantation he had made some money putting on fish fries: "I was the leader, the promoter, the bookkeeper, treasurer and fish fryer," he said. This hustling attitude served him well when it came to patching together musical jobs in New Orleans. He ingratiated himself with Betsy Cole, and her lawn parties spread his reputation. Ory claimed that he was the first to rent an advertising wagon solely for the purpose of promoting his own band, hanging a sign on each side that read, "New Band in Town from LaPlace, Louisiana. Woodland Band. Kid Ory, Manager." And, as we have seen, he took a special interest in advertising-wagon battles, being the first to use a gas-driven truck and routinely adding the zinger of singing *Kiss My Funky Ass* after victories.

He gradually figured out who was making money in music and how they were doing it. Anyone could rent a hall for a dance. Requests for a permit were made directly to the police superintendent and then issued for $5.00. Policemen were assigned to the job at a cost of $2.50 each. Someone like Ory, with light skin and experience dealing with whites in business relationships, had a relatively easy time with these kinds of negotiations. He came upon a scheme for shutting out competition by renting Economy Hall and Cooperator's Hall on the same night, putting his own band in one and keeping the other closed. When the open hall started to overflow with business, he opened the other one too, with another of his own bands. This went on for a year. Eventually he was even able to land a few white "society" jobs—"More money, you know— got away from the cheapskates"—an advantage perhaps also gained by his light skin.

Most bands in New Orleans had a manager and a leader, each filling different roles. To say that a gig "was Ory's job" meant that

Ory had made the contract, received the money, and was responsible for paying the musicians. This was typically work for the manager, though in practice other band members could make arrangements too. The leader had the musical responsibilities, mainly "knocking off" the tempo for each number by pounding his foot and counting the beats; Bolden, with a bit of showmanship, used to slam his cornet on the floor. In 1915 and 1916 Mutt Carey was the leader of Ory's band. When Carey left, Ory tried to do it himself, but he kept messing up. Setting the tempo was an important task. Oliver was admired for being good at choosing just the right one. With the exception of the slow drag, moderate tempos were always favored, in contrast to the faster tempos preferred in places like Chicago. "When musicians from other places . . . played hot, they just played fast," said Emmanuel Sayles. "That's what people called playing hot." But New Orleans musicians could "play hot and at the same time be playing in a groovy tempo where you [could] dance or clap your hands or join."

So when Oliver came into Ory's band, probably in 1917, he naturally took over the role of leader. Apparently he also did more than that, for before Ory knew it, the band was being promoted as the "Ory and Oliver Band." Shrewd enough to recognize his own strengths and weaknesses, Ory acquiesced. The band became extremely popular. "It was the preference band of the people," said Manetta, who played in it in 1917. "The people really liked that Dixieland that we played."

Earlier, Ory had purchased a set of parts for the Red Back Book for twenty-five cents, but the band couldn't handle it. Manetta tried unsuccessfully to teach Carey how to read the melodies and Ory how to read the bass parts. Though the band did not get far with the Red Back Book, we know that their repertory included *Brown Skin Who You For*, *Tulane Swing*, *Eccentric*, *Ole Miss*, *Panama*, *High Society*, some hymns, and some blues. The band played blues at midnight at Economy Hall, Globe Hall, Masonic Hall, and other African-American dance halls, "low down, slow—they would really moan it out," remembered Johnny Dodds, the clarinetist. "The inspiration came mainly from Joe and the drummer, Happy Bolton," who knew "how to drive a band," said Wiggs. Oliver sat out one chorus during every piece, giving space for Dodds to stand out on clarinet with Ory "kicking bass rhythm at the back of him." By 1916 Ory had perfected the current fashion of contrasting loud and soft choruses in a single number, so soft that you could hear feet shuffling on the dance floor. Armstrong went to hear them on Sunday nights at St. Katherine's Hall, and he remembered this technique being used with *Ory's Creole Trombone.*

"That group could play that really jazz sounding style—to us it sounded like heaven," was Wiggs's memory of the Ory-Oliver band. The band seems to have infused New Orleanian dance-band music with more of the African-American vernacular than had ever been done before. It presented the rough and beautiful tradition at its current best. It was from this band that one could hear, in its most sophisticated form, the texture of collective improvisation, as shaped by Oliver playing monkeyshines around Manetta's violin and by Johnny Dodds doing the same thing on clarinet when Oliver carried the lead (especially, perhaps, in the march numbers like *Panama* and *High Society,* brought into dance bands from the parade bands). Hear the driving, flat 4/4 foundational rhythm, brought from church and blues. Hear freak playing with Oliver at his technical peak, and also hear the other markers of "hot" playing—phrasing, attack, and vibrato—described by Charlie DeVore (Chapter 6). When Armstrong and the Lindsay band were imitating the Ory-Oliver band, they were working on all of these things.

Given Ory's business sense and Oliver's musical savvy, it is not surprising to find the band reacting to an intervention that sprang on the scene unexpectedly in 1917. The Original Dixieland Jazz Band had left town just before the Mardi Gras of 1916, headed for Chicago to make a hit with *Brown Skin Who You For.* A year later it made an even bigger splash at Reisenweber's restaurant in New York City, and from there the band found its way into a studio where it made the first phonograph recording of a New Orleans dance band. *Livery Stable Blues* and, on the B side, *Dixie Jazz Band One-Step,* sold more than one million copies. Members of the ODJB were among a handful of white musicians who had been paying close attention to the uptown vernacular, hanging around the Storyville district and even funeral processions. "They were the first to record the music I played," is how Armstrong understood what they were doing. African-American musicians had an appropriately regional name for white musicians like this—"alligators." Johnny Wiggs, the white cornetist who admired Oliver so much at Tulane, remembered how he and his friends "listened to the band around the bandstand instead of talking to the pretty girls." But Wiggs fully acknowledged where this music had come from. The ODJB, on the other hand, took full credit for creating it while denying any African-American influence at all.

Here, in the blockbuster hit of 1917, was the glory that should have gone to Freddie Keppard (Chapter 9), who had turned down an opportunity to record because he was afraid of having his ideas stolen. That was perhaps less of a concern for the ODJB because it was stealing the ideas. The event stands as one of the many American examples of white musicians learning black music and then taking financial and creative credit for it. Perhaps that injustice animated the uptown Negroes and downtown Creoles of color. In any event, these musicians now continued, with renewed vigor, the trend of looking to other parts of the country for greater financial rewards.

And within just a few years, the phonograph would play a role in the presentation of their music. Ory recorded with a band in Los Angeles in 1922; this was followed by the series of recordings by Oliver's band beginning in 1923 and by the even more extensive Hot Five series led by Armstrong, beginning in 1925. But this chronological lag is a bit deceptive. Undoubtedly, the phonograph made its first big impression in the minds of the New Orleanians in 1917. The phonograph was the ascendant technology for the distribution of early jazz, since it miraculously captured the unnotatable attractions of aurality. The ODJB's success immediately launched the trend of learning repertory and styles from recordings, supplementing the traditional approaches of memorizing live performances of other bands, learning arrangements from sheet music, and making up arrangements to go along with a known melody.

The timing was right for the ODJB, since more and more people were buying phonographs. Armstrong himself eventually got "one of those upright Victrolas, which we were very proud of," and he purchased a copy of *Livery Stable Blues*. By the end of 1917 "jazz" bands were being formed as far away as England. White musicians in New Orleans who had never been interested in vernacular music started to incorporate it into their acts. Oliver and Ory reduced the size of their band to mimic the ODJB quintet. "We've got to follow suit, follow suit," said Oliver. Some patrons complained when they got a quintet instead of the seven-piece band they thought they were getting. Lorenzo Staultz the guitarist and Bob Lyons the bass player were both vulnerable. So was Manetta, who played violin, but the band relied on him to teach them new music: "They wanted me all the time, because when they got tangled up with his music I could show them the divisions," said Manetta. The tension caused Manetta to get mad and quit; after that, Emile Bigard was occasionally brought in to play violin. Nevertheless, the ODJB was probably one cause of a diminished role for the violin in early jazz.

❧ After Armstrong settled into Ory's band in the summer of 1918, he began to make a nice reputation for himself. His speed on the cornet was picking up, and his sound was undoubtedly projecting more and more confidence. Other bands sought him out on nights he wasn't playing with Ory. Ory managed to get a contract for the New Orleans Country Club on Saturday nights—"rich folks," Armstrong wrote—which must have required a fairly traditional repertory of dance tunes. Armstrong managed and for the most part fit right in, probably because the band mainly leaned toward vernacular practices, at which he now excelled. "Mello moments I assure you," was how Armstrong remembered his time with this band.

He was solidly at home in the musical world Pops Foster described as rough and beautiful. In one of his memoirs, he reflected on his place in that world and his total acceptance of it:

> I was really *stickin* with cash. Because our tips from those prosperous prostitutes, who came to our joint, gave us lots of tips to play different tunes for them and their *Johns* . . . we made good tips—that is, as far as tips goes, for a barrel house honky tonk. Where nothing but the lowest of guys comes into town on payday looking for anything

to happen. And believe me, it did. And I was right in the middle of it all. With not a thing on my mind but my cornet-piano-drums—to look forward to every night. And I loved it. In fact, I did not know of anything else. And did not want to think of anything else. I was perfectly happy. That was my life and that was that. And I'll gladly live it all over again, so help me.

Yet part of him was restless, and sometime in the fall of 1918 he accepted a job that cut back his participation in Ory's band. The riverboat job with Fate Marable represents a major transition in his musical life, one equal in importance to his eighteen months in the Colored Waif's Home for Boys.

CHAPTER ELEVEN

Movin' On Up

You'll never be able to swing any better than
you already know how until you learn to read.
Then you'll swing in ways you never thought
of before.   —*Armstrong, recalling advice*
from David Jones

When Armstrong accepted Fate Marable's offer to play with his riverboat
orchestra, he was motivated by a push and by a pull. The push came
from his unhappy marriage to a woman named Daisy (formerly
Daisy Parker). They had wed in early 1918, and there were problems from the start. Daisy was a rough prostitute—"the prettiest
and the badest whore in Gretna, Louisiana," said Armstrong—and
some of May Ann's friends did not approve of the match. But May
Ann stayed out of it: "I can't live his life. He's my boy and if that's
what he wants to do, that's that," Armstrong remembered her saying. The newlyweds fought often, and Daisy quickly discovered a
point of real vulnerability: she could get him particularly upset by
hitting him in the mouth, thereby jeopardizing his musical career.
The last straw was when she shredded his Stetson hat with a razor.
The offer from Marable started to look pretty good. Daisy was certainly not the last woman to hear from Armstrong that his horn
comes first.

Marable liked to scout out the dance halls in New Orleans and
the Big 25. He heard Armstrong with Ory's band at Cooperator's
Hall and offered him the job. Armstrong was only seventeen years
old and reluctant to leave home. Several offers came his way during

his last few years in the city, including one from Fletcher Henderson who was in town accompanying Ethel Waters, but he was too nervous to accept them. He had heard stories about the treacheries of traveling jobs, stories about not getting paid and ending up stranded in some desolate place that was hostile to African Americans. The initial job with Marable was less risky because it was a tethered departure: as everyone could see, the Streckfus brothers' excursion boat regularly left its dock at the beginning of Canal Street and regularly returned later that night, right on schedule.

The pull to take this job was that it could help him move forward in the music business. "I jumped at the opportunity, because I thought it was an advancement towards my musical career," he wrote some thirty-five years later. "Because Fate's band had to read, and they *did* read music, perfectly. And Ory's band didn't. It was very fine (I thought) to be in Ory's band—but being in Fate Marable's band meant an advancement to me, a youngster who had big things in mind as far as music's concerned." He told Daisy that if he didn't take the job he might be stuck in New Orleans forever. In other words, he had recognized the career limitations of playing only by ear. He knew a few musicians who had made dramatic progress in army bands. Cornetist Punch Miller rehearsed in one four hours a day and learned the tricks of rhythmic notation, fancy fingering, and good intonation. Armstrong must have had similar expectations for the riverboat job. He returned the cornet Ory had purchased for him, since he had not finished paying for it, and Captain Johnny Streckfus purchased a new one for him.

The *Dixie Belle* was based in New Orleans, and from November through April it took two-and-a-half-hour trips on Friday, Saturday, and Sunday nights. Before departure the band played on the wharf to advertise the event, just as they would at a dance hall. Marable had previously hired the Eagle Band for this job, but it failed because the players could not read music. The new band was named the "Jazz Syncopators," later changed to "Fate Marable and His Jazz Maniacs."

In May of 1919 the program shifted northward. Armstrong was once asked when he had first left New Orleans, and he answered 1919, thinking back, no doubt, to the train ride he took from New

Orleans to St. Louis, where the Streckfus operation was based. David Jones, the mellophone player, was assigned to look out for him. "One of those dicty guys, very much erect in everything he did—a little *too* erect, I'd say," was Armstrong's reading of Jones. Jones had traveled with circuses and other road shows, so it fell to him to escort homeboy Louis safely to St. Louis. Jones was not pleased with this assignment. "He stood by me as if I was just another colored boy going to some other direction and he didn't know me at all," remembered Armstrong. The two eventually became friends, Louis nicknaming him "Bre'r Jones." Their train ride included a stop in Paducah, Kentucky, Marable's hometown, for the purpose of joining the musicians union, which had not been a possibility in New Orleans. When they arrived in St. Louis, they transferred their membership to the local union there.

The work routine in St. Louis was one of longer excursions, the boat leaving at 9:00 in the morning and returning at 6:00 in the evening. After a dinner break they played for the "moonlight ride" at 8:30. "In the four months of summer in 1919," said Pops Foster, "most of the time we worked from eight in the morning until eleven-thirty at night. That was long playing." They also took a few extended trips up the river, stopping by Alton, Illinois; Keokuk, Ft. Madison, Des Moines, and Dubuque, Iowa; Louisiana, Missouri, and, in August, all the way up to Red Wing and St. Paul, Minnesota. Marable's band started out playing on the steamer *Sidney*, which had a capacity of eight hundred patrons, and then moved over to the *St. Paul*, a much bigger boat that held thirty-five hundred.

The boats were, of course, segregated. A couple of years earlier, Captain Streckfus had originally hired Marable to lead a white band. (Johnny St. Cyr claimed that Marable, whose Negro mother was a maid on the boats, was actually Streckfus's illegitimate son, which might explain this experiment of an inverted racial hierarchy.) This new African-American band with Armstrong, Dodds, St. Cyr, and Foster was not "allowed to mingle with the guests . . . Just play that good music for them, the same as we did in New Orleans and all points 'south,' " wrote Armstrong dryly. People in small towns had never before seen African-American musicians dressed

*Fate Marable's orchestra, ca. 1920, with (in front, left to right) Henry Kimball,
Boyd Atkins, Johnny St. Cyr, David Jones, Norman Mason, Louis Armstrong,
George Brashear, and Baby Dodds, with Marable (behind), on piano
(Historic New Orleans Collection, Acc. No. 92-48-L MSS 520 f. 2540)*

up playing European instruments, and many of them simply stood
and stared—or worse. "At first, we ran into a lot of ugly moments
while we were on the band stand," Armstrong wrote, "such as 'Come
on thar, black boy, etc.'" But the next time the boat came into town,
the people were more relaxed and started dancing. Expectations of
the musicians were high and discipline was severe. Baby Dodds
returned to the boat drunk one night and the boss tied him to a
post, threatening to horsewhip him.

Armstrong had been frank with Marable about his inability to
read, and it is hard to imagine that Marable didn't know that already,
since he knew his way around New Orleans. St. Cyr, Dodds, and
Foster all joined the band without reading skills too, so it is clear that
Marable was willing to hire obvious talent and work with it. He had
learned one important lesson from his failed experience with the
Eagle Band: now he mixed readers and nonreaders together. In the
beginning, Joe Howard, the first chair cornetist, played the lead
melody for Armstrong, who memorized it and added a harmony part.
The procedure worked so well that a few of the musicians thought
Armstrong was actually reading parts; it wasn't until Howard got sick
and Armstrong was expected to take over the first cornet part that
they realized he couldn't read. A concerted effort was brought to bear
upon the seventeen-year-old's skills. Bre'r Jones worked with him on
the top deck of the boat for ninety minutes every day on divisions and
phrasing, and Joe Howard continued to help too.

Armstrong said that Marable had hired him because of his tone: "He like the way I played. My tone, and the way I could catch on." The big, fat, round—no peashooter!—confident sound that would come to be admired all over the world was in place, or at least nearly so. "I was piling up all kinds of experiences, that an ambitious kid usually dreams of. So Fate made me a featured man in his Orchestra. And Oh, [what a] thrill to hear those fine applause from the customers." He was the only one who took solos. He was certainly not brought on the boat to impress midwestern white patrons with the improvisational style that would begin to be documented on recordings during the mid-1920s. "We played strictly by music," said Baby Dodds. Yet it is clear that the band eventually did bring a distinctive New Orleanian sound to these towns along the river. Pops Foster said that "the *St. Paul* was known as the rough boat where they played jazz. The *Capitol* was known as a clean boat where they played sweet music." According to Armstrong, even dicty David Jones could swing and improvise. The band did not have the musicians to practice collective improvisation, and it is very unlikely that the Streckfus brothers would have been interested in that anyway. But with the high-level uptown rhythm section of St. Cyr, Foster, and Dodds and with Armstrong, there was plenty of rhythmic drive and swing.

The Streckfus brothers were firmly in control of musical production. "You played music to suit them, not the public," Foster remarked, and it may have been the first time the New Orleanians had encountered such strong intervention. It was certainly the first time they encountered a heavy schedule of rehearsals, essential for learning the fourteen new numbers that the band turned over twice per month. A cashier with a good ear was assigned to keep track of mistakes the musicians made. Marable could be cruel and haughty with them. Streckfus meticulously monitored their tempos with a stopwatch. The biggest problems came when the tempo slowed down and "guys would be out on the floor doing nothing but shaking their butts very slow and dirty," said Foster.

In addition to the exotic attraction of seeing and hearing African-American musicians playing this kind of music, the excursion boats offered a giant hook-up scene. For the fifty-cent price of admission, customers received a book of fourteen dance cards on which they could make notes about arrangements later in the evening, a meeting by the candy counter, at the bar, near the pilothouse, and so forth. "Most everybody came alone, but left with someone on their arm," said Foster. Monday-night excursions from St. Louis were set aside for African Americans. This was a relaxing night for the musicians because they could drink, smoke cigarettes, and socialize with these patrons, who crowded around the bandstand, five or six deep. It was perhaps on these nights, especially, when Armstrong and his buddies brought the uptown routine style to the northern river corridor. Jerome Don Pasquall, a musician from St. Louis, said that hearing Armstrong was a "revelation": "Louis, with all that terrific technique of his (like a clarinet almost), would play so many notes you'd be thrilled and forget all about the melody."

He gained a bigger sense of the world. In Memphis he hung out on Beale Street with Howard and Dodds. In St. Louis he was amazed by the tall buildings and asked Marable what they were—Were they colleges? he wondered. One summer Oliver visited him in St. Louis for four days, his mission to persuade his prize pupil to join him in Chicago. Armstrong declined, but gave his entire lunch to Papa Joe. He continued to compose; he said that he made up the tune *Weatherbird* while playing on the boats. He made a big splash at a party in St. Louis and his reputation as a soloist was starting to spread. In 1920 in Chicago, Paul Mares teased Oliver, telling him, "There's a kid down there in New Orleans, if he ever comes up here you're dead."

The idea that commercial pressures regularly taint the authentic purity of vernacular music is a familiar one. Something like that can happen, of course. But there may also be a more positive dimension in that kind of encounter. Armstrong's riverboat experience shows a musician who grew by meeting the challenges put before him. Playing for the Streckfus brothers and their straw boss Marable meant dealing with a different order of commercial expectation than anything he and his colleagues had previously known. He mastered musical notation and gained precision in the melodic syntax of Eurocentric music. No more faking the unfamiliar keys and scales. The whole structure of the job, with its regular schedule of rehearsing and its downtime for practicing, fostered steady progress. Baby Dodds said that the rehearsals taught the musicians precision and quickness. The experience transformed his ear playing too. Armstrong remembered Jones telling him that "you'll never be able to swing any better than you already know how until you learn to read. Then you will swing in ways you never thought of before." "And he was right," was how Armstrong came to think of the situation. The story of Armstrong on the riverboats stands as a good example of how many of the great popular musicians take their art to higher levels through encounters with the marketplace.

Tom Anderson's and Storyville

When Armstrong was back in New Orleans during the winters, his gains from the riverboat job created opportunities that were well beyond the reach of routine musicians. One was his success with the Tuxedo Brass Band, described in Chapter 1. His solos in a single parade seem to have spread his name around town. "The fact that I belonged to the best brass band in town put me in touch with all the top musicians," he wrote and immediately named, for example, Alphonse Picou, the Creole clarinetist. Now he achieved public success on the same streets where he had, as a child, watched his father strut as grand marshal. The flash of his father's plumes was now trumped by the shine of Louis's brassy cornet, the dance of the father's inventive steps bettered by the creative ragging of the son's tune. His father's success was limited; after the parade, he returned to the turpentine factory where he worked. Louis's success was more marketable, and he was now good enough to be a full-time professional musician in the city of his youth.

His new skills landed him a plump cherry of a job at Tom Anderson's cabaret, just outside the old Storyville district. Storyville had loomed large in his sense of musical life ever since the days when he hung out listening to Oliver, Perez, Keppard, and Johnson while delivering coal. Anderson's new place continued the Storyville tradition. This job probably paid better than any other Armstrong had in the city. "I made so much money I didn't know what to do with it," he remembered.

The first historians of early jazz made a lot out of Storyville, and it has been glued to the music's image ever since. Legalized prostitution seemed like just the right way to link the visceral qualities of the music to licentious New Orleans. Sex sells, and the legend of bawdy Storyville helped sell the revival of New Orleans jazz in the 1940s. Armstrong himself got caught in the exaggerations: he wrote an article for *True* magazine in 1947, to which the magazine gave the ridiculous title "Storyville—Where the Blues Were Born." An illustration mixed the faces of Armstrong, Oliver, Bechet, and Bunk Johnson with sketches of nude women.

But the pendulum can swing both ways, and it has now become common to argue that Storyville actually had very little to do with early jazz; after all, the brothels mainly employed pianists. Earlier writers viewed the forced closing of the district in November 1917 as the catalyst for a mass exodus of musicians out of the city. As a counter to that idea, it has been observed that musicians began leaving several years earlier, as part of the first wave of the Great Migration. Yet some musicians spoke about the 1917 closing in unequivocal terms that must be reckoned with. Hypolite Charles insisted that it left only three places in the whole city where musicians could work full-time: Tranchina's, where Piron's orchestra was playing; Beverly Garden, which hired Celestin's Tuxedo dance band; and the Moulin Rouge at West End. "That's the reason so many musicians went North," he said, and in a separate discussion Sidney Bechet agreed, though he remembered a different set of remaining places. The coincidence of Storyville's closing with the flu epidemic, which also shut down dance halls, must have caused more than a few musicians to search for greener pastures.

Storyville was but one part of a complicated and multidimensional musical world, but it had its importance. It was densely crowded with music during the 1910s, not just in the brothels but also in the many cabarets, honky tonks, and dance halls. Emile Barnes estimated that two-dozen bands played there every night. With few exceptions, the buildings are gone now, the streets remade or renamed. You'll have to use your imagination. But that isn't hard to do, since the musicians supply lots of colorful detail.

The most famous place of all was Lulu White's Mahogany Hall, a spectacular brothel on Basin Street that catered to rich plantation owners who had come to the city for sales or on holiday. Jelly Roll Morton and Manuel Manetta played piano there. But other musicians sometimes did too, including a few clarinet players (Alphonse Picou, Barney Bigard, Big Eye Louis Nelson), cornetists (Kid Rena), and even small bands (Kid Ory's). At Lulu White's, as in most of Storyville, you could experience the color hierarchy of New Orleans in action. All the wealthy clients were white, all the girls were white or light-skinned Creole, most of the musicians were Creole, and all of the servants were Negroes. It was as if slavery had never gone away. (Savvy marketing in New York City would produce, in just a few years, club names to bring this illusion into higher relief—The Cotton Club, The Club Alabam, The Log Cabin, and so on.) Musicians and servants stayed in their place: "As far as to *buy* a little *Trim*—that was absolutely out of the question," Armstrong wrote. He detected a bias against darker-skinned musicians that he thought benefited Jelly Roll Morton, and though it was not universally true, the fact that he believed it says something. "No matter how much his Diamond Sparkled he still had to eat in the *Kitchen*, the same as *we* Blacks," he wrote, with satisfaction.

Wind instruments were actually illegal in the district until 1907. Before that, there was only "soft music," as Louis Keppard described it, mostly strings and pianos and the occasional clarinet. "Things were right on top of each other in the district," said Pops Foster, thus accounting for the prohibition against the louder winds. A bar owner gained permission for Freddie Keppard to play his cornet with a trio in the doorway of his saloon, as a way to draw people inside—a "hustling band," his brother Louis called it—and after that the prohibition was set aside. Foster got into the seven-piece Magnolia Band in 1908, and his musical fortunes changed for the better when Oliver was able to place the band in Storyville. "I never thought [music] would be a way to make a living," said Foster. "I usually had a regular job longshoring or something. My job with the Magnolia Band in the district was the first music job that was a full-time job." The band worked at Huntz's Cabaret, on the corner of Customhouse and Liberty streets. As a customer walked into Huntz's, he saw a bar near the front door and girls standing to the side, in the middle of the dance floor. The band was in the back. Dance tickets were purchased at the bar for twenty-five cents each. Each girl selected for a dance kept half of each ticket, which she turned in at the end of the evening for ten cents a piece. The dances were very short. As arrangements were made for sex, the girl and the customer left the cabaret for her nearby crib, though some cabarets and dance halls had booths and rooms available for this purpose.

Far from irrelevant, Storyville caused a huge spike in the music business during the 1910s. Musicians were drawn to it for the simple reasons that the work was steady and the money good. "The sporting district come to have all the best musicians because the pay was every night," said Big Eye Louis Nelson. "Just take the corner of Iberville and Franklin—four saloons on the four corners, the 25s, 28, The Pig Ankle and Shoto's. Those places had eight bands amongst them. Four on day and four on night." There were also lots of tonks, gambling traps for the visiting plantation owners, sailors, and even wealthy New Orleanians who enjoyed slumming alongside longshoremen. Jelly Roll Morton witnessed an occasional dash of biological class warfare in these tonks when lower-class "bums" discreetly flicked lice on the fancy-suited rich men from St. Charles Avenue.

The big money came through tips. One musician was nicknamed "rat" because of his speed in passing the hat. If an audience applauded, the band played the number again with the expectation of higher tips. German sailors tipped well, Dutch and English sailors only after they got drunk, and French sailors very little. The tips were often accompanied by insults, and a black musician was hardly in a position to respond in kind to a white patron. "These remarks slipped off me like water off a duck's back," said Danny Barker. Johnny Dodds, on the other hand, found it all too degrading and stayed away from Storyville when he could afford to. Money was thrown on the floor for the musicians to humiliatingly pick up. The Magnolia Band hired a guy for one dollar a night just to collect tips.

Clarence Smith liked to say, "Thank you all nice folks for helping the poor" as he passed the hat around, and one day a patron started mimicking him—"and the helpless," said the patron as he dropped his coin. Everybody laughed and the entire crowd took turns thinking up variations on the phrase in exaggerated drawls as the hat came around:

"Thank you Lord for helping the homeless . . . the cripples . . . the lame . . . the blind . . . the legless . . . the wretched . . . the orphans . . . the widows . . . the dying . . . the starving . . . etc." Collecting tips was rarely so much fun, but most musicians put up with it. For Paul Dominguez, an old-line Creole violinist, the choice of whether or not to work in Storyville was simple: "Say for instance I was working with the Olympia Band, working one or two nights a week for two dollars and a half a night. The 25s here in Storyville pay you a dollar and a quarter and tips, but you working seven nights. Naturally, wouldn't I quit the Olympia and go to this tonk? Wouldn't I?"

Many musicians seem not to have merely tolerated the district but to have absolutely enjoyed it. In Storyville, the musician's life fused with pimping and gambling as it could nowhere else, to produce one huge festival of work and pleasure. Sometimes Foster did not leave the district for three weeks straight, sleeping with one or another of his whores in her tiny crib when he got off work at four in the morning. "In those days, all the musicians were healthy guys, with lots of energy nature to do whatever he wished," remembered Armstrong. The network of relationships took on familial qualities. From the bandstand, Foster kept an eye on Big Eye Louis Nelson's whore in her crib across the street; every time she turned a trick he put a chalk mark on the wall, and at the end of the night he gave Nelson the tally. Oliver set up the teenage Foster with his first prostitute, a girl named Edith. But Oliver had a crush on Edith himself and once burst in on the two of them in bed, threatening to fire Foster if he ever slept with her again. He kept nagging until their white boss at Huntz's Cabaret had to tell Oliver to lay off: "Let the boy alone, Joe, Jesus Christ, go on out and get yourself another girl." Camaraderie was deepened by the nightly practice of wandering around and sitting in with other bands, as well as hanging out at the Big 25 after work. On Mondays, everyone's day off, they all headed for a picnic at the lake, where they swam and hired a band for themselves.

Manetta put together a band for the Tuxedo Dance Hall in 1913 and the owner directed him to find the "greatest musicians in town." This was the band of Creoles that, when a sub was needed, refused to allow Manetta to hire any "out of towners"—that is, the uptown immigrants (Chapter 8). The band had an "entertainer" who sang and passed the hat. "We had orchestration, all reading band, no ear at all," said Manetta. Cornetist Arnold Metoyer played a fancy triple-tongued solo. The repertory here and at many places in the district was all popular tunes. Big Eye Louis Nelson led a band at Fewclothes' Cabaret, where a sign hanging over the bar gave the players credit for being able to command all the "latest song hits." Foster remembered playing *Beautiful Dolly* and *Fiddle Up Your Violin* in the district, and Emile Barnes said they had to play "love numbers," songs like *I Know You Belong to Someone Else Tonight*. The Red Back Book was standard fare. Some uptown musicians used the term "classical" for this current repertory, a usage that probably reflects the expectation that the piece was to be played without embellishment, close to the printed page (as when Sidney Bechet says, "He played things more classic-like, straight out how it was written").

To make tips, the musicians had to play requests; to play requests they had to have lots of sheet music so they could perform on demand; and to perform on demand they had to read very well. Hence, the Creole advantage. "They went a lot of places with ease, because of their light skin," said Armstrong about the Creole musicians in Storyville, but training also had something to do with it. The district was dominated by downtown bands like the Superior Orchestra, Peter Bocage's group that sometimes included Bunk Johnson. Their rivals were the Imperial Orchestra, Manuel Perez's group that worked at Rice's Cafe for a time, and the Olympia Orchestra, Freddie Keppard's group that was associated with Billy Phillip's 101 Ranch dance hall. The requirement to read well also created an opportunity for women pianists. Most places in Storyville had a piano, and it was not easy to find male piano players who could read. Oliver hired Emma Barrett on piano at Pete Lala's place on Marais and Conti, and Camilla Todd played piano in Hypolite Charles's Maple Leaf Band at Tom Anderson's. When one or more of the musicians had shaky reading skills (for example, Oliver or Keppard), the pianist could at least play a requested piece from sheet music while the others faked along.

The good tips and the steady work made a gig in Storyville highly desirable, but it was not necessarily at the *very* top of the market hierarchy. Even better money could be made at private parties given by whites in the Garden district. When a job like that came up, you simply got a substitute for your Storyville job. Bechet remembered getting a substitute and then returning to the district after the party to dismiss his sub and stay on until closing time at four in the morning. But Storyville offered the steadiest work. And it was not only a place for playing popular tunes from notated arrangements. We know that Oliver played his freak music there, and that he and Keppard joined battle in cutting contests across the Storyville streets, so there was certainly room for vernacular music. Banjo player Buddy Christian said that Keppard's band "started swing" at Billy Phillip's in 1911 or 1912. Some uptown musicians crossed Canal Street—literally and figuratively—and played with the downtown Creoles in Storyville, making it part of the social-musical mix that was taking place elsewhere in the city too, but with less remuneration. Near the end of his life, when his memory sometimes faded into fantasy, Armstrong believed that "if it wasn't for those good musicians and the Entertainers who appeared nightly in the Red Light District—Clubs, etc.—the District wouldn't have been anything. Music lovers from all parts of the city came to hear them play Genuine Jazz."

Tom Anderson was one of Storyville's movers and shakers, a proprietor with several businesses, a consort to the famous brothel madam Josie Arlington, and an elected member to the state legislature of Louisiana. Storyville was nicknamed "Anderson county" in recognition of his power. After the district officially closed in 1917, Anderson moved his focus to a large place on Rampart Street, just outside of the former district, that was sometimes described as a restaurant, sometimes as a "legitimate hotel." There he carried on all the various traditions of the district—prostitution, music, and gambling. The police estimated that forty prostitutes worked there every night. Armstrong played in a little band lead by Paul Dominguez on violin, with Albert Francis playing drums and his wife Edna Francis piano. Wilhelmina Bart Wynn replaced Edna when she became pregnant. "Both of these girls were much better than a number of men I have heard through the years," Armstrong remembered.

"We played all sorts of arrangements from the easiest to the hardest," remembered Armstrong, "and from the sweetest to the hottest."

The bandstand at Tom Anderson's, with (left to right) Paul Barbarin, Arnold Metoyer, Luis Russell, Willie Santiago, and Albert Nicholas, ca. 1922 (Historic New Orleans Collection, Acc. No. 92-48-L MSS 520 f. 3065, photo by Arthur Bedou)

He liked Dominguez as a leader, since he was easy to get along with and "not a sore head like some of the leaders." Musically, Dominguez was a "little more modern" than other Creole violinists. That must say a lot about the other violinists, for Dominguez (b. ca. 1887) was hardly an enthusiast of uptown ragtime. By 1921 he had come a long way. He was of the generation of Lorenzo Tio Jr., well trained in the downtown tradition. "See, us downtown people, we didn't think so much of this rough uptown jazz until we couldn't make a living otherwise," said Dominguez.

And Armstrong too had come a long way, though he was traveling in the opposite direction. Albert Nicholas played with him for a while at Tom Anderson's, and he was amazed that Armstrong could read through the Red Back Book without missing a single note. Armstrong remembered *Grace and Beauty*, *African Pas*, and *Maple Leaf Rag*—"aw I used to play 'em all." No more drinking too much cheap wine to block out his anxiety about playing with the musicianers, no more running scared. The rich racehorse men put their tips in the kitty in front of the bandstand and requested tunes for their hired girls. Musicians stopped by to sit in, and everyone must have been pretty impressed with Little Louis, who took featured solos.

Competitors

As crucial as his time on the boats was, there was still more to learn on the rough and beautiful side of the musical spectrum. During the riverboat years he continued to play in New Orleans during winters, and this kept him in touch with what was going on in the city. His musical development was really advancing in two directions at once, and in a way that was highly beneficial. Even though some of the most famous players—Oliver, Ory, Bechet, Keppard, and Johnson—had already left, the scene was still bursting with expansive energy. During these maturational years around 1920 he was a professional, fully fired to take his place in the market, and that meant keeping up with the competition, of which there was plenty.

Doctors and Druggists Ball on opening night of the Pythian Temple Roof Garden, with Manuel Perez's band in the balcony, 1923 (Historic New Orleans Collection, Acc. No. 92-48-L MSS 520 f. 2533)

One style of playing that he more or less skipped over was freak music. If you liked freak music in the late 1910s, the man to listen to was cornetist Chris Kelly, an expert with the mute and plunger combination, wah-wah style. Kelly grew up on Deer Range Plantation, "Baptist from birth and cultured in the canebrakes," as Danny Barker phrased it. His signature piece was a freak version of *Careless Love*, played in slow blues tempo. He had relatively weak fingering and did not play a lot of notes, but he made every note and nuance count. On the streets, in certain parts of town, he conquered Armstrong and everybody else, testifying to the continuing appeal of this style. It was now Kelly playing the midnight blues that could cause fights when women inspired by its erotic charge danced with men other than their dates. During off-hours, Kelly could be seen walking down the street wearing a faded-green tuxedo, one black shoe, one brown shoe, and a derby hat. When he died (1891–1927), people waited in a long line to view his body, which nine bands then accompanied to the cemetery.

Some cornet players distinguished themselves by playing in the upper range. Henry "Kid" Rena (1898–1949; originally spelled "René") was one of the best, and there can be no doubt that the challenge of his example caused Armstrong to develop this side of his own technique. "It was a smile for [Rena] to go get a high note," said Punch Miller. Rena's specialty number was the march *Maryland, My Maryland*; he liked to play a phrase at the original pitch level and then repeat it an octave higher. Others could play high briefly or without making much musical sense, but Rena did it cleanly. Some thought he was the best cornet player ever. Preston Jackson said, in the late 1930s, that Rena sounded a lot like the way Roy Eldridge was currently playing, and that both Rena and Armstrong could play high and with good control in 1919. Rena, like Armstrong, was good at inventing variations. He was a few years older than Armstrong, but the two of them had been together in the Colored Waif's Home for Boys.

Punch Miller's strength was fast, agile cornet fingering. He perfected a style of adding quick little runs into phrases. His featured number was *Satanic Blues*. Miller also played freak music with a water bucket as a mute, and he could play powerfully. He remembered an evening in 1919, shortly after he arrived in the city after his release from the army, when he sat in with the band at the Big 25, where Armstrong was playing with Ory, the Dodds brothers, Lorenzo Staulz, and Bob Lyons. The others kidded Armstrong about how well Miller was playing. Armstrong got mad, threatened to quit, and told them to go ahead and take Miller if they wanted to.

The cornet players "were all HELLIONS," wrote Armstrong, with due emphasis. More than a few clarinet players were also fighting for center stage. Downtown, where most of the clarinet players came from, the instrument had always been regarded as a melodic principal alongside the violin, much more so than the cornet, which was more prominent uptown. The difference came from the history of indoor, salon-style music making downtown, in contrast to the outdoor orientation uptown. Downtown clarinetists like Big Eye Louis Nelson, Sidney Bechet, George Baquet, and Lorenzo Tio Jr. regularly played lead in dance bands, taking their place alongside the violin and the cornet. A clarinet can negotiate tricky melodic contours much more easily than a cornet can, especially when leaps of range are involved, and it is easier to play fast. So the lead clarinetists—especially those who were good at improvisation, like Nelson and Bechet—presented an additional challenge to the uptown cornetists. The clarinets were "raising sand in them days," said Punch Miller.

Alphonse Picou gained a little local fame by adapting the piccolo solo in the march *High Society* for clarinet and impressing audiences with a steady stream of leaps and turns. The solo became the main attraction of the piece, not only on the streets but also in dance halls and cabarets. Other clarinetists worked up their own versions, following Picou. Kid Rena figured out how to play it on his cornet by listening to Big Eye Louis Nelson; Alex Bigard heard Rena play it transposed up an octave. Armstrong figured it out too. Bechet remembered Black Benny bragging to him one day about Louis, saying that he could play the *High Society* solo even better than Bechet could—not a modest boast, since Bechet was a fast fingerer. "It was very hard for a clarinet to do and really unthinkable for cornet to do at those times," said Bechet, "but Louis, he did it." Buddy Petit went a step further and became the first cornetist to play a *variation* on the piccolo solo. When the Original Dixieland Jazz Band recorded *Clarinet Marmalade* in July 1918, a solo from that piece grew to similar status as a vehicle for dexterous display. Punch Miller said that Armstrong "used to trick everybody" in 1919 with his own version.

Buddy Petit was also known for fast, excellent fingering, and he had an additional weapon in his arsenal: complicated chords. Old-school, downtown musicians learned the daunting array of chords that are a special focus of Eurocentric music—major and minor, added sevenths of various types, augmented chords, and diminished chords. This knowledge seemed highly remote to routine players who never came close to a lesson in music theory. Routine players usually stuck to the simple harmonies of the blues or, when confronted with a degree of harmonic variety in a tune, faked their way through. Petit, very much one of the routine players, somehow went further and learned to improvise creatively and precisely with fancy chords.

Like Armstrong, Petit had no interest in freak music. But he did know how to skillfully insert blue notes, distorted timbres, and lip slurs into his solos as nuances. His main limitation was range: he never played high, which may have inspired him to find variety in other ways, especially through details of phrasing. Musicians talk about him as a delicate player who did not blast but spun shapely twists and turns. "He had a beautiful tone and was very fast, playing with a running style," said Don Albert. In parades and funerals he was known as the best *second* cornet player in New Orleans, meaning that he was good at creating counterpoint to the main melody, which he usually assigned to clarinetist Zeb Lenares. "Sounded like a sweetheart," said Punch Miller, who demonstrated, decades later, how Petit used to improvise a second cornet part to go with *What a Friend We Have in Jesus.*

Armstrong admired Petit, though he claimed, perhaps with a bit of anxiety of influence, that he didn't hear him very often. Several musicians said that Petit exerted a huge influence on Armstrong's style. Emile Barnes said, "When [Armstrong] makes that chromatic in there, that is Buddy over and over." An interviewer played

Armstrong's *Cornet Chop Suey* (recorded in 1926, but composed several years earlier) for Bebé Ridgley in 1961, without telling him who the soloist was. Ridgley identified it as Petit—"If it ain't him it's somebody just like him." The solo is built on an attractive variety of arpeggiated chords, chromatic ornaments, and subtle rhythmic tension. Listening to the same solo in 1951, Armstrong commented, "Those variations in this recording remind me of the days when we played the tail gate (advertisings) in New Orleans. We kids, including Henry Rena, Buddy Petit, Joe Johnson and myself, we all were very fast on our cornets. And had some of the fastest fingers anyone could ever imagine a cornet player could have."

The argument that Petit influenced Armstrong in a major way makes sense. Both specialized in nicely sculpted improvisations marked by harmonic precision. Both were fast fingerers and skillful in bringing blues touches to any kind of melody. Petit, like Armstrong, had a fertile imagination. "He'd stay in the staff and . . . make you dizzy with the variation he'd make," said trumpeter Albert Walters. Petit got a reputation for taking more than one deposit for a single

The Eagle Band, with Buddy Petit on cornet, ca. 1918
(Courtesy of the Hogan Jazz Archive, Tulane University)

night, then not showing up for any of the jobs. Toward the end of his life he lived in a one-room shack with a wood stove on the north shore of Lake Pontchartrain. An alcoholic, he died a sad, early death (1898–1931). Armstrong happened to be in town on a gig and served as an honorary pallbearer at the funeral. Several musicians felt that Petit was ahead of his time, twenty-five or thirty years ahead of his time, in Don Albert's opinion. Punch Miller said that if he had been able to play high, he "could have been a killer-diller."

All of the young ear-playing cornetists were constantly challenging each other to go further, and any innovation from one must have immediately circulated among all. If Petit or Rena had gone to Chicago before Armstrong did, scoffed trumpeter Ernie Cagnolatti, the public wouldn't have heard of Armstrong so much. Musicians were playing *Heebie Jeebies* and "that kind of stuff up and down the street here, but they didn't know what they were doing," insisted Punch Miller. "Louis went up there and made something out of it."

Miller remembered the first time blues were played by a brass band (or at least he thought it was the first time), around 1921, for a Zulu funeral. This particular jump-up band had a rather stunning three-man cornet section—Rena, Armstrong, and Miller. Henry Martin played snare drum, Black Benny the bass drum. On the ragtime return from the cemetery, Martin had an inspiration, and he decided to signal an up-tempo blues. Black Benny "played the drum all kinds of ways," said Miller, like he was playing for a dance hall (Danny Barker, in an unrelated discussion, said that Benny played his drum with an "African beat"). The tuba player was Eddie Jackson (Armstrong: "used to really Swing the Tuba"), Kid Shots Madison played alto horn, Zeb Lenares clarinet, Gus Metcalf baritone horn (Miller: "He could make it moan—nobody could ever catch on to how he did it"), Frankie Dusen and Willie Cornish, from the old days with Bolden, the trombone. "It was a terrible band," said Miller. A band that must have marked another peak in the rough and beautiful tradition, a different musical universe from the one cultivated by the Tuxedo Brass Band, with their lyres for holding notated arrangements. Within a short time Armstrong was gone to Chicago, trying to explain to musicians there how great the parade bands in New Orleans really were and how much he missed them.

It's easy to imagine why.

A New Urban Blues

In the previous chapter I argued that musical competition in the cutting contests helped drive innovation. Now we can see the details of how that played out for Armstrong in the late teens—high-range playing, fast and tricky fingering, and an expanded harmonic palette. This tendency toward complexity had an impact on blues. Bolden may well have been the first professional cornetist to specialize in blues, while Oliver's generation took the idiom in the direction of freak playing. The generation of Petit and Armstrong then added more melodic complexity. For these younger players, blues was now more nimble and fancy, no longer quite so lush.

Cornetist Chris Kelly kept the simpler style of blues playing in front of audiences and with great success, but he was certainly not perceived as modern. According to Paul Barnes, Kelly's "style was in many respect the opposite of Petit's." Petit was a "good blues man," wrote Armstrong, the player of choice at honky tonks and Economy Hall. Kelly's blues would have been harmonically simple, in step with the old tradition. Harmonic simplicity was probably taken as a virtue: when harmony receded to the background, it served as a simple frame for the main expressive action, carried by melodic and timbral gestures. This was the kind of blues Armstrong grew up with and practiced into the wee hours of the night during his early teens, but by 1916 or so he had gone further. When he sat in with the Ory band, where Mutt Carey was the featured cornet player, his blues caught Carey by surprise. "Now at that time I was the 'Blues King' of New Orleans," remembered Carey. "And when Louis played that day he played more blues than I ever heard in my life. It never did strike my mind that blues could be interpreted in so many different ways."

Blues had acquired a new "structure of feeling," one could say. It had become more than a matter of providing an erotic charge that set the slow drag in motion, or an idiom for exploring vocalized expression. It had long been a place for improvisation ("Blues is what cause the fellows to start jazzing"), a kind of music that placed no harmonic constraints on an amateur or a young player. In the late 1910s it was expanding by the addition of those very harmonic constraints, or at least by the addition of much fancier melodic detail.

The trend may be read as a further urbanization of the idiom, an interest in distancing city from country. If Bolden had given the plantation immigrants a new brand of distinctly urban blues to gather around, this younger generation, fifteen years later, was redefining what it meant to be urban and sophisticated. Bolden's blues reminded people of the soulful call of a preacher or a singer. The new blues of Petit and Armstrong did not sound like singing at all but was full of instrumental virtuosity. No one was saying (as Ory said about Bolden) that the new blues was stolen from the rags-bottles-and-bones man. Armstrong's personal style by the time he left New Orleans carried an air of being *not* rural and *not* that of everyman. The new approach must have been directly associated with the constant, daily competitions on the busy streets—the literal marker of distance between city and country. It was the product of a richly textured musical hierarchy ranging from amateurs to famous professionals, unlike anything known on the plantations. The city created a musical space for lucre, fame, and dignity, the reward for faster, more brilliant, more complicated, more technically controlled playing. Status was *heard*.

The trick was to make the soul of the blues still audible while dressing it in this urban air of controlled complexity. The elaborate garlands Armstrong spun around Bessie Smith's rendition of *St. Louis Blues* in 1925 perhaps capture this playing of five or so years earlier. The great blues queen is said to have preferred the simpler style of Joe Smith. Nevertheless, for many other listeners Armstrong's reach for urban sophistication in New Orleans had prepared him well for Chicago and New York. Not just blues, of course, but the entire array of improvisational practice was now more complicated than it had been with Oliver, and, before him, with Bolden. Punch Miller demonstrated for interviewers how Oliver played *Snag It*, then how

Armstrong would have played it, with more "stuff in it." Musicians in Chicago who were in awe of Oliver immediately heard him as slightly old-fashioned after Armstrong arrived.

❧ Was playing like this produced independently in any other southern city? It is highly unlikely. Oliver, Bechet, Armstrong, and their fellow New Orleanians sounded completely fresh when they traveled around the country because no place else had the same social and musical history, with all of its layers of patronage and practice and its sequential development, the heyday of which coincided with the first twenty-one years of Armstrong's life.

CHAPTER TWELVE

Melody That Changed the World

[Jabbo Smith] played rapid-fire passages while Louis was melodic and beautiful.
—Milt Hinton

On August 8, 1922, Armstrong finished playing for a funeral and made his way over to the Illinois Central Railroad, where the neighborhood ladies who had watched over him when he was young, a few of his musician friends, and his mother and sister all gathered. He was now ready to follow in the footsteps of his mentor, Joe Oliver, who had left four years earlier. Oliver had been trying for several years to get him to leave New Orleans, and now, having just turned twenty-one, Louis was ready.

May Ann gave him a trout-loaf sandwich to eat on the train. Some of the Pullman porters and waiters recognized him from the advertising wagons in town, and they wanted to know about his plans. Oliver could not meet him at the train station in Chicago, so he tipped a porter to show Louis how to get to the Lincoln Gardens, where Oliver's band was playing. Armstrong wore his brown box-back coat, a straw hat, and tan shoes. The musicians playfully called him "Little Louis," his childhood nickname that now carried a bit of humor since he weighed 226 pounds.

Not only Oliver but dozens of musicians, uptown and downtown, had been leaving New Orleans for greener pastures during the previous half-decade or so, clearing out space for the youngsters left behind to rise through the ranks and work out independent styles. Manuel Perez, Freddie Keppard, Mutt Carey, Bunk Johnson, Kid Ory, Jimmy Noone, Sidney Bechet, Alphonse Picou, Lorenzo Tio—all of them had left, some more than once, and some finding that they preferred New Orleans. Rena was called but didn't go; Petit went to California and on a long tour of Gulf Coast venues but always came back; Miller moved to Chicago and also returned. Oliver had tried to get Bunk Johnson and then Rena. There is a

Louis, May Ann, and Beatrice, ca. 1922 (Courtesy of the
Louis Armstrong House and Archives at Queens College/CUNY)

story that he sent Louis a photo of Lil Hardin as special enticement. Many men hoboed their way out of New Orleans, but when a musician was really wanted, he received a one-way train ticket in the mail, as Armstrong did from Oliver. Whatever it was, Oliver's persuasion worked.

But it was not an easy decision. There were plenty of horrifying stories about life in the North. Musicians simply could not stand the long, icy winters. There were complicated problems with unions; Armstrong's friends in New Orleans tried to discourage him with warnings about Oliver scabbing, though Armstrong didn't know what scabbing was. Always in the background lurked the fear of being cheated and left stranded in some unknown place. "I always was afraid to leave home because so many of the boys from home had gone up North and came back in such bad shape," Armstrong wrote, and one can imagine that it only took one example like that to give him a scare.

He was making pretty good money in New Orleans, but there were far greater sums to be made in Chicago. There was also the less tangible matter of opportunity and respect. Musicians who had been leaving were riding the wave of the Great Migration to the urban North, a trip viewed by some as the final break with slavery, a move from a medieval world into a modern one. The immigrants were greeted by "Welcome to Chicago" signs all over town. The South Side of Chicago seemed to be run entirely by African Americans, a "Negro City," as Mahalia Jackson said, with "Negro policemen and firemen and schoolteachers, . . . doctors and lawyers and aldermen." "It was after I got to Chicago that I realized for the first time that the southern whites had a chain on the colored people," she felt. "It reminded me of how they grazed a mule on the levee from a stake—he could eat the grass in a circle all around and no further . . . In Chicago, our people were advancing." Music rang out brightly in this liberating atmosphere, just as it had in the first migratory stage, after the freedmen from the rural plantations moved to southern cities.

With their extra money the immigrants did exactly the same thing they had done in New Orleans: they looked for common ground in the dance halls and the churches. The intense attention to music astonished Armstrong. "There were plenty of work, lots of *Dough* flying around, all kinds of beautiful women at your service. A musician in Chicago in the early twenties were treated and respected just like—some kind of a God," he wrote.

He stepped right into a transplanted community of fellow New Orleanians. The Olivers took him in, and Stella cooked meals for him, just like the old days. Some of the Creoles were working in cigar factories, and some of his friends worked in stockyards. But the musicians in the band he now joined were making so much money that the thought of a day job never crossed their minds. They were riding the crest of the blues fad that had officially begun in 1920, with the release of Mamie Smith's recording of *Crazy Blues*. On the first night of his arrival, Armstrong made his solo debut in Chicago playing blues with Oliver's band. "Let the youngster blow," the crowd shouted out. The blues craze was becoming more and more organized as a commercial market, with touring circuits, advertisements, puff pieces in the nationally distributed *Chicago Defender*, and an explosion of recordings. In April 1923, King Oliver's Creole Jazz Band started their now legendary series of recordings, with Oliver on first cornet and Armstrong on second.

In February 1924 Armstrong and Lillian Hardin were married. His new wife was classically trained and in touch with a sophisticated side of northern show biz. Louis was somewhat in awe of this slender, attractive woman; he described her as a "Big High-powered Chick." Her ambition and skill would now be devoted, for a crucial few years, to launching his solo career. They sketched out tunes on the back steps of their apartment and sent them to Washington, D.C., for copyright. A good sight-reader, she bought a book of cornet solos to run through with him on the grand piano he had purchased for her. Tempos were faster in Chicago, spurring him on to higher levels of dexterity. "Louis was good down here, but after he went up there, he just went to town," said Emile Barnes. He left his New Orleanian cohort of Rena, Miller, and Petit behind, and Rena, back in New Orleans, could only shake his head in jealous disgust. "And because Louis was up North making records and running up and down like he's crazy don't mean that he's that great," Rena said to Danny Barker. "He is not playing cornet on that horn; he is imitating a clarinet. He is showing off."

In 1924 he accepted an offer to play in New York City with a dance orchestra run by Fletcher Henderson. By the time he returned to Chicago in 1925, he was more than ready to stand as a featured soloist. Just as northern musicians had been astounded by Oliver during the late teens, so were they now astounded by Armstrong. With homeboys Johnny Dodds, Johnny St. Cyr, and Kid Ory, and with his wife Lil on piano, he launched in November 1925 the series of recordings known as the "Hot Fives" and "Hot Sevens." This series documents his soaring solo style, which, more than the work of any other single musician, crystallized a new idiom for jazz, a new kind of melody that quickly spread in popularity across the world.

Audiences then and ever since have agreed with bass player Milt Hinton's description of Armstrong's playing as "melodic and beautiful." If before his time on the riverboats his music was "rough and

King Oliver's Creole Jazz Band, ca. 1923, with (left to right) Johnny Dodds, Baby Dodds, Honore Dutrey, Armstrong, Oliver, Lil Hardin, and Bill Johnson, (Historic New Orleans Collection, Acc. No. 92-48-L MSS 520 f. 3295, photo by Daguerre)

beautiful," his style had now changed. The nimble-mindedness that made him such a great improviser also allowed him to musically adapt, first to the demands of the riverboats and then to the heady, more complicated mix of northern show styles.

How much of New Orleans is in the mature solo style of the mid-1920s? Armstrong himself certainly thought that it was there. He remembered recording *Potato Head Blues* in 1927 and thinking about the bandstand in Pelican Dance Hall, where Ory, Dodds, and Oliver were playing; "Every note that I blew in this recording, I thought of Papa Joe," he wrote. Sidney Bechet also spoke about hearing history in this music. His terms are less specific and more emotional, almost mystical. The "good musicianer" always plays "with" history and "after" it—"He's finishing something," Bechet insisted.

> No matter what he's playing, it's the long song that started back there in the South. It's the remembering song. There's so much to remember. There's so much wanting, and there's so much sorrow . . . My people, all they want is a place where they can be people, a place where they can stand up and be part of that place, just being natural to the place without worrying how someone may be coming along to take that place away from them. There's a pride in it, too. The man playing it, he makes a place. For as long as the song is being played, *that's* the place he's been looking for. And when the piece is all played and he's back, it may be he's feeling good . . . Maybe he starts wanting the place he found while he was playing the song.

The music stirred up African-American sorrow so powerfully, said Bechet, that it caused the ruin of many good musicianers, including Buddy Bolden. "When a musicianer made a bad end, it was never a surprise . . . all that night sound there was at the bottom of the song all that long way back making itself heard."

From novelist Ralph Ellison comes the most famous articulation of the living presence of African-American history in music. Ellison's protagonist in *Invisible Man*, high on marijuana, turns on 1,369 light bulbs in the basement where he lives and puts on a recording of Armstrong singing *What Did I Do to Be So Black and Blue*. As he pours red sloe gin over his white vanilla ice cream, he watches the vapors rise and listens to Armstrong, who is literally invisible since the music comes from a phonograph record. He slips *into* the music, through its nodal points where time stands still, into its "underworld" of sound, where he meets an old woman singing a spiritual, a young woman, naked, being auctioned to slaveholders, a preacher speaking of blackness.

It is relatively easy to appreciate the melodic beauties of Armstrong's music, and much harder, at this distance, to hear in it the legacies of slavery. But how much of the African-American past was in the dazzling solo spectacle that Armstrong produced in the mid-1920s? And how was such an achievement possible given the terror and repression of the Jim Crow South, which seemed to be getting worse all the time? If Armstrong and his peers moved to Chicago to make a final break with slavery, that does not mean, necessarily, that they wished to abandon the expressive practices that had been passed down to them from their enslaved ancestors and ultimately from Africa. To the contrary, much of what he and his New Orleanian colleagues were offering had been formed on the plantations. That must have been obvious to the southern immigrants in Chicago, who treated the musicians like Gods and thus created an environment in which the range of jazz could expand further.

The Opportunity of Music

In 1901, the year of Armstrong's birth, slavery had been gone barely thirty-five years. The makers of early jazz were clear and consistent about the historical antecedents to their music—work songs, blues, ragging the tune, and congregational singing in church, all traditions that point directly to the plantations and to slavery. The musical world created by the slaves shaped the environment Armstrong grew up with, in both specific details of sound and general attitudes.

One of those attitudes was a sense that music was a special field of unregulated expression. During slavery and in its aftermath, controlling whites actually encouraged musical autonomy. "People are always putting [the Negro] to music. 'That's your place,' they say," observed Sidney Bechet. African Americans embraced music and held it as high as or higher than any other area of expressive culture. It was another case of taking advantage of the disadvantages.

Music offered enslaved people a way to extend a sense of self into the made world. It became the free space where total control was possible. Artisan slaves were able to enjoy a degree of creative control over the products of their labor, but that opportunity did not exist for the heavily exploited field hands. Yet they did have music, had it even while they worked. During the self-crafted, imaginary moment of musical performance, slavery did not exist. If that seems like a lot to project onto evanescent patterns of sound, we should remember how impressive were the long-term results that flowed from these conditions.

Successful music making depended on all the usual attractions— desired qualities of sound production, technical skill, a sense of confident presence, audience engagement, and so on. But through musical creativity an even deeper sense of agency was possible. Hence, the emphasis on ragging the tune, on adding and filling in, on invention. This value was strong enough to generate the astonishing flow of performer-centered creativity through the post-Reconstruction years, ultimately yielding a range of cultural exploration that included blues, jazz, and gospel. To admire Armstrong as an improviser-innovator is to see him as one of the great masters in this ragging, inventing, creating tradition.

The idea that in music it was possible to control the product of one's labor and assert a sense of autonomous self became part of the professional scene in New Orleans. The musical stage—the advertising wagon, the dance hall, the street—continued to be the place for extending the self into the world. The New Orleanians often speak about the importance of originality. "The New Orleans style is based on originality," said Johnny St. Cyr. "I don't try to copy-cat behind nobody," insisted Lawrence Marrero. And, as Pops Foster explained, "You see each of the guys had their own style. Nobody copied behind each other—everybody had their own style of playing." Armstrong was well suited to these high expectations. Creative adornment bursts out all over in his performances, as if to overwhelm the received text, the trivial or even demeaning content of a popular tune.

"Patience, humility and adroitness must, in these growing black youth, replace impulse, manliness and courage," lamented W. E. B. Du Bois in 1903. Though that formulation is framed in stark, misleadingly binary terms, it sheds light on early jazz. When he interacted with whites, Armstrong learned how to be patient and humble: "Always have a *White Man* who likes you and can and will put his Hand on your shoulder and say—'*This is My Nigger*' and, Can't Nobody Harm Ya." Impulse, manliness, and courage were poured into music. Early jazz was a place for taking creative risks and winning battles, a place for the free play of unrestrained assertion. For dark-skinned common laborers such a place was hard to come by, almost as hard as it had been for their enslaved ancestors.

New Orleans itself did much to extend the sense of musical opportunity. Jim Crow regulation of black behavior was strategic, multidimensional, and effective, yet, in spite of that, New Orleans was a place of possibilities. Most immigrants must regard their new homes in that way, but there were many reasons for the freedmen to think like this about New Orleans, a port city that included people from all over the world—Russia, China, Germany, France, Ireland, the Philippines, Italy, Mexico, the Caribbean. The impact of the city's diverse population on the formation of jazz is usually overestimated through metaphoric talk of "gumbo"; I view it not as a matter of direct influence but as representing a world of expanded options. Mimicking the river, New Orleans was in social flux, which gave it an atmosphere of open-ended future. In music, especially, the space for invention was constantly pried open, a welcoming space for the sonic imagination.

The process of coming together and forging a new culture had been the normal state of things for slaves, who originally came from different parts of Africa and more recently from different parts of the United States before they were sold into the expanding cotton regions of the Deep South. In their turn toward the city, the freedmen arrived from different plantations to discover what they shared and what they could now become. This history of searching for commonalities certainly contributed to the adaptable nature of African-American music. New Orleans circa 1900 represents the earliest opportunity we have to see how demands for musical adaptability played out in detail.

Play the cornet a little louder, a little faster, make it cry like a baby or moan like a preacher, add a diminished chord in a fancy blues, mix techniques associated with second cornet into playing the lead melody—these were the innovative products of the dizzying climate of cultural exploration Armstrong was born into.

The slaves relied on techniques like call and response and heterophony to turn music into community dialogue. Music that is alive with interaction is, again, open-ended; it is never fixed and always responsive to the present situation. Thus, in New Orleans the promise of innovation was built into the musical product from several directions at once. The freedmen arrived there with musical ears that were trained to be open, and this made them agreeable to new styles of music. As jazz evolved into a music made by specialists (rather than the entire community) and by instruments (with little or no vocal participation), it moved away from the stylistic details of the plantations, but it still retained interactive expectations, and the beloved techniques of old were still audible. Even in the sophisticated work of a glamorous soloist, the freedmen could recognize how their social-musical habits had been abstracted and professionalized.

The instrumental rather than vocal focus of New Orleans had huge consequences, of course. African Americans throughout the Deep South commonly distinguished "musicianers" from "songsters," the former being more prestigious, as if to say that anyone can sing while only a few have the means or ability to learn how to control an instrument. The materiality of the instrument, its shine, its expense, the complexity of its valves and mouthpiece, is emphasized, perhaps because of the materiality that slaves had been deprived of and that was, indeed, still precious, and certainly because of the hard-to-find technical knowledge that it demanded. New Orleans was a city that had always been fond of dancing, and the uptown immigrants shared that fondness. Eventually their dance music became much more than that. The phenomenon was not unprecedented: think of all the unlikely creativity and expressive depth that was poured into dance music by eighteenth-century composers like Bach and Mozart, for example. Through instrumental music it was possible to say both less and more than could be said in a song. Jelly Roll Morton recommended forgetting a song about

Robert Charles, "in order to get along with the world on the peaceful side." People did not forget about Bolden's blasting cornet that covered the bloodstained streets of their neighborhoods; to the contrary, they hailed him as their king. Armstrong was raised in the celebratory light of this kind of sonic leadership.

"All American negroes, like all members of oppressed and underprivileged peoples everywhere, are always protesting against their situation in one way or another, by the very modes of their behavior, even if not consciously and deliberately," writes Eric Hobsbawm. "However, in times of relative political stability such as those when jazz was evolved, such protests are often indirect, allusive, complex, esoteric, and extremely difficult for outsiders to recognize as protests." Whether or not outsiders could recognize the implications of Bolden's cornet is moot. The Creoles may have noticed it more easily. Louis Tio ran into the house when he heard those fools messing up good music. Chris Kelly played blues on the streets and the kitchen help came running out, dancing and shoving ring-shout, second-line behavior in Creole faces. Armstrong and Ory taught Robichaux's Creoles a nice lesson.

The most direct statement relating early jazz to the intense racism of the early twentieth century comes from Big Eye Louis Nelson, whose father was murdered in the white rioting following the Robert Charles shootout. The murder was reported in the New Orleans *Daily States* (July 28, 1900, p. 7), but only in reference to an "unknown Negro." Nelson cut out the article, and today his clipping rests in a file folder at the Old U.S. Mint, as part of Louisiana State Museum, barely a few hundred feet from the French market (see the map on page 75 for the location of Gallatin Street), where his father worked a butcher's stall and where the incident began:

SHOT TO DEATH
UNKNOWN NEGRO KILLED ON GALLATIN STREET
*Seen by a Crowd in the French Market
and then Jumped on and Killed.*

An unknown negro was shot and stabbed to death this afternoon on Gallatin street, between Hospital and Ursulines.

The darkey was passing through the French market when he was seen by a crowd of whites. The latter had been greatly excited by the wild reports which came from up-town. It had been rumored that the negroes were engaged in killing whites and that many policemen had been murdered.

The negro ran for his life and the angry mob kept at his heels. The crowd increased every minute.

The darkey turned into Gallatin street and fled past a part of Italians. The fugitive finally fled into a house and managed to get to the second story. He went to the gallery and jumped to the ground.

Before the darkey could get up he was stabbed and shot to death.

The crowd soon dispersed and the body of the victim was sent to the morgue.

A reporter of the States visited the scene, and it was only after great difficulty that he gathered the above details.

"They snatched him off his meat wagon down at the French market and killed him," said Nelson, in an interview much later with Alan Lomax. "Was I angry about it? Well, sure, sure I was. But what could I do? It just wash away. It all just wash away . . . It cause me to dig down deeper in my music more yet . . . Couple of days after my daddy was killed, I was back there at 25's playing harder than ever." The same riots caused the Tio and Dodds families to leave town. That option was apparently not open to Big Eye Louis Nelson, who played harder than ever and became the first great clarinetist in early jazz.

Those who lived under the heavy burden of vigilante terrorism and Jim Crow oppression did not know how their lives were going to unfold. Having moved with hope from the plantations to the city, they still looked to the future. They were all in it together, in their churches, parades, dance halls, clubs, and picnics on Lake Pont-chartrain—"My people stayed by themselves, creating their own fun," as Mahalia Jackson said. There was usually enough food, even if that meant scrapping together rotten turkeys, day-old bread, dis-carded vegetables, and fish heads. At the same moment that the Robert Charles riots made clear how desperate the situation was, Bolden's star was rising. Political power was in decline, musical

*Big Eye Louis Nelson, 1949 (Historic New Orleans Collection,
Acc. No. 92-48-L MSS 520 f. 637)*

power in the ascent. They heard Bolden's brassy defiance as both a
proclamation of vernacular values from the plantations and a new,
urbanized professionalism. When transplanted New Orleanians
heard Armstrong in Chicago in the mid-1920s, they could hear precisely the same combination.

The History of a Melodic Identity

Part of what was melodic and beautiful about Armstrong's playing in the mid-1920s, then, was the special role that music played in
dealing with the repressive legacies of slavery. The descendants of
slaves could also hear many details in his playing that recalled the
expressive culture formed during slavery. His virtuosity and confidence assured them of the ongoing strength of that tradition.

They heard, for example, their own songlike speaking style,
which, in the early 1920s, was being stylized by Bessie Smith and
many others into dramatic speechlike singing. Oliver, the master of

freak music, produced his own version of this idiom on his cornet, and at the Royal Gardens they crowned him king. Armstrong offered it too, though less overtly. In his cornet one could still hear the caressing, arousing gestures of the blues, which still made the chick slap the cheeks of her behind, grind her hips, explode with laughter, all in dialogue with the music and the other dancers. When Armstrong was young, blues was basically a vehicle for these gestures. By the time he left New Orleans he knew how to fold them into any kind of music.

Another component of his mature style is the flat 4/4 rhythmic foundation, which the uptown New Orleanians imported into dance music from blues and church singing. This simple foundation of four undifferentiated beats was played by drums and guitar (and piano when there was one). Not everybody liked it. Drummer Paul Barbarin felt that the traditional Eurocentric practice of accenting beats one and three—known as the two-beat style, because of the weight given to beats one and three—was better because it gives the dancers a firmer reference: "With this kind of music that we play, they know where to come in and put their foot," he said. Ragtime a la Joplin was in two-beat style. But under the spell of the migrating New Orleanians the flat 4/4 intermittently made inroads during the 1920s, triumphing fully in time to launch the swing era in the early 1930s, with bebop following in step after that.

Barbarin raises a reasonable objection, which leads to the question, Why did the uptown musicians favor the flat 4/4? The explanation has to do with the African-derived format of fixed and variable rhythmic groups. In traditional West African music, the fixed pattern is usually much more complex than four undifferentiated beats. But the rhythms are performed without accentual differentiation. That is so because of what happens *against* this foundation: irregular accents in the variable group (or soloist) create unpredictable changes in rhythmic patterning. The same thing happens in jazz. To have the fixed rhythmic group accenting beats one and three might make it easier for unskilled dancers to follow the music, but it also clutters up the foundational pattern, thus interfering with the freedom to construct irregular patterning against it.

The flat 4/4 foundation, boring in itself, provides a springboard for the soloist to bounce off and make easy and fluid shifts of phrasing across the beats and across the "measure" (every four beats). The difference in effect between the two-beat and four-beat foundations is huge, and the change was essential for the new melodic idiom that Armstrong brought to fruition. With "that good 4 beat" under him, Armstrong wrote, Joe Oliver "would create more New Riffs and Ideas than *any* musician I *know* of." The same could be said for Armstrong himself. The "good 4 beat" yields a clearer texture that enhances the listening experience as well as the pleasure of improvising dancers, who, like an improvising soloist, may move in creative tension with the underlying foundational pattern. People listening and dancing in this way must have urged the musicians on in their conversion of dance music to the flat 4/4 in New Orleans and kept it going through the Great Migration.

The flat 4/4 foundation played an important role in collective improvisation, which was an even more distinctive part of early jazz. Collective improvisation had a huge impact on Armstrong's mature solo style. We have already touched on the practice, which may now be reviewed and analyzed more deeply with this important connection in mind.

Collective improvisation, New Orleans style, was conceived according to the model of fixed and variable rhythmic groups. A familiar name for the fixed group is "rhythm section," which, in New Orleans, consisted of drums, bass, guitar (or banjo), piano (if there is one), and sometimes trombone (when it acts like a bass player). These instruments kept the steady, repetitive beat. The variable group of cornet, clarinet, and trombone (when it plays melodically) and second cornet (when there is one) was called the "front line" in New Orleans. These instruments interact with the rhythmic foundation in interesting ways. For example, consider the extremely common practice of syncopation: against the rock-solid foundation of four beats per measure, the main melody is syncopated to create a temporary feeling of two layers of independent rhythmic activity. When the syncopation stops, the melody is back in synchrony with the fixed foundation. As discussed in Chapter 7, this kind of interaction between the two layers was part of the African legacy that survived with potency on the large plantations of the Deep South.

To speak of "rhythmic groups" is a little misleading, for the model involves more than rhythm. The tunes played in New Orleans had regular *harmonic rhythm*, which is to say that the background chords—tellingly called "changes" in later jazz, thus emphasizing the temporal function—changed at a steady rate, typically every four beats (or in multiples or divisions thereof). In this way, chords define the regular flow of measures. Harmonic rhythm organizes the fixed foundation no less than an ostinato does in a West African drum ensemble. The melodic phrases of the tunes played in New Orleans inevitably do the same thing. In fact, most popular music in the United States has been and still is "square" in the sense of being rigidly organized not just around the measure (four beats) but around duple multiples of the measure—eight beats (two measures), sixteen beats (four measures), and so on. Certainly all the rags, marches, hymns, and popular songs played in New Orleans were organized in this way. Jazz musicians thus found, in the repertory they routinely played, not only rhythm but also pitch to articulate a rigid sense of temporal periodicity around multiples of four. They responded by folding that periodicity into the fixed and variable model, the variable part being created by their improvised melodies that worked both with and against the basic four-beat foundation. This approach remained central to the idiom of jazz—one could even say that it helped define it—into the bebop era, and it is still vitally active today.

Early jazz musicians took this larger sense of periodicity and used it to create the unique workings of collective improvisation. It all begins with the melody, which is supposed to be heard "at all times." That always-carried melody maps out the rigid periodicity of two measures, four measures, and so on. Thought of in this way, the instrument playing the lead melody contributes more or less "fixed" patterns through regular phrase structure. The other front-line instruments have a different job to do. They create phrases that soar straight across the regular temporal units of the main melody. As with the workings of an ostinato pattern in a West African drum ensemble, the fixed patterns form a foundation that shapes the listener's perception; no matter how complicated, everything that happens on the variable side is related by the listener to this simple,

recurring foundation. There is no evidence that this format of collective improvisation was practiced anywhere but in New Orleans.
In Ragtime composed by Scott Joplin, the listener hears fixed and
variable layers on the local level of beats, through syncopations,
additive rhythm, and so on. New Orleanians added the larger level
of fixed and variable phrase structures, articulated through melody
and countermelody.

The practice probably emerged as a transformation of heterophony, yet another sonic detail connecting early jazz to church
and plantation ragging. Musicians could capture some of the richness of congregational singing through instrumental doublings,
which were more common in early jazz than is generally realized.
The random embellishments of heterophony were antithetical to
the artisan-like precision of the downtown Creoles, but the practice fit right in with blues-based bending of pitch and string band
ragging of tune. Wallace Collins, one of Bolden's bass players, said
that violinist Tom Adams played the melody straight while Bolden
"ragged" it: "He'd take one note and put two or three to it." Bolden's
clarinetist Frank Lewis sometimes played the melody from violin
parts, which probably put Bolden in a ragging position as well.
Histories of jazz routinely misrepresent the situation by simply
stating that the cornet was the principal melody instrument in
New Orleans, but the evidence shows that the situation was
already, from the very early days, more varied. I doubt that Bolden
receded into the background when Adams or Lewis played the
lead. His loud, rough playing was probably the main attraction,
even when he was ragging embellishments around the straight
lead carried by violin or clarinet.

The arrangement of who played the lead and what the other
melody instruments contributed was unstable throughout Armstrong's
childhood, and in that instability lay the seeds of his mature melodic
style. We saw in the previous chapter how common it was for the
violin to carry the lead; in the absence of a violin the clarinet sometimes took that role. Alto horns, baritone horns, and even the occasional piccolo could do the same. When the clarinet, violin, or
piccolo played the lead melody in a routine band, the cornet player

was ragging, adding, and filling in, just as Oliver did when he made monkeyshines around Perez's lead in the Onward Brass Band. This was sometimes called playing "second." Freddie Keppard played the best second cornet that bass player Wellman Braud ever heard. For Richard Jones, that honor went to Bunk Johnson, who did it just "like Louis, with King Oliver."

To play second sometimes entailed playing an obbligato, a truly independent, melodic counterpoint to the main melody. Obbligato lines were common in notated arrangements, so there were many models, which would have been especially familiar to the reading musicians. George Baquet added clarinet obbligatos to Manuel Perez's cornet renditions of dirges, cornetist Freddie Keppard invented one to go with the song *Sweetie Dear*, and violinist Manuel Manetta did the same for *Panama*. At some point—probably here and there, now and then, in a haphazard, long-term process—the tradition of creating obbligato lines merged with the practice of heterophonic adding, filling in, and making variations, causing pure heterophony to sound old-fashioned and amateurish, a bit too funky. The challenge of making an obbligato was to invent a new melody, not to embellish on the lead melody. And with the sense that several independent melodies are being played in synthesized tension, according to the fixed and variable model, the texture of collective improvisation is fully in place.

In recorded examples of collective improvisation from the 1920s, it is the clarinet that typically soars across the regular phrases of the lead melody in the cornet. The trombone does the same kind of thing in a lower range. It is clear that in the 1910s and before, cornet players were doing this too, while someone else played the lead. Buddy Petit is the cornetist most talked about. As we have seen, Petit was a major influence on Armstrong, so it is interesting indeed to discover Punch Miller saying, after listening to a recording of Armstrong playing some nicely chromatic filler lines between phrases in a 1923 recording of *High Society*, "That's Buddy over and over."

And then there was Sidney Bechet, the soloist who, along with Armstrong, most turned the heads of dancers and listeners as the New Orleanians traveled. Sometimes Bechet played a superb lead, and sometimes he played a superb second. Wellman Braud claimed that Bechet was "the best in the business for second man, play obbligatos, the phrasing and coloring." "Just like Armstrong," agreed Lawrence Duhé.

In other words, Bechet and Armstrong, the two leading soloists to emerge from New Orleans, were also the two best second men, the best at inventing obbligatos, filling in, adding, and phrasing across the regular periodicity of the lead melody. The promiscuous shuffling of instruments and functions, standard practice for the routine bands, led to this dual specialization. The spotlight was on the instrument playing lead, but playing second was just as important and in some ways more difficult since it required improvisational invention. Perez could play powerfully and with beautiful tone, but he could not "get off" the main melody; he was happy to have Oliver do that. When Armstrong did the same thing for the failing Oliver in 1923 in Chicago, he was building on a long line of improvising second players that included Nelson, Bechet, and Dodds on clarinet, Johnson, Keppard, Oliver, and Petit on cornet. That line had one point of origin in the heterophonic ragging of the great Buddy Bolden.

Out of this mixing up of lead and second grew a new melodic style, one that essentially *combined* the two functions. The trick was to preserve enough of the melody to keep the line coherent while adding enough to create the polyrhythmic tensions of phrasing that were achieved through collective improvisation. What the mature Armstrong offered in the mid-1920s was a solo version that captured some of the group effect of collective improvisation. More than anyone else, he brought to fruition the approach to phrasing that was rooted in the fixed and variable model. He was deeply trained in music conceived in this way, from his early lessons in church heterophony all the way through Oliver's monkeyshines and barrelhouse with the Onward Brass Band, and this background put him in a good position to bring the new solo style to fruition.

He was apparently experimenting as early as the mid-1910s. He liked to tell a story about the time Oliver stopped by the honky tonk where he was playing and bluntly wanted to know, "Where's that lead?" "I'd play eight bars and I was gone," Armstrong remembered. "Clarinet things; nothing but figurations and things like that . . . running all over a horn. Joe would say, 'Where's that lead,' and I'd say 'What lead?' 'You play some lead on that horn, let the people know what you're playing.' " This little story frames an issue that was vital for all kinds of African-American vernacular music—*how to forge a fresh melodic idiom*. What would a jazz melody, a blues melody, or a gospel melody be like? That question has sat animatedly at the core of jazz innovation for over a century. Around 1915 Oliver heard in his young scholar the will to adorn too strongly, and he advised him to reign in his bursting creativity and stay closer to the tune.

But Little Louis was good at melodic invention, so he relished the role of second. Sunny Henry could only shake his head in awe of the precocious talent: "I didn't never understand Louis Armstrong, because that son of a gun, he didn't care what you played . . . he would play a obbligato all the time, be off you understand; he wouldn't never come play straight with you. But everything he put it in there, by Ned it worked . . . I don't care [what] you played, by Ned, he'd get in there in that obbligato." Armstrong was hearing something in his mind and reaching for it on his cornet. In 1915, when Oliver stopped by the honky tonk, he had not yet found it; he was probably closer when he played obbligato with Henry a few years later. Armstrong admired Oliver's ability to create "a phrase that stayed with you," which is what he himself eventually learned to do. He eventually discovered how to capture the vigor and richness of collective improvisation in a single line.

But where, then, is the sonic dialogue that was part of church heterophony? Bechet, a dominating soloist if there ever was one, identified its importance in the ragtime he grew up with: "When you're really playing ragtime, you're feeling it out, you're playing to the other parts, you're waiting to understand what the other man's doing, and then you're going with his feeling, adding what you have of your feeling." Being alert to the unpredictability of the performing moment was part of church practice and second-line interaction in the streets, it was practiced in barroom renditions of vocal quartets, it marked the sensuous flow of sonic-kinetic communication between dancers and dance bands, and it was central to the African legacy that shaped expressive culture on the plantations in dance, preaching, verbal sparring, and music of all kinds.

The dialogue is still there in Armstrong's mature solo style, though the conversation is structured differently. The players continued to be inspired by each other. But the main "dialogue" is more abstract. In Armstrong's solos, it works on several levels. First, his melody is in dialogue with the rigid periodicity of the fixed rhythmic group, its beats, harmonic rhythm, and phrase structure, as just described; just like the variable drumming in a West African ensemble, the *meaning* of the improvised solo line can only be construed through its relationship with the fixed foundation. Second, units of his melody are often in dialogue with the previous units, so that one hears his solo as an unending flow of commentary upon itself. And third, his improvised line is in dialogue with the original tune itself, as Armstrong described: "The first chorus I play the melody. The second chorus I plays the melody round the melody, and the third chorus I routines." The whole package is overwhelming in its creative, dialogic energy, even as that energy takes a form very different from what it takes in church heterophony.

This solo transformation of collective improvisation provided jazz with a way of highlighting the individual virtuoso while referencing the communal vernacular. Ralph Ellison summarized that relationship in this way: "Each true jazz moment (as distinct from uninspired commercial performance) springs from the contest in which each artist challenges all the rest; each solo flight, or improvisation, represents (like the successive canvases of a painter) a definition of his identity: as individual, as member of the collectivity and as a link in an endless chain of tradition." Armstrong took the model he had learned in New Orleans to unprecedented levels of solo virtuosity. The plantation immigrants had been in search of a new urban identity in New Orleans, and now the southern immigrants were looking for a new northern identity in Chicago. (Interestingly, he was characterized by some in the North as a rural hick, as if the middle stage, urbanized New Orleanian identity, had never happened.) In each case, the solution was arrived at through the combination that had served so well before: the new cultural product foregrounded distinctly urban sophistication while holding allegiance to lower-class vernacular values.

Playing with Harmony

There is one more central ingredient in the recipe of Armstrong's mature solo style—harmony. His command of harmony—rules governing how pitches are combined together, simultaneously, to form chords—contributed mightily to the sense of sophistication in his improvisations during the mid-1920s. The solos that poured out of his trumpet fit the background harmonies articulated by piano, guitar, and bass with razor-sharp precision. Without this, he would have been a footnote in jazz history. With it, he was able to crystallize an epoch-making model of jazz improvisation that is still going strong. When jazz improvisers following Armstrong's example asked the question, What will a jazz melody be like?, they answered with harmonic precision.

To understand the full significance of this, we need to go back, once more, to the plantations of the Deep South, to the traditions of work songs, congregational singing, string bands, and blues. The people who created these traditions during slavery and their descendants who carried them forward in the post-Reconstruction era knew little or nothing about Eurocentric theory, with its notes, scales, keys, and chords. This is not to say that they held no preference for some combinations of sound over others. But the vast majority probably did not engage very much with harmonic thinking. A few might have picked up bits and pieces of Eurocentric harmonic practice, but the vernacular traditions mainly found sources of expressive energy in other parameters of sound.

Work songs obviously had no need for systematic harmony. In New Orleans, Larenzo talked about his soulful tinhorn blues, and chord formation must have been the furthest thing from his mind. We have little direct information about how the many blues-playing pianists in the honky tonks regarded chords. Outside of New Orleans, pianist Robert "Dudlow" Taylor from Helena, Arkansas, was described as having "a good mind for the blues," though he "didn't know an A-minor chord from a B flat." The simple and eventually standard harmonic pattern of blues (as described in Chapter 3) may have been in place in New Orleans, but it is easy to imagine that there was also lots of leeway, including the choice of ignoring harmony altogether.

Church heterophony and string-band ragging stood as the twin forms, sacred and secular, vocal and instrumental, for organizing ensembles on the plantations. Some practitioners may have stepped outside of heterophony and its assortment of crooks, turns, swoops, and glides and into a pleasing mix of controlled consonance; that mix could have included parallel thirds or fourths, for example. Or they may have leaned on the jagged harmonies and rough, expressive dissonances so admired by Zora Neale Hurston. Those uses of consonance and dissonance, however, did not undermine the basically melodic and textural orientation of the practice, which probably remained strong all the way through Armstrong's youth.

It is true, of course, that the melodies used for organizing heterophony were originally crafted with the Eurocentric harmonic system in mind. Baptist hymns, Sousa marches, and Ragtime songs were rigidly shaped in this way. So the invitation toward harmonic precision was always there, simply because of the melodies that were being performed. What I imagine is that it was only under certain conditions that this invitation was accepted. It must have been perfectly fine to sing the hymns and popular songs with complete disregard for their harmonic implications. The melody allows free participation, which comes on its own African-American vernacular terms, terms that have nothing to do, necessarily, with the intricacies of Eurocentric scale and chord formation. Writer Toni Morrison has said that "the major things black art has to have are these: it must have the ability to use found objects, the appearance of using found things, and it must look effortless." Early jazz, like the other vernacular practices from the plantations, regarded the borrowed melody as something like a found object. The melody offers the chance to build something new and it requires no allegiance whatsoever.

Nevertheless, it seems likely that the details of Eurocentric harmony were gradually and sporadically making their way into routine bands during Armstrong's youth. Each player had to do it on his own. There were clear and very specific incentives. Rough and vigorous heterophony might bring recognition in the streets and lower-class dance halls, but it sounded primitive to audiences at the New Orleans Country Club. Lack of harmonic control automatically put a musician at the end of the substitution list for the better-paying white and Creole gigs. Viewed in this way, harmonic control was analogous to literacy, both musical and verbal: it was a tool for advancing in the economically privileged white world. When Edmund Souchon said that Armstrong sounded rough and "not good" when he substituted for dances at Tulane around 1917, we can assume that he had yet to acquire the harmonic precision that would later make him famous.

For the aspiring routine musician, Eurocentric harmony was a mysterious path to advancement into the professional elite. The problem was how to acquire the knowledge. Pianos were used to give informal lessons in harmony, just as they would be in jazz for a long time. (Miles Davis, for example, was grateful to Dizzy Gillespie for tutoring him in bebop harmonies on the piano in late 1944, soon after he arrived in New York City.) But uptown routine players did not see pianos very often, and they did not know many pianists who really understood chords. Manuel Manetta was one who did. He gave impromptu instruction at the Big 25, which had a piano. Manetta found himself getting hired on jobs not just because he knew a lot of repertory and could hold a band together but because he could teach chords to the routine musicians. "They'd treat me so nice they'd always pay me extra money you know," he remembered, "pay other fellows to hire me on jobs with them."

Behind all interest in harmony was the looming presence of Scott Joplin, whose immensely popular rags featured lots of fancy chords. Jack Carey bought the Red Back Book collection of rags, but he couldn't cut them. The same thing happened to Ory. The public wanted to hear Joplin's rags, and for some it mattered whether or not they were played with harmonic precision. Buddy Petit liked the way Joplin used the diminished chord in *Maple Leaf Rag* and he asked Manetta to teach it to him. He eventually found ways of inserting this chord, which was way beyond the range of most of the routine players, into his improvised second parts. "Buddy Petit was the first trumpet player I ever heard spoke about different chords, minor, major, augmented," said Edmond Hall. In advertising-wagon cutting contests and in parades too, Armstrong had Petit's example in front of him, and if he wanted to keep up with the competition, there was only one way to go.

Which is not to say that everyone made the same choice. "Most everybody around [New Orleans] doesn't know what a note is, to say nothing of a chord," claimed Johnny Wiggs. Clarinetist Omer Simeon explained his own approach: "I don't think about the chords when I play, it comes natural." Simeon never did learn harmony, he said, because he had never studied piano, banjo, or guitar. Certainly he was not alone. It is likely that few of the uptown wind players learned to conceptualize chords precisely, and this did not necessarily trouble them. Doing so, they must have felt, ran counter to their sense of melodic, textural, and timbral priority.

But by the time Armstrong arrived in Chicago in 1922, he had gone beyond the level of most of his colleagues. If he first heard harmonically daring and precise improvisation from Petit, the riverboat jobs gave him the chance to work on doing that himself. George Guesnon explained how the time he had spent working on the boats spurred his own playing toward harmonic precision. A report from Albert Walters suggests how this might have worked for Armstrong. Asked if he had taken piano lessons, Walters answered, "Naw, I didn't have a teacher on piano but a fella by the name of David Jones used to teach me when I was working around with him. He used to teach me chords, how to form them and invert them." Good old Br'er Jones, dicty and put off by Louis's low-class hustler crudeness, probably came through for him in the end. Whatever he learned on the riverboats was brought along further with the solos and exercise books his wife Lil had him run through on their grand piano in Chicago.

Milt Hinton, born in Vicksburg, Mississippi, moved with his family to Chicago, where he heard Armstrong playing in 1927. He described the scene:

> Here we had come up in a society in Chicago from, as I say, the twen-ties, where we were emulating, if you would say it, the white studio orchestra in the pit playing overtures. But then in our own ethnic way,

after the overture was over, there would be a big trumpet solo by Louis Armstrong on *Saint Louis Blues* and going into one of these fantastic things which was quite creative. But the people would come on Sundays to the theater and they would be dressed. They would have on their tuxedoes with wing collars and it was like we were emulating white folks, like it was a big white theater you know. Then the orchestra played this little overture and then all of a sudden, we'd go right straight back into our own thing. Black people wanted to be like white people because they felt that this was the way to be; that you were right and you were white and this was the only way it could be . . . We emulated white people because this was a very conditioned thing that had been brought down to us that this was the only way of life.

Louis had enough of the academic thing to read the music properly, and so this was the style. We were going to be just like downtown. And we'd sit there, my mother would have me by the hand, and we'd sit and listen to this overture, which had a European environment. Then the people would be a little restless, and say "Well, that sounds nice," and applaud it. Then somebody would say "Hey baby, play so and so" and when Louis stood up and played one of his great solos, you could see everybody letting their hair down and say "Well, it's great to be like that, but this is what really relates to us."

Louis's "academic thing" was a matter of musical literacy and also something else. Notice how Hinton's phrase resonates with similar remarks from the period. John Stark promoted Joplin's rags to white America with the claim that "these instrumental rags . . . are the perfection of type . . . They have the genius of melody and the scholarship of harmonization. They are used in the drawing rooms and the parlors of culture." W. C. Handy embedded the same terms in a vivid metaphor:

At first folk melodies like these were kept in the back rooms of my mind while the parlor was reserved for dressed-up music. Musical books continued to get much of my attention. There was still an old copy of Steiner's *First Lessons in Harmony*, purchased back in Henderson for fifty cents.

The sequential mix of musical-social inflections that Hinton and his fellow immigrants heard in Chicago was held by Handy in different parts of his mind. Handy's mental parlor, reserved for "dressed-up music"—the equivalent of Hinton's "tuxedoes with wing collars . . . like we were emulating white folks"—was also the place where he stored Steiner's *First Lessons in Harmony*. Meanwhile, Joplin's "scholarship of harmonization" reflected his own interest in placing his music in real white parlors, where the player piano resided. The period neatly packaged a cohesive and easily decipherable semiotic chain: white styles of dress and a white style of gentile socializing went hand in hand with music that had enough of that academic thing, defined as literacy and Eurocentric harmony.

In the long run, however, musical literacy was a peripheral matter for Armstrong. As he once joked, when asked if he knew how to read musical notation, "Not well enough that it interferes with my music." This stood in strong contrast with Joplin's vision of a written kind of distinctly Negro music that could take its place alongside the Eurocentric classics. The New Orleanian achievement did not hinge on literacy; to the contrary, it foregrounded aurality, and it was served not by the technology of sheet music but by the phonograph. Harmony, on the other hand, became crucial, if not for the New Orleanians Armstrong left behind, then for the generation of jazz improvisers who emulated him. The music Hinton and his fellow immigrants approved as something that "really relates to us" had vernacular traits such as blues phrasing and the fixed and variable model, but it also had tremendous harmonic precision.

Harmony is therefore a fascinating part of the story of how the ragging tradition made its way from the plantations to New Orleans and then to the urban North. A group of people created compelling music that did not depend on Eurocentric harmony at all; their descendants later gave birth to a style of melodic improvisation that was built on harmony in a central way. What are the social implications of this? Specifically, does it index an ideology of assimilation? Or perhaps it reflects a more neutral melting-pot mentality, one that has often been articulated with respect to New Orleans jazz through the metaphor of gumbo, a Louisiana stew. Or is something else altogether going on?

It is impossible to be sure that an interest in assimilation did *not* spark some interest in Eurocentric harmony among uptown routiners; little evidence survives that would speak to this directly, so it cannot be ruled out. Throughout this book, I have made the different argument that Armstrong was not the least bit interested in cultural assimilation of any kind. He was raised by the antiassimilationist Saints, taught to be grateful for what he had and not to envy others. He disdained dicty African Americans who put on airs. Around age seventeen we find him moving full steam ahead into the rough and beautiful tradition, though he also picked up signs that his playing was a bit too rough for some audiences. He accepted Marable's offer to play on the riverboats with the hope that the training he would get there might open up better-paying jobs. He was driven not by the ideology of assimilation but by a desire to enter the white market. Had it been otherwise, had assimilation been part of his mindset, certainly his musical development would have turned out very differently than it did.

At the Colored Waif's Home for Boys, Peter Davis advised him to learn not just "ragtime" (the unnotated plantation tradition of ragging the tune) but also "classical" (notated music) music. This has always been the normal situation for African-American musicians in the United States: there is tremendous financial incentive to learn white musical codes, which is not at all the same as the motivation to assimilate. Cross-cultural patronage is not the same as cross-cultural assimilation. In order to work in some venues, uptown routiners had to iron out the rough dissonances. Once that was achieved, they figured out how to use chords on their own terms. This analysis takes harmony out of the realm of assimilation and gives it a different ideological charge: harmony is regarded as sonic material—a found object—to be worked into vernacular practice.

We have already seen how, in a basic way, harmony was folded into the fixed and variable model. Harmonic rhythm provides another way to mark rigid periodicity, the model's core feature. Guitar, piano, and bass play the regularly spaced chords, and the soloist gains a sense of congruence between the variable melody and fixed foundation by prominently including the notes of those chords. Independence between the two layers is produced through rhythmic details and phrase structure. But jazz musicians eventually went further when they discovered how to enhance the independence of their variable, solo layer by manipulating harmony.

Harmonic departures from the fixed foundation are not especially common in Armstrong's mature solos from the 1920s, but those that do occur are revealing. They show his willingness to violate the conventions of Eurocentric harmonic practice to an important end. An excellent example comes in the first phrase of one of his most famous solos, from a 1926 recording of the song *Big Butter and Egg Man*. He begins with a series of three ascending gestures that are fairly in step with the two-bar harmonic rhythm of the background. Subtle rhythmic tension is achieved within the two-bar modules. The three ascents are then answered by a melodic goal, a leap to a high f, which is followed by a balancing, arpeggiated descent of an F chord. On this level of design, the phrase is straightforward. But two additional details make the arrival on this goal very striking. First, the high f comes one bar earlier than is predicted by the pattern of the three ascents. Armstrong had first introduced rhythmic tension *within* the two bar modules; now he introduces it by working *against* them. Even more impressive is the radical harmonic clash that his climactic F chord creates, for it stands in biting dissonance with the background chord of C, thus violating the norms of Eurocentric harmonic practice. One measure later, while he completes his arpeggiating descent of the F chord, the background harmony catches up with him, so to speak, thus bringing the fixed and variable layers back into synchronization.

If one were to only look at a transcription of the notes on a page, one would suspect a mistake. That is not, however, the impression one gets from listening. Not only is Armstrong's harmonic clash calculated through details of melodic design; it is also played with such full, brimming confidence that no listener has ever heard it as wrong. The solo may have been more of a composition than an improvisation, for jazz historian Brian Harker has argued that Armstrong worked on it over an extended period, getting it just right, in the old-school tradition of his home city. The chiseled perfection of the phrase is the result of honing it no less patiently than a sculptor polishes a slab of marble.

The harmonic chaos turns out not to be chaos at all; instead, this moment shows harmony being used to intensify the fixed and variable model. The early arrival on *F* folds harmony into the workings of layered phrase structures. Armstrong has ventured into the sacred inner court of the mansion of the muses and snatched away harmonic secrets for his own vernacular use. For the Creoles, for Joplin, for Handy, and for all the others who were not trained as he was, Eurocentric harmony is a primary system of pitch syntax that must not be violated. For Armstrong, *the fixed and variable model is primary*. Eurocentric harmonic syntax is secondary and subservient to that, and here he shows how to use one in the service of the other. Crystallized in this brief moment is a brilliant synthetic stroke, one that emerges as a logical step from his entire training even while it places him at the forefront of jazz improvisation in 1926.

This orientation continued to animate the leading innovators in jazz. A decade later, Lester Young explored ways of making his solos even more independent from the harmonic foundation, thereby opening up a fresh sense of bluesy detachment. Around the same time, Coleman Hawkins and Art Tatum were experimenting with adding chords into their improvised melodies to produce two layers of harmonic rhythm, each moving at different speeds and thereby enhancing the fixed and variable model. Hawkins and Tatum also opened the door to bebop with the dizzying practice of substitution harmonies, another technique that may be understood in terms of the fixed and variable model.

In all of these examples—which were foregrounded and central to jazz innovation around 1925–1950—pitch relations are folded into a conceptual model that was derived ultimately from West Africa. It may be that very few people thought about these details in that way, but they are central to the history that explains how the music works as it does. Duke Ellington did not like the word "jazz," and he did not like putting limiting definitions on music. "I used to have a definition," he said, "but I don't think I have one any more, unless it is a music with an African foundation which came out of an American environment." The point of view advanced here is that harmony, as learned in an American environment, was brought into the workings of an African foundation.

Jazz musicians learned how to craft a new melodic idiom—*a new melodic identity*—through purposeful use of harmony. Blues and heterophony are still audible in the mature Armstrong's solos, but the crucial, central feature that launched the jazz solo tradition was the stubborn insistence on the priority of the fixed and variable model, even while absorbing harmonic sophistication into it. Without this, jazz would not have distinguished itself either from music that was less harmonically inflected, such as the blues, or, on the other side of the musical-social spectrum, from Broadway-show styles that use harmony in a straightforward and traditional way. Jazz could easily have found a comfortable, virtuoso niche alongside either one of these models, but the leading innovators carved out an independent musical field by continually exploring ways of folding harmony into a musical conception that came from the plantations of the Deep South and ultimately from Africa.

We can now see one explanation why Armstrong abandoned the freak music that brought so much fame to Joe Oliver: he was busy concentrating on something else. Freak inflections would only get in the way of the blisteringly precise harmonic improvisation and polyrhythmic phrasing he was working on. The kind of music he came to specialize in still took Oliver as a point of departure, but it was his monkeyshines, barrelhouse, and creative second playing rather than his freak music. In 1919 the southern immigrants in Chicago were so moved by Oliver's freak music that they crowned him king. By the mid-1920s, Armstrong had rearranged the sonic terms of African-American vernacular modernity. He synthesized the academic thing with something that still really related to the southern immigrants, and the success of this synthesis inadvertently pushed freak music to the margins.

❧ The good-natured, locationally specific metaphor of jazz as gumbo stands as a subtle alternative to assimilation. The metaphor attractively marks jazz as a product of American diversity. The United States may lack the high "art" traditions that grew out of centuries of rigid class differentiation in Europe, but as one huge melting pot it has produced the musical gumbo of jazz. Certainly New Orleans has long been noted for its diversity. A poem from

1829 parodied the city with an inventory of Frenchmen, Spaniards, West Indians, Creoles, Yankees, Kentuckians, Tennesseans, lawyers, priests, friars, nuns, Negroes "in purple and fine linen," slaves "in rags and chains," robbers, pirates, sailors, pretty girls, ugly fortune-tellers, pimps, white men with black wives—"*et vice-versa* too." Clarinetist Barney Bigard described the city in similar terms: "It's such a mixture, a melting pot of peoples and races: artists, sailors, writers, whores, poets, pimps, and just about every kind of person you can think of. It's like a 'gathering place for lost souls.'"

But in the present reading, jazz was no musical gumbo but the product of direct and vigorous transformation of the plantation vernacular. Given their heritage of ragging the tune, the uptown routine musicians found it natural to embrace and transform many different kinds of music. It is easy to misconstrue their open-armed, open-eared attitude, as is evidenced by arguments that put forward marches, hymns, and ragtime—even Italian opera, ritual singing of Jewish cantors, and French folk songs—as essential components of early jazz. Unquestionably, some of these idioms put Eurocentric harmony in Armstrong's ear, but at the level of stylistic influence they were largely interchangeable in this regard. Repertorial diversity alone does not make for a musical gumbo. My sense is that Armstrong's musical development would not have been one bit different had he never heard an Italian aria or a French folk song. The confusion extends through all levels of analysis, micro and macro. Both rhythmic tension and harmony are prominent in jazz—didn't they come from different parts of the Old World, one from Africa and one from Europe, which would make jazz an American fusion of the two?

That way of thinking can easily drift toward a kind of racial determinism in which the Creoles of color, part African and part French, are seen as the biological representation of a cultural fusion and hence central in the formation of jazz. But we have already noted the traditional Creole agenda, which positioned them very differently. "You have the finest ideas from the greatest operas, symphonies and overtures in jazz music," claimed Creole Jelly Roll Morton. "There is nothing finer than jazz music because it comes from everything of the finest class music." Morton knew more

Longshoreman (New Orleans Public Library,
photo by George François Mugnier)

about the history of jazz than he let on when he said that, but he said it nevertheless. How differently Armstrong cast the matter, socially and musically. "It all came from the Old Sanctified Churches," he wrote on one occasion; and, on another, jazz "isn't anything new. At one time they was calling it levee camp music." There was probably never a time when jazz was one thing and one thing only, when it did not include a range of possibilities. The topic of this book, however, is not that entire range but rather the part of it that shaped Louis Armstrong.

Jazz as Armstrong learned it was a creation of the ratty people, as Isidore Barbarin would have called them, the "roustabouts unloading banana boats on the wharves—all of my folks," which is how Armstrong once identified his community, the common laborers, domestics, hustlers, and prostitutes who found themselves confined by the color line to the economic bottom of society. His success was theirs too. It was a victory for the people who nourished him, the Saints in church who applauded his singing as a child, the rags-bottles-and-bones men who held him spellbound with soulful talk, his buddies in the vocal quartet, his teacher at the Waif's Home, the honky tonk musicians, parade musicians, and little routine musicians who circulated around town every day on advertising wagons. A victory for those people who loved to move their bodies in time with rhythmically exciting music, who spoke in musical ways, who admired instrumentally inflected singing and vocally inflected instruments, who regarded blue notes as the strongest notes you could play. People who looked forward to Sundays in church, where the music they made brought the sum of their community to a greater whole, who relied on music to proudly proclaim who they were in public events, who admired musicians with professional skills but could also appreciate music played by an amateur, as long as he showed willingness and heart. Out of their values and practices came the fruits of an expressive culture that are with us still.

BIBLIOGRAPHY

General Sources

Abbott, Lynn. 1992. "'Play That Barber Shop Chord': A Case for the African-American Origin of Barbershop Harmony." *American Music* 10: 289–325.

———. 1993. "'Brown Skin, Who You For?' Another Look at Clarence Williams's Early Career." *Jazz Archivist* 8, nos. 1–2 (December):1–15.

Abbott, Lynn, and Doug Seroff. 1996. "'They Cert'ly Sound Good to Me': Sheet Music, Southern Vaudeville, and the Commercial Ascendancy of the Blues." *American Music* 14: 402–54.

———. 2001. "Brown Skin (Who You Really For?)." *Jazz Archivist* 15: 10–16.

———. 2002. *Out of Sight: The Rise of African American Popular Music, 1889–1895.* Jackson: University of Mississippi Press.

Abbott, Lynn, and Jack Stewart. 1994. "The Iroquois Theater." *Jazz Archivist* 9, no. 2 (December): 2–20.

Abrahams, Roger. 1977. "The West Indian Tea Meeting: An Essay in Civilization." In *Old Roots in New Lands: Historical and Anthropological Perspectives on Black Experiences in the Americas*, ed. Ann Pescatello, 173–208. Westport, Conn.: Greenwood Press.

———. 1983. *The Man-of-Words in the West Indies: Performance and the Emergence of Creole Culture.* Baltimore: Johns Hopkins University Press.

———. 1992. *Singing the Master: The Emergence of African American Culture in the Plantation South.* New York: Pantheon Press.

Ake, David Andrew. 1998. "Being Jazz: Identities and Images." Ph.D. diss., University of California, Los Angeles.

Albertson, Chris. 2003. *Bessie.* New Haven: Yale University Press.

Allen, Walter, and Brian Rust. 1987. *"King" Oliver.* Revised by Laurie Wright. Essex: Storyville Publications.

Anderson, Gene. 1990. "Johnny Dodds in New Orleans." *American Music* 8: 405–40.

———. 1994. "The Genesis of the King Oliver's Creole Jazz Band." *American Music* 12: 283–303.

Antony, Arthé Agnes. 1978. "The Negro Creole Community in New Orleans, 1880–1920: An Oral History." Ph.D. diss., University of California at Irvine.

Armstrong, Louis. 1936. *Swing That Music.* London: Longmans, Green.

———. 1946. "New Orleans' Own Louis Armstrong: 30 Years a Jazz Great." *Negro South* 4, no. 8 (April): 16–17, 33, 37.

———. 1947. "Storyville—Where the Blues Were Born." *True* (November): 32–33, 100–105.

————. 1950. "New Orleans Function." Recorded with the All Stars on April 26, re-released on the album *The Complete Decca Studio Recordings of Louis Armstrong and the All Stars*, Mosaic MD6–146.

————. 1954. *Satchmo: My Life in New Orleans*. New York: Prentice Hall.

————. 1955. "They Cross the Iron Curtain to Hear American Jazz." Interview. *U.S. News and World Report*, December 2, 40–54.

————. 1961a. "How Jazz Came to Life." *Music Journal* (March): 13.

————. 1961b. "Daddy, How the Country Has Changed!" Interview. *Ebony* (May), 81.

————. 1966. *Louis Armstrong, a Self-Portrait: The Interview with Richard Meryman*. New York: Eakins Press.

————. 1999. *Louis Armstrong in His Own Words*. Ed. Thomas Brothers. Oxford: Oxford University Press.

Arnesen, Eric. 1991. *Waterfront Workers of New Orleans: Race, Class, and Politics, 1863–1923*. New York: Oxford University Press.

Ayers, Edward L. 1992. *The Promise of the New South: Life after Reconstruction*. Oxford: Oxford University Press.

Bakhtin, M. M. 1986. "Response to a Question from the *Novy Mir* Editorial Staff." In *Speech Genres and Other Late Essays*, ed. C. Emerson and M. Holquist, trans. V. McGee, 1–9. Austin: University of Texas Press.

Baraka, Amiri [aka Leroi Jones]. 1963. *Blues People: Negro Music in White America*. New York: Morrow Quill Paperbacks.

Barber, Karin. 1989. "Interpreting Oríkìo as History and as Literature." In *Discourse and Its Disguises: The Interpretation of African Oral Texts*, ed. Karin Barber and P. F. de Moraes Farias, 13–23. Birmingham University African Studies Series no. 1. Centre of West African Studies, University of Birmingham.

Barker, Danny. 1986. *A Life in Jazz*. Ed. Alyn Shipton. New York: Oxford University Press.

————. 1998. *Buddy Bolden and the Last Days of Storyville*. Ed. Alyn Shipton. London: Cassell.

Barlow, William. 1989. *Looking Up at Down: The Emergence of Blues Culture*. Philadelphia: Temple University Press.

Bechet, Sidney. 1960. *Treat It Gentle: An Autobiography*. New York: Twayne.

Berlin, Edward. 1980. *Ragtime: A Musical and Cultural History*. Berkeley: University of California Press.

————. 1994. *King of Ragtime: Scott Joplin and His Era*. New York: Oxford University Press.

Berliner, Paul. 1994. *Thinking in Jazz: The Infinite Art of Improvisation*. Chicago: University of Chicago Press.

Bernhardt, Clyde. 1986. *I Remember: Eighty Years of Black Entertainment, Big Bands, and the Blues: An Autobiography*. Philadelphia: University of Pennsylvania Press.

Bethell, Tom. 1977. *George Lewis: A Jazzman from New Orleans*. Berkeley: University of California Press.

Bigard, Barney. 1986. *With Louis and the Duke: The Autobiography of a Jazz Clarinetist*. Ed. Barry Martyn. New York: Oxford University Press.

Blassingame, John. 1973. *Black New Orleans, 1860–1880*. Chicago: University of Chicago Press.

Blesh, Rudi. 1946. *Shining Trumpets: A History of Jazz*. New York: Knopf.

Blesh, Rudi, and Harriet Janis. 1950. *They All Played Ragtime*. New York: Knopf.

Borneman, Ernest. 1959. "The Roots of Jazz." In *Jazz*, ed. Nat Hentoff and Albert J. McCarthy, 1–20. New York: Rinehart.

———. 1970. "Jazz and the Creole Tradition." *Jazzforschung* 1: 99–112.

Bourdieu, Pierre. 1984. *Distinction: A Social Critique of the Judgement of Taste*. Trans. Richard Nice. Cambridge: Harvard University Press.

Brooks, Edward. 2002. *The Young Louis Armstrong on Records: A Critical Survey of the Early Recordings, 1923–1928*. Studies in Jazz, no. 39, Institute of Jazz Studies. Lanham: Scarecrow Press.

Brothers, Thomas. 1994. "Solo and Cycle in African-American Jazz." *Musical Quarterly* 78: 479–509.

———. 1997. "Ideology and Aurality in the Vernacular Traditions of African-American Music (ca. 1890–1950)." *Black Music Research Journal* 17: 169–209.

———. 1999. *Louis Armstrong in His Own Words*. New York: Oxford University Press.

Brown, H. Rap. 1972. "Street Talk." In *Rappin' and Stylin' Out: Communication in Urban Black America*, comp. Thomas Kochman, 205–9. Urbana: University of Illinois Press.

Brubaker, Rogers, and Frederick Cooper. 2001. "Beyond 'Identity.'" *Theory and Society* 29: 1–47.

Büchmann-Møller, Frank. 1990. *You Just Fight for Your Life: The Story of Lester Young*. New York: Praeger.

Bushell, Garvin. 1988. *Jazz from the Beginning*. As told to Mark Tucker. Ann Arbor: University of Michigan Press.

Calhoun, Craig. 1997. *Nationalism*. Minneapolis: University of Minnesota Press.

Carey, Mutt. 1946. "New Orleans Trumpet Players." *Jazz Music* 3, no. 4: 4–6.

Chamberlain, Charles. 2000. "Searching for 'The Gulf Coast Circuit': Mobility and Cultural Diffusion in the Age of Jim Crow, 1900–1930." *Jazz Archivist* 14: 1–18.

———. 2001. "The Goodson Sisters: Women Pianists and the Function of Gender in the Jazz Age." *Jazz Archivist* 15: 1–9.

———. N.d. "Beyond Storyville: Race, Jobs and Jazz in New Orleans during the First World War, 1917–1919." Unpublished paper.

Charters, Samuel. 1963. *Jazz New Orleans, 1885–1963: An Index to the Negro Musicians of New Orleans*. New York: Oak Publications.

Chernoff, John. 1979. *African Rhythm and African Sensibility: Aesthetics and Social Action in African Musical Idioms*. Chicago: University of Chicago Press.

Chevan, David. 1989. "Riverboat Music from St. Louis and the Streckfus Steamboat Line." *Black Music Research Journal* 9: 153–80.

Chilton, Charles. 1947. "Jackson and the Oliver Band." *Jazz Music* 6: 5–9.

Chilton, John. 1987. *Sidney Bechet: The Wizard of Jazz*. New York: Oxford University Press.

Cimbala, Paul. 1979. "Fortunate Bondsmen: Black 'Musicianers' and Their Role as an Antebellum Southern Plantation Slave Elite." *Southern Studies* 18: 291–303.

Clark, Andrew. 2001. *Riffs and Choruses: A New Jazz Anthology*. London: Continuum.

Cogswell, Michael. 2003. *Louis Armstrong: The Offstage Story of Satchmo*. Portland: Collector's Press.

Collier, James Lincoln. 1983. *Louis Armstrong: An American Genius*. New York: Oxford University Press.

Collins, Lee. 1974. *Oh, Didn't He Ramble: The Life Story of Lee Collins as Told to Mary Collins*. Ed. Frank Gillis and John Miner. Urbana: University of Illinois Press.

Connerton, Paul. 1989. *How Societies Remember*. Cambridge, UK: Cambridge University Press.

Creecy, James R. 1860. *Scenes in the South, and Other Miscellaneous Pieces*. Philadelphia: Lippincott.

Dailey, Jane. 2000. *Before Jim Crow: The Politics of Race in Postemancipation Virginia*. Chapel Hill: University of North Carolina Press.

Dance, Stanley. 1969. "Duke Ellington." *Stereo Review* (December).

Davis, Allison, and John Dollard. 1940. *Children of Bondage: The Personality Development of Negro Youth in the Urban South*. Washington: American Council on Education.

Davis, Miles, with Quincy Troupe. 1989. *Miles, the Autobiography*. New York: Simon and Schuster.

Desdunes, Rodolphe Lucien. 1973. *Our People and Our History: A Tribute to the Creole People of Color in Memory of the Great Men They Have Given Us and of the Good Works They Have Accomplished*, trans. and ed. Sister Dorothea Olga McCants. Baton Rouge: Louisiana State University Press. Translation of *Nos hommes et notre histoire* (Montreal: Arbour and Dupont, 1911).

DeVeaux, Scott. 1997. *The Birth of Bebop: A Social and Musical History*. Berkeley: University of California Press.

Dixon, Melvin. 1985. "Singing Swords: The Literary Legacy of Slavery." In *The Slave's Narrative*, ed. C. Davis and H. Gates, 298–318. New York: Oxford University Press.

Dodds, Baby. 1992. *The Baby Dodds Story: As Told to Larry Gara*. Rev. ed. Baton Rouge: Louisiana State University Press.

Dollard, John. 1957. *Caste and Class in a Southern Town*. 3rd ed. New York: Doubleday.

Domínguez, Virginia. 1986. *White by Definition: Social Classification in Creole Louisiana*. New Brunswick, N.J.: Rutgers University Press.

Donder, Jempi de. 1983. "My Buddy: An Attempt to Find Buddy Petit." *Footnote* 14, no. 3: 24–34; 14, no. 4: 4–13.

Douglass, Frederick. 1982. *Narrative of the Life of Frederick Douglass, an American Slave, Written by Himself*. Ed. Houston A. Baker Jr. New York: Penguin. First published in 1845.

Du Bois, W. E. B. 1906. "Niagara Movement Speech." available at http://teaching americanhistory.org/library/index.asp?document=496. Accessed July 2004.

———. 1961. *The Souls of Black Folk*. New York: Dodd, Mead. (Orig. publ. 1903.)

Dugan, James. 1946. "Old Man Jiver." *Collier's* (9 February): 27, 51–52.

Eagleson, Dorothy. 1961. "Some Aspects of the Social Life of the New Orleans Negro in the 1880's." M.A. thesis, Tulane University.

Edwards, Brent Hayes. 2002. "Louis Armstrong and the Syntax of Scat." *Critical Inquiry* 28: 618–49.

Edwards, Laura. 1997. *Gendered Strife and Confusion: The Political Culture of Reconstruction*. Urbana: University of Illinois Press.

Ellington, Edward Kennedy "Duke." 1973. *Music Is My Mistress*. New York: Doubleday.

Ellison, Ralph. 2002. *Invisible Man*. New York: Random House. (Orig. publ. 1947.)

Emery, Lynne Fauley. 1988. *Black Dance from 1619 to Today*. 2nd, rev. ed. Princeton: Princeton Book. (Orig. publ. 1972.)

Epstein, Dena. 1977. *Sinful Tunes and Spirituals: Black Folk Music to the Civil War*. Urbana: University of Illinois Press.

Escott, Paul. 1979. *Slavery Remembered: A Record of 20th-c Slave Narratives.* Chapel Hill: University of North Carolina Press.

Evans, David. 1978. "African Elements in Twentieth-Century United States Black Folk Music." *Jazzforschung* 10: 85–109.

———. 1987. "Charley Patton, the Conscience of the Delta." In *The Voice of the Delta: Charley Patton and the Mississippi Blues Traditions, Influences and Comparisons,* ed. Robert Sacré, 111–214. Liège, Belgium: Presses Universitaires Liège.

Fanon, Frantz. 1967. *Black Skin White Masks.* Trans. Charles L. Markmann. New York: Grove Press.

Feather, Leonard. 1965. "Life with Feather: Part V of a Critic's Autobiography: Remembering 'Pops.' " *Down Beat* (15 July): 19–22.

Fiehrer, Thomas. 1991. "From Quadrille to Stomp: The Creole Origins of Jazz." *Popular Music* 10: 21–38.

Floyd Jr., Samuel. 1995. *The Power of Black Music: Interpreting Its History from Africa to the United States.* New York: Oxford University Press.

Foner, Laura. 1970. "The Free People of Colour in Louisiana and St. Dominigue: A Comparative Portrait of Two Three-Caste Slave Societies." *Journal of Social History* 3 (Summer): 406–30.

Fortes, M., and G. Dieterlen, eds. 1965. *African Systems of Thought: Studies Presented and Discussed at the Third International African Seminar in Salisbury, December 1960.* London: Oxford University Press.

Foster, Pops. 1947. "Forty-eight Years on the String Bass." *Jazz Record* (March): 18 and 32.

———. 1971. *Pops Foster: The Autobiography of a New Orleans Jazzman.* Ed. Tom Stoddard. Berkeley: University of California Press.

Friedlander, Lee. 1992. *The Jazz People of New Orleans.* Afterword by Whitney Balliett. New York: Pantheon Books.

Gabbard, Krin. 1995. "Signifyin(g) the Phallus: Mo' Better Blues and Representations of Jazz Trumpet." In *Representing Jazz,* ed. Krin Gabbard, 104–30. Durham: Duke University Press.

Giddins, Gary. 1988. *Satchmo.* New York: Doubleday.

———. 2000. *Satchmo: Louis Armstrong.* New York: Columbia Music Video.

Gillespie, Dizzy. With Al Fraser. 1979. *To Be or Not to Bop.* New York: Doubleday.

Gilroy, Paul. 1993. *Small Acts: Thoughts on the Politics of Black Cultures.* London: Serpant's Tail.

Gioia, Ted. 1989. "Jazz and the Primitivist Myth." *Musical Quarterly* 73: 130–43.

Goffin, Robert. 1946a. *La Nouvelle-Orléans: Capitale du Jazz.* New York: Éditions de la Maison Française.

———. 1946b. 'Big Eye' Louis Nelson. *Jazz Record* (June): 7–9.

———. 1977. *Horn of Plenty: The Story of Louis Armstrong.* New York: Da Capo. (Orig. publ. 1947.)

Greenough, Jane. 1947. "What Did Ory Say?" *Record Changer* (November): 5–6.

Guralnick, Peter. 1992. *Searching for Robert Johnson.* New York: Dutton.

Gushee, Lawrence. 1985. "A Preliminary Chronology of the Early Career of Ferd 'Jelly Roll' Morton." *American Music* 3: 389–412.

———. 1987. "When Was Bunk Johnson Born and Why Should We Care?" *Jazz Archivist* 2, no. 2 (November): 4.

———. 1988. "How the Creole Band Came to Be." *Black Music Research Journal* 8, no. 1: 83–100.

———. 1989. "New Orleans-Area Musicians on the West Coast, 1908–1925." *Black Music Research Journal* 9, no. 1: 1–18.

———. 1991. "Black Professional Musicians in New Orleans c. 1880." *Inter-American Music Review* 11, no. 2: 53–64.

———. 1994. "The Nineteenth-Century Origins of Jazz." *Black Music Research Journal* 14, no. 1: 1–24.

———. 1998. "The Improvisation of Louis Armstrong." In *In the Course of Performance: Studies in the World of Musical Improvisation*, ed. Bruno Nettl with Melinda Russell, 291–334. Chicago: University of Chicago Press.

Hahn, Steven. 2003. *A Nation under Our Feet: Black Political Struggles in the Rural South from Slavery to the Great Migration*. Cambridge: Harvard University Press.

Hair, William Ivy. 1976. *Carnival of Fury: Robert Charles and the New Orleans Race Riot of 1900*. Baton Rouge: Louisiana State University Press.

Hall, Gwendolyn Midlo. 1992a. *Africans in Colonial Louisiana: The Development of Afro-Creole Culture in the Eighteenth Century*. Baton Rouge: Louisiana State University Press.

———. 1992b. "The Formation of Afro-Creole Culture." In *Creole New Orleans: Race and Americanization*, ed. Arnold Hirsch and Joseph Logsdon, 58–90. Baton Rouge: Louisiana State University Press.

Handy, W. C. 1957. *Father of the Blues: An Autobiography*. London: Sidgwick and Jackson.

Harker, Brian. 1997. "The Early Musical Development of Louis Armstrong, 1901–1928." Ph.D. diss., Columbia University.

———. 1999. "'Telling a Story': Louis Armstrong and Coherence in Early Jazz." *Current Musicology* 63: 46–83.

———. 2003. "Louis Armstrong and the Clarinet." *American Music* 21, 137–58.

Hazzard-Gordon, Katrina. 1990. *Jookin': The Rise of Social Dance Formations in African-American Culture*. Philadelphia: Temple University Press.

Herskovitz, Melville. 1941. *The Myth of the Negro Past*. New York: Harpers.

Higginbotham, Evelyn. 1993. *Righteous Discontent: The Women's Movement in the Black Baptist Church, 1880–1920*. Cambridge: Harvard University Press.

Hirsch, Arnold, and Joseph Logsdon. 1992. *Creole New Orleans: Race and Americanization*. Baton Rouge: Louisiana State University Press.

Holloway, Joseph E. 1990. *Africanisms in American Culture*. Bloomington: Indiana University Press.

Hurston, Zora Neale. 1983. *The Sanctified Church*. Berkeley: Turtle Island.

Ingersoll, Thomas N. 1996. "The Slave Trade and the Ethnic Diversity of Louisiana's Slave Community." *Louisiana History* 37: 133–61.

Jackson, Joy J. 1969. *New Orleans in the Gilded Age: Politics and Urban Progress, 1880–1896*. Baton Rouge: Louisiana State University Press.

Jackson, Mahalia. With Evan Wylie. 1967. *Movin' On Up*. New York: Hawthorn Press.

———. 1973. *The Life I Sing About*. Caedmon Records, TC 1413-1973.

Jameson, Frederic. 1981. *The Political Unconscious: Narrative as a Socially Symbolic Act*. Ithaca: Cornell University Press.

Jasen, David, and Gene Jones. 2000. *That American Rag: The Story of Ragtime from Coast to Coast*. New York: Schirmer.

Johnson, Jerah. 1992. "Colonial New Orleans: A Fragment of the Eighteenth-Century French Ethos." In *Creole New Orleans: Race and Americanization*, ed. Arnold Hirsch and Joseph Logsdon, 12–57. Baton Rouge: Louisiana State University Press.

———. 1995. *Congo Square in New Orleans*. New Orleans: Louisiana Landmarks Society.

———. 2000. "Jim Crow Laws of the 1890s and the Origins of New Orleans Jazz: Correction of an Error." *Popular Music* 19: 243–52.

Jones, Max, and John Chilton. 1971. *Louis: The Louis Armstrong Story. 1900–1971*. Boston: Little, Brown.

Jones, Tad. 2000. "Digging for Satchmo's Roots in the City That Spawned Him." *New York Times*, August 15.

Jones, Will. 1949. "It's the Bunk, but It Helped." *Minneapolis Tribune*, July 20, 16.

Kelley, Robin D. G. 1993. "'We Are Not What We Seem': Rethinking Black Working-Class Opposition in the Jim Crow South." *Journal of American History* 80 (June): 75–112.

Kenney, William. 1993. *Chicago Jazz: A Cultural History, 1904–1930*. New York: Oxford University Press.

Kinser, Samuel. 1990. *Carnival, American Style: Mardi Gras at New Orleans and Mobile*. Photographs by Norman Magden. Chicago: University of Chicago Press.

Kinzer, Charles. 1993. "The Tio Family: Four Generations of New Orleans Musicians, 1814–1933." Ph.D. diss., Louisiana State University.

———. 1996. "The Tios of New Orleans and Their Pedagogical Influence on the Early Jazz Clarinet Style." *Black Music Research Journal* 16: 279–302.

Kmen, Henry A. 1966. *Music in New Orleans: The Formative Years, 1791–1841*. Baton Rouge: Louisiana State University Press.

———. 1972. "The Roots of Jazz and the Dance in Place Congo: A Re-Appraisal." In *Yearbook for Inter-American Musical Research*, ed. G. Chase, vol. 8, 5–6. Austin: University of Texas Press.

Knowles, Richard H. 1996. *Fallen Heroes: A History of New Orleans Brass Bands*. New Orleans: Jazzology Press.

Koenig, Karl. 1981. "The Plantation Belt Brass Bands and Musicians, Part 1: Professor James B. Humphrey," and "Professor James B. Humphrey—Part II." *Second Line* 33: 24–40; and 34: 15–19.

———. 1982. "The Plantation Bands, Part IV: Harrison Barnes, Sunny Henry and The Eclipse Marching Band of Magnolia Plantation." *Second Line* 34: 37–45.

———. 1983. "Chris Kelly: Blues King of New Orleans Jazz." *Second Line* 35: 4–21, 24–26.

Kubik, Gerhard. 1990. "Drum Patterns in the 'Batuque' of Benedito Caxias." *Latin American Music Review* 11, no. 2: 115–81.

———. 1993. "Transplantation of African Musical Cultures into the New World." In *Slavery in the Americas*, ed. Wolfgang Binder, 422–34. Würzburg: Königshausen and Neumann.

———. 1999. *Africa and the Blues*. Jackson: University of Mississippi Press.

Lachance, Paul. 1988. "The 1809 Immigration of St. Domingue Refugees to New Orleans: Reception, Integration, and Impact." *Louisiana History* 29:109–41.

———. 1992. "The Foreign French." In *Creole New Orleans: Race and Americanization*, ed. Arnold Hirsch and Joseph Logsdon, 101–30. Baton Rouge: Louisiana State University Press.

Lanier, Sidney. 1973. *Florida: Its Scenery, Climate, and History*. Gainesville: University of Florida Press. (Orig. publ. 1875.)

Lardner, John. 1951. *White Hopes and Other Tigers*. Philadelphia: Lippincott.

Lax, John. 1974. "Chicago's Black Jazz Musicians in the Twenties: Portrait of an Era." *Journal of Jazz Studies* 1: 107–21.

Leiding, Harriette Kershaw. 1910. *Street Cries of an Old Soutern City*. Charleston: Daggett.

Levin, Floyd. 1994. "'I Wish I Could Shimmy Like My Sister Kate,' The First Recorded Hit of the Jazz Age." *Second Line* 46: 58–60.

Levine, Lawrence. 1977. *Black Culture and Black Consciousness: Afro-American Folk Thought from Slavery to Freedom*. New York: Oxford University Press.

Lewis, George. 1946. "Play Number Nine." *Jazz Record* (January): 7–10.

Lindfors, Bernth. 1983. "Circus Africans." *Journal of American Culture* 6: 9–14.

Logsdon, Joseph, and Caryn Cossé Bell. 1992. "The Americanization of Black New Orleans, 1850–1900." In *Creole New Orleans: Race and Americanization*, ed. Arnold Hirsch and Joseph Logsdon, 201–61. Baton Rouge: Louisiana State University Press.

Lomax, Alan. 1970. "The Homogeneity of African-Afro-American Musical Style." In *Afro-American Anthropology: Contemporary Perspectives*, ed. Norman Whitten and John Szwed, 181–202. New York: Free Press.

———. 1993. *Mister Jelly Roll: The Fortunes of Jelly Roll Morton, New Orleans Creole and "Inventor of Jazz."* Berkeley: University of California (Orig. publ. 1950.)

———. 1997. *Southern Journey 61 Highway Mississippi: Delta Country Blues, Spirituals, Work Songs and Dance Music*. Vol. 3 of the Alan Lomax Collection. Cambridge, Mass.: Rounder CD 1703.

Lovett, Leonard. 1978. "Black Holiness-Pentecostalism: Implications for Ethics and Social Transformation." Ph.D. diss., Emory University.

MacMurray, Mona. 1982. "Chester Zardis." *Second Line* 24: 28–35.

MacMurray, Mona, and Sue Hall. 1984. "Josiah 'Cie' Frazier." *Second Line* 36: 10–15.

Marquis, Donald. 1978. *In Search of Buddy Bolden*. Baton Rouge: Louisiana State University Press.

McCusker, John. 1998. "Kid Ory's Baptismal Certificate." *New Orleans Music* 7, no. 4: 17.

Mitchell, Reid. 1995. *All on a Mardi Gras Day: Episodes in the History of New Orleans Carnival*. Cambridge: Harvard University Press.

Montgomery, William. 1993. *Under Their Own Vine and Fig Tree: The African-American Church in the South, 1865–1900*. Baton Rouge: Louisiana State University Press.

Moore, Fred. 1945. "King Oliver's Last Tour." *Jazz Record* (June): 10–12.

Morgenstern, Dan. 1965. "Yesterday, Today, and Tomorrow: An Interview with Louis Armstrong." *Down Beat* (15 July): 15–18.

Morris, Bob. 1991. "Manny Gabriel's Story." *Second Line* 43: 11–25.

Morton, Jelly Roll. 1947. "I Discovered Jazz in 1902." In *Frontiers of Jazz*, ed. Ralph de Toledano, 104–6. New York: Oliver Durrell. (Orig. publ. 1938.)

Murray, Albert. 1976. *Stomping the Blues*. New York: Random House.

Nettl, Bruno. 1974. "Thoughts on Improvisation: A Comparative Approach." *Musical Quarterly* 60: 1–19.

Newton, Francis [aka Eric Hobsbawm]. 1975. *The Jazz Scene*. New York: Da Capo. (Orig. publ. 1960.)

Oliver, Paul. 1984. *Songsters and Saints: Vocal Traditions on Race Records*. Cambridge, UK: Cambridge University Press.

Ong, Walter. 1982. *Orality and Literacy: The Technologizing of the Word*. London: Metheun.

Ostendorf, Berndt. 1993. "Urban Creole Slavery and Its Cultural Legacy." In *Slavery in the Americas*, ed. Wolfgang Binder, 389–401. Würzburg: Königshausen and Neumann.

Palmer, Robert. 1982. *Deep Blues*. New York: Penguin.

Panetta, Vince. 2000. "'For Godsake Stop!': Improvised Music in the Streets of New Orleans, ca. 1890." *Musical Quarterly* (Spring): 5–29.

Parsons, Kahne. 1989. "Distinct Favorites." *Jazz Archivist* 4, no. 2 (December): 6.

Pastras, Philip. 2001. *Dead Man Blues: Jelly Roll Morton Way Out West*. Berkeley: University of California Press.

Peretti, Burton. 1992. *The Creation of Jazz: Music, Race and Culture in Urban America*. Urbana: University of Illinois Press.

Radano, Ronald. 2000. "Black Noise/White Mastery." In *Decomposition: Post-Disciplinary Performance*, ed. Sue-Ellen Case, Philip Brett, and Susan Leigh Foster, 39–49. Bloomington: Indiana University Press.

———. 2003. *Lying Up a Nation: Race and Black Music*. Chicago: University of Chicago Press.

Raeburn, Bruce Boyd. 1991. "Jazz and the Italian Connection." *Jazz Archivist* 6, no. 1 (May): 1–6.

———. 1992. "Dancing Hot and Sweet: New Orleans Jazz in the 1920s." *Jazz Archivist* 7, nos. 1–2 (December): 10–13.

———. 1997a. "Jewish Jazzmen in New Orleans, 1890–1940: An Overview." *Jazz Archivist* 12, no. 1 (May): 1–12.

———. 1997b. "Sidney Bechet." *Gambit* 8: 15–17.

———. 2000a. "King Oliver, Jelly Roll Morton, and Sidney Bechet: Ménage à Trois, New Orleans Style." In *The Oxford Companion to Jazz*, ed. B. Kirchner, 88–101. New York: Oxford University Press.

———. 2000b. "A Century in Retrospect: The First Fifty Years of New Orleans Jazz." *Jazz Educators Journal* 31, no. 4 (January): C2–C10.

———. 2001. "Louis and Women." Paper read at the "Louis Armstrong and the Jazz Age" symposium, University of North Carolina at Chapel Hill, March 2.

———. 2002a. "Early New Orleans Jazz in Theaters." *Louisiana History* 43, no. 1 (Winter): 41–52.

———. 2002b. "Playing with Words." Paper read at the Natchez Library and Cinema Celebration, March 1, Natchez, Mississippi.

Rampersad, Arnold. 1993. Introduction to *The Souls of Black Folks*, by W. E. B. Du Bois. Gütersloh: Knopf.

Ramsey Jr., Frederic. 1939. "King Oliver and His Creole Jazz Band." In *Jazzmen*, ed. F. Ramsey and C. Smith, 59–91. New York: Harcourt.

———. 1940. Interview with George Baquet. *Down Beat* (15 December): 10 and 26.

———. 1941. "Baquet and his Mob 'Carved' King Bolden!" *Down Beat* (1 January) 6.

Ramsey Jr., Frederic, and Charles Edward Smith, eds. 1939. *Jazzmen*. New York: Harcourt.

Rankin, David. 1976. "The Forgotten People: Free People of Color in New Orleans, 1850–1870." Ph.D. diss., Johns Hopkins University.

Roach, Joseph. 1996. *Cities of the Dead: Circum-Atlantic Performance*. New York: Columbia University Press.

Rohrer, John, and Munro Edmonson et al. 1960. *The Eighth Generation: Cultures and Personalities of New Orleans Negroes*. New York: Harper.

Romaine, Paul. 1974. "Johnny Dodds Is Dead, but His Soul Goes Swinging On." *Storyville* 54 (August–September): 227–28.

Rose, Al. 1974. *Storyville, New Orleans: Being an Authentic, Illustrated Account of the Notorious Red-Light District.* University, Ala.: University of Alabama Press.

Rose, Al, and Edmond Souchon. 1967. *New Orleans Jazz: A Family Album.* Baton Rouge: Louisiana State University Press.

Russell, William. 1939. "Louis Armstrong." In *Jazzmen,* ed. F. Ramsey and C. Smith, 119–42. New York: Harcourt.

———. 1971. *New Orleans: Til the Butcher Cut Him Down.* Videocassette. Written and directed by William Russell, produced by Phillip Spaulding. New York: Rhapsody Films.

———. 1994. *New Orleans Style.* Comp. and ed. Barry Martyn and Mike Hazeldine. New Orleans: Jazzology Press.

———. 1999. *"Oh Mister Jelly": A Jelly Roll Morton Scrapbook.* Singapore: JazzMedia Aps.

Russell, William, and Stephen W. Smith. 1939. "New Orleans Music." In *Jazzmen,* ed. F. Ramsey and C. Smith, 7–38. New York: Harcourt.

St. Cyr, Johnny. 1966. "Jazz as I Remember It." *Jazz Journal* (September): 6–9.

Sanders, Cheryl. 1996. *Saints in Exile: The Holiness-Pentecostal Experience in African American Religion and Culture.* New York : Oxford University Press.

Schact, Beulah. 1946. "Story of Fate Marable." *Jazz Record* (March): 5–6, 14.

Schafer, William. 1974. "Thoughts on Jazz Historiography: 'Buddy Bolden's Blues' vs. 'Buddy Bottley's Balloon.'" *Journal of Jazz Studies* 2, no. 1: 3–14.

———. With assistance from Richard B. Allen. 1977. *Brass Bands and New Orleans Jazz.* Baton Rouge: Louisiana State University Press.

Schwerin, Jules. 1992. *Got to Tell It: Mahalia Jackson, Queen of Gospel.* New York: Oxford University Press.

Scott, James C. 1990. *Domination and the Arts of Resistance.* New Haven: Yale University Press.

Shapiro, Nat, and Nat Hentoff, eds. 1955. *Hear Me Talkin' to Ya: The Story of Jazz as Told by the Men Who Made It.* New York: Dover.

Simpson, Erik. 2002. "Playing Lead: Bandleadership in New Orleans, 1900–1925." Unpublished seminar paper, Duke University.

Small, Christopher. 1998. *Musicking: The Meanings of Performing and Listening.* Hanover, N.H.: University Press of New England.

Somers, Dale A. 2000. "Black and White in New Orleans: A Study in Urban Race Relations, 1865–1900." In *The African American Experience in Louisiana, Part B: From the Civil War to Jim Crow,* ed. Charles Vincent, 518–36. Lafayette: Center for Louisiana Studies. First published in *Journal of Southern History* 40 (February 1974): 42.

Souchon, Edmond. 1964. "King Oliver: A Very Personal Memoir." Repr. in Martin Williams, ed., *Jazz Panorama: From the Pages of the Jazz Review,* 13–20. New York: Da Capo, 1979.

Stearns, Marshall. 1956. *The Story of Jazz.* London: Oxford University Press.

Stearns, Marshall, and Jean Stearns. 1994. *Jazz Dance: The Story of American Vernacular Dance.* New York: Da Capo. (Orig. publ. 1968.)

Stewart, Jack. 2001. "The Strangest Bedfellows: Nick LaRocca and Jelly Roll Morton," *Jazz Archivist* 15: 23–31.

———. 2004. *Funerals with Music in New Orleans.* New Orleans: Save Our Cemeteries, Inc., and Jack Stewart.

Stewart, Rex. 1972. *Jazz Masters of the Thirties*. New York: Macmillan.

———. 1991. *Boy Meets Horn*. Ed. Claire P. Gordon. Ann Arbor: University of Michigan Press.

Stuckey, Sterling. 1987. *Slave Culture: Nationalist Theory and the Foundations of Black America*. New York: Oxford University Press.

Sullivan, Lester. 1988. "Composers of Color of Nineteenth-Century New Orleans: The History behind the Music." *Black Music Research Journal* 8: 51–82.

Thompson, Robert Farris. 1966. "An Aesthetic of the Cool: West African Dance." *African Forum* 2: 85–102.

———. 1983. *Flash of the Spirit: African and Afro-American Art and Philosophy*. New York: Random House.

———. 1990. "Kongo Influences on African-American Artistic Culture." In *Africanisms in American Culture*, ed. Joseph E. Holloway, 148–84. Bloomington: Indiana University Press.

Tregle Jr., Joseph G. 1992. "Creoles and Americans." In *Creole New Orleans: Race and Americanization*, ed. Arnold Hirsch and Joseph Logsdon, 131–88. Baton Rouge: Louisiana State University Press.

Tucker, Mark. 1991. *Ellington: The Early Years*. Urbana: University of Illinois Press.

Turner, Frederick. 1982. *Remembering Song: Encounters with the New Orleans Jazz Tradition*. New York: Viking.

Wallace, Maurice. 2002. *Constructing the Black Masculine: Identity and Ideality in African American Men's Literature and Culture, 1775–1995*. Durham: Duke University Press.

Walser, Robert, ed. 1999. *Keeping Time: Readings in Jazz History*. New York: Oxford University Press.

Ward, Geoffrey C. 2000. *Jazz: A History of America's Music*. New York: Knopf.

Wells, Dickey. 1991. *The Night People: The Jazz Life of Dicky Wells*. As told to Stanley Dance. Washington: Smithsonian Institution Press.

Williams, Raymond. 1973. *The Country and the City*. New York: Oxford University Press.

Wilson, Olly. 1978. "The Significance of the Relationship between Afro-American Music and West African Music." *Black Perspective in Music* 1: 1–21.

Wiltz, Christine. 2000. *The Last Madam: A Life in the New Orleans Underworld*. New York: Faber and Faber.

Work, John Wesley. 1998. *American Negro Songs: 230 Folk Songs and Spirituals, Religious and Secular*. Mineola, N.Y.: Dover. (Orig. publ. 1940.)

Zander, Marjorie Thomas. 1962. "The Brass-Band Funeral and Related Negro Burial Customs." M.A. thesis, University of North Carolina at Chapel Hill.

Archival Sources

References are to interviews unless otherwise noted. For explanation of the abbreviations used in this section, see page 321.

Albert, Don. HJA 1961, May 11.

———. HJA 1967, December 30.

———. HJA 1972a, May 27.

———. HJA 1972b, September 18.

————. HJA 1973, August 6.

————. HJA 1974, June 2.

Allen, Ed. HJA 1961, January 14.

Anderson, Andy. HJA 1960, April 30.

Armstrong, Louis. WRC 1939, January 18 (interview for *Jazzmen*).

————. LAHA 1949? Tape 495.

————. LAHA 1951a. Tape 202 (interview in Honolulu).

————. LAHA 1951b. Tape 238.

————. LAHA 1953. Tape 96 (dubbing of radio interview).

————. IJS 1954 (Armstrong's typescript that was used to make *Satchmo: My Life in New Orleans*).

————. LAHA 1954. Tape 528 (dubbing of radio interview).

————. LAHA 1957. Tape 295.

————. LAHA 1960. Tape 564 (dubbing of interview from July 2, 1960).

————. HJA 1960a, August 2 (interview for WQED *Our Heritage*).

————. HJA 1960b, August 9 (interview for WQED *Our Heritage*).

————. HJA 1960c, August 16 (interview for WQED *Our Heritage*).

————. LAHA 1965, February 20. Tapes 3-8 and 3-9.

————. LAHA 1968, May 6 (letter from Larry Amadee). This fascinating letter has been published by Giddins (1988, 212–23), who discusses the issue of authority. Armstrong has recopied a letter from Amadee and glossed it without indicating the two different voices. I have examined the letter but cannot offer any improvement on Giddins's good (though speculative) attempt to distinguish Armstrong from Amadee.

————. LAHA 1970a, May 25. Tape 487 (*Mike Douglas Show*).

————. LAHA 1970b. Tape 426 (letter to Max Jones).

————. WRC 1970 (interview transcribed in mss 506, folder 14).

————. LAHA n.d. Tape 124.

————. LAHA n.d. Tape 336 (interview for *This Is NY* radio program).

Barbarin, Isidore. HJA 1959, January 7.

Barbarin, Paul. HJA 1957, March 27.

————. HJA 1959, January 7.

Barnes, Emile. HJA 1960a, July 29.

————. HJA 1960b, August 22.

————. HJA 1962, January 3.

Barnes, Emile, with Paul Barnes. HJA 1959, October 1.

Barnes, Harrison. HJA 1959, January 29.

Bechet, Leonard. ALA ca. 1948 (interview with Alan Lomax).

Bechet, Sidney. HJA 1945, November 19 (conversation with John Reid).

————. WRC n.d. (interview for *Jazzmen*).

Bechet, Sidney, et al. HJA 1944, June (joint interview, Louis Nelson, Manuel Perez, Alphonse Picou, Willie Santiago).

Bertrand, Jimmy. HJA 1959, September 9.

Bigard, Alex. HJA 1961, February 7.

Brunious, John. HJA 1959, May 26.

Cagnolatti, Ernie. HJA 1961, April 5.

Casimer, John. HJA 1959, January 17.

Charles, Hypolite. HJA 1963, April 13.

Charles, Jessie. HJA 1967, December 15.

Christian, Narcisse J. "Buddy." WRC 1938, mss 519, folder 21 (interview for *Jazzmen*).
Clayton, Jimmy. HJA 1961, June 23.
Clementin, Ferrand. HJA 1973, August 2.
Cornish, Bella. HJA 1959, January 13.
Dawson, Eddie. HJA 1959, August 11.
————. HJA 1961, June 28.
————. HJA 1962, January 31.
————. HJA 1972, April 5.
Desvigne, Sidney. HJA 1958, August 18.
DeVore, Charlie. HJA 1962, July 4.
Dodds, Johnny. WRC n.d. (interview for *Jazzmen*, ca. 1938(?); mss 515, folder 15).
Dodds, Warren "Baby." WRC n.d. Untitled memoir, Manuel Manetta papers mss 516, folder 744.
————. HJA 1958, May 31.
Dominique, Anatie "Natty." HJA 1958, May 31.
Duhé, Lawrence. HJA 1957, June 9 (with Wellman Braud).
————. HJA 1960 (only date given).
Foster, Abbey "Chinee." HJA 1960, June 29.
Foster, George "Pops." WRC 1938, mss 519, folder 13 (interview for *Jazzmen*).
————. HJA 1961, April 27.
Garland, Ed. WRC 1958, August 16.
Glass, Henry "Booker T." HJA 1962, March 22.
Glenny, Albert. ALA ca. 1948 (interview with Alan Lomax, Leonard Bechet joining).
Hamilton, Charlie. HJA 1965, March 21.
Hardin, Lillian. WRC 1938 (interview for *Jazzmen*).
————. HJA 1959.
————. LAHA 1971? Tape 3-1 (dubbing from older audio clips, including an interview with Lil Hardin).
Henry, Charles "Sunny." HJA 1959, January 8.
————. HJA 1959, October 21.
Henry, Oscar "Chicken." HJA 1959, July 11.
Hightower, Willie. HJA 1958, June 3.
Humphrey, Earl. HJA 1963, March 28.
Jackson, Preston. WRC 1938 (interview for *Jazzmen*).
————. HJA 1958, June 2.
James, Louis. HJA 1959, May 25.
Johnson, Victoria Davis. WRC 1938, mss 519, folder 20 (interview for *Jazzmen*).
Johnson, William Manuel "Bill." WRC 1938, mss 519, folder 28 (interview for *Jazzmen*).
Jones, Louis. HJA 1959, January 19.
Jones, Richard M. WRC 1938, mss 519, folder 29 (interview for *Jazzmen*).
Joseph, John "Papa John." HJA 1958, November 26.
Keppard, Louis. HJA 1957, August 4.
————. HJA 1961, January 19.
Lala, Johnny. HJA 1958, September 24.
Laurent, August. HJA 1960, March 21.
Lawrence, Marshall. HJA 1960, June 28.
Lindsay, Joe. WRC n.d. (interview for *Jazzmen*).

Loyacano, Arnold. HJA 1956, September 29.

Manetta, Manuel. WRC 1957–1970, mss 516, folders 648–738.

Mares, Paul, WRC n.d. (notes taken from *Jazzmen*, folder 31).

Marrero, Lawrence. HJA 1959, January 2.

Matthews, Bill. HJA 1959, March 10.

Miller, Ernest "Punch." HJA 1959a, August 20.

———. HJA 1959b, September 25.

———. HJA 1960a, April 4.

———. HJA 1960b, August 23.

Miller, Sing. HJA 1964, December 11.

Mitchell, George. HJA 1959, July 1.

Morand, Herb. HJA 1950, March 12.

Morton, Ferdinand "Jelly Roll." LC ca. 1938 (transcription of interviews conducted at the Library of Congress; circulating photocopy with no transcriber named).

Nelson, Louis. HJA 1960, April 18.

Nicholas, Albert. HJA 1972, June 26.

Noone, Jimmie. WRC 1938 (interview for *Jazzmen*).

Oliver, Stella. HJA 1959, April 22.

Ory, Edward "Kid." HJA 1957, April 20.

Palmer, Roy. HJA 1955, September 22.

Parker, Willie. HJA 1960, March 29.

Penn, Sammy. HJA 1960, April 21.

Perez, Manuel. WRC 1938, mss 519, folder 34 (interview for *Jazzmen*).

Picou, Alphonse. HJA 1958, April 4.

Piron, Armond J. WRC 1938, mss 519, folder 35 (interview for *Jazzmen*).

Rena, Henry "Kid." WRC 1938, mss 519, folder 36 (interview for *Jazzmen*).

René, Joseph. HJA 1960, April 7.

Ridgley, William "Bebé." HJA 1959, June 2.

———. HJA 1961, April 11.

Robichaux, Joe. HJA 1959, March 19.

St. Cyr, Johnny. ALA ca. 1948 (interview with Alan Lomax).

———. HJA 1958, August 27.

Shoffner, Bob. HJA 1959, September 8.

Singleton, Arthur "Zutty." WRC 1938, mss 519, folder 37 (interview for *Jazzmen*).

Souchon, Edmond. HJA 1958, May 7.

———. LSM n.d. Typed memoir, Louisiana State Museum. Partly published as Souchon 1964.

Stevenson, Burke. HJA 1959, June 12.

Summers, Eddie. HJA 1960, September 16.

Valentine, Thomas "Kid Thomas." HJA 1957, March 22.

———. HJA 1959, November 8.

Vigne, Arthur. HJA 1961, November 29.

Walters, Albert. HJA 1959, January 5.

Wiggs, Johnny. HJA 1962, August 26.

Williams, Clarence. WRC 1939, mss 519, folder 17 (interview for *Jazzmen*).

Williams, George. HJA 1959, March 17.

Wilson, Cassius. HJA 1962, April 5.

Zeno, Alice. HJA 1958, November 14.

NOTES

ALA: Alan Lomax Archive, Hunter College
HJA: William Ransom Hogan Jazz Archive, Tulane University
IJS: Institute of Jazz Studies, Newark, N.J.
LAHA: Louis Armstrong House and Archives, Queens College
LC: Library of Congress
LSM: Louisiana State Museum, New Orleans
WRC: Williams Research Center, Historic New Orleans
    Collection, New Orleans

Introduction
4 Something similar had happened: Johnson 1995, 39.
4 By the 1840s: Johnson 1995, 42.
4 On slave plantations: Stuckey 1987, 3–97; see also Floyd 1995, 6.
8 *Times-Picayune* of New Orleans: Reprinted in Walser 1999, 8.

Chapter 1: Tuxedo Brass Band, 1921
9 Isidore Barbarin: Knowles 1996, 46–47. According to his grandson, Danny
    Barker, Barbarin also worked for a "burial establishment"; Barker quoted in
    Shapiro and Hentoff 1955, 14.
9 "toward the end of 1921": Armstrong 1954, 218.
9 city's dirt streets: Armstrong IJS 1954, 58, 74.
9 Emile Barnes refused: Barnes, Emile HJA 1960a.
9 Hypolite Charles thought: Charles, Hypolite HJA 1963.
9 Aaron Clark was convinced: Knowles 1996, 45.
9 Walter Blue Robertson actually did die: Barbarin, Paul HJA 1959.
12 He learned his instrument: Knowles 1996, 44.
13 "I really felt": Armstrong 1954, 219.
13 "When I played with the Tuxedo Brass Band": Armstrong 1954, 219.
14 "I hope the day": Blassingame 1973, 174.
14 the most notorious incident: Higginbotham 1993, 48.
14 "in order to get along": Morton in Lomax 1993, 70.
14 citywide rioting: In his study of the Robert Charles massacre, William Ivy Hair
    (1976, xiv) concluded that "white reaction to Charles vividly illustrated the hard-
    ening of racial attitudes which occurred around that time."
14 Armstrong remembered: Armstrong IJS 1954, 14. On a similar incident from the
    1930s in New Orleans, see Davis and Dollard 1940, 122.

15 "could pass around the streets": Keppard HJA 1957. Jelly Roll Morton (LC ca. 1938), another Creole of color, also remembered New Orleans as an easy place to get around.

15 "I didn't know": Barbarin, Isidore HJA 1959.

16 "turned colors": Armstrong IJS 1954, 4–5; emphasis in original. The central source for information about Armstrong's early life in New Orleans is the typescript he wrote for the production of his published autobiography *Satchmo: My Life in New Orleans* (Prentice Hall, 1954). This typescript is titled "Life Story of Louis Armstrong (autobiography)," and it is held by the Institute of Jazz Studies at Rutgers University. This study relies on the typescript rather than the published book, except in cases where the surviving copy is incomplete.

16 At age seventeen: Armstrong IJS 1954, 64.

16 "Just a few drunks": Armstrong IJS 1954, 64.

16 Two years later: Armstrong 1954, 221–22. For a similar story about movement and danger, see Miller, Ernest "Punch" HJA 1959a.

16 "At *ten* years old": Armstrong 1999, 17; emphasis in original.

17 "drum sticks, baseball bats": Morton LC ca. 1938 (quotation); Armstrong 1999, 27. For more references, see Mitchell 1995, 154.

17 "if you followed a parade": Armstrong 1954, 225 (quotation); see also Rankin 1976, 76.

17 Creole neighborhoods: Armstrong 1999, 200. See also Collins 1974, 11.

17 Many Creoles: Bigard 1986, 7; Singleton WRC 1938; Zeno HJA 1958.

17 Benny Williams: Barker 1986, 62–63.

17 "Nobody would do us nothing": Garland WRC 1958.

17 By performing this little service: Jones, Will 1949, 16.

17 he was known to break away: Ridgley HJA 1961, 17.

17 Freedom of movement: Cimbala 1979, 292.

18 "the only man, musician or not": Armstrong 1954, 226.

18 "six foot six inches": Barker 1986, 63.

18 "Blondie": Nicholas HJA 1972.

18 "I too could go": Armstrong 1954, 226.

18 more than a few musicians: Barker 1998, vii.

18 On one level: Jameson 1981, 78–80.

19 "I walked on stage": Armstrong 1961b, 84–86.

19 "Every Negro in the South": Dollard 1957, 359.

19 After he moved: Kenney 1993, 114.

20 "All the chicks": Armstrong IJS 1954, 11.

21 "Second line": Charles, Jessie HJA 1967.

21 The ring shout: Stuckey 1987, 3–97. Floyd 1995, passim, and esp. 19–45.

21 "you gonna have": Quoted in Lomax 1993, xiv.

21 subversive rudeness: Dailey 2000, esp. Chapter 4.

22 shoulder bumping: Dailey 2000, 129–30.

22 "Good darkies ": Dailey 2000, 131.

22 city of Place Congo: Souchon LSM n.d.

23 "Lots of people dancing": Charles, Hypolite HJA 1963.

23 "played for those blues": Barker in Shapiro and Hentoff 1955, 51–52.

23 led by John Robichaux: Robichaux himself was not a downtown Creole, but, as Big Eye Louis Nelson said, "He use mostly downtown men." Nelson in Lomax 1993, 109.
23 "You dig what I'm digging?": Armstrong IJS 1954, 62–63.
23 "We proved to them": Armstrong IJS 1954, 62–63.
24 "Mr. Barbarin, Dear Friend": Armstrong 1999, 43.
24 different sections of New Orleans: It has often been pointed out that by 1900 both downtown and uptown were diverse places. Yet, musicians on each side of Canal Street seem to have thought otherwise. This is not surprising, since within their professional networks, downtown and uptown were vivid markers. Danny Barker (quoted in Shapiro and Hentoff 1955, 4), for example, explained simply, "The city was split by Canal Street, with one part of the people uptown and the Creoles downtown."
26 Black Benny Williams: Armstrong IJS 1954, 30.
26 Joe Oliver: quoted in Bernhardt 1986, 91.
26 Captain "Sore" Dick: Armstrong IJS 1954, 55
26 Isaiah Hubbard: Armstrong IJS 1954, 57
26 Henry Zeno: Armstrong, quoted in Shapiro and Hentoff 1955, 44.
26 "Snow": Armstrong IJS 1954, 26
26 Nicodeemus: Armstrong IJS 1954, 29
26 Tony Jackson: Morton quoted in Lomax 1993
26 Clerk Wade: Armstrong IJS 1954, 41; also Armstrong 1999, 121
26 Leontine Richardson: Armstrong IJS 1954, 60
26 Buddy Bolden: Ory HJA 1957
26 Arthur Brown: Armstrong IJS 1954, 37
26 Nelly Williams: Armstrong IJS 1954, 31
26 Lorenzo Tio: Bigard 1986, 16.
27 Morris Moore: Armstrong IJS 1954, 41
27 Isaac Smooth: Armstrong IJS 1954, 54
27 Mrs. Martin: Armstrong IJS 1954, 12
27 John Cootay: Armstrong 1999, 233
27 Dave Perkins: Dodds 1992, 7
27 John Robichaux: Souchon HJA 1958, May 7.
27 "When I first saw her": Armstrong 1999, 139.
27 "Isidore referred": Barker 1986, 27.
28 established figures in the downtown tradition: Knowles 1996, 8.
28 "We were both": Ridgley HJA 1959.
28 "white gentleman": Ridgley HJA 1959 and 1961.
29 "That was a good deal": Armstrong 1954, 219.
29 "the [uptown and downtown] musicians": Dodds 1992, 13.
29 intimidated by the idea: Knowles 1996, 39.

Chapter 2: The Saints

31 "It all came from": Armstrong 1999, 170
31 "Everybody in there sang": Jackson, Mahalia 1967, 33
31 "I'm a Baptist": Armstrong 1955, 59.
31 Louis was baptized: Jones, Tad 2000, 1. Tad Jones's research has been presented in

the *New York Times*, August 15, 2000 (Section E, p. 1, c. 4) and in a lecture given for the Louis Armstrong Centennial Conference, New Orleans, August 4, 2001.

31 the first five years: Armstrong IJS 1954, 3. Armstrong wrote that he did not see his mother May Ann (her given name was Mary Ann Albert) "for a long time" after she left him with his grandmother, that his grandmother sent him to school, which implies a stay at least until age five, and that he did not see his sister until he was five years old.

32 "That's where I acquired": Armstrong IJS 1954, 3.

32 Jewish singing: Armstrong 1999, 3–36.

32 A family named Karnofsky: At the end of his life he misremembered Irving Berlin's 1927 *Russian Lullaby* as a folk song that the Karnofsky family had taught him when he was seven years old, and he made other claims about the importance of this family that were clearly caused by failing memory; see Brothers 1999, 191–93. Hence, I seriously doubt his claims (Armstrong 1999) that he worked for this family as early as 1907. More likely, this experience dated to ca. 1915.

32 Sanctified: I am using the term "Sanctified" as synonymous with "Pentecostal" and "Holiness," which seems to be how the musicians use them. Further on these terms, see Lovett 1978, 4.

32 The arrangement is practical: Connerton 1989, 39.

33 Life was an adventure: Armstrong IJS 1954, 7.

34 "If my mother was Hustling": Armstrong IJS 1954, 1. In the passage, "selling fish" is crossed out and replaced with "hustling."

34 "try to keep her out": Jackson, Mahalia 1973.

35 Elder Cozy: Lynn Abbott (1992, 324, n. 153) identifies Elder Cozy as Rev. William M. Cosey, pastor at Mt. Zion Baptist Church, 512 Howard Street (now LaSalle Street).

35 "had the whole church": Armstrong IJS 1954, 12.

35 "the preachers had to duck": Armstrong IJS 1954, 12. On water baptism, see Sanders 1996, 59.

35 domestic work: Armstrong IJS 1954, 1; Sanders 1996, 33. Giddins (1988, 48) reports that May Ann is listed as a laundress in the 1910 census.

35 "All of you wash-ladies": Oliver 1984, 169.

35 "all but slaves": Armstrong IJS 1954, 89.

35 After emancipation: Jackson, Mahalia 1967, 14–16.

36 "cold and proper": Simon Brown in Stuckey 1987, 33.

36 62 percent of all African-American churchgoers: Montgomery 1993, 105.

36 "jubilee time": Henry, Charles "Sunny" HJA 1959, January 8; Charles, Hypolite HJA 1963; Parker HJA 1960.

36 "They'd word it out": Barnes, Harrison HJA 1959.

36 two main religious-musical practices: In reference to her visit to New Orleans in the 1850s, Fredrika Bremer wrote about the "tornado" of "shrieking and leaping, admonishing and preaching," elements, in her opinion, of "true African worship." Blassingame 1973, 6–7, 149, and 151; Stuckey 1987, 53–64.

37 city directory: Marquis 1978, 31.

37 Baptist houses of worship: Higginbotham 1993, 14.

37 missionaries targeted the morals and habits: Higginbotham, 1993, 96 and 194.

37 Shiloh Baptist Church: Higginbotham 1993, 201.

37 At the First Baptist Church: Higginbotham 1993, 201.

37 "sweet": Jackson, Mahalia 1967, 32–33.
37 "Before you realized": Armstrong 1999, 170; emphasis in original.
38 what many lower-class Negroes indeed did: Sanders 1996, 14–15.
38 "crude and undeveloped": Higginbotham 1993, 43.
38 Lay preachers: Higginbotham 1993, 25.
38 ranked the churches: Gillespie 1979, 30–31.
39 "I first learned the meaning": Gillespie 1979, 31.
39 "Those people had no choir": Jackson, Mahalia 1967.
39 "They used the drum": George "Pops" Foster (1971, 20–21) described how, at
     another Sanctified church in New Orleans, "they'd clap their hands and bang a
     tambourine and sing."
39 Saints used their bodies: Higginbotham 1993, 44.
39 "Everybody in there sang": Jackson, Mahalia 1967, 33.
40 "Louis was very strong": Muranyi in Giddins 2000.
40 he learned to sing: Armstrong HJA 1960a; Armstrong LAHA 1970a.
40 tied to bodily motion: "African traditional cults are *danced faiths*," writes Robert
     Farris Thompson (1966, 85). "Music without motion is unnatural among
     Negroes," Zora Neale Hurston (1983, 104) insisted.
40 several purposes: Sanders 1996, 8, citing James Murphy.
40 Kid Ory told a story: Cited in Russell 1971.
41 "the slaves were not converting": Dixon 1985, 302; emphasis in original.
41 For the Ewe people of West Africa: Chernoff 1979.
41 "I always did love": Jackson, Mahalia 1973.
41 "The jagged harmony": Hurston 1983, 80; italics in original.
41 "When I sang in church": Armstrong IJS 1954, 3.
41 heterophony: See, for example, recordings of Rev. R. C. Crenshaw and his con-
     gregation made by Alan Lomax in the early 1950s and distributed as the CDs
     Roots of the Blues (New World Records) and *Sounds of the South* (Atlantic
     Records).
42 "The congregation joined in": Epstein 1977, 302.
42 "It all came from": Armstrong 1999, 170; Armstrong LAHA 1965.
42 Brock Mumford: Manetta WRC mss 516, folder 701.
42 Buddy Bolden: Ory HJA 1957.
43 "a moan in his cornet": Matthews HJA 1959.
43 "The preacher would have": Jackson, Mahalia 1973.
43 "perfect rhythm": Shapiro and Hentoff 1955, 37.
43 Buddy Bolden: Manetta WRC mss 516, folder 729.
43 Joe Oliver: Russell 1994, 58; Barbarin, Paul HJA 1957.
44 "That's all he'd do": Charles, Hypolite HJA 1963.
44 Amateur brass bands uptown: Schafer 1977, esp. p. 46; a contrary position is
     taken by Bethell 1977, 37.
44 "get more out of a piece": James HJA 1959.
44 playing hymns heterophonically: Recordings from the 1950s of uptown street
     bands show various degrees of heterophony, as do re-creations by Louis
     Armstrong and his All Stars of funerals that Armstrong heard in his youth. *The
     Birth of Jazz*, vol. 4 of *The Music of New Orleans*, rec. by Samuel Charters (New
     York: Folkways Records); "New Orleans Function," Armstrong 1950.
45 By the time Armstrong's mother: Armstrong IJS 1954, 9.

45 "The secret of good jazz music": Dodds, Warren "Baby" WRC n.d., 30; see also Johnny St. Cyr in Russell 1994, 72.

45 The conception: Small 1998.

45 "set": Hurston 1983, 104.

46 "The more enthusiastic his audience is": St. Cyr in Russell 1994, 90; see also Russell 1994, 72.

46 "natural feelings": Hurston 1983, 80.

46 "To maintain their poise": Chernoff 1979, 158.

46 "Yea—I am just like the *Sister*": Armstrong 1999, 175; emphasis in original. For another version of this story, see Armstrong 1999, 120.

48 "I always stuck": Morand HJA 1950.

48 "They're not different": Armstrong HJA 1960b.

48 "Louis, you've been described": Armstrong HJA 1960c.

49 Du Bois understood: Cited and discussed in Kelley 1993, 88–89.

50 "a certain Spoon for this": Armstrong 1999, 97.

50 "she [Lucille] still has a sense": Armstrong 1999, 160.

50 "protest against the high-brow tendency": Hurston 1983, 103.

50 "resistance to the closures": Thompson 1983, 222.

51 "It was something I noticed": Wilber in Chilton, John 1987, 186.

51 capitalism causes: Jameson 1981, 62.

52 predominantly female: Higginbotham 1993, 7. It has been estimated that the membership in African-American Baptist and Sanctified churches was at least two-thirds female; see Higginbotham 1993, 7. In analyzing the gender-related attitudes and experiences of Armstrong's youth, I have benefited from the work of Bruce Boyd Raeburn, who moves in parallel through some of the issues developed in the present study in "Louis and Women," a paper read at the symposium "Louis Armstrong and the Jazz Age," University of North Carolina at Chapel Hill, March 2, 2001.

52 "Old Lady" Magg, Mrs. Laura, and Mrs. Martin: Armstrong IJS 1954, 44.

52 These "old sisters": Armstrong 1954, 228.

52 both dance hall and church: Marquis 1978, 79; Ory HJA 1957.

52 only twenty minutes between: Garland WRC 1958. Funky Butt Hall was also a place where "hustlers, gangsters and hard working musicians" could be laid out for wakes, remembered Preston Jackson (Jackson WRC 1938).

53 Easter represented: Foster, George "Pops" HJA 1961; Foster 1971, 36, 57.

Chapter 3: Larenzo's Soul

55 "Blues is what cause": Quoted in Lomax 1993, 109.

55 three different street musicians: Armstrong IJS 1954, 46. The passage comes in the section dealing with the years 1916–1917, but the reference to before the "orphanage" makes clear that this is a chronological digression. See also Armstrong 1966, 11. The "Waffle Man" may have been "Buglin' Sam" Dekemel, also known as "Buglin' Sam, the Waffle Man," who was born ca. 1900; on Dekemel, see Rose and Souchon 1967, 34, picture on p. 318. Manetta (WRC mss 516, folder 720) reports that Dekemel's father had a wagon before him.

55 "an old, tin, long horn": Armstrong IJS 1954, 46.

56 "stole": Ory HJA 1957.

57 "rags-bottles-and-bones men": Morton in Lomax 1993, 77. Armstrong was

familiar with Lomax's book, and the similarity in phrasing between his recollection and Morton's suggests that Morton jogged his memory. Both Ory and Morton described the horns as "Christmas" horns.

57 Morton heard their music: Morton LC ca. 1938. Lawrence Gushee (1985, 391–94), however, has discovered evidence that Morton spent considerable time uptown. He alludes to a potential line of inquiry, similar to that being suggested here, when he says that "young Morton knew several musical worlds, and one can suggest that the great force of his playing results from his early experiences not only with a more refined and European parlor and dance music but also with the hard-driving stomp and blues music he speaks about somewhat disparagingly, but plays with great conviction, in the Library of Congress recordings."

57 Kress horn: A small irony: the Kress family used their tremendous wealth to collect old master paintings, which they eventually donated to a number of American museums; they would not have known about this connection to early jazz. The beautiful Kress building still stands on Canal Street, "awaiting preservation and adaptive use," as a Web site put it.

57 Johnny Wiggs: Wiggs HJA 1962.

57 The long tinhorns: According to Morton, cited in Clark 2001, 29.

57 "untrue" pitches: Ory HJA 1957.

57 "the most gifted people": Wiggs HJA 1962.

58 "isn't anything new": Armstrong 1966, 57.

59 work songs preserved: Borneman 1959, 10.

59 "This may account for": Douglas in Epstein 1977, 162.

59 jail mates in New Orleans singing blues: Foster 1971, 80.

59 "queer minor catch": Leiding 1910, 6.

59 "Blues come out of the fields": References for Hopkins et al. in Barlow 1989, 18 and 27.

59 Henry Sloan: Evans 1987, 139–41.

60 "In these 'hollers'": Work 1998, 35.

60 Mississippi River was a gathering place: Morton LC ca. 1938.

61 a good little blues player: Foster 1971, 51.

61 prostitutes had fun with him: Armstrong 1954, 198; Armstrong 1999, 124; Armstrong 1947, 104; Armstrong IJS 1954, 24.

61 Handy heard a singer-guitarist: Handy 1957, 74.

61 Singer Gertrude "Ma" Rainey: Work 1998, 32.

62 For the tinhorn men, "blues" meant: It seems unlikely that anyone in this musical environment ever conceived or heard of such a thing as a blues *scale*, such as one commonly encounters in modern textbooks. The gestural orientation of the music made it fundamentally different from the kind of music the Creoles were learning, where scales were many and central.

62 history of this idiom: Kubik 1999, 63, working with earlier research of Paul Oliver.

62 swinging triplet feeling: Kubik 1999, 73.

62 "The blue notes": Foster 1971, 73.

62 Muddy Waters: Palmer 1982, 260.

62 "they couldn't catch it": Clementin HJA 1973.

63 incorrect one-dimensionality: Murray 1976.

63 "the women jump out the window": Matthews HJA 1959.

63 "an admiration for the Blues": Armstrong 1999, 124.

64 "He'd go around singing": Collins in Blesh 1946, 157.

64 blur between speech and music: Holloway 1990, 25.

65 "Literacy, which trains one": Palmer 1982, 101–3.

65 Armstrong learned the idiom early on: Armstrong wrote (1999, 122) that most of his schooling took place in the Colored Waif's Home for Boys, which he entered at age eleven.

66 "I used to stay around": Rose 1974, 160; emphasis in original.

66 Various lower-class references: The lower-class identity of blues did not depend solely on association with lower-class patrons; blues was wrapped up in a way of speaking associated with illiteracy and poverty. This analysis is compatible with the idea that speaking styles—especially lower-class speaking styles—tend to stay consistent as an index of social identity.

66 "Blues is what cause": Nelson in Lomax 1993, 109.

67 sing through operas: Handy 1957, 13–14.

67 "many a fine musicianer": Bechet 1960, 91.

68 "there wasn't an eastern performer": Bushell 1988, 19.

68 "The trumpet or clarinet will sometimes delay": Dodds, Warren "Baby" WRC n.d., 31.

68 "Bubber and I sat there": Bushell 1988, 25.

68 "I shall never forget": Ellington 1973, 47.

68 Young (b. 1909) grew up: Büchmann-Møller 1990, 4–6.

69 Young stubbornly: Büchmann-Møller 1990, 19–23; Brothers 1997.

69 "I'm not what you call": Gillespie in DeVeaux 1997, 174.

70 "a way of hesitating": Hardin WRC 1938; Jackson WRC 1938. There is room for suspicion about the consistent claims for an influence of Johnson on Armstrong in these 1938 interviews, which are summarized by Bill Russell on notes preserved at the Williams Research Center. It is likely that Russell, who had already spoken with Johnson, was asking leading questions, as he often does on the taped interviews from the 1950s. On Armstrong's denial of influence from Johnson, see Armstrong 1999, 40–41 and 197–98. On the other hand, Ory also cited this kind of phrasing as Johnson's specialty. Russell 1994, 178.

71 Training that is exclusively oral: For a general discussion of orality along these lines, see Ong 1982, esp. Chapter 3.

71 the conclusion: A good review of this way of thinking is Gioia 1989.

71 "soulful song": Albert HJA 1972a.

72 "Louis will take a popular piece": Wiggs in Russell 1994, 168.

72 Soloists like Hawkins and Gillespie: For a technical discussion of Armstrong's merging of blues sensibility with different kinds of music, including a comparison with Hawkins, see DeVeaux 1997, 78–84.

72 "In the city they didn't do much singing": Miller, Ernest "Punch" HJA 1960b. Hypolite Charles (HJA 1963) confirms this: "We didn't sing the blues, we *played* the blues."

72 Bolden's band: Eddie Dawson (HJA 1959) said that the first band he heard play blues was Bolden's playing at Betsy Cole's lawn party, on Magnolia Street.

73 "realized that I could play." Armstrong 1999, 12.

73 blues played by Larenzo on a long tinhorn: Armstrong mentioned playing one of these tinhorns himself. Armstrong 1999, 16.

Chapter 4: Street Hustler

74 "Lots more music back then": Manetta WRC 1969, folder 695 (June 24).
74 "All day Sunday": Miller, Ernest "Punch" HJA 1960a.
74 "When I was coming up": Armstrong IJS 1954, 11.
74 a funny story: Armstrong 1999, 179.
75 a tradition of herbal medicine: Escott 1979, 108.
75 "grab four bedposts": Armstrong 1966, 52.
75 daily food staples: Armstrong 1999, 22.
76 "Sex time": Armstrong IJS 1954, 11.
76 "never worry about": Armstrong 1999, 186; emphasis in original.
76 "nigger rich": Armstrong 1999, 72, 74–75.
76 "If you're poor": Bigard 1986, 72.
76 "Marandy, you'd better": Armstrong 1999, 7.
77 grand marshal: Bechet 1960, 65–66.
78 "He was a *Freak*": Armstrong 1999, 8; emphasis in original.
78 march the aides to the club: Armstrong 1954, 225.
79 One club has: Armstrong 1954, 225.
79 Joe Oliver, featured cornetist: Armstrong 1999, 38.
79 "You want to *see*": Bechet 1960, 66; emphasis in original.
79 The country boys: Knowles 1996, 78.
79 As many as fifteen bands: Armstrong HJA 1960b.
79 typical band formation: Knowles 1996, 24, citing Sunny Henry and Albert Warner. Also: Miller, Ernest "Punch" HJA 1960a; Barbarin, Paul HJA 1957; Red Allen in Friedlander 1992, 117–19.
79 Sandwiches and whiskey: Armstrong 1954, 225.
79 second line with his buddies: Armstrong LAHA 1968, also in Giddins 1988, 222.
80 several will become well-known toughs: On Black Benny and Nicodeemus, see Bunk Johnson in Ramsey 1939, 120; also Morton LC ca. 1938, 233.
80 Black Benny: Morton LC ca. 1938, 233.
80 The police sometimes disperse: Barker 1986, 34.
80 "That meant lay off": Singleton WRC 1938.
80 "the Broadway of New Orleans negroes": Quoted in Kinser 1990, 143.
80 the only musician who does this: Armstrong LAHA 1960.
80 Onward Brass Band: Armstrong LAHA 1951b.
80 Mardi Gras: "All musicians were employed on Mardi Gras day," remembered Lawrence Duhé (HJA 1960).
80 white bands: Armstrong 1999, 33. Preston Jackson (cited by Peretti 1992, 32) also said that the Mardi Gras parade was the only opportunity he had to hear white bands.
80 Prostitutes: Armstrong LAHA 1970a.
80 "big white monkey suit": Armstrong 1999, 211.
80 "coal cart drivers": Armstrong 1999, 211.
81 first King Zulu: Kinser 1990, 233.
81 "Zulu": Barker 1986.
81 "get off of his big, fine boat": Armstrong 1999, 211.
81 "royal barge": Kinser 1990, 381, n. 47.

81 carnivalesque release of class tensions: "The Negroes preserve in its truest essence the primitive spirit of the Carnival," wrote Henry Rightor (quoted in Kinser 1990, 142) about New Orleans in 1900.

81 "Each member has a burlesque": Armstrong IJS 1954, 56.

81 one of the Zulus parodied: Armstrong 1999, 211; Armstrong IJS 1954, 56. For other examples of this kind of African parody through dance, see Thompson 1966, 96.

82 "This one's for you, Rex!": Armstrong 1999, 213.

82 Memphis: Raeburn 2002b is the source of this information on Memphis; I thank Dr. Raeburn for providing me with a copy of his paper.

82 "You know, Mr. Armstrong": Jackson in Raeburn 2002b.

83 crown of King Zulu: Armstrong 1999, 212.

83 two-sided signifying: Samuel Floyd Jr. (1995) offers an extended analysis of different types of African-American music in terms of signifying.

84 "funeral with music": Friedlander 1992, 118. Funeral descriptions: Barbarin, Paul HJA 1957; Henry, Charles "Sunny" HJA 1959, October 21; Knowles 1996, 12 and passim; Miller, Ernest "Punch" HJA 1960b; Keppard HJA 1961; Russell 1939, 123, on Armstrong and Johnson and dirges. Red Allen in Friedlander 1992, 115–19.

84 "perfect death": Morton LC ca. 1938, 184.

84 "a very slow 4/4 tempo": Foster in Russell 1994, 100.

84 "While we were sitting": Armstrong 1961a, 13.

84 band plays the hymn: Armstrong HJA 1960c.

84 "Bass drum": Armstrong 1961a, 13.

84 the hymn of choice: Armstrong 1966, 9–10.

84 The procession: Dodds WRC n.d., 11.

85 George Baquet: Bigard 1986, 17.

85 "It would go so sweet and high": Singleton WRC 1938.

85 this band as his favorite: Armstrong 1936, 15.

86 recording from the 1950s: *Satchmo: A Musical Autobiography*, vol. 1, Jazz Unlimited (JUCD 2005), recorded April 26, 1950. On the accuracy, see Bigard 1986, 120.

86 "Yeah, Pops": Armstrong 1961a, 13.

86 "ragtime will always be popular": Jasen and Jones 2000, xxi.

86 "The dancers moved": Wingfield in Stearns and Stearns 1994, 18.

86 Armstrong and his friends: Zutty Singleton in Ramsey and Smith 1939, 27.

87 second line: Armstrong HJA 1960c.

87 "Forty instruments all bucking": Bechet 1960, 67.

87 The entire event: Charles, Hypolite HJA 1963.

88 bands could be heard: Barbarin, Paul HJA 1957; see also Shapiro and Hentoff 1955, 38.

88 "beat the bell": Loyacano HJA 1956.

88 "Mama didn't": Armstrong LAHA 1960.

88 Bunk Johnson remembered: Ramsey 1939, 120.

89 "To a tune like": Armstrong 1966, 8.

89 descriptions of slave dancing: Epstein 1997, 40.

89 "Everything is acted out": Hurston 1983, 49–50.

90 This gave children: Armstrong IJS 1954, 8; Armstrong 1966, 8.

90 hearing Buddy Bolden in this way: Armstrong IJS 1954, 8.
90 Armstrong took the dance steps: Robert Goffin (1977, 44) describes Armstrong's dance routine in detail. But the problem here is the usual one with Goffin: it is impossible to know when he is reporting accurately, with information directly from Armstrong himself, and when he is making things up.
90 selling newspapers: Armstrong 1999, 151.
90 how to multiply his earnings: Armstrong IJS 1954, 9.
90 cleaned graves: Armstrong 1999, 18.
90 scraped brick dust: Armstrong 1966, 13.
90 "The Eagle Boys fly high": Ramsey 1939, 25.
91 "People ran out of their houses": Manetta WRC mss 516, folder 671; see also Bigard 1986, 8.
91 Paul Barbarin had one: Barbarin, Paul HJA 1957.
91 "humming band": Ory HJA 1957.
91 Armstrong and his friends: Armstrong IJS 1954, 14.
91 quartet sang for tips: Chilton, John 1987, 208; Foster 1971, 92.
91 Their favorite song: Armstrong 1966, 14.
91 They had a walking order: Armstrong IJS 1954, 13.
91 "Policemen catch you": Garland in Peretti 1992, 26. Armstrong 1966, 13.
92 disguise themselves with long pants: Armstrong 1966, 14.
92 Armstrong's performance pose: Armstrong IJS 1954, 14; see also Armstrong 1966, 14.
92 ear cupping: For discussion, with references and a photo, see Kubik 1999, 89.
92 "some of the finest singing": Armstrong IJS 1954, 47.
92 barbershop quartet singing: Abbott 1992.
92 "It was typical": Melton in Abbott 1992, 290.
92 "about every four dark faces": McClain quoted in Abbott 1992, 290.
92 "When you find you can't afford": Berlin quoted in Abbott 1992, 301.
92 "jack of all trades": Armstrong IJS 1954, 47.
93 " 'Twas in a great big rathskeller": Abbott 1992, 312–13.
93 searching for those same beautiful chords: Armstrong 1966, 13.
93 "like a barbershop quartet": Ory HJA 1957.
93 basic understanding of the format: Armstrong HJA 1960b.
93 "I have witnessed": Johnson in Abbott 1992, 299.
94 "crazy ideas of harmony": Morton LC ca. 1938, 181.
94 Roland Hayes: Abbott 1992, 313–14.
94 vocal quartet: Armstrong IJS 1954, 17. The association between quartet singing and wind bands was such that some brass band musicians in rural Louisiana referred to their bands as "quartets." Abbott 1992, 318.
94 Karnofsky family: Armstrong 1999, 15.
94 Louis's innate ability: Armstrong 1999, 15.
94 1925 recording of *Heebie Jeebies*: The recording is discussed most recently in Edwards, Brent Hayes 2002.
94 Jelly Roll Morton objected: Morton LC ca. 1938, 211. This passage from the Library of Congress recordings has been reissued in vol. 4 of the CD set *The Jazz Singers*, ed. Robert O'Meally, Smithsonian Collection of Recordings, 1998.
95 Armstrong responded: Armstrong WRC 1970.
95 Red Happy Bolton made a name: Paul Barbarin in Russell 1994, 58.

95 "Little Louis": Zutty Singleton in Shapiro and Hentoff 1955, 48.
95 his emergent alcoholism: See, e.g., St. Cyr in Russell 1994, 68.
95 "It's a little thing": Bechet 1960, 92.
95 a long rivalry: Bigard 1986, 71.
96 His story of being arrested: Armstrong HJA 1960a.
96 no choice but to protect themselves: Davis and Dollard (1940, 23–98) make the point that lower-class children were raised to defend themselves, in the absence of police protection and in rough environments.

Chapter 5: Jail

98 "Few Juveniles Arrested": It is interesting that the article gives Armstrong's age as twelve, implying a birth year of 1900, which is what he always insisted and stands in contradiction to the evidence marshaled by Tad Jones that he was actually born in August 1901. Perhaps this implies that by this time, Armstrong was already mistaken about the year of his birth.
98 sentenced to live in the Colored Waif's Home for Boys: Knowles (1996, 102) suggests that Armstrong's time in the Home was divided into two periods, and that he was released in the middle into the care of his grandmother.
98 his father, Willie: His father would "hire and fire the colored guys who worked under him if they didn't do their work right . . . from the time my father and mother separated, I did not see him until I had grown to be a pretty good size." Armstrong IJS 1954, 2.
98 difficult period for her: Collier 1983, 34–35. Chester Zardis, who was at the Waif's Home with Louis, was under the impression that Louis didn't have any parents, just a sister. MacMurray 1982, 29.
98 "those bad characters": Armstrong IJS 1954, 1.
99 police were reluctant to go there: Dawson HJA 1962 and 1972.
99 also known as a place: Roach 1996, 207.
99 "gambling hells of Franklin Street": Panetta 2000, 19.
99 "nothing but the toughest of kids": Armstrong IJS 1954, 16.
99 "contented cows . . . Yea": Armstrong IJS 1954, 16.
99 He remembered: Armstrong 1936; Armstrong IJS 1954, 22.
100 Those who tried to run away: Armstrong IJS 1954, 18.
100 "more like a kind of health center": Armstrong IJS 1954, 22.
100 the boys learned how to read and write: "Most of my schooling was done in the Waif's Home (boy's jail)." Armstrong 1999, 122.
100 Bechet . . . never learned to read: Romaine 1974, 227.
100 "played school": St. Cyr HJA 1958.
100 "I went to High School": Armstrong LAHA 1954.
100 included singing: Armstrong IJS 1954, 16.
101 patterned its routine on military practice: Jones and Chilton 1971, 52.
101 a brass band for the boys: Armstrong LAHA 1954.
101 "a little of every kind of music": Armstrong IJS 1954, 16.
101 "gitbox": Rena, Henry "Kid" WRC 1938.
101 he wanted to be a drummer: Armstrong WRC 1939.
101 the ragman's tinhorn: At the end of his life, he insisted (contrary to many earlier statements) that his first cornet was given to him in 1907, but the many inaccuracies in this document point to a lapse in memory; see Brothers 1999, 192–93. In

1939 (Armstrong WRC 1939) he told William Russell that he wanted to be a drummer before he entered the Waif's Home. In 1954 (Armstrong IJS 1954, 16), he says plainly, "I'd never tried to play a cornet before."

101 Humphrey taught his brass bands: Knowles 1996, 76.

101 "My better judgment": Armstrong IJS 1954, 17.

102 Davis gave him a bugle: Armstrong IJS 1954, 19.

102 Soon he was playing lead melody: Armstrong HJA 1960a.

103 regularly used for fund-raising: Armstrong IJS 1954, 19.

103 White patronage: Paul Cimbala (1979, 293): "By encouraging music and dancing, masters hoped to keep moody slaves happy, lazy slaves productive, and idle slaves out of mischief."

103 Bebé Ridgley: Ridgley HJA 1959.

103 Warmouth sponsored a band: Knowles 1996, 75.

103 Brady hired Professor Humphrey: Knowles 1996, 78.

104 basic instruction: Knowles 1996, 91.

104 "first thing Peter Davis taught me": Armstrong IJS 1954, 67.

105 Oliver once said: Jackson HJA 1958.

105 "ability was evident": Quoted in Peretti 1992, 33; see also Ory HJA 1957.

105 His shining moment: The event was remembered by several interviewees in the 1950s and 1960s, and a newspaper story covered it briefly.

105 "whores, pimps, gamblers": Armstrong IJS 1954, 20.

105 Someone ran to wake up his mother: Armstrong IJS 1954, 20.

105 One observer remembered: Casimer HJA 1959.

105 the main distinguishing feature: Remembering Armstrong in this parade, Kid Ory said, "I heard this trumpet behind me, you know, good solid tone." Ory in Russell 1994, 177. Hypolite Charles (HJA 1963) said in the 1950s that Armstrong's tone in the early days was "practically the same like he was using now."

106 "Snowball": Souchon HJA 1958.

106 "peashooter sound": Albert HJA 1972a.

108 social transition represented by the Home: See also Raeburn 2001.

108 as a place to give young adolescent boys fatherly attention: Davis and Dollard 1940, 91.

108 "life in general": Armstrong IJS 1954, 16.

108 personal visits at Davis's house: Armstrong IJS 1954, 22.

108 When Louis heard: Armstrong IJS 1954, 23.

109 "When I got out": Armstrong HJA 1960a.

Chapter 6: Lessons with Oliver

110 "Everything I did": Jones, Will 1949, 16.

110 got him a job delivering coal: Armstrong LAHA 1953; Armstrong IJS 1954, 25.

110 "What is the name of that thing": Armstrong IJS 1954, 24.

111 "Henry Ponce is one": Armstrong IJS 1954, 25.

111 "kid band": Foster 1971, 51; see also Morgenstern 1965, 17.

112 the first of many such arrangements: Armstrong LAHA 1957; Armstrong IJS 1954, 25.

112 Cornetist Don Albert: Albert HJA 1967.

112 remembered playing until daybreak: Armstrong LAHA 1954.

112 Honky tonks: Foster 1971, 91.

112   around Liberty and Perdido the tonks were: Armstrong IJS 1954, 8.
112   a "quail": Armstrong LAHA n.d., Tape 336; Armstrong IJS 1954, 46. Was he say-
      ing "quill" and remembering bamboo pipes from the countryside? (On quills, see
      Chapter 7.)
113   "honky tonk music": Foster 1971, 73.
113   Foster remembered: Foster 1971, 50. Foster says that this was "about 1914,"
      though Lawrence Gushee (1989, 15) has suggested that Foster's dates are often
      two or three years too early.
113   "The only thing Louis could play": Foster 1971, 51.
113   "In New Orleans": Foster 1971, 54.
114   On the first night: Armstrong IJS 1954, 61.
114   "real beautiful women": Armstrong IJS 1954, 25.
114   In an account: Armstrong 1954, 198, and 1999, 124; Armstrong 1947, 104;
      Armstrong IJS 1954, 24.
114   "Come here, you cute": Armstrong 1954, 198.
114   "We two silly kids": Armstrong IJS 1954, 27.
114   He was actually a little relieved: Armstrong IJS 1954, 39, and 1999, 13ff. On the
      chronological problems in the latter account, see Brothers 1999, 191–93.
114   Storyville . . . was bursting: Armstrong 1999, 120; Foster 1971, 29; Armstrong IJS
      1954, 66–67.
114   Armstrong wandered around delivering: Armstrong IJS 1954, 40.
115   He usually started the fire: Armstrong 1947, 100, and 1999, 14.
115   "I'd just stand there": Armstrong 1947, 100.
115   Four years older than Armstrong: This paragraph is based on three sources for
      Souchon: Souchon HJA 1958, Souchon LSM n.d., and Souchon 1964.
115   Souchon and his buddy disguised: Souchon LSM n.d., 41.
115   "held up an expanse of trousers": Souchon HJA 1958.
115   Armstrong came to Oliver's attention: Armstrong 1999, 38.
115   He was not shy: Armstrong HJA 1960c.
116   Most of them brushed him away: Armstrong 1999, 136; Armstrong 1999, 40.
116   "after a man retires": Miller, Ernest "Punch" HJA 1960a.
116   Oliver started showing up: Armstrong LAHA 1951a; Jones, Will 1949, 16.
116   "Everything I did": Jones, Will 1949, 16.
116   began to make himself at home: Armstrong 1999, 38, 85; Armstrong IJS
      1954, 42.
117   Oliver's biography: Oliver HJA 1959 on place and year of Oliver's birth.
      However, Clyde Bernhardt (1986, 90) said that Oliver told him that he was fifty-
      four years old in 1931, and that he was born in New Orleans. Fred Moore (1945,
      10) says that Oliver was fifty-one years old in 1931. John "Papa John" Joseph
      (HJA 1958) claimed that Oliver was born on a big plantation in Burnside, near
      Donaldsonville.
117   His father . . . and his mother: Oliver HJA 1959.
117   After that he moved in with his sister: Ramsey 1939, 59.
117   He learned to play cornet in a brass band: Ramsey 1939, 59; Johnson, Victoria
      Davis WRC 1938; Christian WRC 1938. Perkins also arranged for white bands.
      Schafer 1977, 34.
117   Perkins controlled the uptown market: Knowles 1996, 83.
117   "straight man in music": Dodds 1992, 7.

117 Perhaps Oliver learned something from Perkins: Oliver HJA 1959; Knowles 1996, 81, citing Baby Dodds; Knowles (1996, 93–94) also cites reports that Oliver took lessons with George McCullum.

117 a strict reputation: Knowles 1996, 82, citing Red Clark.

117 he started out by learning: Oliver HJA 1959.

117 to teach the only student he ever had: Oliver HJA 1959.

118 Oliver was a slow learner: Ramsey 1939, 60; Dawson HJA 1959.

118 "rough and rugged": Souchon LSM n.d., 201.

118 Johnson: Ramsey 1939, 60.

118 Oliver later joked: Ramsey 1939, 84.

118 as a bandleader, Oliver: Foster 1971, 78.

118 Oliver enjoyed listening: Manetta in Dawson HJA 1959.

118 "When I was with the Magnolia Band": Foster 1971, 41 and 44.

118 the band went through a series of cornetists: Manetta in Dawson HJA 1959; Manetta WRC mss 516, folder 701.

118 "Here comes so and so": Manetta WRC mss 516, folder 701.

118 in the year 1907 they invited him: Ramsey 1939, 61.

118 when he first met him: Dawson HJA 1959.

119 some "variations" on the hymn: Ramsey 1939, 61. Stella Oliver (HJA 1959) remembered that she objected to Oliver's playing of church hymns, presumably due to the mixing of sacred and secular.

119 could also match the Eagle Band: Charles, Hypolite HJA 1963.

119 more and more musical opportunities opened up: Ramsey 1939, 61; Foster 1971, 29. The pace of Oliver's musical development is difficult to gauge and in need of systematic research. What is offered here is only one way to read the situation.

119 Freddie Keppard: Dawson HJA 1959 and 1961.

119 "Now here is where Joe": Ramsey 1939, 61; see also Knowles 1996, 48.

119 "technique that was much smoother": Souchon LSM n.d., 201.

119 continued to advance in the uptown vernacular: Schafer 1977, 39–40; Knowles 1996.

120 "modified lead": Summers HJA 1960 (quotation); see also Miller, Ernest "Punch" HJA 1959a and 1960a; Dodds, Warren "Baby" WRC n.d., 25; Bigard 1986, 95.

120 Manny Gabriel remembered: Knowles 1996, 51.

120 Oliver was the "barrelhouse man": Barbarin, Paul HJA 1959.

120 "making them monkeyshines": Knowles 1996, 51. On Perez playing the melody straight, see also Foster 1971, 77. On Oliver and Perez in the Onward Brass Band, referred to as a "ragtime team," see also Armstrong LAHA 1968. Johnny Lala (HJA 1958) said that Perez was "a real, real 'carry the melody,' you know what I mean. And he had good hot men with him. And you take Joe Oliver, at that time, was a young feller, and another feller by the name of Freddy Keppard."

120 "Your feet is time": Abby "Chinee" Foster in Russell 1994, 50.

121 "them fellows played straight stuff": Miller, Ernest "Punch HJA 1960b.

121 "didn't want to hear any one person": Nicholas HJA 1972.

121 "We already got a clarinet": Oliver in Raeburn 2000a, 94.

121 surprised by how organized the band sounded: Hardin HJA 1959.

121 "I was so wrapped up": Armstrong 1999, 50.

121 a great blues cornetist: Souchon LSM n.d., 75; see also Bud Scott in Shapiro and Hentoff 1955, 37.

122 Freak music: Dawson HJA 1962; Hightower HJA 1958; Miller, Ernest "Punch" HJA 1960a; Bertrand HJA 1959; Foster 1971, 78.

122 "could do most anything": Miller, Ernest "Punch" HJA 1960a.

122 preservations of the practice: For example, Gerhard Kubik (1990) has analyzed Brazilian batuque drumming in terms of "timbral-melodic sequences."

122 worked up a routine: Hightower HJA 1958; see also Bethell 1977, 25–26.

122 Oliver sometimes got angry: Chilton, Charles 1947, 5.

122 "weirdest music I had ever heard": Handy 1957, 74.

122 editorial on the "Dime Museum": Panetta 2000, 8–9.

123 "His guitar seemed to talk": Shines in Guralnick 1992, 59.

123 "Joe could make his horn": Carey in Shapiro and Hentoff 1955, 42.

123 a version of "Eccentric Rag": Jackson HJA 1958; also Armstrong 1999, 52–53.

123 a skit: Armstrong 1999, 52–53.

124 Oliver's talking-cornet rendition: Barbarin, Paul HJA 1957.

124 A paper crown: Paul Barbarin and Barney Bigard both believed that Paddy Harmon, who patented the Harmon mute, got the idea from watching Oliver, and that some of Harmon's millions should have gone to the creator himself. Bigard 1986, 29; Miller, Ernest "Punch" HJA 1960a.

124 Miley, who had learned by watching Oliver: On Miley and Oliver, see Tucker 1991, 101. Charles Chamberlain (2000) reports that Cootie Williams, later to be Ellington's freak specialist on trumpet, was first exposed to the idiom by traveling musicians from New Orleans visiting his hometown of Mobile, Alabama.

124 he decided to take Louis under his wing: Armstrong 1999, 71.

124 Tio Jr. charged fifty cents: Bigard 1986, 15.

124 Perez taught anyone: Dominique HJA 1958.

124 "I'm going to make a cornet player": Natty Dominique in Russell 1994, 140; Dominique HJA 1958.

125 Desvigne began taking two lessons: Knowles 1996, 48.

125 Another student: Dominique HJA 1958.

125 "I loved him as a daddy": Dominique in Russell 1994, 146.

125 The first step in the Creole pedagogy: This review of Creole pedagogy is based on Nicholas HJA 1972; Bigard 1986, 14–15; Albert HJA 1972b; Dominique HJA 1958; Desvigne HJA 1958; Cagnolatti HJA 1961; Dodds, Warren "Baby" WRC n.d.; Keppard HJA 1957.

125 Arnold Metoyer: Cagnolatti HJA 1961.

125 even Perez could send a student home: Dominique HJA 1958.

125 "nervous type of Creole fellow": Dodds, Warren "Baby WRC n.d., 67.

125 best of the Creole musicians: Dominique HJA 1958.

125 Vic Gaspard: Summers HJA 1960.

125 They worked on breath control: Nicholas HJA 1972.

125 Gaspard taught his students: Summers HJA 1960.

125 After the ability to sight-read: Dominique HJA 1958.

126 certainly much harder to come by: Dodds 1992, 13.

126 Oliver himself was never a fluent reader: Shoffner HJA 1959; Carey in Shapiro and Hentoff 1955, 42.

126 "I'm the slowest goddamned reader": Oliver in Bernhardt 1986, 94.

126 not at all unusual for uptown musicians: Bigard 1986, 11; Manetta WRC mss 516, folder 703; Nicholas HJA 1972.

126 "A whole lot of guys": Foster 1971, 74.
127 "didn't know division": Dawson HJA 1972.
127 several sources: For example, Foster 1971, 106; Armstrong 1966, 26.
127 doubtful that he did much reading with Oliver: Stella Oliver (HJA 1959), however, said that Oliver taught Armstrong with books, and Armstrong (1966, 17) says this also.
127 Oliver answered all of his questions: Armstrong 1936, 26. See also DeVore HJA 1962.
127 "Like Louis and all those guys": Wells 1991, 43.
127 "the modern way of phrasing": Armstrong 1936, 26.
127 exchange with interviewer Richard Allen: DeVore HJA 1962.
128 "no trumpet player had the fire": Armstrong 1999, 37–38.
128 "they called it 'attack'": Bailey in Shapiro and Hentoff 1955, 102.
128 He learned solos: Armstrong 1999, 38 and 136; Armstrong IJS 1954, 62.
129 his debt to Oliver: See also letter from Andrew Kimball in Ramsey 1939, 85; Mitchell HJA 1959.
129 "His style hypnotized me": Armstrong LAHA 1968.
129 Armstrong overstated his musical debt: Collier 1983, 67.
129 Other musicians commented: Rudy Jackson in Chilton, Charles 1947, 5.
129 "'Well, Papa Joe, Mother's here'": Armstrong 1999, 87.
129 Oliver nurtured his student: Armstrong 1999, 69.
129 When Louis needed money: Armstrong IJS 1954, 43–44.
129 "I can [never] stop loving": Armstrong IJS 1954, 42.
130 Gabe showed the same degree of kindness: Armstrong 1999 and 1954, 202.
130 in New Orleans, Oliver had been: Armstrong IJS 1954, 38, 63; Armstrong LAHA 1968; Armstrong 1999, 38; Russell 1994, 138.
130 "nobody will ever know": Wiggs in Russell 1994, 161.
130 Oliver's teeth: Armstrong HJA 1960a.
130 "Joe wasn't in his prime": Armstrong HJA 1960a; see also Bernhardt 1986, 90; Foster 1971, 78.
130 Oliver's solo: Hardin LAHA 1971?.
131 without Oliver's sponsorship: Collier 1983, 68.
131 "If it hadn't been for Joe": Russell 1994, 138.

Chapter 7: Ragtime and Buddy Bolden

132 "There has been ragtime": Berlin 1980, 23.
132 "Bolden put 'em out": Duhé HJA 1957.
133 musicians from other places were stunned: Bushell 1988, 19 and 25; Mitchell HJA 1959; Buster Bailey in Shapiro and Hentoff 1955, 77–79; Ellington 1973, 47.
133 "'Jazz,' that's a name": Bechet 1960, 3.
134 During the decades following Reconstruction: My information on locations in this paragraph was culled from many different oral histories and from Rose and Souchon 1967.
134 Charlie Hamilton's father: Hamilton HJA 1965.
134 "quills": Anderson 1990, 410; Kubik 1999, 90 and 92. Alan Lomax recorded Sid Hemphill playing quills in 1959, in Senatobia, Mississippi; commercial release on Lomax 1997 (with photograph).
134 Clarinetist Louis James: Abbott and Seroff 2002, 101; James HJA 1959.

135   "hotbed of dark, uneducated cornfield Negroes": Souchon LSM n.d., 73.
135   African Americans came by the thousands: This is an inference based on growth
      in population; statistics cited by Peretti 1992, 25; see also Hahn 2003, 337–38.
136   "huddling for self-protection": Du Bois 1961, 114.
136   New Orleans during Armstrong's childhood: Henry, Charles "Sunny" HJA 1959,
      January 8.
136   outdoor venues: Duhé HJA 1957; Miller, Ernest "Punch" HJA 1959a.
137   James Humphrey: Manetta WRC mss 516, folder 697; other details about
      Humphrey in Koenig 1981.
137   "Any trumpet player": Hightower HJA 1958.
137   Louisiana held the largest plantations: Hall 1992b, 60.
138   "thorough-bred Africans": Olmstead in Stuckey 1987, 60.
138   Vestiges of Congo culture and language: Thompson 1983, 104. For analysis of the
      Senegambian ethnicity of the early slave population brought to Louisiana, see
      Hall 1992a.
138   Many words associated with voodoo: Kubik 1993; Thompson 1983, 105.
138   slave culture of the Deep South: Thompson 1983, 108.
138   blues singer Robert Johnson: Thompson 1983, 110.
138   African cultural legacy that shaped plantation life: Hall 1992a and 1992b;
      Thompson 1990; Evans 1978; Lomax 1970; Floyd 1995.
138   "They're all trying to take": Quotation in Brothers 1999, 216. For similar lack of
      interest in the African legacy that shaped jazz, see Ory HJA 1957. In the 1910s,
      taking the name "Zulu Aid and Pleasure Club" was an indication of distance from
      Africa, not an embrace of it; men in Armstrong's neighborhood took on the
      Mardi Gras mask of primitive Zulus as a means to perform parody. On Zulu
      imagery in late-nineteenth-century United States, see Lindfors 1983.
138   My impression: I do not see evidence of interest in organizing politically around
      an African identity, such as what motivated emigration agendas in Mississippi,
      Kentucky, and elsewhere; see, for discussion, Hahn 2003, 333.
139   immigration of some three thousand slaves: The timing of the reports on Place
      Congo coincides with the aftermath of this immigration, suggesting that what-
      ever African practices were already in place in New Orleans now received a
      tremendous boost. Lachance 1988, 111.
139   Many of those slaves had originally: Jean Price-Mars, as cited in Thompson 1990,
      149. Kmen 1972, 14. Thompson (1983, 103) observes that "Congo" was often
      used to designate any slave taken from the west coast of Central Africa.
139   "more brutally savage": Latrobe in Johnson 1995, 2.
139   By the 1840s: Johnson 1995, 42.
140   where the balance stood: See Kmen 1966, Chapter 12, for a good review of
      African-American music in antebellum New Orleans. On the Louisiana slave
      trade generally, see, most recently, Ingersoll 1996 and Hall 1992.
140   cornetist Charles "Buddy" Bolden: For introduction to Bolden, see Marquis
      1978.
141   Bolden's mental health dramatically deteriorated: Armstrong IJS 1954, 8.
141   Some believed: Ory HJA 1957.
141   "Bolden put 'em out": Duhé HJA 1957.
141   "polka hound": Guralnick 1998, 22.

141 Johnny St. Cyr and others: St. Cyr in Russell 1994, 72; Ed Hall in Russell 1994, 209.

141 "The schottische was a very beautiful": St. Cyr in Russell 1994, 72.

141 these traditional dances: General discussion of this kind of transformation in Stearns and Stearns 1994, 18–24.

141 "had a jazz way": Armstrong IJS 1954, 29.

141 "could play a waltz": Foster 1971, 51.

141 bands used to change waltz tunes: Dodds 1992, 10.

142 Bolden could play "sweet": On Bolden as a sweet player and variety of dances, see Raeburn 1992, 10.

142 the percussive precision of foot against wood: Abrahams 1992, 93–94; see also Emery 1988, 92, 104, 110, 111.

142 in his study of West African religion: Thompson 1983, xiii.

142 "There wasn't any such thing": Miller, Ernest "Punch" HJA 1960a.

142 "I'd try to dance the quadrilles": Foster 1971, 41.

142 "They dance by themselves": Quoted in Hazzard-Gordon 1990, 30; I have altered the quotation to standard spelling.

142 "you could grab the chick": Foster 1971, 73.

142 Dancing techniques common throughout the African diaspora: This list is derived from Stearns and Stearns 1994, 14–15.

143 "'Way down, 'way down low": Song quoted in Ramsey 1939, 13. Marquis (1978, 108) reports that the song was written by Percy Cahill and listed in New Orleans by 1906. Gushee (1994, 15, n. 15) quotes some lyrics from Cahill.

143 "them chicks would get way down": Armstrong 1966, 8.

143 "guys squatting on the floor": The syntax of the song suggests that he is telling the band to play softly, but I am skeptical about that, since there are many contrary statements that the band always played loudly; soft playing for variety was a later development.

143 crouching position: Thompson 1983, 125.

143 number of references to animal dances: Stearns and Stearns 1994, 21 and 26.

143 "developed into its highest state of efficiency": Quoted in Gushee 1994, 19–20.

143 "The older people loved": Lyons in Goffin 1946a, 56.

143 the new dance in the 1890s: Gushee 1994, 19.

144 John Philip Sousa: Berlin 1980, 49.

144 A journalist estimated: Berlin 1980. 45.

144 pianists were attracted: JRM in Blesh and Janis 1950, 148.

145 ragtime flowed through St. Louis: "We bought most of our music from St. Louis," said the New Orleanian bass player Pops Foster (in Russell 1994, 101).

145 "There has been ragtime music": Joplin in Berlin 1980, 23.

145 Charles Ives heard . . . and documented: Transcription and discussion in Berlin 1980, 23.

145 Hoffman published several arrangements: Examples of Hoffman's arrangements in Berlin 1980, 64.

145 The technique: For a fuller description of this model, see Brothers 1994.

146 "in west Africa the superposition": Kubik 1999, 43.

146 Patting Juba: Epstein 1977, 141; Floyd 1995, 50–57.

146 Drummer Chinee Foster: Foster in Russell 1994, 50.

146 "I have heard": Epstein 1977, 142–43. In nineteenth-century accounts, "Juba" is

usually capitalized, a reference to the minstrel performer William Henry Lane, who moved and tapped with virtuoso elegance and precision and took the stage name Juba. For additional references, see Emery 1988, 96–98 and 185–90.

146   "I do not know": Beverly Tucker to Edgar Allan Poe in Epstein 1977, 142.

147   "At the start of a recording session": Stearns 1956, 5; emphasis in original.

148   The "ragtime era": Berlin (1980) emphasizes this point; a good example of the range of music thought of as "ragtime" is given in Schafer 1977, 18.

148   Bolden's repertory: Manetta WRC mss 516, folders 729–733.

148   He and his band: Manetta WRC mss 516, folder 729.

148   "ripping" a vigorous break: Manetta WRC mss 516, folder 729.

148   "He was famous": Barbarin in Barker 1986, 28.

148   Frankie Dusen: Manetta WRC mss 516, folders 701 and 709.

148   Algiers supported two "colored" dance halls: Ramsey 1940, 26. Local mythology included the idea that a woman could kill a man by taking the little decorative bow out of his hat, and stories were eventually told that this was what had killed Bolden. Men were known to hold their hats while dancing. Perhaps Bolden's musicians kept their hats on for protection. Garland WRC 1958.

149   lowered their suspenders: Foster in Russell 1994, 104.

149   Bolden himself wore a hat and went tie-less: Morton LC ca. 1938, 212.

149   "The girls and women": Morton LC ca. 1938, 212.

149   When the well-mannered Manetta: Manetta WRC mss 516, folder 729.

149   Brock Mumford: Manetta WRC mss 516, folder 729.

149   ran with rough women: Manetta WRC mss 516, folder 701; see also Foster 1971, 48.

150   "the only way he could get away from her": Manetta WRC mss 516, folder 734.

150   both rough places: Manetta's brother found Funky Butt Hall much too rough and hated to go to there. Manetta WRC mss 516, folder 648.

150   "You should see the place": Ory HJA 1957.

150   "nothing but waltzes": Foster in Russell 1994, 103; Wilson HJA 1962.

150   As the dances modulated down and dirty: It is tempting to relate this midnight transition to the Congese system of four moments of the sun, one of which was midnight and associated with female energy; see Thompson 1983, 109.

150   erotic combination of blues and the slow drag: Brunious HJA 1959.

150   Legends grew around his power over women: Jones, Richard M. WRC 1938.

150   "Bolden was still a great man": Scott in Shapiro and Hentoff 1955, 37; see also John Joseph in Russell 1994, 118. Louis Jones said that Bolden's blues made him famous: Jones, Louis HJA 1959.

151   "We took our time": Dodds, Warren "Baby" WRC n.d., 22. Lawrence (HJA 1960) also speaks of playing different pieces in "blues time."

151   "packed like sardines": Manetta WRC mss 516, folder 729; Barnes, Emile with Paul HJA 1959.

151   "guys . . . doing nothing": Foster 1971, 107 and 42.

152   "blues time": Lawrence HJA 1960.

152   "That was his": Manetta WRC mss 516, folder 729.

152   several reliable witnesses: Manetta WRC mss 516, folder 729; Jones, Louis HJA 1959; Cornish HJA 1959.

152   the only "ratty music": Manetta WRC mss 516, folder 648.

152   Blues offered the challenge: On these connections, see Ory HJA 1957; Scott in Shapiro and Hentoff 1955, 37; Marquis 1978, 28; Matthews HJA 1959.

152 "blues is what cause": Big Eye Louis Nelson in Lomax 1993, 109.

152 "Buddy Bolden, nobody read in his band": Joseph HJA 1958.

152 He scored his most famous: "Everything they played they had music in front of them . . . Had George Baquet and all those guys," said Ory (HJA 1957).

152 Each park: St. Cyr HJA 1958; Ridgley HJA 1959. More on Lincoln and Johnson parks, see Marquis 1978, 59–63.

152 Buddy Bartley . . . impressed the crowd: On Bartley, see Schafer 1974.

153 "a pimp and notoriety as he could be": St. Cyr HJA 1958.

153 The two segregated parks competed heavily: Ridgley HJA 1959. Bruce Raeburn informs me (personal communication) that the two parks were marked by different class status, Lincoln more "respectable" and Johnson more "ratty."

153 "I used to have to play": Armstrong IJS 1954, 45.

153 physical strength: Bourdieu 1984, 384.

153 "jazz musicians have to be a working class": St. Cyr in Lomax 1993, 123.

153 loud playing represented both: Ory felt that Bolden's success was not due to musical skill but to his loud playing: "He wasn't really a musician . . . He didn't study, I mean, he was gifted, playing with effect, but no tone, you know . . . He played loud . . . And people loved it, they went for it." Ory HJA 1957.

154 "King Bolden": Manetta WRC mss 516, folder 729.

154 Loud cornet playing: Knowles 1996, 51.

155 Robichaux sometimes won: Scott in Shapiro and Hentoff 1955, 37; Marquis 1978, 81; Willie Santiago in Bechet et al. HJA 1944.

155 Ory admired Robichaux's orchestra: Ory HJA 1957.

155 Bolden played a diverse repertory: "Bunk Johnson got his style from Buddy with his sweetness, but could never play rough and loud like Bolden," said Bill Matthews (cited in Raeburn 1992, 10), confirming that it was not just his repertory but also his playing style that was diverse.

155 a rallying point around which lower-class values gathered: Don Marquis (1978, 64–67) has produced the following profile of Bolden's audiences, based on a police report on a disturbance at Odd Fellows and Masonic Hall: the 106 patrons mostly held common laboring jobs, such as stevedores, valets, housekeepers, and cooks, and only 14 were able to read and write.

156 "didn't play jazz": Morton LC ca. 1938, 212.

156 "Jazz was also called 'ragtime'": Valentine HJA 1957.

156 "Joe Howard didn't play nothing": Manetta WRC mss 516, folder 687.

156 "There's two kinds of music": Bechet 1960, 3.

156 "Robichaux would play": Miller, Ernest "Punch" HJA 1959b.

156 "Ragtime . . . that's the onliest": Duhé HJA 1960.

157 "Ragtime originated uptown": Piron WRC 1938.

157 "They would make me carry": Armstrong IJS 1954, 47.

157 "a musician with a tone": Armstrong IJS 1954, 67.

157 "I wouldn't say I know what jazz is": Armstrong 1955, 60.

157 the meaning of ragtime: Sometimes they use the term in both ways—as the popular genre and as the uptown New Orleanian performance practice—which is unsurprising though confusing. For example, Pops Foster, who is otherwise such an excellent source for uptown music, uses "ragtime" not in this sense but in the traditional way that it is used by Jelly Roll Morton when he (1971, 41) says, "From about 1900 on, there were three types of bands around New Orleans. You

had bands that played ragtime, ones that played sweet music, and ones that played nothin' but blues."

159 "He's supposed to be playing different": Miller, Ernest "Punch" HJA 1960b.

159 slave-musician had no recourse to copyright: There is a fascinating exception to the impossibility of slaves being able to copyright a composition. Contrary to law, Basile Barès copyrighted a piano piece in New Orleans, in 1860. Sullivan 1988, 65.

160 "Their band consisted of just three pieces": Handy 1957, 76–77.

160 performed in this same over-and-over way: Foster 1971, 74–77; Wiggs HJA 1962.

160 "just couldn't make no ending": Foster 1971, 52–53.

160 Oliver gauged the dancers' reception: Dodds, Warren "Baby" HJA 1958.

160 He kept a brick near to hand: Dawson HJA 1961. A story, difficult to document, circulating from years later has the young John Coltrane confessing that he had soloed for so long because he just didn't know how to finish. Miles Davis had some brusque advice: "take the horn out of your mouth."

160 "The will to adorn": Hurston 1983, 50–54.

161 visual collages: See Cogswell 2003; Armstrong 1999.

161 "Invent" is the verb: They also used the phrase "getting off," as in "getting off from the melody"; for example, Charles, Hypolite HJA 1963. "Variation" can be used in the same way, as when Emile Barnes (HJA 1960b) says, "You can take a number and variate, go in and out of the melody."

162 "I have heard": Epstein 1977, 294–95; emphasis in original.

163 "You have to give [Bolden] credit": Ory HJA 1957.

Chapter 8: "Most of the musicians were Creoles"

164 "Most of the musicians": Armstrong 1999, 32.

164 "The Downtown boys": Foster 1971, 42.

164 Creoles: On the contested history of the term "Creole," see Domínguez 1986. "Creole" was not synonymous with "Creole of color" for whites in New Orleans. But Armstrong thought of the term in that way, which is itself revealing. My usage will follow his, with "Creole" and "Creole of color" being used interchangeably.

164 Pops Foster explains how: The same thought is articulated by Foster, Abbey "Chinee" HJA 1960 (no relation to Pops Foster); see also Dawson HJA 1972.

164 "get well": Johnson in Ramsey 1939, 61.

164 New Orleans as made up of three main social groups: Armstrong 1999, 5.

166 "In a world where it means so much": Du Bois 1961, 138.

166 "We were the Indians": Armstrong 1999, 58.

166 Most of the whites he knew: Armstrong 1999, 5 and 11.

166 "There is scarcely one public relation": Cable in Tregle 1992, 178.

167 "an Italian white boy" and other quotations from Armstrong here: Armstrong 1999, 160, 213–14.

168 "an old white fellow": Armstrong IJS 1954, 32.

168 "Everybody was telling old man": Armstrong IJS 1954, 32.

168 "Great White South's Perpetual Proclamation": Barker 1998, viii.

168 getting hired for a house party: Hightower HJA 1958.

168 "I'll tell you, what got the most": Hightower HJA 1958.

169 whites didn't care what the musicians played: Foster 1971, 54.
169 Several musicians explained: Manny Gabriel in Morris 1991, 18; Glenny ALA ca. 1948; Leonard Bechet ALA ca. 1948.
169 steady exposure to white audiences: Armstrong 1999, 33.
169 The settlers were advised to: Johnson 1992.
170 "The blood of the savages": Johnson 1992, 35.
170 "first class Octoroons": Blesh and Janis 1950, 170.
170 *gens de couleur libres*: Domínguez 1986, 23.
170 Signs of French-American tension: Kmen 1966, 61; Domínguez 1986, 111.
170 In the decades after the American purchase: For an important qualification of this familiar depiction of the American pattern of settlement, see Tregle 1992, esp. 154–59.
171 "Creole" included both whites and *gens de couleur libres*: "Unchallengeable white supremacy, in short, had made it possible to accommodate a pan-racial creolism," is how Joseph Tregle (1992, 172) sums up the situation.
171 in antebellum New Orleans: Tregle 1992, 138–39.
171 1860 census: Domínguez 1986, 116.
171 qualifications for leadership: Domínguez 1986, 134. A thorough review of the complicated political dynamics during this period is given by Logsdon and Bell 1992.
171 Some of them articulated: "Our future is indissolubly bound up with that of the Negro," wrote one Creole of color in 1864. Quote from Domínguez 1986, 136. See also Logsdon and Bell 1992, 228; Hair 1976, 71.
172 "I didn't know": Barbarin, Isidore HJA 1959.
172 "it is debatable": Albert HJA 1972a.
172 "Creole of color": Bigard 1986, 5; see also Lomax 1993, 101–2.
172 he had no African ancestry: Lomax 1993, 3, 126, 263. See also Armstrong 1999, 24; Ake 1998, 46, citing Richard Allen and Lizzie Miles, who cites Morton's claim that he was white; Peretti 1992, 59, citing Lovie Austin.
172 Morton's denial: Gushee (1985, 391) suggests that Morton's "account of his pedigree may be as much due to shame as to ignorance."
173 on the wrong side of voting rights: Jackson, Joy J. 1969, 21.
173 "When one brother could pass": Davis and Dollard 1940, 135.
173 An older woman interviewed in the 1970s: Domínguez 1986, 168.
173 narrative of French descent: Rohrer and Edmonson et al. 1960, 223.
173 artisan class: Davis and Dollard (1940, 88) refer to occupations such as carpenter and plasterer as "lower-middle class" in their elaborate class-based analysis of New Orleans Negro society.
173 For much of the nineteenth century: Foner 1970, 407.
174 of the Creoles Armstrong knew: Dominique HJA 1958; Foster 1971, 83; Peretti 1992, 30; Picou HJA 1958; Dominique HJA 1958, 5; Picou HJA 1958; Shapiro and Hentoff 1955, 18.
174 "New Orleans is probably the only city": Kinzer 1993, 130. See also James Trotter in *Music and Some Highly Musical People* (1878), quoted in Kinzer 1993, 90 and 93.
174 history of the Tio family: The Tio family history is easily accessible thanks to the work of Charles Kinzer; Kinzer 1993 and 1996.
174 Lorenzo Tio Jr.: Kinzer 1993, 252 and 263.

174 ancestry: Kinzer 1993, 44ff.
175 By the late 1880s: Kinzer 1993, 143 and 138, quoting the *Weekly Louisianian*.
175 Louis rolled cigars and Lorenzo worked as a bricklayer: Kinzer 1993, 145 and 168.
175 national tour with the Georgia Minstrels: Kinzer 1993, 159–61.
175 helped form the Lyre Musical Society: Kinzer 1993, 169ff.
175 Louis and Lorenzo: Kinzer 1993, 191.
175 "Let me get under the bed": Dominique HJA 1958.
175 settled on rolling cigars: Bigard 1986, 8.
175 Lorenzo's son: Kinzer 1993, 210.
175 he impressed the other musicians: Kinzer 1993, 214.
175 listed in the city directory as a painter: Kinzer 1993, 237.
175 Several musicians who regularly played with the Tios: Charles, Hypolite HJA 1963; Knowles 1996, 80–81.
176 the typical reaction toward: Davis and Dollard 1940, 155.
176 Clarinetist Achille Baquet: Keppard HJA 1961.
176 census of 1900 . . . By 1910: Kinzer 1993, 301, n 9.
176 "knew he was very bright": Keppard HJA 1961.
176 "He went too far, I guess": Keppard HJA 1961.
176 "The lines between": Logsdon and Bell 1992, 239–40.
177 During Reconstruction: Domínguez 1986, 135–36.
178 story about trombonist George Fihle: Manetta WRC mss 516, folders 729–733 and 652.
178 "Didn't want to have any parts": Dodds, Warren "Baby" WRC n.d., 22.
178 what was driving his mother's irritation: Dodds, Warren "Baby" WRC n.d., 22.
178 Frank Dusen: Manetta WRC mss 516, folder 695.
178 the dark-skinned Oliver: Nicholas HJA 1972.
179 Albert remembered: Albert HJA 1973.
179 Piron . . . orchestra . . . and . . . Robichaux's orchestra: "Both bands were made up of light Negroes," said Dr. Edmond Souchon (HJA 1958), the wealthy doctor who grew up on St. Charles Avenue, and though that wasn't true completely it was true mainly.
179 Light-skinned Creole musicians: Picou HJA 1958. It remains to be discovered how extensively the social category "colored" played out in this way.
179 When brass instruments: Keppard HJA 1961.
180 they were now colored in a dangerous way: Bourdieu 1984.
180 musicians Armstrong knew from downtown never heard one: Picou, whose father was French and whose grandfather owned slaves, was one exception. Picou HJA 1958; on Picou's grandfather, Perez WRC 1938.
180 Creoles like Barbarin and Perez were happy: Pops Foster managed to find a spot for himself in a band that was largely Creole, which put him in a number of downtown dance halls. The required repertory downtown, in his experience, was "6/8 marches." Foster WRC 1938.
181 social distinction: Bourdieu 1984, 228.
181 artisan-class position: The word "artisan" has the etymological advantage of sharing roots with the word "art," both carrying the ancient sense of learned craft. It would be nice to know more about the Société des Artisans, which was flourishing as early as 1867; about Artisans Hall, which was where Louis Tio's orchestra

sometimes played; and about Creole-of-color connections tu Prinre Hall Masonry, an organization that was saturated with artisan symbolism and imagery. On Société des Artisans, Hirsch and Logsdon 1992, 193, and Logsdon and Bell 1992, 235; on Artisans Hall, Knowles 1996, 58, and Lomax 1993, 106–7; on Prince Hall Masonry, Wallace 2002.

181 dissonances that are not to be ironed out: Hurston 1983, 80.

181 strongest notes you can play: Foster 1971, 73.

181 effects that made Joe Oliver's cornet: Carey in Shapiro and Hentoff 1955, 42.

181 "And he'd say to the guy": Bigard in Kinzer 1993, 207; see also Kinzer 1996, 284.

181 "just whatever come in your head": Morand HJA 1950; see also Armstrong 1999, 175.

182 a light-skinned Creole boy told: Davis and Dollard 1940, 240.

182 "colored people used to get their real kicks": Armstrong IJS 1954, 5.

182 Moments like this: Kelley 1993, 103.

182 Yet they were also moments: Davis and Dollard 1940, 136.

183 "a waltz and schottische king": Armstrong LAHA 1968; emphasis in original.

183 "there are some nice dark people": Davis and Dollard 1940, 136.

183 Parents regulated the mating of their children: Keppard HJA 1961; Albert HJA 1974; Miller, Ernest "Punch" HJA 1960a; Barker 1986, 41; Foster 1971, 63 and 65.

184 "kind of bright": Keppard HJA 1961.

184 Nelson . . . had relatively dark skin: Lomax, who interviewed Nelson, described him as having dark skin; Lomax 1993, 109.

184 Being an integrated member: Goffin 1946a and 1946b.

184 "Nigger hunting time": Armstrong 1999, 17.

184 Armstrong was never in Keppard's class: Lomax 1993, 188.

184 "when you come darker than Keppard": St. Cyr in Lomax, 1993, 125 and 253.

184 "Jelly didn't like Negroes": Lomax 1993, 125 and 253. Jack Stewart (2001) provides a good discussion of Morton's ambivalent attitudes.

184 Yet Morton admired: Raeburn 2000a, 96.

184 would "be friends and all": Barnes, Emile HJA 1960a.

185 "the cats in his band": Barker in Shapiro and Hentoff 1955, 52.

185 "Creole bands wouldn't hire": Bethell 1977, 25.

185 they let darker people know: Jackson HJA 1958.

185 "had an inferiority complex": Bernhardt 1986, 101 (quotation); Nicholas HJA 1972.

185 "That shit would always come out": Armstrong LAHA 1970b.

185 "real light skinned": Armstrong IJS 1954, 12.

186 "They did not want a Black piano player": Armstrong 1999, 24.

186 Creole and Negro musicians rarely played together: Manetta told a revealing story about Frankie Dusen's band, ca. 1900, when Dusen had hired Creole clarinetist Alphonse Picou as a substitute for a gig in Algiers. The Negro patrons in the dance hall were nervous because Picou looked white: "Oh Jesus, some kind of white man playing with them," Manetta remembered hearing. Manetta WRC mss 516, folder 709.

186 "Sometimes we used to mix": Charles, Hypolite HJA 1963.

186 "the [uptown and downtown] musicians mixed only": Dodds 1992, 13.

186 categorical identity: Brubaker and Cooper 2001.

187 "Creoles didn't want their children": René HJA 1960 (quotation); see also Schafer 1974, 11; Foster 1971, 16.
188 "Nice lesson for them": Armstrong IJS 1954, 62–63.
188 "speaks directly from and to": Newton [Hobsbawm] 1975, 268; Hobsbawm reminds us that it is easy for outsiders to miss behavioral protests from oppressed people, since they are often indirect and concealed.
189 Creole society was not quite so monolithic: Logsdon and Bell 1992, 233.
189 Nelson's father moved: Lomax 1993, 108. For information on Nelson, Lomax is the main source; see also Goffin 1946a and 1946b, which, however, have many inaccuracies.
189 plantation-to-city immigrants: Logsdon and Bell 1992, 232.
189 "After four or five months": Nelson in Lomax 1993, 108; emphasis in original.
190 Charley Payton: In Goffin (1946a, 55), based on an interview with Bob Lyons, Payton is named "Billy Peyton." In Rose and Souchon (1967, 99) he is called "Henry Peyton," as he is by Kid Ory (in Russell 1994, 171). Payton is mentioned briefly by Dawson (HJA 1961) and by John Joseph (HJA 1958).
190 "a very lowdown type": Morton in Lomax 1993, 76–77; see also Jones, Louis HJA 1959.
190 Frustrated with the legitimate route: Lomax 1993, 109. Nelson claimed that Buddy Bolden played in the Payton band too, perhaps as an accordionist who was just beginning to take up the cornet. The claim that Bolden was an accordianist is interesting since this was also Payton's instrument and since Nelson claims Bolden learned from Payton. Wind instruments were not yet allowed in the Storyville district until 1905, but perhaps this did not include the block where the Big 25 was located. Nelson's claim is supported by Lyons, however. See Goffin 1946b, 9, and 1946a, 56; Lomax 1993, 110.
190 Seventh Ward Creole neighborhood: Laurent HJA 1960.
190 Nelson eventually: Charles, Hypolite HJA 1963; Albert HJA 1961; Russell 1994, 145.
190 good at freak music: Barnes, Emile HJA 1962.
190 good at playing fast and making variations: Duhé HJA 1957; Lomax 1993, 114.
190 improvisationally inventive: Barnes, Emile HJA 1962.
190 "Big Eye Louis Nelson": Foster 1971, 87.
190 he then changed to cornet: Keppard took cornet lessons with Adolphe Alexander Sr., a friend of Isidore Barbarin's described by Danny Barker as "very French in manner . . . whom I never saw smile once and who was serious and touchy." Keppard HJA 1961; Barker 1986, 26 and 28. Pops Foster (WRC 1938) and several others said that Keppard imitated Bolden. Paul Dominguez in Lomax 1993, 105–6; Johnson, William Manuel "Bill" WRC 1938.
190 "When he": Keppard HJA 1961.
190 particularly obnoxious to uptown Negroes: Chilton, John 1987, 30.
191 two different cornet styles: Wiggs HJA 1962.
191 Louis offered a Creole perspective: Keppard HJA 1957.
191 "had a style": Dodds 1992, 52.
191 "It sounded like heaven": Wiggs HJA 1962.
191 "bigger": Singleton WRC 1938. Wiggs (HJA 1962) also claimed that white musicians from New Orleans imitated Keppard.
192 "Little differences": Armstrong LAHA 1953.

192 Bechet's stylistic model: Palmer HJA 1955; Bechet 1960, 79–80.
192 Reminiscing in 1944: Bechet et al. HJA 1944.
193 "used to rehearse, and rehearse": Bechet et al. HJA 1944.
194 "rough babies": Foster 1971, 41.
194 "real gut-bucket band": Bechet HJA 1945.
194 playing with Oliver: Bechet HJA 1945.
194 He has been portrayed as: Sidney's older brother Leonard, described by John Chilton (1987, 4) as "studying to become a dentist," was actually a lowly dental assistant until one day the dentist decided to quit; he liked Leonard so much that he gave the business to him. Bechet, Leonard ALA ca. 1948. See also Lomax 1993, 116, quoting Leonard Bechet: "Well, you know, we were very poor."
194 He quit school: Bechet, Leonard ALA ca. 1948.
194 Leonard tried: Laurent HJA 1960; Manetta WRC mss 516, folder 652; Keppard HJA 1961; Chilton, John 1987, 18; Lomax 1993, 117–19.
194 "bad luck place": Barnes, Emile HJA 1960a.
194 Yet the musicians: Dawson HJA 1959.
194 "He didn't know what key": Bocage in Raeburn 1997b, 15.
194 He studied briefly: Bigard 1986, 15; Chilton, John 1987, 7.
194 "No, no, no": St. Cyr in Russell 1994, 68.
194 "See how many ways": Richard Hadlock in Chilton, John 1987, 233.
195 the expanding taste for blues-based ragtime: An interesting comment comes from Pops Foster (1971, 54): "It was a rule in New Orleans if you didn't play any blues you didn't get any colored jobs, and if you didn't play lancers you didn't get Cajun jobs. White jobs didn't care what you played." See also p. 44.
195 "real Creole people": Manetta WRC mss 516, folder 695; see also folder 652.

Chapter 9: Musicians as Men

197 "Under the present": Quoted in Somers 2000, 520; italics in original.
197 "The trumpet": Armstrong in Walser 1999, 154.
197 "We claim exactly": Quoted in Dailey 2000, 91; emphasis in original.
197 "With the right to vote": Du Bois 1906, 93.
198 "have to be a working class": St. Cyr in Lomax 1993, 123.
198 typical place for female music making: As if to confirm the place of women as singers, women who collected berries and sold them on the streets sang to attract customers, in contrast with the rags-bottles-and-bones men who played their tinhorns.
198 even a few women: Chamberlain 2001.
199 how to make arrangements: Armstrong IJS 1954, 70.
199 his skill in blues: Armstrong 1999, 124. See also Henry Glass (HJA 1962), who said that all you had to do to get women was be a musician.
199 "He said to me": Armstrong 1999, 160, 213–15.
199 "All the musicians": Foster 1971, 32.
199 "She wasn't very much": Armstrong IJS 1954, 36.
200 "the sharpest pimp": Armstrong 1999, 121; Armstrong IJS 1954, 41; see also Ory in Russell 1994, 179, "Kirk" being, no doubt, Clerk Wade.
200 "waltzes and everything": Manetta WRC mss 516, folder 695.
200 Bold clothing: Kelley 1993, 86.
200 "low class hustler": Dodds, Warren "Baby" WRC n.d., 16–17; also Russell 1994, 20.

200 "They knowed how": Morton LC ca. 1938, 477–80; Armstrong IJS 1954, 41.
200 As a special attraction: Manetta WRC mss 516, folder 687; Morton LC ca. 1938, 480; Lomax 1993, 236.
200 "fifth class whore": Morton LC ca. 1938, 480.
201 "brassy, broad and aggressively": Baraka [Jones] 1963, 154.
201 Some pianists: Foster 1971, 93–94; Ory HJA 1957.
201 smoke opium: Morton (LC ca. 1938, 410) noticed a distinction within the drug-using pianists: "The higher class ones always used opium and the lower ones resorted to cocaine, crown, heroin, morphine and so forth and so on."
201 And more than a few pianists: Jones, Richard M. WRC 1938.
201 The Frenchman's: Manetta WRC mss 516, folders 687 and 695.
201 "Them freaky people": Manetta WRC mss 516, folder 687.
201 "The band musicians thought": Foster 1971, 99. "Of course when a man played piano, the stamp was on him for life, the femininity stamp," lamented Morton (quoted in Pastras 2001, 16). Alan Lomax asked Leonard Bechet (ALA ca. 1948) if Jackson was a "fruit," to which Bechet replied that it "wasn't known, but you sort of suspected it, since he played the piano delicately."
202 "Master and mistress": Emery 1988, 91. Also, p. 104: "Old Charlie Snipes was the lead man, and he was the biggest cut-up in the quarters." See also pp. 105 and 109.
202 This usage has been traced to Africa: Abrahams 1992, 121 and 96.
202 "One will continue": Creecy 1860, 22; emphasis in original.
202 "If we said": Dodds 1992, 18.
202 "we played": Brown 1972, 205.
203 "free aggressive expression": Davis and Dollard 1940, 83.
203 guitarist Lorenzo Staulz: Barker 1998, 9–10; see also Manetta WRC mss 516, folders 701 and 709.
203 "He just loved": Bernhardt 1986, 91.
203 "Don't kid me": Bigard 1986, 29.
203 Verbal skill: Dawson HJA 1961; also St. Cyr in Russell 1994, 65. This paragraph is indebted to Simpson 2002.
203 "Jones got a lot of work": Dawson HJA 1961.
203 "couldn't sing": Humphrey HJA 1963.
203 association of verbal invention: Abrahams 1992. John Rohrer and Munro Edmonson found in their study of lower-class gangs in New Orleans that effective dozens play was a primary means for establishing leadership. Rohrer and Edmonson et al. 1960, 162.
203 No one ever talks about: Albert HJA 1972b; Dodds 1992, 25.
204 "It seemed as though": Armstrong IJS 1954, 66.
204 When two bands met: Marrero HJA 1959.
204 it was not unusual: Bechet 1960, 65.
204 they exchanged numbers back and forth: Bechet 1960, 63.
204 Buddy Petit: George Lewis in Shapiro and Hentoff 1955, 25.
204 Oliver instructed Louis: Armstrong IJS 1954, 40–41. Armstrong once hid in a wagon waiting for Kid Rena to come near; at the right moment he jumped up and went head to head with Rena. Jackson HJA 1958.
204 Spontaneous battles: Dodds 1992, 19.
204 Sometimes two bands: Marrero HJA 1959.

204 "I ain't gonna stop": Garland WRC 1958.

204 "They couldn't get out": Ory HJA 1957.

204 He liked to pour salt: Bigard 1986, 8; Armstrong 1999, 28; Jackson HJA 1958.

204 A substantial public: Ramsey 1939, 29; see also Bigard 1986, 8; Barker 1986, 57–59.

204 Food and drink: Bechet 1960, 63.

205 "It was a terrible thing": Barker 1998, 11–12.

205 Clarinetist Jimmie Noone: Barnes, Emile HJA 1960a.

206 "They could play anything": Bechet 1960, 64.

206 "Get out of that neighborhood": Ramsey 1939, 29; see also Bethell 1977, 26.

206 "Get in B-flat": Oliver in Shapiro and Hentoff 1955, 45–46; see also Ramsey 1939, 62–63.

206 Oliver remembered: Bernhardt 1986, 100.

206 The likely places: Williams, Clarence WRC 1939; Shapiro and Hentoff 1955, 12–13.

207 he thoroughly embarrassed: Stewart, Rex 1972, 46–47; Shapiro and Hentoff 1955, 205–6.

207 Johnny Dunn: Bigard 1986, 30; Barker 1986, 130–31.

207 "one or two hundred choruses": Barker 1986, 130.

208 this was why: Morton LC ca. 1938, 386.

208 The most famous example: On Keppard and the first recording, see Ramsey 1941, 6; Johnny St. Cyr in Lomax 1993, 189. Gushee (1988, 89–90) challenges this legend, though it is told by many musicians, including Armstrong (LAHA 1970b). Gushee makes the good observation that, in any event, many vaudeville artists were paranoid about their best routines being stolen.

208 "Once you got a certain solo": Armstrong 1966, 43. For an extended analysis of this phenomenon, see Harker 1999.

208 "Inspired improvising": Bechet 1960, 64.

208 "could raise so much sand": Ridgley HJA 1959.

209 "Selecting one of their number": Abrahams 1992, 91–92, citing Burwell, *A Girl's Life in Virginia Before the War* (New York: Stokes, 1895). See also Douglass 1982, 57.

209 "Moreover, each singing": Hurston 1983, 80.

209 "The way I see it": Armstrong 1999, 38. And in a separate discussion: "He was a Creator, with unlimited Ideas." Armstrong 1999, 174. See also Armstrong IJS 1954, 67.

209 "Joe broke them that night": Williams in Allen and Rust 1987, 335; see also Mitchell HJA 1959. It was claimed that Oliver could extend blues solos to twenty choruses or more. Allen and Rust 1987, 333, quoting Glyn Paque.

210 "is supposed to be heard": Dodds, Warren "Baby" WRC n.d., 30.

210 "Lack of closure": Barber 1989, 19.

210 "Nobody could touch him": Armstrong IJS 1954, 40.

210 break was integral to jazz: Morton LC ca. 1938, 190.

210 "blues is what cause": Lomax 1993, 109.

210 "The band often repeated": Quoted in Gushee 1994, 20.

211 "But there will be other tunes": Morgenstern 1965, 18.

211 Musicians were not the only men: In addition to first-person accounts, the following section on the fraternal societies relies on Blassingame 1973, 167–68; Zander 1962.

211 "remarkable 'thickening'": Hahn 2003, 461–63.
211 "Everybody in the city": Morton in Lomax 1993, 20.
211 "Pleasure clubs": Mitchell 1995, 150–51.
211 Some of the clubs: Ridgley HJA 1961.
212 Armstrong joined: Armstrong IJS 1954, 74; Armstrong 1966, 8.
212 Membership could cost: Zander 1962, 100.
212 Armstrong was known as: Armstrong 1999, 21; Armstrong 1954, 233–35.
212 Savvy musicians: Charles, Hypolite HJA 1963; Knowles 1996, 15.
212 "Tuxedo, Onward, Eureka": Charles, Hypolite HJA 1963.
212 Over in Algiers: Knowles 1996, 66; Henry, Charles "Sunny" HJA 1959, January 8.
212 Odd Fellows having a funeral: Barbarin, Isidore HJA 1959; Knowles 1996, 12; Marquis 1978, 32. 1880s: Eagleson 1961, 77. A good source for details about the clubs is Henry, Charles "Sunny" HJA 1959, October 21.
212 pimps' club: Manetta WRC mss 516, folder 687.
212 last parade he saw: Armstrong 1954, 224; see also Vigne HJA 1961.
213 Morton ranked clubs: Morton LC ca. 1938, 230.
213 Masons were prohibited: Ridgley HJA 1961 and Zander 1962, 87; Ridgley also said that the Masons did not allow music on the march from the church to the cemetery, only after the burial.
213 Black Benny's funeral: Danny Barker in Shapiro and Hentoff 1955, 16.
213 When Henry Zeno died: Ridgley HJA 1961.
214 One came from England: Stewart, Jack 2004.
214 an African-American funeral: Latrobe in Zander 1962, 32.
214 "pulling [Johnson] out of church": Foster 1971, 48.
214 "Rejoice at the outgoing!": Jackson, Mahalia 1967, 30.
214 women, preachers, and Catholics: Schwerin 1992, 25; Zander 1962, 36; Jackson, Mahalia 1967, 30; Charles, Jessie HJA 1967; Valentine HJA 1959; Miller, Ernest "Punch" HJA 1960b; Henry, Charles "Sunny" HJA 1959, October 21. Contrary testimony is given by Vigne (HJA 1961), who said that his Catholic father died in 1916 and was buried with music; his father was a musician who played in three brass bands, however, perhaps accounting for the exception. "Usually when a musician was buried they had a band," said Vigne. Jack Stewart (2004) cites the 1903 ban on "profane" music by Pope Pius X as a possible intervention.
214 he left the Catholic Church: Dawson HJA 1972. References in the oral histories to men joining church only after they stopped playing music include Miller, Ernest "Punch" HJA 1960a; Summers HJA 1960; Valentine HJA 1959. It is difficult to gauge how many of the Creole musicians were religious; Manuel Perez was described by Louis Nelson as belonging to people who were "very very up to the minute, running back and forth to the church. A little bit of this is a sin and a little bit of that is a sin." Nelson in Lomax 1993, 111.
215 funerals with music: My account of the funeral with music leaves out the question of how much participation there was, both in the clubs and in the funerals, from Creoles of color downtown. Downtown musicians were hired by the clubs to play for funerals, but it is not clear how many of them belonged to clubs or if those clubs sponsored funerals with music. Some general remarks are made by Logsdon and Bell 1992, 234ff.
215 Betsy Cole: Miller, Ernest "Punch" HJA 1960b. Another noteworthy female exclusion involves the Zulu Mardi Gras rituals, which did not include a female

Queen Zulu to go along with King Zulu until 1923; until 1936, the position was taken by a cross-dressing man; Kinser 1990, 233–34.

215 The fraternal clubs: Sabers: Souchon LSM n.d.; Souchon 1964.

215 Cash to pay for a band: Miller, Ernest "Punch" HJA 1960b; Foster 1971, 67. Friedlander 1992, 118.

215 people wouldn't give a dollar: Ory in Russell 1994, 179. Danny Barker (1986, 53) told a story about a tourist asking a grand marshal, "'This dead man must have been quite a big figure to rate a big funeral like this, huh?'" The marshal's response, according to Barker, was "the usual one: 'Oh no, he was just an ordinary fellow.'"

215 first documentation of the performance: Stewart, Jack 2004.

216 The dignity being performed: Higginbotham 1993.

216 musicians he knew: Armstrong LAHA 1949.

217 "I'm putting it on tape": Armstrong LAHA 1970b.

217 "was very confident in himself": Foster, George "Pops" WRC 1938.

217 "the old Southern-type nigger": Melrose in Lomax 1993, 232.

218 "It is probably not too much": Dailey 2000, 94; emphasis in original.

218 Once while Louis was playing: Armstrong HJA 1960b.

218 "way up there": Armstrong 1999, 38.

218 Freddie Keppard: Christian WRC 1938. For a provocative interpretation of sexual symbolism in jazz and especially high trumpet playing, see Gabbard 1995.

Chapter 10: "Rough and beautiful"

219 "[Joe Johnson] played": Foster 1971, 48.

219 "Some people like music": Charles, Hypolite HJA 1963 (reel 4, p. 22).

220 "All them little routine fellows": Manetta WRC 1957, mss 516, folder 671 (January 27).

220 "Lots more music": Manetta WRC 1969, mss 516, folder 695 (June 24).

220 With smaller bands: Armstrong IJS 1954, 73.

220 tacked to the side of the wagon: Some tunes became associated with the wagons. Armstrong (1999, 135) said that when he and the Hot Sevens recorded *Weary Blues* in 1927, he was reminded of the wagons and "was looking direct into New Orleans."

220 an advertising job with Bechet: Chilton, John 1987, 21; Armstrong IJS 1954, 60.

220 holes in their pants: Jones, Richard M. WRC 1938.

221 "We both would meet": Armstrong 1999, 31.

221 Bands typically advertised: Manetta WRC 1959, mss 516, folder 671 (January 27).

221 "All day Sunday": Miller, Ernest "Punch" HJA 1960a; see also Knowles 1996, 18.

221 "a lot of ratty brass bands": Barnes, Emile HJA 1960a.

221 Fifteen-year-old Baby Dodds: Dodds, Warren "Baby" WRC n.d.

221 A parade band could get by: Charles, Hypolite HJA 1963.

221 "in the rough style": Howard quoted in Koenig 1983, 7.

222 "could express themselves loudly": Barker 1998, vii.

222 When there was more than one: Foster 1971, 18.

222 Mrs. Betsy Cole: Garland in Russell 1994, 94–95.

223 gambling, picnicking, dancing, and drinking: Johnson 1995.

223 Well before 1900: Ridgley HJA 1961.

223 The train delivered them: Foster 1971, 68.
223 Bands still looking for work: Foster in Russell 1994, 105.
223 bands routinely: Garland WRC 1958.
223 little "camps": Miller, Ernest "Punch" HJA 1960a.
223 Adjacent camps: Miller, Ernest "Punch" HJA 1959a.
223 even a few white bands: Raeburn 2000a, 95.
223 lively racial mix: Bigard 1986, 20; see also Barnes, Emile HJA 1960a.
224 "The organized bands": Miller, Ernest "Punch" HJA 1960b.
224 Big Eye Louis Nelson: Lomax 1993, 108–9.
225 "not like New York": Jones, Richard M. WRC 1938.
225 musicians found work: Anderson 1990, 418.
225 Louis worked: Armstrong 1999, 11 and 16.
225 Karnofskys started to sell coal: Armstrong 1999, 13–15.
225 "big bottle": Foster in Russell 1994, 101.
226 Foster remembered: Foster 1971, 27.
226 Armstrong recalled: Armstrong IJS 1954, 25.
226 Bill Matthews recalled: Knowles 1996, 39.
226 "The musicianers from the other bands": Bechet 1960, 65.
226 "WHAT THE HELL IS THIS?": Armstrong IJS 1954, 61–62; emphasis in original.
226 "Louis would get nervous": Manetta WRC 1959, mss 516, folder 671 (January 27).
226 Black Benny sometimes tied Louis: Ory HJA 1957. On the chronology of the Ory band, see Anderson 1990.
227 Oliver had worked up a solo: Armstrong LAHA 1951a.
227 "Why don't you keep off Katie's head?": As sung by Kid Ory in 1959 and transcribed by Floyd Levin in Levin 1994, 59.
227 "there were always poor boys": Manetta WRC 1968, mss 516, folder 687 (December 27).
227 Bolton was a few years older: Manetta WRC 1968, mss 516, folder 687 (December 27). The estimate of Bolton's birth—1885—in Rose and Souchon (1967, 18) is surely much too early.
227 "If you had": Charles, Hypolite HJA 1963.
227 "Red Happy was bad, man": Miller, Ernest "Punch" HJA 1960b.
227 first time he ever heard: Barbarin, Paul, HJA 1957.
227 success of that band: Wiggs in Russell 1994, 161.
227 Red Happy was also good: Paul Barbarin in Russell 1994, 58; Wiggs in Russell 1994, 163–64. Recall (from Chapter 3) the use of scat in the vocal quartet Armstrong and Bolton sang with, a few years earlier.
227 Bolton had an influence: Wiggs in Russell 1994, 164.
227 "the greatest showman of them all": Armstrong IJS 1954, 14.
227 "He played them nice": Manetta WRC 1958, mss 516, folder 667 (April 8).
228 It is indeed interesting: Information and quotations in this paragraph and the next are derived from Abbott 1993 and Abbott and Seroff 2001, unless otherwise noted.
229 Musically rich New Orleans: Kinzer 1993, 261; Robichaux HJA 1959; Abbott 1993, 12. See also Ory HJA 1957 on Piron's stealing of compositions.
229 Armstrong sold his song: Armstrong 1966, 18–19; Armstrong WRC 1939.

229 theft was not isolated: Stewart, Jack 2001, 27; see also Ory HJA 1957.

229 Piron insisted: On the historical background of the song's text, see Levin 1994, 58; Rose 1974, 11. Manetta (WRC 1958, mss 516, folder 667, April 8) said that " 'Sister Kate' was Louis's number: Louis made that himself. Because he named it 'Take your finger out of Katie's Head.' "

229 a lot of that going on: See Abbott and Seroff 1996, 434–38.

229 A musically illiterate composer: Williams said (Shapiro and Hentoff 1955, 57) that "Piron was important to me because he could write the songs down for me." See also Allen HJA 1961. Foster's memory (Foster 1971, 100) of Clarence Williams taking rapid musical dictation for publication must have him confused with Piron, since others too described Williams as musically illiterate.

230 "I wasn't brought up": Armstrong in Morgenstern 1965, 18.

230 Others created breaks: Charles, Hypolite HJA 1963.

230 Big Eye Louis Nelson: Manetta WRC mss 516, folder 757; Barnes, Emile HJA 1962.

230 Freddie Keppard: Manetta WRC, mss 516, folder 757.

230 Tony Jackson: Parsons 1989, 6.

230 "If you've got": Letter from Oliver to Buddy Petit (May 1926) in Ramsey 1939, 78; see also Oliver's letter to Bunk Johnson in Ramsey 1939, 84.

230 After Armstrong hooked up: Armstrong 1999, 132.

231 "music by Louis Armstrong, words by Lillian Hardin": Armstrong had several other collaborators too: he and one Philmore Holley submitted *Drop that Sack* (December 8, 1923), he and Preston McDonald submitted *Papa, What Your are Trying to do to Me I've Been Doing it for Years* (December 13, 1923), and he and Paul Barbarin submitted *Don't Forget to Mess Around When You're Doing the Charleston* (March 10, 1926). My thanks to Robert Shaw for bringing the Library of Congress holdings of these pieces to my attention.

231 "amateur contest": Armstrong 1999, 30.

231 "used to dance": Ridgley HJA 1961.

231 "jive routine": Armstrong 1936, 34.

231 "mug and make some": Armstrong IJS 1954, 29.

231 Oliver and his band: Photograph in Rose and Souchon 1967, 264.

231 "as a comedian": Abbott 1993, 2; see also Gushee 1985, 401–2. Photos of Morton with blackface makeup appear in Russell 1999, 334, 476, and 477.

231 ample opportunities: Abbott and Stewart 1994.

232 a six-piece band: Armstrong 1936, 26; Lindsay WRC n.d.; Armstrong IJS 1954, 41; Russell 1994, 138; letter from Larry Amadee (May 6, 1968) in Giddins 1988, 221.

232 "We were": Armstrong IJS 1954, 42.

232 "That is one reason why": Armstrong IJS 1954, 82.

232 "perhaps not good then": Souchon HJA 1958.

232 only needed to know a small number of tunes: Hamilton HJA 1965.

232 One musician recalled: Keppard HJA 1961.

233 "It was like having beans and rice": James HJA 1959.

233 "That's what I did wrong": Dodds in Foster 1971, 50.

233 "There were a lot of players": Foster 1971, 49–50.

233 assigned to memorize the part: Koenig 1983, 18.

233 Jack Carey sent out Punch Miller: Miller, Ernest "Punch" HJA 1960a; see also Duhé HJA 1960.

233 It was not unusual: Greenough 1947, 5.
233 Clarence Williams: Frank Walker in Shapiro and Hentoff 1955, 239.
233 Similar service could be procured: Jones, Richard M. WRC 1938.
233 This way of learning music: Anderson 1990, 415; Hardin WRC 1938.
233 more successful routine bands: Armstrong HJA 1960b; Danny Barker in Shapiro and Hentoff 1955, 20; Charles, Hypolite HJA 1963; Barnes, Emile HJA 1960a.
234 "For a long time": Foster 1971, 75 (quotation); see also St. Cyr HJA 1958, 28; Bigard 1986, 10; St. Cyr in Russell 1994, 73; Charles, Hypolite HJA 1963; Barnes, Emile HJA 1960a.
234 But the bands Armstrong admired: Souchon 1964, 79.
234 violin players had the advantage: Dodds, Warren "Baby" WRC n.d.; Manetta WRC 1962, mss 516 (September 6).
234 "play a whole lot of melody": Foster 1971, 75.
234 "they never got so loud": St. Cyr in Russell 1994, 73. See also Dodds, Warren "Baby" WRC n.d.; Garland WRC 1958; Garland in Russell 1994, 97. Some musicians had trouble controlling their instruments and could not play softly; Willie Cornish is mentioned by Manetta WRC 1962, mss 516 (September 6).
234 "they are no longer string bands": Manetta WRC 1962, mss 516 (September 6).
234 "The way we used to play": Baby Dodds WRC (in Manetta WRC, mss 516, folder 744, 25).
234 "the sweet and soft": Ed Garland in Russell 1994, 97.
234 "He's got so much faking": Chinee Foster in Russell 1994, 52.
234 "musical men": Chinee Foster in Russell 1994, 52; Johnny Dodds made a similar point about George Baquet, but he put a social spin on it: "He couldn't play hot, so much playing with the whites." As summarized in Dodds, Johnny WRC n.d.
235 "slows down": Wiggs in Russell 1994, 166.
235 "With those heavy arrangements": Bigard 1986, 88. It is clear that Armstrong learned to read music fairly well during his time on the riverboats, beginning 1918. But some musicians who played with him much later were convinced that he had never learned. I doubt that he simply forgot; what seems more likely is that he preferred to learn pieces by ear. Certainly Armstrong would have been totally puzzled by the modern-day pedagogical practice of having jazz students transcribe famous solos in order to learn them. His approach, and the approach of most of the great soloists, was to memorize such solos by ear, a completely different procedure. Frank Foster told me that Armstrong once quipped, when asked if he knew how to read musical notation, "Not well enough that it interferes with my music."
235 a musician cannot play well: Dodds, Warren "Baby" WRC. n.d.
235 Robert Palmer: Palmer 1982, 101–3.
235 Plato in Ancient Greece: Ong 1982, 24 and 79–81.
235 "Narrative originality": Ong 1982, 41–42.
235 analyzes the "pre-emptiveness" of literacy: Ong 1982, 12.
236 Theirs was not the road: Kinzer 1993, 239; see also Bigard 1986, 10.
237 "The downtown bands": Ridgley 1961, 23.
237 if a violinist was desired: One reason why the violin eventually became marginal in jazz lies in the inaccessibility to uptowners of both the instrument and the training to play it; another relates to the importance of outdoor jobs uptown, where the violin was of limited use.

237 The traditional downtown bands: Bechet 1960, 63–65.

237 "Red Back Book": Barnes, Emile HJA 1960a.

237 "I used to play": Manetta WRC 1959, mss 516, folder 671 (January 27); see also Dawson HJA 1959.

237 "Any learned musician": Armstrong IJS 1954, 62–63.

238 "Way late around New Orleans": Foster 1971, 44. A different perspective is offered by Dodds (1992, 10): "There were certain halls in New Orleans where you had to play [mazurkas, quadrilles, polkas, and schottisches]. Some of the Creole people went only for that music. If you couldn't play them you just didn't get the job."

238 Eventually even Jimmy Palao: Manetta WRC 1969, mss 516, folder 695 (June 24); Dawson HJA 1962. Jelly Roll Morton (in Shapiro and Hentoff 1955, 251): "Violinists weren't known to play anything illegitimate even in New Orleans."

238 After the Joe Lindsay band: Armstrong IJS 1954, 43–44.

238 Bebé Ridgley: Ridgley 1961, 17.

239 "with a big broomstick": Stevenson HJA 1959; see also Manny Gabriel in Morris 1991, 15.

239 He washed dishes: Armstrong IJS 1954, 35.

239 He overdosed on the sweets: Armstrong IJS 1954, 35.

239 While driving "Lady,": Armstrong IJS 1954, 35.

239 For lunch he ate: Armstrong IJS 1954, 35–36.

239 closing of Storyville: Armstrong IJS 1954, 38.

239 worldwide flu epidemic: Armstrong IJS 1954, 38 and 48; Foster 1947, 32; Foster 1971, 108.

239 "Everybody was down": Armstrong IJS 1954, 48.

239 job for a few weeks: Armstrong IJS 1954, 44–48.

239 "a lot of blues": Armstrong IJS 1954, 48, and 1999, 124.

240 But in short time: Armstrong IJS 1954, 48.

240 work-or-fight laws: Chamberlain (n.d.) discusses how these laws affected musicians in New Orleans, including Armstrong. Armstrong IJS 1954, 38–39, 52, 62–64. See also Dawson HJA 1962; Ory in Russell 1994, 178.

240 worked as a stevedore: Armstrong IJS 1954, 39.

240 He and Kid Ory: Chamberlain n.d.; Armstrong IJS 1954, 52.

240 "The war is over": Armstrong IJS 1954, 63–64.

240 drying up of musical jobs: Other people gave different reasons for Oliver's departure, including a police raid that put Oliver in jail; Oliver HJA 1959; Stevenson HJA 1959.

240 "When the law commenced": Armstrong IJS 1954, 44.

240 Oliver left: Armstrong IJS 1954, 60; Noone WRC 1938; Stella Oliver (HJA 1959) said also that Oliver and Noone left together. Gene Anderson (1994), however, argues that Oliver may not have left New Orleans until early 1919.

240 Ory offered the position: Armstrong IJS 1954, 60.

240 he knew Oliver's solos by heart: Armstrong IJS 1954, 61.

240 "I lived Joe Oliver": Armstrong IJS 1954, 61.

241 "could look direct": Armstrong 1999, 128.

241 In 1918 Kid Ory: See McCusker 1998 and Anderson 1990 for biographical details on Ory.

241 History books routinely misrepresent: Historians identifying Oscar Celestin as a

Creole, probably because of his name, have been lured into the same trap; but he immigrated from Napoleonville, Louisiana, lived uptown, was shunned by the downtown Creoles, and was buried in a Baptist church.

242 He never learned to read music: Ridgley HJA 1961.

242 He was born: Anderson 1990, 419; McCusker 1998, 17.

242 Ory told Sidney Bechet: Bechet 1960, 90–91.

242 "Speak French": Dominguez in Lomax 1993, 102.

242 "I said": Ory HJA 1957.

243 His father's cousin: Ory HJA 1957; Greenough 1947, 5; Ory in Russell 1994, 172; Garland WRC 1958; Garland in Russell 1994, 94.

243 "I was the leader": Ory HJA 1957; Ory in Russell 1994, 171–81.

243 He ingratiated himself: Armstrong IJS 1954, 12. For a description of the parties, see Armstrong 1966, 11.

243 he was the first: Ory HJA 1957.

243 Requests for a permit: Marquis 1978, 35.

243 He came upon a scheme: Ory HJA 1957.

243 "More money, you know": Ory HJA 1957.

243 a gig "was Ory's job": Manetta WRC 1969, mss 516, folder 714 (May 30).

244 "knocking off": George Baquet in Shapiro and Hentoff 1955, 38.

244 In 1915 and 1916: Garland WRC 1958; Garland in Russell 1994, 96.

244 Oliver was admired: St. Cyr in Russell 1994, 72.

244 With the exception of the slow drag: Bechet WRC n.d.; on tempos, see also Chevan 1989.

244 "When musicians from other places": Sayles in Chamberlain 2000, 10.

244 So when Oliver came: Anderson 1990, 421.

244 he did more than that: Raeburn 2000a; Anderson 1990, 421.

244 "It was the preference band": Manetta in Russell 1994, 124.

244 Earlier, Ory had purchased: Manetta WRC 1969, mss 516, folder 714.

244 Though the band did not get far: *Eccentric* must be the ragtime hit of 1912 by J. Russel Robinson, also known as *That Eccentric Rag*. Robinson was apparently living in New Orleans at the time. Wiggs in Russell 1994, 163; Preston Jackson in Shapiro and Hentoff 1955, 42; Brothers 1999, 203–4.

244 "low down, slow": Dodds, Johnny WRC n.d.

244 "The inspiration came": Wiggs in Russell 1994, 161.

245 "kicking bass rhythm": Nicholas HJA 1972.

245 Armstrong went to hear them: Armstrong 1999, 133–34.

245 "That group could play": Wiggs HJA 1962.

245 an intervention that sprang on the scene: Raeburn 1991, 3.

245 Members of the ODJB: Jones, Richard M. WRC 1938; Manetta WRC 1969, mss 516, folder 709; Jack Weber in Shapiro and Hentoff 1955, 60–61; Schafer 1977, 35.

245 "They were the first": Armstrong 1966, 24.

246 "alligators": Dodds 1992, 25.

246 "listened to the band": Wiggs HJA 1962.

246 the glory that should have gone to Freddie Keppard: Johnson, William Manuel "Bill" WRC 1938; Jones, Richard M. WRC 1938; Armstrong IJS 1954, 23.

246 The ODJB's success: Ridgley HJA 1959.

246 "one of those upright Victrolas": Armstrong IJS 1954, 72.

246 By the end of 1917: Newton [Hobsbawm] 1975, 61.
247 White musicians in New Orleans: Raeburn 1997a, 4.
247 "We've got to follow suit": Oliver in Manetta WRC 1959, mss 516 (January 27); see also Raeburn 1991, 4, and 2000a, 91; Manetta in Russell 1994, 124.
247 "They wanted me all the time": Manetta WRC 1959, mss 516 (January 27).
247 Nevertheless, the ODJB: Raeburn 1991, 4.
247 After Armstrong settled into Ory's band: Armstrong IJS 1954, 61.
247 "rich folks": Armstrong IJS 1954, 68.
247 "Mello moments": Armstrong IJS 1954, 61.
247 "I was really *stickin* with cash": Armstrong IJS 1954, 89; emphasis in original.

Chapter 11: Movin' On Up

249 "You'll never be able to swing": Armstrong 1936, 48, 68.
249 his unhappy marriage: Armstrong 1936, 37.
249 "the prettiest and the badest": Armstrong 1999, 124.
249 "I can't live his life": Armstrong 1966, 24.
249 The newlyweds fought often: Armstrong IJS 1954, 78.
249 not the last woman: Armstrong IJS 1954, 36. Neither was Daisy the only woman in New Orleans to hear that the horn comes first. Cornish HJA 1959.
249 He heard Armstrong with Ory's band: Ramsey and Smith 1939, 99, quoting Fate Marable; see also Armstrong 1936, 36–37.
249 Several offers came his way: Armstrong 1936, 34–35; Henderson in Shapiro and Hentoff 1955, 202–3.
250 He had heard: Armstrong 1966, 27.
250 "I jumped at the opportunity": Armstrong IJS 1954, 80.
250 He told Daisy: Armstrong IJS 1954, 82.
250 Cornetist Punch Miller: Miller, Ernest "Punch" HJA 1960a.
250 He returned the cornet: St. Cyr in Russell 1994, 69.
250 The *Dixie Belle*: Armstrong 1936, 37–38. Foster (1971, 107) remembered the name of this excursion boat as the "Belle of the Bend."
250 Before departure the band played: Armstrong LAHA n.d., Tape 336.
250 Marable had previously hired: Foster 1971, 105.
250 The new band: Foster 1971, 107.
250 he answered 1919: Armstrong LAHA 1965.
251 "One of those dicty guys": Armstrong IJS 1954, 85; emphasis in original.
251 work routine: Foster, George "Pops" WRC 1938.
251 After a dinner break: Armstrong IJS 1954, 85.
251 "In the four months": Foster 1971, 111.
251 They also took: Foster 1971, 109; Dodds 1992, 21.
251 Marable's band: Dodds 1992, 21.
251 segregated: Schact 1946, 6. David Chevan (1989, 158) reports that the Streckfus boats were desegregated only in 1969, by court order.
251 Marable . . . was actually Streckfus's illegitimate son: St. Cyr ALA ca. 1948; see also Foster 1971, 108; Dodds 1992, 23. Marable had apparently been working on the boats since age sixteen. Feather 1965, 19. Zutty Singleton in Shapiro and Hentoff 1955, 76.
251 "allowed to mingle with the guests": Armstrong IJS 1954, 88.

251 People in small towns: Dodds 1992, 28; Dodds, Warren "Baby" HJA 1958.
251 "At first, we ran": Armstrong IJS 1954, 84.
252 Baby Dodds returned: Dodds 1992, 23.
252 Armstrong had been frank: Armstrong IJS 1954, 80–81.
252 all joined the band without reading skills: St. Cyr HJA 1958; Dodds, Warren "Baby" WRC n.d.
252 He had learned one important lesson: Armstrong IJS 1954, 81.
252 In the beginning, Joe Howard: Armstrong IJS 1954, 80–81.
252 The procedure worked so well: Jackson HJA 1958.
252 Bre'r Jones worked with him: Armstrong IJS 1954, 80–81; Armstrong 1936, 47–48; Dodds 1992, 24.
253 "He like the way I played": Armstrong IJS 1954, 82.
253 "I was piling up": Armstrong IJS 1954, 81; see also Dodds 1992, 26.
253 the only one who took solos: Dodds 1992, 26.
253 "We played strictly by music": Dodds 1992, 23; see also Dodds, Warren "Baby" WRC n.d.
253 "the *St. Paul* was known": Foster 1971, 111 (quotation); see also Shoffner HJA 1959.
253 even dicty David Jones: Armstrong 1936, 47; Armstrong IJS 1954, 80.
253 "You played music to suit them": Foster 1971, 106 (quotation); Chevan 1989, 159; Armstrong 1999, 70.
253 It was certainly the first time: Foster 1971, 106; Dodds, Warren "Baby" WRC n.d.
253 A cashier with a good ear: Foster 1971, 112.
253 Marable could be cruel: Armstrong IJS 1954, 81.
253 "guys would be out": Foster 1971, 107.
253 For the fifty-cent price of admission: Foster 1971, 108.
254 "Most everybody came": Foster 1971, 108.
254 Monday-night excursions: Foster 1971, 113; see also Chevan 1989, 157ff.
254 "revelation": Harker 2003, 142.
254 In Memphis: Armstrong LAHA 1965, Tape 3-8.
254 In St. Louis: Armstrong IJS 1954, 86.
254 One summer Oliver visited: Armstrong 1999, 71.
254 He continued to compose: Armstrong LAHA 1960.
254 He made a big splash: Armstrong 1936, 53.
254 "There's a kid down there": Mares WRC n.d.
255 rehearsals taught the musicians: Dodds 1992, 26.
255 "you'll never be able to swing": Armstrong 1936, 48, 68.
255 "The fact that I belonged": Armstrong 1954, 220.
255 "I made so much money": Armstrong 1947, 102.
256 got caught in the exaggerations: Armstrong 1947.
256 As a counter to that idea: Gushee (1989) presents thorough documentation about New Orleanian musical migration to the West Coast.
256 only three places: Charles, Hypolite HJA 1963.
256 "That's the reason": Charles, Hypolite HJA 1963.
256 Sidney Bechet agreed: Sidney Bechet WRC n.d.; see also Foster 1971, 37; Chilton, John 1987, 27; Ridgley HJA 1959.
256 The most famous place of all: Armstrong 1999, 24.
257 Jelly Roll Morton and Manuel Manetta: Rose 1974, 90.

257 But other musicians sometimes did: Picou HJA 1958; Albert HJA 1974; Ory in Russell 1999, 171-81; Keppard HJA 1957.

257 color hierarchy of New Orleans: Armstrong 1966, 12.

257 "As far as to *buy* a little *Trim*": Armstrong 1999, 24; emphasis in original.

257 "No matter how much": Armstrong 1999, 24. Note again the careful placement of emphasis, which says, first, that Morton's charade about his identity fools no one; second, that even though there are two kinds of blacks, Negroes and Creoles of color, they are equally less than equal in the eyes of whites. Armstrong would not have had any direct knowledge of Morton's assignment to the kitchen, since he was very young when Morton left the city.

257 "soft music": Keppard HJA 1961; Dawson HJA 1959, 3. See also Marquis 1978, 35, on restrictions for brass instruments. Marquis (1978, 59) reports a permit issued in 1907 to Nancy Hank's Saloon, at the corner of Marais and Customhouse, "to sing, with cornet, and band, also for electrical piano." Louis Keppard's memory is close to this documentation: he thought that Keppard played at Hannon's saloon on the corner of Marais and Customhouse. Marquis's discovery of the permit may thus be taken as documentation of Keppard's first job in Storyville. Foster said that Oliver first played in the district in 1908.

257 "Things were right on top": Foster 1971, 29.

257 A bar owner gained permission: Keppard HJA 1961.

257 "I never thought": Foster 1971, 26–37. Lawrence Gushee has observed a tendency in Foster's accounts to date events years too early. My impression is that he also sometimes dates things correctly. The issue of when and how cornets were first allowed into the district needs systematic investigation.

257 Huntz's Cabaret: This place was known to many musicians as "Huntz and Nagel's." Place names and ownership changed frequently in Storyville, and Huntz and Nagel's can be very confusing. Rose (1974, 87) reports that The Casino, on the lakeside, uptown corner of Iberville and Liberty, was at one time known as Huntz' Cabaret, and that Groshell's Cabaret and Dance Hall, on the downtown corner, was one time known as Hanan's Cabaret. Foster (1971, 34) reports that Eddie Groshey was the boss at Huntz and Nagel's—this must be Eddie Groshell, who did at one time own Groshell's Casino and at one time worked with Hans Nagel.

257 As a customer walked into Huntz's: Foster 1971, 31.

258 "The sporting district": Nelson in Lomax 1993, 109.

258 lots of tonks: "Every tonk had a band," said Barney Bigard (1986, 23).

258 an occasional dash of biological class warfare: Morton LC ca. 1938, 416.

258 The big money: Charles, Hypolite HJA 1963.

258 German sailors tipped well: Foster 1971, 30.

258 "These remarks slipped off me": Barker 1986, 37.

258 all too degrading: Dodds, Johnny WRC n.d.

258 Money was thrown on the floor: Charles, Hypolite HJA 1963.

258 The Magnolia Band: Foster 1971, 30.

258 Clarence Smith liked to say: Barker 1986, 38.

259 "Say for instance": Dominguez in Rose 1974, 107.

259 "In those days": Armstrong 1999, 120.

259 kept an eye on Big Eye Louis Nelson's whore: Foster 1971, 33–34.

259 "Let the boy alone": Foster 1971, 34.

259 "greatest musicians in town": Manetta WRC 1958, mss 516, folder 652 (March 21).

259 This was the band of Creoles: Manetta WRC, mss 516, folders 729–733; Manetta WRC 1959, mss 516, folder 678 (June 9); Manetta WRC 1958, mss 516, folder 652 (March 21).

260 "We had orchestration": Manetta WRC 1958, mss 516, folder 652 (March 21).

260 The repertory here: Rose 1974, 74.

260 remembered playing: Foster, George "Pops" WRC 1938.

260 they had to play "love numbers": Barnes, Emile HJA 1960b.

260 the term "classical": Dodds 1992, 20: "We didn't call them pop numbers though, we called them classical numbers." This clarifies what Peter Davis was suggesting when he told Armstrong to learn how to "play any kind of music, whether it's classic or ragtime." Armstrong IJS 1954, 67.

260 "He played things": Bechet 1960, 79.

260 "They went a lot of places": Armstrong 1999, 32.

260 The district was dominated: Hypolite Charles (HJA 1963) said that Johnson "learned his music there, as Peter could make anybody play."

260 Their rivals: Ramsey and Smith 1939, 32–33; Foster in Russell 1994, 102.

260 women pianists: Keppard HJA 1957; Charles, Hypolite HJA 1963.

261 getting a substitute and then returning: Bechet WRC n.d.

261 "started swing": Christian WRC 1938.

261 "if it wasn't for those good musicians": Armstrong 1999, 24–25.

261 Tom Anderson was one: Information in this paragraph from Rose 1974, 43–47.

261 the various traditions of the district: Dodds, Johnny WRC n.d.; Armstrong 1947, 102.

261 "Both of these girls": Armstrong 1954, 216; Armstrong 1999, 83.

261 "We played all sorts of arrangements": Armstrong 1999, 83.

262 "not a sore head": Armstrong 1954, 216.

262 "See, us downtown people": Dominguez in Lomax 1993, 105.

262 amazed that Armstrong could read: Nicholas HJA 1972.

262 "aw I used to play 'em all": Armstrong 1999, 149.

262 The rich racehorse men: Armstrong 1954, 216. Armstrong also played at Anderson's briefly before going on the boats, in 1918. This may have been when, according to Pops Foster (1971, 82), Willie Foster (his brother) played violin with Armstrong there and taught Armstrong the melodies.

264 Chris Kelly: Miller, Sing HJA 1965; Stevenson HJA 1959. Barker claimed that Cootie Williams, the great freak trumpeter from Mobile, Alabama, who played with Ellington for many years, got his style from Kelly when the latter went on regional tours. Barker in Shapiro and Hentoff 1955, 51; see also Albert HJA 1961. Some of the evidence in this section on competitors is also reviewed in Harker 2003, but with somewhat different readings and toward different conclusions.

264 "Baptist from birth": Danny Barker in Shapiro and Hentoff 1955, 50.

264 His signature piece: Bigard HJA 1961.

264 He had relatively weak fingering: Stevenson HJA 1959.

264 On the streets: Barbarin, Paul HJA 1959.

264 It was now Kelly: Brunious HJA 1959.

264 During off-hours: Brunious HJA 1959; Barker in Shapiro and Hentoff 1955, 51.

264 When he died: Lewis 1946, 9.

264 Henry "Kid" Rena: Stevenson HJA 1959; Walters HJA 1959; Miller, Ernest "Punch" HJA 1960b. Jackson WRC 1938. See also Harker 2003, 142.
264 "It was a smile": Miller, Ernest "Punch" HJA 1960b.
264 Rena's specialty number: Miller, Ernest "Punch" HJA 1960b.
264 best cornet player ever: Stevenson HJA 1959; Jackson WRC 1958.
264 Preston Jackson said: Harker 2003.
264 was good at inventing variations: Nelson HJA 1960.
264 the two of them had been together: Barker 1986, 58–59; Giddins 1988, 213–14; Ory in Russell 1994, 177.
264 Punch Miller's strength: Albert HJA 1961; Stevenson HJA 1959; Miller, Ernst "Punch" HJA 1960b.
264 He perfected a style: Clayton HJA 1961; Russell 1971.
264 Miller also played freak music: Nelson HJA 1960.
265 He remembered an evening: Miller, Ernest "Punch" HJA 1959b.
265 "were all HELLIONS": Armstrong IJS 1954, 67; emphasis in original.
265 More than a few clarinet players: Barnes, Emile with Paul, HJA 1959.
265 Downtown clarinetists: Barnes, Emile HJA 1962; Duhé HJA 1957; Miller, Ernest "Punch" HJA 1960a.
265 "raising sand in them days": Miller in Harker 2003, 140.
265 Alphonse Picou: Dodds 1992, 10.
265 Other clarinetists: Kinzer 1993, 223.
265 Kid Rena: Rena, Henry "Kid" WRC 1938; Bigard HJA 1961.
265 Bechet remembered: Barnes, Emile HJA 1960a.
265 "It was very hard": Bechet 1960, 92; Donder 1983, 9. Preston Jackson (HJA 1958) said that Roy Palmer learned the *High Society* solo on his trombone.
266 "used to trick": Miller, Ernest "Punch" HJA 1960b.
266 Buddy Petit: For biographical information on Petit, who was born on a plantation 100 miles from New Orleans, see Donder 1983. Petit was Joe Petit's stepson; Manetta (WRC 1969, mss 516, folder 709 [April 3]) described Joe as "one of those Creole fellows." It is not straightforward, however, to group Buddy Petit with the Creoles; see Foster in Russell 1994, 101: "Downtown there's a different class of musicians. Buddy Petit wasn't in a class with them." See also Bethell 1977, 53–55, and Charters 1963, 93–95.
266 Petit, very much: Walters HJA 1959; Bigard HJA 1961; Anderson HJA 1960; Miller, Ernest "Punch" HJA 1959b and 1960a; Donder 1983, 8–10; Brunious HJA 1959.
266 Petit had no interest: Miller, Ernest "Punch" HJA 1960a and 1960b.
266 Musicians talk about him: Nicholas HJA 1972.
266 "He had a beautiful tone": Albert in Valentine HJA 1959.
266 "Sounded like a sweetheart": Miller, Ernest "Punch" HJA 1960b.
266 Armstrong admired Petit: Armstrong 1999, 31.
266 Several musicians: Casimer HJA 1959; Barnes, Emile with Paul HJA 1959; Manetta WRC, mss 516, folder 709; Nelson HJA 1960; Bigard 1986, 88; Ridgley HJA 1961; Lewis 1946; Donder 1983, 7–8.
266 "When [Armstrong] makes": Barnes, Emile with Paul HJA 1959; Donder 1983, 8.
267 recorded in 1926: Harker 2003, 144, citing David Chevan.
267 "If it ain't him": Ridgley HJA 1961.
267 "Those variations": Armstrong 1999, 133.

267 "He'd stay in the staff": Walters HJA 1959.
267 Petit got a reputation: Jackson HJA 1958.
268 Toward the end of his life: Foster 1971, 81; Albert HJA 1972a.
268 An alcoholic, he died: Foster 1971, 82; Ridgley HJA 1961; Donder 1983, 25.
268 Several musicians felt: Nicholas HJA 1972; Albert HJA 1972a; Walters HJA 1959.
268 "could have been a killer-diller": Miller, Ernest "Punch" HJA 1960a.
268 If Petit or Rena: Cagnolatti HJA 1961.
268 "that kind of stuff": Miller, Ernest "Punch" HJA 1959a.
268 the first time blues were played: Miller, Ernest "Punch" HJA 1960b.
268 "played the drum all kinds of ways": Miller, Ernest "Punch" HJA 1960b.
268 played his drum with an "African beat": Barker in Shapiro and Hentoff 1955, 52. Miller, Ernest "Punch" (HJA 1960b) supports this by demonstrating Williams's drumming in scat with lots of funky afterbeats. On the other hand, Baby Dodds (1992, 8) said that Williams "only played in street bands and there was nothing special about his drumming except that he would always do something to fill in and make some novelty out of it. I heard him when I was very young but his style of drumming was nothing that inspired me." It should be remembered that Dodds left New Orleans in 1918, with Armstrong on the riverboats; perhaps he did not hear Williams in 1921. George Williams (HJA 1959) said that Williams played a lot of fancy beats, and Henry "Kid" Rena (WRC 1938) said that Williams was considered the greatest bass drummer in New Orleans.
268 "used to really Swing the Tuba": Armstrong 1999, 27. Also on Jackson see Dodds 1992, 12; Knowles 1996, 107 and 116–19.
268 "He could make it moan": Miller, Ernest "Punch HJA 1959b, also HJA 1960b.
269 Within a short time: Armstrong 1999, 43.
269 Bolden may well have been: Carey 1946.
269 "style was in many respect": Barnes in Koenig 1983, 9.
269 "good blues man": Giddins 1988, 215.
269 "Now at that time": Carey 1946, 4; see also Miller, Ernest "Punch" HJA 1960a.
269 "structure of feeling": The phrase comes from Williams 1973.
270 The trick was: Walters HJA 1959.
270 The great blues queen: Collier 1983, 147; Albertson 2003, 82.
271 "stuff in it": Miller, Ernest "Punch" HJA 1960b.
271 Musicians in Chicago: Tommy Brookins in Shapiro and Hentoff 1955, 100–101.

Chapter 12: Melody That Changed the World

272 "[Jabbo Smith] played": Hinton quoted in Shapiro and Hentoff 1955, 135.
272 On August 8, 1922: Armstrong LAHA n.d., Tape 124.
272 May Ann gave him: Armstrong LAHA 1968; Armstrong 1954, 227–28.
272 Armstrong wore his brown box-back coat: Preston Jackson in Shapiro and Hentoff 1955, 97.
272 The musicians playfully called him: Lillian Hardin Armstrong in Shapiro and Hentoff 1955, 101.
272 Not only Oliver but dozens of musicians: Miller, Ernest "Punch" HJA 1959b.
273 Oliver had tried: William Russell quoted in Friedlander 1992, 107.
274 he received a one-way train ticket: Armstrong 1936, 68.
274 Armstrong's friends: St. Cyr HJA 1958; Armstrong HJA 1960a.

274 "I always was afraid": Armstrong 1999, 53.
274 The immigrants were greeted: Bigard 1986, 27.
274 "Negro City": Jackson, Mahalia 1967, 46.
274 "It was after I got to Chicago": Jackson, Mahalia 1967, 49.
275 "There were plenty of work": Armstrong 1999, 74; emphasis in original.
275 He stepped right into: Knowles 1996, 57–58.
275 "Let the youngster blow": Armstrong 1999, 53.
275 legendary series of recordings: A good introduction to these recordings is Brooks
     2002.
275 "Big High-powered Chick": Armstrong 1999, 86.
275 A good sight-reader: Russell 1939, 125; Armstrong 1999, 89.
275 "Louis was good down there": Barnes, Emile HJA 1960a.
275 "And because Louis": Rena in Barker 1986, 59.
277 "Every note that I blew": Armstrong 1999, 128, see also 135, 136.
277 "good musicianer": Bechet 1960, 202–3; emphasis in original.
277 "When a musicianer": Bechet 1960, 203–4.
277 Ellison's protagonist: Ellison 2002, 6–10.
278 "People are always putting": Bechet 1960, 8.
279 Yet they did have music: To paraphrase Maurice Wallace (2002, 66), patterns of
     sound transformed the exploited laborer from *animal laborans* to *homo faber*.
279 "The New Orleans style": St. Cyr in Russell 1994, 74. See also Abbey Foster in
     Russell 1994, 54: "Always make a style of your own. Like when I had my cards
     printed, I had printed, 'I originate while others imitate.'"
279 "I don't try to copy-cat": Marrero in Russell 1994, 85.
279 "You see each of the guys": Russell 1994, 101.
279 well suited to these high expectations: An argument related to this one is
     advanced in Edwards, Brent Hayes 2002.
279 "Patience, humility and adroitness": Du Bois 1961, 153.
279 "Always have a *White Man* who likes you": Armstrong 1999, 160, 213–14.
282 "in order to get along": Morton in Lomax 1993, 70.
282 "All American negroes": Newton [Hobsbawm] 1975, 267.
283 "They snatched him": Nelson in Lomax 1993, 91–92.
283 "My people stayed by themselves": Jackson in Schwerin 1992, 32.
285 "With this kind of music": Barbarin in Russell 1994, 58.
286 "that good 4 beat": Armstrong 1999, 65; emphasis in original.
287 "at all times": Dodds, Warren "Baby" WRC n.d., 30; see also St. Cyr in Russell
     1994, 72.
288 "He'd take one note": Collins in Blesh 1946, 156 and 181. This contradicts claims
     that Bolden played the melody straight. It is certainly possible that he sometimes
     played the melody straight, with other musicians contributing heterophony, and
     sometimes made the heterophonic ragging himself.
288 clarinet sometimes took that role: For references to clarinetists Nelson, Baquet,
     Tio, and Bechet carrying the lead, see Manetta WRC, mss 516, folder 652; Duhé
     HJA 1957; Barnes, Emile HJA 1962. According to Richard Hadlock (cited in
     Chilton, John 1987, 30), Sidney Bechet said that the lead belonged to the violin,
     but if there was not a violin then the clarinet took over. Buddy Petit had clar-
     inetist Zeb Lenares play the lead so that he could play "second" on his cornet.
     Miller, Ernest "Punch" HJA 1960a.

288 Alto horns, baritone horns: Miller, Ernest "Punch" HJA 1959b and 1960a; Manetta WRC, mss 516, folder 697.
289 Freddie Keppard played the best second: Braud in Russell 1994, 112. Keppard would "get a long way from the melody and the clarinet would take the lead," said Emile Barnes (HJA 1962).
289 "like Louis, with King Oliver": Jones, Richard M. WRC 1938.
289 George Baquet: Singleton WRC 1938; Manetta WRC, mss 516, folders 648 and 757; Barnes, Emile HJA 1962.
289 the cornetist most talked about: Valentine HJA 1959, 4; Penn HJA 1960.
289 "That's Buddy over and over": Miller in Donder 1983, 8.
290 "the best in the business": Duhé HJA 1957 (with Wellman Braud).
291 "I'd play eight bars": Morgenstern 1965, 17; see also Armstrong 1966, 56, and Armstrong LAHA 1951a, which includes this description of Oliver coming to the honky tonk where Louis was playing: "He'd hang around and he'd listen to me play a while. He'd tell me, 'Listen boy, play some more lead. Stop so much that variation. Play some lead.' And I thought about that a lot. And then he'd show me, blow a while, Oh he'd have them hopping around there."
291 "I didn't never understand": Henry, Charles "Sunny" HJA 1959, January 8.
291 "a phrase that stayed with you": Armstrong 1999, 38.
291 "When you're really playing": Bechet 1960, 141.
292 Armstrong's mature solo style: A good discussion of this in Collier 1983, 178–79, 181–82, 244; see also Harker 1999.
292 "The first chorus": Armstrong quoted by Harker 1999, 47.
292 "Each true jazz moment": Ellison cited in Ake 1998, 62.
293 "a good mind for the blues": Payne in Palmer 1982, 191.
294 "the major things": Morrison in Gilroy 1993, 181.
295 grateful to Dizzie Gillespie: Davis 1989, 58.
295 He gave impromptu instruction: Manetta WRC, mss 516, folders 705 and 720.
295 "They'd treat me so nice": Manetta WRC, mss 516, folder 709.
295 Buddy Petit liked the way: Manetta WRC, mss 516, folder 709; see also Miller, Ernest "Punch" HJA 1960a and 1960b.
295 He eventually found: Guesnon in Russell 1994, 77.
295 "Buddy Petit was the first": Hall in Russell 1994, 206; Miller, Ernest "Punch HJA 1960a.
296 "Most everybody around": Wiggs HJA 1962.
296 "I don't think about": Simeon in Russell 1994, 202.
296 the time he had spent: Guesnon in Russell 1994, 77.
296 "Naw, I didn't have a teacher": Walters HJA 1959.
296 "Here we had come up": Hinton in Lax 1974, 118.
297 "these instrumental rags": Stark quoted in Berlin 1994, 71.
297 "At first folk melodies": Handy 1957, 75–76.
298 "Not well enough": Personal communication from Frank Foster, November 15, 2004.
299 He disdained: Armstrong IJS 1954, 86.
299 notated music: Bechet 1960, 79; Dodds 1992, 20.
300 1926 recording of the song *Big Butter and Egg Man*: Brothers 1994.
300 Armstrong worked on it: Harker 1999, 75. To the evidence Harker presents should be added this, from notes taken by Bill Russell from an interview with Zutty Singleton (WRC 1938): "Played with Clarence Jones, Louis Armstrong,

Howard, Jimmie Bell and Carroll Dickerson. In the Metropolitan Theater. After the Met, the whole band quit, got another job with Sammy Payton at the Persian Palace, Club Bagdad. Had two bands . . . Louis used to come out there every night (he wasn't with our band) and play *Butter and Egg Man*. Every night. He would come there to pick me up. All the white guys were crazy about his playing. He would come on in and set in the band and play and we would have a ball."

301 mansion of the muses: *Times-Picayune*, 1918, reprinted in Walser 1999, 8.

301 A decade later, Lester Young: this paragraph based on Brothers 1994.

301 pitch relations are folded: Brothers 1994. It is important to emphasize the analytical ramifications that flow from this point—that the solo utterance is conceived in terms of interaction. It is not offered as an autonomous, self-standing utterance that depends for its success on narrative coherence. To be sure, narrative coherence may be mixed into the solo, but it is not the main governing principle; it is, in fact, absolutely expendable. That is why methods of analysis that have been developed to understand music conceived as narrative—Schenkerian analysis, for example—fail so miserably when applied to jazz. It is always possible to find a bit of coherence, but that way of hearing the design must proceed from the more basic and universally governing principle of active musical interaction. In any event, coherence is inevitably achieved through the a priori design of the harmonic foundation (a blues pattern or the chorus a song like *I Got Rhythm*), where it is obvious to the point of being uninteresting. The soloist automatically keys into this coherence through congruence with the foundation, and an additional layer of melodic coherence is not required.

301 "I used to have a definition": Ellington in Dance 1969, 69.

302 A poem from 1829: Creecy 1860, 275.

303 "It's such a mixture": Bigard 1986, 5.

303 "You have the finest ideas": Morton in Lomax 1993, 66; see also 190, where Lomax quotes Walter Melrose as saying that "Scott Joplin was [Morton's] God; and, really, things like *Maple Leaf Rag* and *Grace and Beauty* were his models."

304 "It all came from the Old Sanctified Churches": Armstrong 1999, 170. Armstrong was fond of saying that Rock and Roll was nothing but "old soup warmed over," derivative of music in the Sanctified Church; for example, Armstrong LAHA 1965.

304 "isn't anything new": Armstrong 1966, 57.

304 "roustabouts": Armstrong LAHA n.d., tape 336.

INDEX

〜〜〜〜

Page numbers in *italics* refer to illustrations; page numbers beginning with 321 indicate endnotes.